What's So Bad About Being Poor?

Our Lives in the Shadows of the Poverty Experts

Deborah M. Foster

D & D Publishing

Book Cover by Steve Kuhn

1st edition 2024

Contents

Preface

CHARLES MURRAY INTERFERED WITH my career plans. During my first year of college, I was taking a required economics class. Early in the semester, when the subject turned to poverty, my professor assigned an essay from Murray, a conservative political scientist, think tank researcher, and future supporter of eugenicist theories. At the time, Murray main claim to fame was being a "poverty expert" whose criticism of welfare programs buttressed the Reagan revolution.[1]

Until I encountered the notorious Dr. Murray, my plan had been to research schizophrenia in order to find an effective treatment or a cure for my father's schizoaffective disorder. But I was so appalled by Murray that I decided to focus instead on taking him down a notch. His theories about poverty simply weren't accurate. I knew this because I grew up poor. Murray's wrongheadedness bugged me enough to change my life course.

The title of Murray's essay was, "What's So Bad about Being Poor?"[2] It appeared in 1988, in the aftermath of Ronald Reagan's two-term assault on the welfare state. In it, Murray suggested that being poor in the United States was not so bad after all, because welfare benefits were too generous. He blamed the plight of poor people on their own behavior, suggesting there was something inherently wrong with them. There were strong racial overtones to the article, portending the firestorm to come when he expanded on those sentiments in his 1994 coauthored book, *The Bell Curve.*[3] "What's So Bad about Being Poor?" was one of many rhetorical questions or hypotheticals raised by Murray about welfare dependency. My professor snapped them up and decided our assignment would be to answer Murray's questions.

The essay made me so angry, and I got out some of my feelings in my response paper to Professor Lund. But Murray had left a mark. I had been alerted to the fact that there were people in the United States who actually believed what I had suffered through was "not so bad."

What's so bad about being poor? What kind of person would even ask such a ridiculous question? What kind of person would casually observe "that there is nothing so terrible about poverty per se"? What kind of person would argue that "material resources . . . should be put last" in discussions of poverty policy. This point of view could not stand. I had to be part of correcting the record.

I had to become one of the people considered legitimate enough in my expertise to convince everyone that Charles Murray was a fool. I had to become a poverty expert in my own right. I wanted to explain that his ideas were toxic misconceptions, but I knew my personal experience alone would not be respected. I would need to become an academic.

Interestingly, Murray claimed that personal experience was precisely what was missing from the knowledge base of policy thinkers. The first line of his essay read, "One of the great barriers to a discussion of poverty and social policy in the 1980s is that so few people who talk about poverty have ever been poor." He himself had never really been poor (which was why he proposed "thought experiments" to understand what it might be like to be poor), but he was definitely right about the value of personal experience.

College can often be an awful experience for a poor student. I was fine academically and picked up what I needed to quickly. Yet, I nearly dropped out numerous times since I felt like I didn't fit in. Thankfully, fortunately, I had the help of a woman named Phyllis Gray. She worked with the federal educational opportunity program Upward Bound, which I had participated in during high school. I stuck it out through undergrad and eventually was ready to pick a graduate school.

One day, I was walking past the bulletin board in the social sciences building when a flyer caught my eye. It was from the University of Michigan. It said I could get a joint doctorate in Social Work and Psychology—at the same time. I could pursue my goal of working with serious mental illness, *and* learn how to combine my life experience with scholarly evidence to put Murray in his place. Michigan had its own poverty expert, Sheldon Danziger. He was the anti-Murray.

I applied to the program despite the skepticism coming from my undergraduate advisers in both psychology and social work. Each told me to apply to other graduate schools, because Michigan was very difficult to get into. I shouldn't get my hopes up. I did as they suggested. When I was accepted to University of Michigan, it was against the odds. Thankfully, the School of Social Work used affirmative action for many types of underrepresented groups in higher education, including those from a low socioeconomic status.

I didn't realize that you don't really get to focus on your own goals in graduate school. You find senior professors to mentor you, and you work on their research. Eventually, your dissertation becomes something related to your mentor's research. Thankfully, I had a good mentor. I would never have finished graduate school without Dr. Carol Mowbray, co-leader of the Center for Poverty, Risk, and Mental Health. She made sure I understood how to do research inside and out. But it was *her* area of research I was working on.

I thus wasn't able to aim my work toward countering Charles Murray. The deeper I got into academia, the more I was bifurcated into having two areas of expertise: 1) poverty and social policy; and 2) mental health. My publications were not in social policy either. They were all coming out in the mental health area. I was restless with frustration.

Meanwhile, Charles Murray wouldn't leave me alone. In 1993, he published an article about "the coming white underclass." This spurred an article in the *U.S. News & World Report*[4] that identified my hometown, Waterloo, Iowa, as having the seventh-largest population of poor white people in the country. Murray was writing about people like me, and he was blaming the rise of the white underclass on single parenthood. The implication of his work was that these were dumb white people who weren't getting married but were procreating dumb, violent, drug-addicted children. Read in light of Murray's controversial 1994 book *The Bell Curve*,[5] the strong implication was that these poor white people were genetic failures.

Murray was particularly focused on the inability of poor whites to form families. Single women were destined for poverty, he argued. He didn't realize that conservatives had set up welfare in the stupidest way possible if their goal was to encourage marriage. My own parents had once gotten separated in part because of the rules made for welfare. When Reagan came into office, conservatives prevented two-parent families from receiving aid. My family couldn't get aid unless my mom was single.

I know about these cuts, because, in 1981, my parents became ineligible for Aid to Dependent Children of Unemployed Parents, the program that was then often simply referred to as "welfare" for two-parent families. Murray was insulting poor women of all races for being single mothers when that was the last thing they wanted to be.

As a graduate student, I taught social policy to master's-level social work students. I told them about theories of poverty, including Murray's, and then presented research evidence to dismantle Murray. I threw in personal experience to hammer the points home. My students gave me great reviews. This wasn't exactly making change on a large scale, though.

When I became a professor, I continued to read Murray and his employer, the American Enterprise Institute, spewing forth about how easy it was for Americans to live in poverty, yet I had no effective way to respond. I was at a different university with another renowned poverty expert, but we weren't working together. I was being drawn into research on the quality of care in social services. This was a worthy cause, but not a step toward shutting down Murray's falsehoods.

Charles Murray said that readers should do a thought experiment in which they imagined they were poor. But I don't want readers to use their imaginations. I want them to listen to a testimonial like mine about the reality of being poor.

I had been writing a book about my family since I was ten years old. Because of the age I was when I first developed this goal, I believed that it was a mission that came straight from God. At that age,

I was praying daily, out loud, and I imagined I heard God's reply. At the time, I wasn't too far removed from being a fundamentalist Mormon.

I wanted to pattern my book after Andrew Solomon's *The Noonday Demon: An Atlas of Depression*,[6] a memoir that doubles as a scientific study. But I ended up making different decisions than he did. In his book, he tried to use real names as often as possible. I couldn't do that. I have used a lot of pseudonyms, mixed in with as many real names as I could muster. Welcome to my family and our mental health struggles.

My book is about poverty and mental illness in a white, American family, my own. It is also about coming of age, coming apart, and coming to the point of finishing this book. Nothing is this book was easy to experience, and I wish I could portray the true emotional impact of the array of experiences, but I'm so damaged by them, my emotions are frozen. Everything in this book suggests why I took personal offense at Charles Murray's question and why the best response to him was to tell my family's story.

It is so bad to be poor.

Chapter One: Early Onset of Mental Illness

FIFTY YEARS AGO, MY mom and dad created thick, heavy books of family history with page after page of our relatives listed with their families. At first glance, this seems like an extremely boring hobby. You're just systematically listing family members with birth, marriage, and death dates. Over and over.

They created the genealogy books in Salt Lake City, Utah, where they met in 1970 at the famous genealogy library of the Church of Jesus Christ of Latter-day Saints' (LDS). Their relationship began because of the Mormons.

My father in a suit

My mom in church robe

Figure 1. Pictures of my father and mother in their youth

This should have been a romantic story of a chatty blonde with a cute gap in her front teeth falling in love with the dark-haired, seductively good-looking man who is equally entranced. Except that's not how it happened. They both had a secret. They were two very troubled people when they met.

In 1965, my father, John, graduated from high school, and voluntarily joined the Air Force, as his father had done during World War II. It was not an easy time for Dad. His best friend from high school had just been killed in a car accident.

Dad wanted to follow in his father's footsteps. Diabetes had prevented his father from being a pilot during WWII, but our dad could join the Air Force to serve during Vietnam. Maybe he could even learn to fly planes. He tried to do everything right. He had been an altar boy and a Boy Scout. Dad voluntarily joined the Air Force, but when his parents were not happy that he had enlisted, it broke his heart. Dad had the weight on ancestry on his side, though.

When I conducted my own genealogical research, I found that on my dad's side going back to the Revolutionary War —and even well before then in the Pequot War in 1636—our family has been involved in battles.

During his time in the Air Force, Dad was stationed in Texas, Arizona, and Colorado. He was nearly deployed twice to Thailand. The orders were canceled both times when war plans changed. One day, when he was twenty-one years old, my father heard a man whistling. The whistling began to agitate and then infuriate him. He attacked the man he thought was whistling. Witnesses said the man wasn't making a sound.

Dad was sent to psychiatric lockup. Based on his obvious psychotic breakdown, he came away with a diagnosis of schizoaffective disorder, which combined the often-paranoid delusions and hallucinations of schizophrenia with the deep despair and self-loathing of depression.[7]

Dad told the psychiatrists about his military buddy Alex from the planet Orarus-Orr in another star system. He also told them about going in a UFO to Zorcon and Mare Crisium, planets supposedly prophesied in the Book of Samuel in the Bible. In 1969, the Air Force gave him an honorable medical discharge after three-and-a-half years of service.

Other people may have simply concluded Dad was becoming mentally ill when this incident occurred, but he told me that his "visions" went all the way back to early puberty.

Figure 2. Picture of the angel Moroni trumpeting

As Dad told it, a Mormon friend from the military had taken him to visit Salt Lake City during leave. He had seen the magnificent Mormon temple with the statue of the angel Moroni trumpeting to the people to come to the Lord. He understood Joseph Smith, the founder of the Mormons, and his visions of angels. *He had them too.* He felt the Mormon faith call to him.

Dad was particularly obsessed with the "Lost Tribes of Israel," and he believed he made contact with them on other planets. He would talk about this all the time. The Lost Tribes of Israel were part of his dreams. They were part of how he interpreted every Bible verse. To show his devotion to Israel, he made an official-sized canvas flag that had blue and white stripes with a Star of David in the corner of it. It represented the Lost Tribes of Israel with whom he'd had contact in outer space. Dad hung the flag in a prominent place on the wall wherever he lived.

Dad fit in perfectly with huge numbers of his countrymen who followed faith leaders. Plenty of other Americans are obsessed with Israel too. Kurt Andersen wrote a book called *Fantasyland: How America Went Haywire—A 500 Year History*,[8] in which he explained that a generation of Americans began obsessing about the End Times right about the same time Mom and Dad did. It wasn't specific to their mental illnesses. It was part of the culture too.

Andersen explained that Americans became actively involved with fundamentalist faiths again. Check. He said they were taking the Bible literally more often. Check. He said they were exploring the occult and mysticism. Check. He said they were seeing every war in the Middle East as a sign of the apocalypse. Check.

Apparently, at the time Dad came to Utah, his parents were going to kick him out of the house. They didn't understand his medical discharge from the military, or why he seemed to be lying around in bed a lot. That was the *affective* part of the schizoaffective disorder. Once, many years later, when I was about eighteen, our grandmother leaned over to me and whispered, "I think your father has schizophrenia. He hasn't been right since he was a child." With that, his mother turned away ashamed. We never spoke of it again.

Once he was married, Dad could not have resented the fact that he had a wife and children more. It wasn't his idea to have a family. He always swore he loved our mother and us kids, but that didn't mean he didn't feel manipulated into having us.

In 1968, when, my mother Laura[9] was twenty-three years old, she returned to Iowa months early from a two-year Lutheran mission to teach English in New Guinea. It had not gone well there. Once she arrived, she realized the arrogance of telling other people what to believe. They already had their own belief systems and she felt shy about imposing hers on them.

The first year went okay, but two new missionary women arrived the second year. They were not there to be helpful to the local people or to spread Christianity. They were exploring their freedom and rebelling against authority. They drank. They smoked. They played poker all night long, flouting a law that prohibited card-playing in New Guinea. The law was enacted because many gambling husbands traded their wives, who had been put up as collateral for bets. The new girls teased our mother for her devotion to the Bible and the missionary rules. Mom had counted on them to help grade the stacks of children's school essays; instead, they were like children themselves. The more Mom dwelled on the situation, the more upset she got. It wasn't long before she ended up in the hospital with an opportunistic case of mononucleosis. Her Australian doctor diagnosed her with major depression.

She took the yellow-and-white pills he prescribed until she became convinced they were making her depression worse—even making her feel suicidal. Decades later, research would show that antidepressants can make depressive symptoms worse in people with bipolar disorder,[10] but Mom's bipolar disorder II was not yet recognized.[11]

The doctor scoffed at the notion that the pills could be making her worse, saw the palmful of pills she had been hiding in her drawer, and made her take all of them at once. This psychiatrist was so aggressively arrogant that Mom crumbled instead of resisting further. "These pills are perfectly safe. They do not cause depression," he insisted. "Take them!"

She did.

That "solution" actually worked, briefly. She was awake for days, happy and full of energy.[12] She exercised three times a day for a week. She did all her work, plus the work of those "lazy, mean missionary girls." The elderly German woman she was staying with commented, "Why, I haven't seen someone go from so sickly to so healthy so quickly in my whole life."

Beaming, Mom said, "We can do anything with God's help." The crash that followed approximately five days later led her to take every pill she had in an attempted overdose.

In Laura's mind, the only precipitant for her depression was her poor health and the other missionary girls. However, reports by her sisters and brothers contradict this perspective. As her sister told me when we discussed Mom's depression, "She was a sensitive child, often withdrawn. She seemed down much of the time."

But I was more interested in how Mom ended up halfway around the globe from her family and in a totally different culture. I remembered how scared I was to live in Germany with a class of college students I knew, including a dear friend, for only six months. Not alone. Our mother was brave. Gutsy. I knew this, but she had cracked up overseas, and I also wanted to understand that.

Mom told stories about how she grew up driven to seek approval, running into the house and asking if she was doing a good job after she swept each concrete block on the sidewalk. She took it as a personal failure when no one accepted the cream and sugar she offered at her mother's tea parties. She'd cry silently in the closet from the rejection if no one was interested. She endlessly tried to get attention, most often by faking sickness or injury.

Mom would cozy up to the heat register to make her forehead hot and feverish. She would lie on the ground under a swing set, making it look as though she had fallen off. After she twisted herself into a position on the ground as if she'd been injured, she'd wait for someone to rescue her, eventually giving up when no one seemed to notice her lying there.

Her father's narcissistic focus on his own ideas and his business meant his daughter often went unnoticed. Even at the age of seventy-five, Mom still displayed a picture of her father with her perched on his knee. Our grandfather suffered from bipolar symptoms that his daughter inherited. His migraine headaches drew his attention away as well. It wasn't that he didn't love his children. They were sometimes brought along on business trips. It was the pervasive neglect, and his insistence on having things his way that eventually led to the self-imposed moniker, "Crazy Dad."

Whatever the factors that led to her suicide attempt in New Guinea, Mom returned home earlier than planned in 1968. While she was in the southern hemisphere, half of her family had converted from the Lutheran to the Mormon faith, led by her brother, Paul[13]. When she got back to the States, she dutifully attended an LDS church service in Cedar Falls, Iowa.

Her father's influence had always cast a long shadow on her worldview, and with both of her parents converting, it felt lonely and marginal to remain Lutheran. The family members who weren't converting had married and moved away. Besides, she said that the Mormon missionaries who came to visit were lovely people, *always so sincere*.

Trying to make a new start in the United States, Laura moved to Minneapolis and took a job at the Hennepin County Juvenile Detention Center, a maximum-security facility for both male and female offenders. One of the most interesting people she met was the "real" Charlie Brown. He worked with the male offenders, so they didn't get to see each other often.

On Christmas Eve 1968, when only a few detainees remained over the holidays, Charlie Brown played the piano and sang. He reminded our mother of the cartoon character, and she learned that he and Charles Schulz were indeed good childhood friends and that Schulz had received his permission to base his *Peanuts* character on him. Mom said he was truly a wonderful human being—just one that seemed to have more than his fair share of melancholy.

Mom was back into a state of suicidal crisis by the spring of 1969, about a year after leaving New Guinea. Working at the juvenile detention center, county employees were supposed to go to a county health clinic. However, the doctor did nothing for Mom but send her home for the weekend, asking her to return on Monday. The only trouble was that suicidal feelings are a life-and-death problem, so this was like sending someone home with a heart attack. Even though she said, "I feel just like I did a year ago," it was not judged to be an emergency.

She turned to Dr. Green, a private physician, and called him when things were becoming too much to cope with. She asked him if he was busy. He bluntly stated he was, so she apologized and hung up, quietly determined never to bother anyone again. She devoured a bottle of sleeping pills and turned on the gas in the apartment she shared with three other "inhospitable women."

That landed Mom in the hospital, where the story gets confusing. She remembers being discharged shortly after that. She began seeing Dr. Green on an outpatient basis, but she quickly ended up in a six-week recuperation at Glenwood Hills Psychiatric Hospital. Glenwood Hills was a beautiful new facility dedicated to treating mental illnesses.

At one point, Laura met someone who recommended that she see one Reverend Pfotenhauer, a Lutheran minister who had a deliverance ministry in his basement in St. Paul. She described the meeting with Rev. Pfotenhauer as follows:

"He began to speak to the 'demons' in me, asking them questions. I was a bit shocked when my voice answered—without my volition—that his name was Bavasiki. He identified himself as the 'spirit of suicide.' . . . They proceeded and a second demon was identified. This one, called Kenona, refused to come out. He just said . . . 'It isn't time yet.' That seemed to be the end of it, and the session was over . . . He [Kenona] was the 'spirit of depression.'"

That's Mom's interpretation of her experience, and she says she was never suicidal after that. She doesn't seem to remember that she *was* suicidal again during our childhoods.

On a visit home to her family in Iowa, she was introduced to a recent Mormon convert, a nice young man. This was my future father, just home from the service. They saw each other at a ward (local congregation) event and exchanged small talk. Shortly afterward, Dad decided to move to Utah. Mom decided she was maybe not interested in him anyway because he was Mormon, and she was still trying to figure out her own faith in the wake of her family's conversion. At any rate, she was living in Minneapolis, not near Utah.

Mom didn't seriously consider converting from Lutheran to Mormon, until she went to a Billy Graham crusade and saw a table of literature with an anti-Mormon section. She compared what she'd experienced with Mormons to what she was reading in this denigrating literature. To her, those brochures were proof that people lied about Mormons. Therefore, the Mormon Church must be speaking the truth and was being persecuted. It was enough to tip Mom over the edge, and she decided to become a Mormon.

She began studying the texts of her new religion with devotion: the Bible,[14] the Book of Mormon,[15] the Doctrine and Covenants,[16] and the Pearl of Great Price.[17] Ultimately, she pursued her "desire for spiritual sustenance"[18] by moving to the Mormon mecca: Salt Lake City.

At this point, neither of our parents were aware that this religion is based on white supremacy. Joseph Smith created a religion with a story in which dark-skinned people in the Americas killed off light-skinned people. (Needless to say, there is no archeological evidence whatsoever for this having happened). Those dark-skinned people became Native Americans.

In January 1970, Dad took a job at the Visitor Center near the Temple in Salt Lake City. Later that month, Mom arrived in town to "deepen her understanding of her new faith," while using the Mormon Church's world-renowned library of family genealogy to learn about her family tree. The Mormon ritual of baptizing the dead has led them to amass the largest collection of records related to family history available anywhere.

Mom stopped into the Visitor Center to get information about the area. Again, our parents crossed paths. The fact that these two Iowans, who grew up blocks away from each other, both landed in Utah and crossed paths in the Mormon Visitor Center, compelled them to spend time together, especially at the genealogy library.

When church elders got word of the two new converts meeting by chance, they were confident God was asserting His will to have these two people marry. The odds of meeting in Iowa about six months before running into each other again in Utah had to be supernaturally small, right? They were both in Salt Lake City trying out a new faith as a remedy for old troubles. *There, in Salt Lake City, coincidences were interpreted as destiny.*

A tradition of the Mormon Church is to offer a "patriarchal blessing" when a patriarch of the church provides guidance about life,
ostensibly channeled straight from God. The patriarch is part of
a hierarchy not unlike the Catholic Church, with its single leader,
cardinals, and bishops.

The purpose of a patriarchal blessing is to restate one's connection to the tribes of Israel, provide gifts of spiritual knowledge,
and offer specific advice to individuals about their circumstances.
At a general conference of the Mormon Church, President Ezra
Taft Benson stated, "Study [your patriarchal blessing] carefully and
regard it as personal scripture to you—for that is what it is . . . then
read it regularly that you may know God's will for you."

Dad's blessing included a recommendation to marry and begin
a family. It was this spiritual mandate that led him to ask Mom to
become his wife. Mom had her own "vision" foretelling that this
marriage was God's plan, but she was more enthusiastic than John.
He silently felt manipulated into the whole thing by the church
elders. Within five months of meeting in Utah, they married with
two witnesses in attendance.

Given what I'd eventually learn about their past, this clearly was
the beginning of one of the most ill-advised couplings imaginable.
Prone to zealotry because of the desperation of their search, they
had neither the will nor the wherewithal to resist the elder's blessing.

During their short courtship, they learned almost nothing about
each other. Even our father's disclosure that a UFO had abducted
him failed to scare Mom away. Likewise, Dad did not call things off
after learning Mom participated in an exorcism. What did they have
in common besides growing up near each other in Iowa?

They knew they both liked to read. They both loved genealogy.
They both felt they were on a quest for the truth. Mostly they
enjoyed asking existential questions such as, "Which is God's true
church?" and "Which modern-day prophet should one follow?"

Much later, Mom would say, "I think it all boils down to that
your dad and I simply never were really 'in love,' although at the time
it seemed like a good idea. Who knew back then?" Dad only wanted
to join the Mormons because the angel Moroni called to him and

they talked about the Lost Tribes of Israel. He never counted on this whole family-responsibility angle. He could deal with getting married to this woman. He could love her. But he didn't think about the fatherhood duties. He wasn't up for them. He wasn't well.

Our parents met a couple named Kurt and Angie shortly after they got married. These two were hard-core survivalists who believed they needed to prepare for the coming invasion of the government due to the collapse of society. This was going to happen near the impending apocalypse. The omnipresent, always imminent apocalypse.

They had stored away a year's worth of supplies, and Mom and Dad attempted to do the same. Their survivalist friends told Mom she would be giving birth in the woods by the time of her due date if she got pregnant. They took our parents around to different stores to buy supplies for the coming Armageddon. Mom and Dad looked for land to purchase together with Kurt and Angie. Only a few months later, Mom was pregnant. When I arrived before the End Times, I surprised everyone.

Home pregnancy tests were not available over the counter at the time, so Mom went to some extreme lengths over a weekend to find out if she was expecting. She had heard about a Hungarian physician named Dr. Ignatz von Peczely, who re-founded the "science" of iridology. Iridology was "reading" the iris of the eye to detect medical conditions. Although discredited,[19] and probably in part because it was discredited, Mom sought someone who could perform this craft. The man she found told her that iridology only detects disease, not naturally occurring phenomena like pregnancies. She dragged our dad everywhere over the weekend, looking for someone to tell her if she was pregnant or not, but she ended up having to wait until Monday.

When I was older, Mom shared a letter with me about how she told our dad that they had a firstborn on the way:

"I rushed home from the doctor's office in the happiest state I had ever experienced. My feet never touched the ground. At home, I found your father reading a newspaper at the kitchen table. Coming up behind him, wrapping my arms around his chest, I announced, 'We are having a baby.' Immediately, he threw my arms from around him with such force as to send me flying backward across the room. His face became a deep purple, his eyes glowered, and his fists clenched. He left the house for the remainder of the day."

He was clearly not ready for the responsibility so soon. He didn't have a solid job yet. Anyone can understand where he was coming from. In the Mormon belief system, as the man, he was responsible for the family. At least in his family growing up, his parents had worked equally to support the family.

My college-educated mother wasn't exactly prepared to have me either. She thought that when I was born I wouldn't open my eyes for the first few days, just like a newborn puppy. She was amazed when I came into the world with big blue eyes full of curiosity. It seems like a significant gap in the education of a woman licensed to teach elementary school.

Thankfully, things got much better after I was born. Mama told me later: "You were completely doted upon by both your father and your mother. I remember when I had you wrapped up like a mummy in your blankie and I placed you between the pillows on our big double bed. Your dad just looked over at you—so tiny against that big bed [and cried, saying], 'You don't know what that little girl has done for me.'"

His attitude had changed quite a bit by then.

During the early part of her pregnancy, Mom went for prenatal care with a medical doctor. Once. Perhaps through years of influence from her very patriarchal father, Mom accepted alternative medicine much more than traditional medicine. Grandpa Meyer was famous for saying things like: "A lack of aspirin doesn't cause headaches"; "They took fifty years to accept the thermometer"; and, "Remember, the establishment mocked the man who said hand-washing was key to preventing disease[20]."

At the appointment, an argument ensued between Mom and the doctor, whom she saw as hyper-arrogant, over the best way to proceed with her delivery. The doctor said, "If you're going to be so pigheaded about it, why don't you go home and deliver your own baby?"

The suggestion became her new conviction. She found a naturopath who agreed to deliver her firstborn at home. This doctor, Rulon Allred, would later become famous for his violent death at the hands of a faction of fundamentalist Mormons. My parents had no idea Allred had five wives and was the leader of a polygamous cult. In 1977, a rival cult leader ordered one of his wives to kill Allred.[21] Allred's name appears on my birth certificate, though it was actually one of his associates who delivered me.

Until 1890, polygamy was a doctrine of the Mormon Church. However, after about sixty years of being mocked by other Christians and out of a desire to join Utah with the United States, the Church opted to outlaw polygamy or, as many advocates like to call it, "plural marriage."

A group of followers who disagreed with the change in the church's stance broke off, many moving north to Canada or south to Mexico to live out their beliefs in communal settings. Those who remained in Utah frequently skirmished with each other, and once with the federal government. In a 1979 stand-off, federal agents ended up killing one such Utahan, John Singer. This fed our parents' anti-government attitudes.

Our parent's association with Dr. Allred, led the elders of their church ward to call them in for "a meeting." The elders questioned the circumstances of their connection to Allred and warned them about interacting with him. Defiant toward authority in their own ways, my parents likely became only more determined to learn about fundamentalist Mormons. This was the first rumbling of my family's avalanche of later problems. In many ways, it was predictable that they would be vulnerable to a cult.

Shortly after getting married, Mom brought home a little blue book from the Salt Lake City Public Library that in her words "caught her eye." She saw *Book of Onias*,[22] authored by Robert C. Cross-field, and she felt "drawn" to it. Mama felt the Holy Spirit, (or as Mormons frequently said, the Holy Ghost), calling her to read his book.

Crossfield was a self-proclaimed prophet and seer, a man who was extreme enough to have been rejected from all the Fundamentalist Latter-day Saint (FLDS) sects. In his 1969 book, Crossfield revealed that LDS leadership was misleading the Mormon Church. The Mormons, he argued, had abandoned Joseph Smith's teachings when they agreed to give up polygamy in exchange for being part of the United States. He chastised the faithful for abandoning polygamy and called on Latter-day Saints to heed the words of the church's founding prophets, Joseph Smith and Brigham Young.

Smith's revelations focused on marriage. Essentially, Smith told his followers that God wanted humanity to practice polygamy with men having multiple wives, just as occurred in the Old Testament. Smith married more than three dozen women himself.

Also known by his self-decreed name — the "Prophet Onias" — Crossfield wrote about receiving a series of revelations from God beginning in 1961. He received divine guidance "straight from the Lord" that men were to have multiple wives as Abraham of the Old Testament had. He appealed to fellow Mormons to look at sections promoting "plural marriage" in the *Doctrine and Covenants*, an LDS holy book. Onias knew directly from the source that God was unhappy with this betrayal because having multiple wives was "the Most Holy Principle." Most LDS members rejected Onias's teachings, and the Church eventually excommunicated him. Onias's presence threatened the leadership of sects of the fundamentalist Mormons too. They let him visit their compounds, but he didn't seem to have permission to stay.

Enamored with Crossfield's apparent connection to God, our parents wrote to him in 1971 and invited him down to Salt Lake City to share his revelations in person. Excited to have potential new followers, the Prophet Onias obliged and said he would come to Salt Lake City to visit. He traveled with two of his daughters from a small town in Alberta, Canada, to Utah shortly after I was born.

Onias's girls were dressed in the traditional clothing of funda-mentalist Mormons: long dresses that covered them from neck to toe, and they didn't wear any makeup. Their long hair was braided and twisted into an attractive style. They were the picture of de-mure, polite, submissive women trained to serve their male superi-ors.

Mom was impressed when Onias took me as an infant into the bedroom and cuddled me to his chest as he rested from the long drive. She liked how fatherly and family-oriented he was. He cer-tainly reacted to me in an immediately positive way that differed significantly from how Dad had initially responded. For this reason alone, she was drawn to Onias.

Our parents said goodbye to Onias, enthralled with him. "The Most Holy Principle" he taught about polygamy as God's highest law appealed to them. Even Dad was intrigued. But he was now supposed to go out and find *another* wife to have children with. I imagine my father thought he could exercise more choice this time. Having just gotten married to Dad, Mom wasn't sure she felt ready to share him. But she was eager to get on with the process of starting their plural marriage if that was what God wanted.

They kept in touch with Crossfield but chose not to move to Canada to live with what Crossfield hoped would be his growing congregation. They were going to be a part of Onias's scattered flock—a flock spread out all over North America, and beyond, too. They began several years of studying Onias's teachings. When he received a new revelation, he mailed a copy to our parents.

Shortly after Onias's visit, Dad declared that Salt Lake City was too oppressive for him. Too many rules, too much dogma. He liked coffee. He wanted to smoke Camel Straights again like he had in the Air Force. Mormons did not do such things. Strangely enough, fundamentalist Mormons have not always followed the same rules about avoiding alcohol, caffeine, and tobacco that the mainstream LDS Church has.

Besides, the park they loved to take me to, Liberty Park, became the scene of a double murder—a mixed-race couple jogging together, the crime motivated by racism. Mom was certain it was a legacy from the racist past of Utah. Our parents decided to move home to Iowa. But if that's where Dad was going to avoid feeling oppressed, he was heading to the wrong place.

Chapter Two: Dad Just Can't Adjust

MOM AND DAD OPTED to live in a home near Dad's grandparents in Nashua, Iowa. They loved living there. They spent time in Cannon Park with me. They got ice cream together at the Dairy Queen. They talked about everything over coffee, but God especially occupied their conversations. Dad considered our little family perfect. The only thing that could ruin all this was the announcement of another pregnancy. The maintenance job Dad had would not support a family of four, and there were no other jobs available in Nashua.

They were going to have to move closer to his parents by turning to the city where the jobs were—Waterloo. Our dad decided he would take classes at Hawkeye Community College here to study civil engineering when he was not at work. Dad would end up feeling like he failed at this because he could never get a turn using the equipment he needed for class. It's a near certainty, though, that his disorganized mind and psychotic thinking were a substantial factor in his inability to complete college classes.

Once in Waterloo, Dad felt miserable being so close to his parents. They had been living in the house his grandparents had lived in, while his parents lived less than ten miles away in Cedar Falls. Only a few years prior, his folks had kicked him out of their house after he got home from the service. The rest of the family didn't know the details of what happened during that time; they only knew that Dad did not get along well with his parents. He especially felt like he could never please them, win their approval, or raise his status within the family.

Dad had already converted from the strong—let's say rigid--Catholic tradition in his family to being a fundamentalist Mormon. He tried to keep this fact hidden from his parents, while avoiding invitations to Mass. He'd had his fill of Catholicism from going to Catholic school all the way to high school graduation. He dodged questions about where he and Mom got married, by whom, and in what faith. If his parents had known he was building up the courage to add a second wife, they would have exploded on the spot.

Mom's insistence on delivering her children at home instead of a hospital was already drawing our grandma's side-eye glances of disapproval. It was plain that Grandma thought a lot of what Mom said was strange. Mom is a talker, and when she's nervous, she'll go nonstop. Grandma could have heard a thought stream of Mom's ideas about alternative medicine. And religion. And lots of other questionable topics.

Grandma, on the other hand, was a woman of science. If she'd had her choice, she would have had a doctorate in Family Science or Family Ecology, where her expertise in preserving cloth from the 1800s would be in research journals. She did achieve a graduate degree in Home Economics, which was the Family Science of her school, but she'd wanted to continue her education.

Being a wife and mother got in the way. For a woman who overcame polio to walk again, succumbing to barriers was considered anathema. In the end, for most of her life, Grandma MacIntyre[23] was a full-time, adjunct professor at the University of Northern Iowa in the Home Economics department. Eventually, the university named a small museum collection after her that housed her textiles from the 1800s and early 1900s, but it's extremely difficult to access.

Mom insists that when she met Dad's family she could automatically notice a strong favoritism toward Dad's younger brother, Stan. She said Dad never spoke of any dynamic like that, but she picked up on it. Over time, Mom would hear about how Stan was allowed to do things Dad never got to do, like play football, get braces, get his higher education partially paid for, and even socialize during high school.

Not long after my brother, David, was born in 1973 (at home, in our parents' bedroom, without a midwife) we all moved again. This time, instead of leaning on Dad's parents, we leaned on Mom's. For our new home, Mom and Dad moved into the apartment above Grandpa Meyer's chiropractic office/home in Sheboygan, Wisconsin, where my memories began. Where Dad had a great job at a chemical factory. Where Dad got so sick.

To hear Mom tell it, everything went wrong sometime in the spring of 1975 when I was four years old. There was a noise, a cross between a thud and a crack, that came from the living room. Dad had fallen.

The 911 emergency line didn't exist yet. You just had to call the ambulance. Mama grabbed towels from the bathroom and pressed them against our father's face as she cradled his head and shoulders in what was left of her lap, since her tummy was inflated with baby Samuel[24]. When the towels were soaked, she pulled the red bandana from her long, straight blonde hair and pressed it against his nose. "Don't just stand there staring, help him!" she yelled at Grandpa, her pale blue eyes flashing with anger. Grandpa stooped down, took Dad's hand from mine, and touched his wrist. "He's got a steady pulse." Dad's groans grew louder.

Emergency sirens wailed in the distance. They were so far away! But eventually, people in uniforms were whirling around, trying to figure out how to get the stretcher cradling our father down the long flight of stairs. I ducked out of the way into my room.

After the blaring sirens, the crackling of the emergency radios, the yelling voices, and the stomping feet faded from our home, I crept back out to where Dad had fallen. Grandpa had his camera out. I was worried about Dad and grossed out by the blood. "Look at this," Grandpa said. When I glanced to where he was pointing, I saw the imprint of my father's two front teeth embedded in the blood-smeared hardwood floor. Grandpa finished snapping pictures. I'd share them, but they were damaged in a flood.

Mom came home alone when it was dark. She was quiet, but I wasn't sleeping. When she stole a look into our room, she saw my eyes were open. "Is Daddy okay?"

"I don't know, sweetie. I just don't know." She started to tell me a story, but didn't finish it, just curled up with me on my twin bed and fell asleep.

As the days passed, Dad remained in the hospital. I missed putting together puzzles with him and listening to him read me bedtime stories. I also missed his mischievous nature.

Before he got sick, we spent our evenings as a family, gathered on worn furniture and braided floor rugs to watch TV programs that Mom considered wholesome enough. *Little House on the Prairie*, *Star Trek*, and *The Waltons* all passed her scrutiny. Long before it became popular to ask, "What would Jesus do?" my mom was doing her own version of trying to be like Jesus. Hollywood was a known polluter of children's minds, so she asked herself what Jesus would let us watch.

While Mom was an authoritarian about keeping her children pure, Dad was more permissive. He would let me sneak out to watch detective shows like *Quincy, M.E. or Charlie's Angels* with him after Mom went to sleep. I became a lifelong lover of crime dramas and mysteries. And TV.

Figure 3 Dad with David and me

Our family's second-floor apartment was located above the room where Grandma slept, and the office where Grandpa was a chiropractor. He got his degree at a prestigious school for chiropractic medicine in Texas. So did Grandma Meyer[25], but she never practiced as a chiropractor. She only served as Grandpa Meyer's receptionist. Grandpa brought in his mother to care for his children and kept his wife by his side at work.

Grandpa's greatest insights came from his study of Eastern medicine. He believed deep and rhythmic breathing held benefits for the immune system and physical well-being generally, so he created a chair that reclined bodies into a position perfect for deep diaphragmatic breathing, with your legs supported in the air and your head rested at a declining angle. In other words, the chair almost turned a person upside down. It looked fun, but it was too big for children to use. There were plenty of other things to play with in Grandpa's chiropractic office. First, there was the adjustment table, contoured to the human body, which could move a standing person into the position of lying down when Grandpa stepped on the right button.

Once patients were slowly lowered flat, Grandpa would twist and manipulate their necks and spines. Crack . . . pop . . . over and over. Then, there were gushing thank yous to Grandpa for making their pain feel better. Grandpa also had an X-ray machine, and he would sometimes allow us to put the film of an anonymous neck or spine up on the backlight.

There were reminders in the apartment behind the office of what must have been Grandma Meyer's personality before she developed brain cancer. She was completely of Finnish origin, and the Finns love their saunas. Grandma's sauna wasn't a room like those at the local spa. Her sauna sat nestled into a corner of the mudroom separating Grandpa's chiropractic office from where they lived. It was the small kind of sauna that you sat in naked, with your head sticking out the top. Our grandma was not well enough to tell me tales of how good the moist heat would be for my health, but Mom reminded me often. When the sauna wasn't turned on, it was a perfect spot for hide-and-seek.

Chapter Three: Narcissistic Abuse

ASIDE FROM HIS MEDICAL equipment, Grandpa knew a few ways to entertain children between patients on slow days. He kept a stock of colorful balloons at the office reception desk that he blew up and twisted into animal shapes.

He also made a habit of swinging children back and forth through the air by their ankles. Not only was it obvious to him that most youngsters loved the thrill of flying, but he also believed that the swinging motion provided corrective benefits for little spines knocked out of whack during routine slips and falls. When he was too tired to swing, Grandpa loved to bounce children on his lap; randomly, he would pull his knees apart to allow a sudden, but safe, plunge.

After they took Dad away without bringing him back for a few months, Mama packed up the car trunk with blankets, a picnic basket, and a cooler. She put our favorite drinks, little grape juice cans with plastic pull tops, into fresh ice in the cooler. Mama pushed forward the driver's seat of our Chevy Impala and told David, then me, to hop in the back.

As she drove, we passed by billboards and signs with bright company logos that gave way to alternating patches of trees and farmland. We passed a few fields with quite a few cows. We were going for a trip to the hospital where Dad was staying.

David and I usually teased each other on car rides. Sometimes I would poke or tickle him, anything to make him giggle. This time, we each looked out our windows in silence.

Eventually, Mom turned into a long driveway surrounded by perfectly spaced, large trees growing in flawlessly mowed, thick, green grass.

It was a large, regional hospital for people with tuberculosis. Mom argued with the receptionist and the nurses. We children were not allowed to go and see Dad because he was under quarantine. The nurses said that the problem making our dad sick could also hurt children if we got near him. Mama was not pleased. The nurses were irritated. After Mama disappeared around a corner, I heard the nurses whispering, "What was that woman thinking coming in here pregnant and with small children?"

The waiting room got boring after a long while, so I took David outside to roll down a hill behind the hospital. I ended up dizzy after turning and tumbling just once. David gurgled in bliss on his third trip down. Mom found us outside and hustled us back into the car. She smiled much more than she before on the way back from the hospital. She was relieved as she told us that Dad would be coming home soon.

The doctors had figured out that he actually didn't have tuberculosis as they had assumed, which was the whole reason he had been sent to a TB hospital in isolation. Instead, he had hepatitis and valley fever, also known as *coccidioidomycosis*, an infection in his lungs.[26] He had originally contracted both conditions while serving in the Air Force. When his immune system weakened from working in a paint factory full of chemicals, both illnesses flared up.

We stopped at a park on the way home and had a picnic. I started to feel better after a peanut butter sandwich and grape juice. There were many bushes in the picnic area with bright red berries. David and I brought samples of different berries back to Mom so she could look in a wildlife survival guide to check if the little fruits were edible. None of the berries we found that afternoon were potential food. But Mom noticed that in the wild, dandelions *were* considered a source of food. After trying them, both David and I spat them back out. Bitter. Yuck. Nevertheless, with that book, in the event our family decided to hide away in the wilderness, we were ready to live off the land.

Dad was back at home in a few days and spending a lot of time in bed. When he came out at night to watch his favorite detective show, about Jim Rockford and his dad Rocky, I peeked around the piano to look at him. He had a yellow tint around his blue eyes where it should have been white, and his skin was a sickly yellow too.

"*Red or yellow, black or white, they are precious in his sight, Jesus loves the little children of the World . . .*"[27] I sang the little tune to myself. So, this was a yellow person. Since he looked tired and grumpy, it was a good thing that God loved him.

A few weeks later, Mama dislocated her knee while moving furniture around, so two of her sisters came to stay with us. At the time, I didn't realize that Mom was sending out pleas for help, and that everything was falling apart, especially for Grandma. From a preschooler's point of view, life was carefree: Head Start, books, puzzles, toys, and television. But, much later on, owing to our extended family's pack-rat tendencies, I found a February 1975 letter from Mom to our aunt revealing a very different picture:

"*If you knew what an effort it is sometimes merely to get up out of a chair, or to bend over from what I can figure out, the organs and tissues don't get an adequate supply of blood, and it's sort of like when the juice goes down, the lights everywhere don't burn as brightly, the iron doesn't get as hot, the radio slows down, etc. to be MENTALLY DEPRESSED; and to have DIGESTIVE DISTURBANCES, COLD HANDS AND FEET, and VAGUE PAINS*[28][29]. *Boy, is that me, eh?*"

Our visiting aunts cooked and helped us with our baths. Feeling happier with some help, Mom would frequently sit at the old upright piano in our living room playing songs until her wrists hurt. She also knew how to play the accordion. The whole family, including our grandparents, would often gather around her to dance and sing. They especially liked a rousing polka number. Soon, Mom complained that her crutches made her underarms hurt, especially since she was bursting with the baby almost ready to be born. She stayed in bed, lying next to Dad while he slept and slept.

I was lucky enough to be picked for Head Start, the preschool program for poor kids. I was enrolled in the local program when fall came. As I got ready for school on the first morning, I followed my routine of watching *Sesame Street*. I was so disappointed that leaving for school meant missing the rest of the program I loved so obsessively that I almost changed my mind about going to preschool.

But at the end of my short school day, I discovered that I could turn on the television to find that the second half of *Sesame Street* was on. This "divided *Sesame Street*" effect led me to believe that television shows stopped when you turned off the set and resumed when you returned. This arrangement alleviated any misgivings I had about school, so I was free to enjoy my new activity. I liked being around the other children, and I couldn't get enough of the sand table.

My fortunate enrollment in Head Start was the result of three things. The first was my parents' shame-ridden decision to seek out food stamps at my grandma's encouragement. My parents considered themselves conservatives who were firm believers in the notion that you should get by on your own without relying on government programs, so I was blessed they gave in to sheer need. Second, my grandma had pointed out that they were entitled to benefits because Dad had enlisted to serve his country during a war. Third, the state policy at the time was to *bundle social programs*, which meant you were offered all the services available to a person on the date of application. So, when my mom applied for food stamps, she was also applying for Head Start, Medicaid, etc. That policy brought an educational intervention into my life that I needed but would not have otherwise gotten.

While I was at school, my little brother, David, being only three years old, spent his mornings throwing a tantrum because he wasn't allowed to go to school too. Then he spent the rest of his day with Mom while she ran the household. Dad went to work at the K.W. Muth Company, which manufactured chemicals and paints. Mom said that once, when she picked Dad up from work, she saw a man light a cigarette at the entrance to the factory, and the flames flashed up two feet in the air. She didn't like Dad working around dangerous fumes, but, as he put it, he never went to college, so he didn't have many options. Since this factory was where he got sick, he had to quit, so Dad didn't have a steady job anymore.

One day in September not long after her birthday, Mom suddenly left to go to the hospital. She was angry about it. She wanted to give birth to all her children at home, but her sisters said they weren't helping her give birth at home with a messed-up leg. Mom was convinced the hospital would be horrible, and it turned out to be exactly that. The day she went into labor, she arrived at the admitting desk on crutches, and the nurse misinterpreted her needs. So, she sat in the lobby for quite a while having contractions. Finally, her sister went up to the desk and raised a stink. Apologies were made. They didn't even let her kiss Samuel when she went to hold him for the first time. It was too unsanitary, they said.

She came back after being at the hospital for a few days. Not long after, David had to go to the hospital for spinal meningitis. It got serious, such that David could die, and Mom cried almost continuously. I felt guilty for all the times that I had left my little brother out of my play. I made a vow to change when my brother returned from the hospital. Eventually, about two weeks later, David got better.

Still, Mom was not done dealing with major stressors. Grandma Meyer was dying, and we expected her to pass away within weeks. Watching her mother deteriorate broke our mom's heart. In my oblivious state of early childhood, I was uplifted by the parade of visitors who came to see Grandma. Most of the visitors were family: our aunts, uncles, and cousins who stayed around for musical sessions with Mom at the piano or on the accordion. They read to me. They nourished our environment. They were our village. For months these family members had come to stay with our dying

Grandma, our pregnant, injured mother, and our sick father. This was all going to come to a screeching halt.

Mom was happy Samuel was born when he was since her mother got to hold him a little bit before she died, about a month later. In October 1975, Grandpa Meyer bundled up his childhood sweetheart, put her in the back seat of his car and drove her across Wisconsin and halfway across Iowa so she could die in Iowa, enabling him to collect on a life insurance policy. Then, when she died, instead of paying for a hearse to come and get her body, he asked around until he found someone who would loan him a pickup truck for him to haul her body. (I can't stop picturing poor Grandma bouncing around in the back of the truck as he drove to the funeral home). Eventually, my Grandpa Meyer took my grandma to Minnesota to bury her. I was too young to go, and I missed Mom and Grandpa while they were gone.

Arguably, most Americans are raised within an evangelical-authoritarian hierarchy. That is to say, we learn that: "*1) God is above all else; 2) We only live this life for the afterlife; 3) After man serving God, woman serves man; 4) Children serve parents; 5) The poor serve the rich; 6) Whites are over other races; 7) Straight is over gay; 8) Humans are over nature; 9) The healthy are over the sick*"[30]. This hierarchy is not unknown. It mostly just goes undescribed. Out of this hierarchy comes misogyny, sexism, racism, child abuse, homophobia, spiritual abuse, and a whole host of social ills. However, all these problems are driven at least in part by the violence and abuse of a personality dynamic: the narcissistic abuse cycle.[31] This refers to the bond of the bully and his victim.

Evidence of Grandpa Meyer's narcissistic abuse is left behind in his many letters to family. In these letters, he degrades and berates anyone expressing dissent, but he elevates and praises anything he perceives to reflect glory onto him. Mom once told Grandpa that he didn't have to be so stubborn, so he kicked her hard in her backside, showing her that dissent meant physical punishment.

What becomes clear is that this is not only my family's own sickness but society's as well. Unfortunately, Grandpa Meyer was attracted to a theory that the poor were genetically inferior. He probably believed he was genetically superior as a German man and a man with money. Little did he understand his own family was going to get the genetic purification axe. In reality, Mom and Dad were both mentally ill and poor.

Later in life, Grandpa Meyer became addicted to talk radio host Rush Limbaugh, subscribing to his every opinion. Without realizing it, Grandpa was being groomed to buy into what has become known as the Great Replacement Theory. This theory was first highlighted in the 1987 book, *The Birth Dearth*,[32] by the American Enterprise Institute's Ben Wattenberg. Wattenberg wrote:

"The main problem confronting the United States today is that there are not enough white babies being born in this country. If we don't change this, and change this rapidly, white people will lose their numerical majority in this country, and this will no longer be a white man's land.

"There are three things we can do to solve this. Number one: We can pay women to have babies as they have been doing in Western European nations for years. Unfortunately, we would have to pay women of all colors to have babies, so we don't want to do that. The second thing we could do is increase the number of legal immigrants that are allowed into this country every year.

"Unfortunately, the vast majority of those wanting to come to this country are people of color, so we don't want to do that. Sixty percent of the fetuses that are aborted each year are white. If we could keep that sixty percent alive, we could solve the birth dearth."

Grandpa Meyer would have been ready to hear rhetoric that said immigrants from South America, South Asia, and the Arabian Peninsula would overtake the white population of the United States.[33] Both of his sons embraced that rhetoric a generation later. And his grandsons two generations later.

But our grandfather wasn't focused initially on immigration. He was concerned with white women and their birth rate, especially relative to Black women and their birth rate. His politics were focused on race within the United States. His daughter would produce six white children.

Folks don't realize it, but it isn't Darwin they are referencing when they talk about survival of the fittest.[34] That can be attributed to Herbert Spencer, a eugenicist. He believed that you should not build things such as libraries for the poor,[35] as it just encouraged the genetically inferior to try to rise above their limitations.

Grandpa Meyer looms large in our lives because he was politically divisive. But so are other family members. Uncle Paul's decision to join the Mormon Church also weighs heavily. These men influenced Mom so much that she didn't have any notion of an identity outside what they'd written for her. This, in turn, would influence the rest of our family.

"My first memories are mostly of being rescued by your grandpa," our mother told us later in life. "He had to carry me into the house after I fell off a swing, and another time, I got a nasty dog bite. He was a giant of a man, especially to a little girl, and it felt good to have him come to my rescue. I must admit, I started to manufacture emergencies to get his attention. Unfortunately, as the fourth child out of six, it was easy to be overlooked."

Our egotistical grandpa was a domineering man. He was physically imposing as well, over six feet tall, with a broad chest and legs that allowed him to make record-breaking mile runs at the community college he attended. Not only was he athletic but he was also handsome. Besides having a voice that carried far, he was also clearly in command of not just his family but also his interactions with other people. He fancied himself a salesperson, although he was not. He talked too much, wouldn't let people get a word in, and ended up annoying many a listener. But he was also a genius. He invented things like his diaphragmatic breathing chair.

Born in 1915, our Grandpa Meyer[36] grew up in the Minnesota north country among white pines and iron miners. He could see no limit to his potential on his good days, but cameras often caught his lurking depression.

Figure 4. Grandpa Meyer

His family had invested in real estate and came through the Great Depression in better shape than most Americans. When he graduated high school in 1933, he was able to earn an associate's degree. Access to any form of higher education in the middle of the Depression showed that his family's wealth was above the norm. There were also relatives from the Twin Cities, who came to visit in limousines.

When C.K. Klein, one of his uncles and a St. Paul banker, passed away, the obituary in the *Minneapolis Star Tribune* described him as one of the state's wealthiest men. Our grandpa was said to have inherited a nice sum, although I never knew how much.

Being just a bit better off than the other workers never left our grandpa's mind. He taught his children, including Mom, that they were better than other people. He was unquestionably a snob, and the money contributed to this belief. The fact that he was good at athletics and academics didn't help. He might have been completely insufferable if he didn't have an empathetic streak. He also had two brothers and their wives living with his family. This living situation meant Grandpa spent his time around aching miners, hearing their frequent complaints of sore backs. He knew at a young age that he would become a chiropractor and treat back pain. He went to Texas Chiropractic College in San Antonio, Texas.

Grandpa had been a highly successful chiropractor in Waterloo for about ten years when, in 1955, two major events happened. First, Mom's sister Cleo[37] caught Grandpa providing more than chiropractic services to a woman known in the area to be a prostitute. Mom, being young, wasn't privy to what was going on, but she knew her new baton got bent in half when Grandpa hit my Aunt Cleo with it. The baton beating may have been because of what Cleo saw, or it may have been because she came home pregnant as a sixteen-year-old at about the same time. Second, with family scandals and his own bad back dogging him, Henry decided to quit his chiropractic practice, move north to forty acres of land, and start a family business building RVs. The timing was perfect in his mind because Eisenhower had just created the national interstate highway system.

A proud man, Grandpa came home from the many RV shows he attended with his RV prototype, "The Escort," and told his family that his idea was ahead of its time. He did hold two patents on RV upgrades that were unique designs, allowing for collapsible extensions of the sides and back of a unit. They are still in use on RVs today. Privately, he must have worried that his business would have to offer something special because the competition was growing rapidly.

After reading about Grandpa's aerodynamically designed recreational vehicles in John Gartner's 1969 book, *All About Pickup Campers, Van Conversions, and Motor Homes,*[38] customers from Alaska to New York would drive to Iowa to pick up their custom-made vehicles. The pinnacle of his business career occurred when the *Ford Times* featured one of his models on the cover of their flagship auto industry magazine, and then the Kmart Corporation put a picture of his RV on the cover of one of their small US road atlases.

Instead of implementing what could be learned from that rapid growth into his business plan, he customized each RV with improvements from the previous model. This business strategy might have been profitable if he'd charged enough to compensate for the research and development. He did not. He never managed to get into major production as a result.

Because of his uneven business achievements, our mercurial Grandpa would spend hours yelling and preaching, often in the middle of the night, criticizing and blaming Grandma for what he perceived were her efforts to sabotage the family business. Grandma had been nervous about getting out of the established chiropractic business where they had done well and going into the risky new venture of building recreational vehicles. The RV business struggled over ten years, and Grandma worked hard to support it. They experienced three fires that burned his business workshops to the ground. So, because Grandma had been reluctant initially, Grandpa would take his setbacks out on her. Grandma never argued back; it was always a one-sided battle.

When Grandma asked their oldest son, Paul, to go and get a "real job" to support the family, it set Grandpa off even more. He would rant about Clara Ford, Henry Ford's wife, and how she was a true believer in her husband's business ideas.

Over and over, he would say, "Clara the Believer stood by her man, never let him feel unsupported. And look what happened with their family. They were the richest family, or close to it, during the Depression."

Grandpa felt the need to bring investors into the business. The company, Organizers and Underwriters, Inc., exercised a lot of power over decisions. It changed the logo and the business cards, and moved the location of the business to a place that was to quite a distance from where Grandpa lived. He was losing control of the inventions he had created. It wasn't his business anymore. Worse than that, these investors were *purposely* killing the business, perhaps to benefit the competition.

Our widowed great-grandma (Grandpa's mother) had lived with the family for many years, helping to cook, clean and watch the children. Even she thought he was too prone to infuriated, violent fits. Once she shook her fist at him and vowed to haunt him from her grave for his stubbornness. When she died unexpectedly one night, it was a hard loss for everyone, but particularly crushing for Grandpa. It turned out that she'd had an allergic reaction to a penicillin shot that a doctor gave her on a house call. The fact that mainstream medicine was responsible for her death did not go unnoticed by our anti-medical establishment chiropractor grandfather either.

Then, one windy, wintry day not long after her Grandma died, Mom came home early from school to find Grandpa had gone out of control. The house was a mess, chairs were overturned, and a pot of soup had been thrown all over. The scene was very frightening to her, so she drove into town to get their pastor. When they returned, no one was around. Foot tracks led out to the grove behind the house. They couldn't figure out what had happened. Pretty soon, Mom's brother Paul showed up and said he'd been called home from school by their mother, who had run to a neighbor's house for help. The pastor and our uncle finally found Grandpa in the top of one of their barns cowering and sobbing, and they sent him to the state mental hospital.

He wouldn't tell a soul what he was told about his diagnosis, but Grandpa often repeated that the psychiatrists believed he was "an ingenious man who struggled to be understood." He also was proud of the fact he only "cheeked" the medications the psychiatrists were trying to give him, instead of swallowing them. There was no way Henry Meyer was taking mainstream medicine. It's hard to say what the therapists were telling him, but he only heard their positive assessments of him, which is typical of a narcissist. Nonetheless, this hospitalization became a source of extreme bitterness for Grandpa.

Eventually, Mom learned that Grandpa's diagnosis had been "agitative depression."

In 1968, after Mom's goodbye party for her Lutheran mission to Papua New Guinea, Grandpa Meyer stepped on Grandma Meyer's head when she was napping on the floor, and then told her if she was going to let other people walk all over her, he would too.

Chapter Four: Our Only Family Vacation

MOM WAS MISERABLE. HER husband was sick. Her mother had died. Her son, David, had almost died from a bout of meningitis. She felt like a single parent to three children. Her father had betrayed her by not giving her husband a job as he'd promised. Society was changing. Women needed to work outside the home to support their families. The fact that Mom was mentally ill was a wrinkle in this emerging social demand.

Everything was going wrong. The doctors were recommending that Dad avoid exposure to air coming off the lake for the benefit of his lung condition. Mom decided it seemed like a good time to get away, a good time for what would be our only real family vacation.

She packed five sleeping bags into the back seat of the Impala, allowing David and me to see our surroundings, despite our short statures. There were no child safety seat or seat belt laws in those days. By today's safety standards, driving this way was foolishly death defying. But there was a ready supply of grape and vegetable juice in small metal cans with plastic pull tabs, and more food in the trunk alongside our tent. It was time for an adventure.

As we drove through Wisconsin, Dad amazed me as he told me the starting point and destination of every railroad track we encountered; I thought he was simply brilliant. Whenever we had to stop the car to wait for a passing train, he told us where the train was headed. Maybe he should have been a train conductor.

We drove to a Manitowoc, a city on the coast of Lake Michigan, that had a ferry service to the Upper Peninsula of Michigan. I was impressed to learn that a ship could hold cars as well as people. Dad drove the car right onto this huge boat. Our family stood together at the side of the ship and watched the water turn as it cut through each wave.

On the other end of the lake, camping and sightseeing began. Dad was never fond of highways or other frequently traveled roadways, so he took us along back roads and dirt trails. We stopped to pitch a tent for the night at various campgrounds, and eventually, our journey took us into Canada. On a day trip in Ontario, we took the Algoma Central train into the mountains to see the Agawa Canyon.

The driving itself was made all the more pleasurable by Mom's singing. She would get us started with a rousing version of, "We Ain't Got a Barrel of Money," or "This Land Is Our Land." Dad didn't like to sing, but he never objected to our off-key renditions of the folk songs Mom loved. When we weren't singing, David and I played word games that had us giggling uncontrollably. Incessant chatter annoyed Dad, and he often commanded us to be quiet with his thunderous voice. His threats to stop the car were rarely, if ever, realized.

Dad liked the quiet, but he also loved listening to music on the radio from time to time. Sometimes he'd play his Gordon Lightfoot eight-track cassette. Mama was convinced "rock" music was unholy, but she would begrudgingly let him listen to it for short periods of time. There has never been a time of greater contentment for me than those handful of days on the highway with the sun warming our faces and Neil Diamond crooning love songs on the radio. I was five years old. David was three. Samuel was a baby. If only it had stayed that way. If only our parents could have gotten along like they did on that trip. If we could have stayed the way we were as we traveled around Michigan, Ontario, and Wisconsin, we would have been happy. But Dad was still sick, and mental illness lurked darkly in our lives.

Chapter Five:
Everything Comes
Apart

I T WAS THE TWO hundredth birthday of the United States, and the whole country was having a bash. We were still living in Sheboygan, Wisconsin. On the evening of the 4th of July, 1976, fireworks lit the sky over Lake Michigan. Our family sat in lawn chairs on our back patio.

The back patio usually served more utilitarian purposes. On laundry day, clotheslines were strung. Mom believed clothes were not handled suitably unless they dried in fresh air and sunlight. She used an old-fashioned wringer washing machine in the basement, and I assisted her with running clothes through the wringers to squeeze out the water. Then I would help her hang them up to dry. She lowered the height of one of the clotheslines just for me.

That Bicentennial night, the back patio was ideal for family togetherness. We had a picture-perfect view of the fireworks without having to walk down to the lake. Dad got out of bed to sit with us. Nothing seemed finer than having three generations of our family sitting as a small tribe. The setting exuded the kind of security a strong, free country and a tight-knit family always promised to provide. It was a conservative's dream.

That's when our folks broke the news to us. We were moving across the state. The only life I had known was in Sheboygan. My best friend was there. I went to Head Start there. I loved my kindergarten class there. I was supposed to start first grade that fall at the school right across the street from where I had gone to kindergarten. Instead, Mom and Dad started packing up everything we owned. I cried for so long and so hard when I heard about the move that I gave myself a tremendous, throbbing headache.

David didn't seem to mind it at all. He did as he had always done—tagged along after me no matter what I did. Baby brother Samuel, nearly a twin to David with pale blonde hair and azure blue eyes, not quite a year old, was especially indifferent about moving. I was the only one who was miserable—at least at first. I was going to be starting the 1976 school year in an unfamiliar place. The most traumatic experience in my short life was happening.

I broke out crying all over again on moving day and continued to cry while looking out the back window for the entire drive across the state. That's whenI learned to associate crying with painful headaches. Crying became something I swore to avoid in the future.

I hated La Crosse, Wisconsin—no matter how many times its beauty was pointed out to me. I didn't care about immense rivers. They were supposed to replace the ocean-like lakes of Sheboygan, but I was a lake girl. Dad told me there were giant catfish living in the Mississippi that some thought were big enough to eat a person, but I wasn't impressed. It looked like La Crosse was surrounded by little mountains, which they called bluffs. The unusually tall bluff in the area was named Granddad Bluff, and hang gliders were often seen floating down from its slopes. Our new home was situated directly below it. I had to admit, I liked the gliders trailing down the tree-lined giant hill.

In October 1976, my first-grade teacher called me into an office with the school nurse. The nurse inspected my body and announced that I needed to leave right away because I was contagious. They called Mom at work to come and get me. While we waited for her to arrive, the teacher and the nurse discussed whether our family was clean or not. I had impetigo, and they were saying good hygiene would have prevented it. It wasn't true— we weren't dirty— but I was embarrassed for our family. I'd never heard anyone question whether we were clean before. That night, our parents got into the loudest, scariest fight I had ever heard. Mom was screaming that

Dad's lack of help with caring for the family led to this humiliating incident. I was secretly pleased that at least I didn't have to go to school.

Mama had seemed like such a happy person, at least when she was in Sheboygan, but no longer. We didn't have a piano in La Crosse. Maybe that was the problem. Above all, Mom was a traditional woman who considered her work to be childcare and household management. She believed her time belonged to her family. After I was born, she didn't have a job outside the home until we moved to La Crosse. It wasn't that she had never worked before. She had. It just had not gone well because of her mental health. She had to become the full-time breadwinner while Dad trained for a new occupation through a local vocational program. She must have believed he would take over some of the day-to-day parenting since he was at home a lot, but the fact that I also got twelve cavities around this time suggested he did not.

Mostly, he asked *me* to deal with changing diapers, feeding the baby, or tidying up the house. He was quick to yell, usually barking military commands, such as "Front and Center" to gather us together or "Attention" to silence us. We must have been a pretty slipshod and undisciplined military unit because he was continually dismayed at how long it took us to come to order. He would yell, and his face would turn dark red.

He was busy reading *Chariot of the Gods?,*[39] a book about the absurd idea that aliens built the ancient pyramids. Since he believed he had been abducted by aliens, this was well within his belief structure. An interesting finding from scientists studying reported alien abductions is that individuals with night terrors are significantly more likely to also report UFO abduction experiences. Dad may have had night terrors.[40]

He did make me feel special when we joined a group through the local YMCA called the Indian Guides and Princesses, a name that I now see as embarrassing and culturally appropriated. This group was for fathers and daughters to do the same kinds of things Girl or Boy Scouts do. It was supposed to cheer me up and bring us closer, which it did.

The only thing that made living in La Crosse tolerable was that Mom and Dad were singlehandedly adding to the oil crisis on weekends as they drove all over the Midwest.

During the weekdays, Dad attended community college while Mom worked at a home for children with multiple disabilities. The weekends were for family road trips. It was our new family tradition to travel in the Chevy Impala around Wisconsin, Iowa, and Minnesota on day trips. The family drove up and down the Mississippi River, stopping at riverside parks for picnics. We visited nearly every lock and dam, those structures that manipulate the depth and flow of the river. There were also regular trips to a little café in Lansing, Iowa, for huge, warm cinnamon rolls.

On one of our trips around Thanksgiving time, Mom said we were going on a ride to visit Grandma and Grandpa MacIntyre, Dad's parents in Cedar Falls. During the whole trip down, Dad kept reminding us of the rules—and there were a lot of them. "Don't touch anything. Take your shoes off at the door. If you are asked any questions, let either your mother or me answer them. In fact, be silent. Show them how obedient you can be. Both of your grandparents like obedient children."

The closer we got to his parents, the more Dad's shoulders rose up in tension and the tighter his jaw clenched. As we parked in front of their tiny, lime-green house, he repeated the instructions again. I had only met this grandma and grandpa as a toddler, so I didn't know what to expect.

Grandma answered the door. She was a sizable person, over six feet tall with white hair and glasses. She smiled broadly and gave each of us an awkward hug. Grandma had polio when she was a little girl and the illness left her with a stiff arm and leg. The doctors had predicted she would not be able to walk, but she refused to listen. Grandma knew she wouldn't be able to go to school if she couldn't walk, and that was just unacceptable. She went to school that fall. Still, it was more than the stiffness of her body that made the hug clumsy. This was not a woman who expressed physical affection much in her life.

Following behind her was our grandpa. He was the perfect picture of a farmer with OshKosh B'gosh overalls over a plain, pale-blue oxford shirt, even though he worked across the street at the Viking Pump factory and not on a farm. He had a few strands of hair combed over his bare head, and he wore glasses. He extended his hand for a shake rather than offering a hug. Before he fell in love with Grandma, he had strongly considered becoming a priest. One of his sisters, in fact, became a nun. But as he drove the tractor in his family's fields, Grandma would often wave to him from her horse-drawn buggy, driving to and from the local country school where she was a teacher. He found himself eager to wave back.

They were an awkward couple physically even if well-matched temperamentally. She stood nearly a foot taller than he did before putting on her shoes. She was sharp-tempered, quick to snap, and decidedly independent-minded. He was passive, gentle, and patient. She could manage a household with a professional touch. She was an expert with her advanced degree in home economics. Grandma raised her children as a first priority, but she brought in extra money by teaching piano lessons and sewing clothes before she became an adjunct professor once her children were raised. Grandpa MacIntyre had secured a meatpacking job during the years when meatpacking still paid well and workers were treated with respect. Well before Rath Packing Company and the other old packing companies were slowly going out of business, Grandpa became a plumber working for Viking Pump in Cedar Falls.

Grandpa's decision not to pursue higher education was not about an aversion to reading. He loved books. He taught himself about all types of birds and their calls. He loved to take children to feed the ducks in the park near the house. Grandma used to remind her children they were lucky they weren't poor people when within a block-and-a-half lived a family of eight kids in a three-room shanty that would flood when the Cedar River topped its banks. These children would go through the foundry slag pile looking for bits and pieces of brass, copper, etc., for salvage. Dad did, too, but he wasn't doing it to support his family.

Dad was an industrious young entrepreneur making money in all the ways a child could. He expanded into the scrap-metal collection business, where he once loaded six hundred pounds onto his little red coaster wagon, which he hauled about four city blocks to the scrapyard. He recalled how such an unusual spectacle drew the attention of the factory workers he had to pass by on the way. He also made money through an afternoon paper route, shoveling snow, and other odd jobs.

We all tried to walk from the front hallway into the minuscule kitchen, but there was not enough room. "Move along Deborah. David, sit on the sofa," Dad said. The adults stayed in the kitchen to "ooh" and "aah" over baby Samuel. Moving into the living room and glancing around, I noticed there were very few patches of floor that were not covered by furniture. I whispered to David: "This is a sardine can." He giggled.

The adults finished their oohs and aahs and came in to join us, Grandpa in his recliner, Grandma on "her corner" of the sofa next to the end table, and our parents around a table squeezed between the sofa and a desk. After a moment of pained silence, Grandma asked how we liked living in La Crosse. I instinctively lied and said it was nice. David nodded in agreement.

"And how's school?" Grandma inquired. I looked at Mom and Dad. Their eyes narrowed slightly. "Don't you dare mention the impetigo!" was in their expression.

"Just great, Grandma," I said, lying again. Why wasn't Mama jumping in? She loved to talk. She talked to everyone.

When Mom started to speak, and then cleared her throat, David chimed in first by saying, "Deborah just had a bunch of cavities!" I glared at him, and he fell silent again. The quiet was broken by excessively loud chimes from a grandfather clock next to a small piano. Then, bells rang to signify the time.

Grandma rose and walked toward the kitchen while asking, "I suppose you all are getting hungry?" She got out bread, mayonnaise, and lunch meat, making sandwiches for everyone. She poured juice into tiny little plastic glasses. There was only room for three people at the table, but they pulled it out and crammed another chair in front of the window. No one could move around the kitchen now.

Mom told David and me we were going to eat at the table in the living room, but Grandma said no. "They will eat with us. You and John can sit with the baby in the other room."

We were hungry, so David and I picked up our sandwiches right away. Grandma hollered, "Don't you say grace before you eat?"

"What's grace?" David asked. Grandma and Grandpa looked at each other, shaking their heads in disapproval. Then, they each moved a hand to their head and chest as they said:

"Bless us, O Lord, and these Thy gifts, which we are about to receive from Thy bounty, through Christ our Lord. Amen."

David and I remained silent. Grandpa asked in a weak voice, "Don't you even know the words?" which I quickly answered with, "Oh, we just forgot." Grandma and Grandpa just shook their heads and looked sorrowful.

Mom reminded Dad that we needed to get back to La Crosse, and he readily agreed. Time to get going. There were sighs of relief as we pulled away. They chastised us for all the things we did wrong during the visit. We shouldn't have talked about cavities, religion, etc.

On the way home, we stopped for a picnic at a lock and dam south of La Crosse. I almost never traveled without my Ernie doll from *Sesame Street*. After we finished our picnic, David and I decided to walk along the guardrail that prevented falls into the river. As we walked together, we began teasing each other, and David grabbed Ernie out of my hands. With a pitcher's arm, David threw my prized doll over the fence, where it fell into the waters of the Mississippi River. I was not the type of child to scream or become hysterical, but I began wailing. But within a few minutes, he came flying back over the fence, where he landed with a sloppy, wet thud. Apparently, some boaters had seen the stuffed puppet bobbing in the water and decided to rescue him. I thanked God with all my might and hugged the soaking wet doll so tightly that a stream of smelly river water squeezed out all over my clothes.

Our parents developed a habit in La Crosse that they didn't have in Sheboygan; they began arguing constantly and visibly in front of David, Samuel, and me. Something was wrong with Mom. She wouldn't stop yelling and crying. One thing was sure, she didn't like the fact that Dad had taken up smoking cigarettes again. She said they made her sick. She urgently reminded Dad that he had a lung infection, and smoking was bad for him. He said school was stressing him out, and he needed the stress reliever. I knew Mom was also angry and disappointed with the condition of our apartment, which she felt Dad only made worse. When he wasn't studying for school, Dad spent most of his time reading the Bible and *Strong's Exhaustive Concordance of the Bible.*[41] He rarely spoke and interacted with me, and with the boys even less.

I won Dad over by having the best possible temperament as a baby—quiet, rarely crying, and making noise only in the form of a laugh or a giggle. If he had grown to tolerate me as his eldest child, primarily because of my ongoing mellow and obedient personality, he disliked David for being a loud, rambunctious child with little appreciation for authority. It didn't mean he didn't love David, but he struggled to warm up to him. He seemed to be taking a wait-and-see attitude with his second son, Samuel. Regardless, he spent only brief periods of time with us. His childcare skills were non-existent, while mine started to improve as I took care of Samuel for him. What six-year-old nurturer wouldn't want a living doll?

The only thing you had to do to make Dad angry was get "boisterous." His favorite word. For some reason, when my brothers got together, there was racket. David was habitually noisy, chattering loudly with anyone. I wasn't entirely innocent either. Dad found this deeply disturbing. His mother had never allowed such behavior in her house when he was growing up. Children occupied themselves quietly under Grandma's steely stare. Dad was used to seeing a woman lay down the law with just the stance she took, like a notorious sheriff coming through the double doors of a saloon. According to Dad, by letting the children "act like a bunch of hellions," Mom wasn't doing her job as primary caretaker.

Mom couldn't handle the detached father she saw before her. He wouldn't even hold his children. She remembered her father as a very engaged dad. He decided what the family was going to do on weekends. He was the unquestioned leader. He doled out punishments. She questioned her father only once and got that kick to the ass. Although Mom didn't remember their family having any meals together, she said there was strong evidence that they ate, because there were always so many dishes to wash. Still, her dad took her family on frequent road trips, showed them how to have empathy for people, like down-and-out hitchhikers, and joined them in singing songs on the way.

She compared my dad to what her father was like and noted he had neither the self-assuredness of a wise elder nor the initiative of an entrepreneur. Dad was locked in his own mind so much of the time. He told her a few times, "I'm depressed." Mom panicked when she heard that. Her father had become so agitated and depressed during her teens that he needed to be committed to the state hospital. She thought about how her father had broken down, and she was worried to see it happening to another family—hers. Mom thought she would have to become the primary source of income. She'd watched how things deteriorated in her own family when Grandpa's business went poorly. She was scared about shouldering the entire burden of raising children and meeting the financial needs of the family.

A month later, in November, shortly after we returned from the trip to Grandma and Grandpa MacIntyre's house, there was a horrible day that grew into a terrible week. Mom was clearly upset about something. She was picking fights with Dad, loudly telling him he didn't help her enough. The next day was no better. Mom cried and shouted that the family didn't love her because we didn't help her with all the household chores. She said she was overwhelmed working full-time while raising three children under six years old. Dad wasn't even responding. He seemed to be imagining that he wasn't there at all.

After shouting at him a little longer, Mom came into the room I shared with David and began yelling that it was a mess. She turned toward me and ordered me to gather together each and every one of our toys because I was naughty for leaving them around. Quickly, I picked up all the toys and began throwing them onto the bed until I could put them into their proper place. Mama always said, "There's a place for everything, and everything should be in its place."

She screamed at me for a while, and then scooped up all the toys. She grabbed a couple large garbage bags, tossed the toys into the bags, and declared she was taking them to children who would appreciate them. I pleaded for my dolls and stuffed animals, while David begged for his favorite playthings. "Too late," she said. If given to charity, there would be little girls and boys who would take better care of them.

I was horrified. I couldn't stand the thought of being stripped of all my earthly belongings. I implored with reason. I begged with tears. I promised to do better. Nothing worked. I hid Ernie and another doll in my closet, but Mom found those as well. I couldn't stop sobbing. Ernie was my only friend. Mom did not relent but instead left the apartment with our toys and belongings. I was so angry I screamed that I hated her, but only David heard. I wished she could've been there to hear my harsh words because she deserved each irate jab.

My rage turned to fear when she didn't come home that night. This feeling intensified as one day passed into another. Dad was around, but he was so quiet. He was never the type of person others approached to process tense or anxiety- producing situations. I went to school, but distraction kept me from remembering anything that happened while I was there. As I walked to and from school, my neck was stiff from my compulsion to look down at the concrete for every step. I mentally scolded myself to look up occasionally, but my eyes were fixed on the cracks in the sidewalk.

After Mom disappeared, I looked around the apartment and realized that it was really messy. While she was away, I gathered all the laundry, did the dishes, and vacuumed the entire apartment. Since I was only six years old, my laundry skills were poor. I put all the clothes together, and of course, I didn't sort by color. I was also unskilled with the use of detergent. After I finished the laundry, I put the wet loads into two baskets and waited excitedly for Mama's return. Needless to say, she was not pleased when she finally came home. She just looked at the soapy piles of clothes and the soap-filled washing machine and broke down in tears.

I felt guilty. I was determined to change, to stop being such a rotten kid. I could not be good enough fast enough. Later that day, Mom and Dad left the house quickly once again and didn't return for a long time. A stranger came to stay with David, Samuel, and me.

As it turns out, Mom and Dad were in Minneapolis, visiting a Lutheran pastor named Reverend Pfotenhauer. Mom had met Reverend Pfotenhauer when she went to his deliverance ministry. The first time she attended the ministry, she was very depressed, and she wanted the reverend to perform an exorcism to make her depression go away. This second exorcism was a shot in the dark to finally rid her of "the spirit of suicide" as she called it and her other demons. Based on what happened afterward, this second session with the reverend was no more effective than the first one had been.

In the meantime, primal scream therapy had become popular. Some friends convinced our parents to try it. This is how Mom described its effect on her depression:

"You remember how depressed I used to get, and felt so 'full' always? I didn't know what it was, but John [Dad] explains it that 'sin' is matter. Like Joseph Smith taught that our spirit is made of matter. This matter takes up room. Well, we saved ourselves that money and are in the process of getting the same results, just through prayer and the priesthood. I went through my primal scream, which I'd rather call a 'freedom scream.' John helped me. I believe I relived my birth."

Not much later in the month, Mom packed a few of our more portable belongings, got her three children ready, and left Dad. We didn't t even ask why we were leaving without him. But I did ask where we were going. After years spent chasing Dad's affection and involvement, Mom was at the end of her rope. When she received a phone call from the "Prophet Onias" around this time, she left Dad in every way but legally, declaring the marriage to be hell.

Mom said we were going to Canada. We boarded a train that took most of the night and into the next morning to finally stop. At last, part of the family arrived in Canada, where some man was waiting to pick us up. He was a stranger to me, but Mom gave the man a big hug, so I figured they must be friends.

The man who picked us up at the train station in Lethbridge, Alberta, had thinning, whitish hair and glasses, and he seemed nice. This was Bob Crossfield, the Prophet Onias. He drove our little troop to his home in the small town of Vulcan, Alberta. Other than having much more snow on the ground, everything looked the same as in the United States. All the houses in Vulcan were decorated for Christmas.

When we arrived at his house, we were introduced to Mrs. Crossfield, their children, and a host of other people of all ages staying with them. Then, smiling broadly and pointing to Mr. Crossfield, Mom announced, "Kids, this is your new daddy."

Chapter Six: The Prophet Onias

WHEN MOM INTRODUCED US kids to Robert Crossfield, she turned to me and said, "He held you when you were an infant in Salt Lake City. He's a modern-day prophet." Eventually, he became a founder of the School of the Prophets, whose members have since gained infamy as murderers.

Not long after we arrived in Canada, Mom became Crossfield's, or as he preferred, "the Prophet Onias's," second wife. He was still married to his first wife, and of course Mom was still married to Dad. Nonetheless, Bob and Mom had a "wedding" ceremony in a hotel room. Then they traveled to Utah to celebrate their marriage with a honeymoon. While they were gone, one of Crossfield's sons became a regular babysitter. He was asked to watch David and me a few times when Mrs. Crossfield was out. His sleeping area was in the attic, and I slept right across the stairway in a walled-off room.

He started teaching me how to play chess. He started off slow, showing me the pieces that looked like horses and telling me they were knights. I fingered the plastic pieces, memorizing what he'd said about pawns, bishops, and rooks. Eventually I was playing a decent game for a six-year-old.

"Now, your queen, that's your most valuable piece," he said. "You want to protect it at all costs. You also want to use it strategically." But I liked the horses the best.

We played over and over until Jason[42] had shown me all the ways I could move my pieces and all the ways I could lose my pieces. Of course, he beat me handily. "Don't worry, kiddo. It's your first time. There's no such thing as beginner's luck in chess. You just have to keep playing to get better and better." For some reason, I didn't mind losing to this teen. He was much older than I was, for one thing. It wasn't like I was losing to my little brother. Jason also treated me very nicely, including when he won.

"Let's play again." I must have said it thirty times that first night. David had long been asleep, and I should have been very sleepy, but it was very exciting to stay up late playing chess.

"No, sweetie. It is time for bed. We'll play again tomorrow," Jason replied.

The first time I saw a man's erect penis was five minutes later. I suppose he wasn't a man. He was sixteen, maybe seventeen. Jason was holding it in his hand, and swiftly stroking it. I had no idea if it was something I was supposed to see, and yet my instincts told me something was wrong. You see, he wasn't just touching himself. With his other hand, he was stroking my vagina.

He started out massaging my legs right after we played chess. He told me I would find it relaxing and it would help me go to sleep. When he pulled down my panties, I was embarrassed, but he said it was all right. He rubbed me gently. He said I was getting older, and I was ready for something new. Then, he started touching himself, breathing hard, and getting funny looks on his face. When he stopped having his hands on his penis, I was still awake. He kept rubbing my vagina because he said soon it would make me tired enough to sleep. I was tired, and it did put me to sleep. But I have no doubt that I tossed and turned.

I taught David how to play chess when he got a set for Christmas a couple of years later. David became incredibly good at the game. So good, in fact, that he was beating the president of the University of Northern Iowa chess club when he was in sixth grade. Me, I rarely played chess after Jason's predatory lessons.

Therapists and experts know sexual abuse often causes a child to become sexualized at a young age, leading them to see the world through a sexual lens.[43] They learn that relationships are not based in love, but in sex. It's a warped worldview, and it's made all the more painful by the fact that it degenerates cyclically. The more you're abused, the more you end up in abusive relationships, and so forth. There's another key ingredient to this, a corollary of sorts. No one ever teaches you how to be normal. No one ever teaches you how to be a healthy woman, functioning well in a relationship. In my case, my mom was not able to teach me any of these things.

By the time Crossfield moved our family to an apartment in another small Alberta town, still minus Dad, I was beginning to get suspicious about our mom's intentions. I'd thought we were just on a vacation to Canada. But we weren't going home. And Bob occasionally came and stayed with the family.

I was unaware Mom was writing letters to her family at this point, finally informing them of her new marital status. Here is some of what she wrote on February 10, 1978:

"By denying a woman her proper head (Bible says man is head of woman, and God is head of man ... in addition, woman is head of her children, all in order), the church (by forbidding polygamy) has caused her to seek a less worthy man to be her wrongful head. Hence the children suffer, not having a proper and righteous man to head them. I know women's libbers would croak at this whole idea, but they don't realize the privileges that come to women with this. They say it's better that one woman has a man, and another has to go without, than to seek some crumb that's worse than nothing in many cases. Through revelation, God would give you the right head, so everything would be in order. [And] we've received revelation that this is true principle.

"Remember when we were in Salt Lake and I talked about the book of Onias that we'd read? Well, we've met the man who published the book, and basically, that's who we're with now. We believe his book to be a true revelation from God."

One night, when Crossfield was with us, I had a terrible nightmare and went to Mom's room. When I quietly opened the door, I saw that she and Crossfield were busy in the bed. It was the first time I saw two naked adults moving around like that. They didn't see me, and I tiptoed back from the doorway, closing the door very quietly. I was suddenly angry that it wasn't my dad in the bedroom instead of Mr. Crossfield. I also felt disgusted by what I saw. Somehow, it seemed connected to being touched by a boy in my private place. After I had seen them having sex, I copped an attitude every time Crossfield was around.

I pretended to be asleep when he showed up, even though it was clear that I was not. One afternoon, they shook me for a full fifteen minutes while I pretended to be asleep. He tried to curry favor with me by giving me a doll, and then a coloring book. But I didn't show any sign of stopping my tantrums, silent treatment, and sassiness.

Onias and Mom approached me with unbelievable news not too long after that. I was to be sent to a boarding school in the next province for what amounted to reeducation. It was Crossfield's idea to send me to the commune in British Columbia where I could be trained to be a properly submissive young lady and future child bride. This whole situation confused me since I had still half-heartedly believed we were on vacation.

Bob drove me to an FLDS family's home that seemed a long way from Mom. They were, of course, complete strangers to me. They tried to make me feel comfortable in their trailer home. The women and girls all wore long dresses and bonnets. They were nice enough, but I was not optimistic as the reality of the situation became clearer. Bob wished me the best of luck at the new school I'd be going to, and then left me behind with this foreign family. I didn't cry for very long when he pulled away, even though I felt a knot in the pit of my stomach watching him go. Mom was nowhere around. And thus began my lifelong issues around abandonment.

A charismatic patriarch, deemed a prophet, typically leads each community or location where FLDS families live, although some prophets hold sway over more than one community. Crossfield was a prophet without a community. His followers were spread all over mostly the US and Canada based on who had read his book, felt moved by it, and became a disciple of the Prophet Onias. Nonetheless, he had limited connections with the FLDS community in British Columbia—enough so that this family had taken me in.

I liked the first few days with the new people because they congratulated me for being a brave girl. They tried to help me adjust to being left there and to the rules. There were a lot of rules. They showed me around what turned out to be a small farm nestled in the foothills of the Skimmerhorn Mountains. A few other families lived on the same property in trailer homes. Rules included wearing special clothes, such as pantaloons and dresses that went from neck to ankle. Some men were considered leaders, and they were to be obeyed. I was required to be obedient and to "smile sweetly at all times," or "stay sweet," as I heard said all the time now. There were three young girls in the family, and I slept in a room with all of them, in a top bunk I shared with one daughter. The other two girls got the bottom bunk.

This family made their own ice cream, so I thought maybe this home was going to be all right, but I still missed Mom and the boys. I was giving less and less thought to Dad, at least on a regular basis. It was just too hard to think about him.

The school was different from any I had been to before. It was like the school on *Little House on the Prairie*, only twice the size. This school had *two* rooms: one for older students, and one for younger, who would now include me. They showed me my desk, and all the students surrounded me to say hello. It was hard to be the center of attention, and I wanted it to end quickly. But it also felt good to have everyone be so welcoming.

We often met in a large white meeting hall that looked like a barn. It was adjacent to the church and was used for large group activities or for lunch. Everything was done communally, which can be enticing in its own way, but it looked like there was a small crowd everywhere we went, with nearly every person there wanting to hug you. Sometimes this felt pretty good, but my advice to you is this: Be wary of lots of hugs from gatherings like this. Such "love bombing" is a primary recruiting tool for cults everywhere.

Figure 5. My father and I working on a puzzle

I was told one of the other little girls was my cousin. I didn't believe this, but I liked my new friend. Her name was Virginia, and I laughed as I told her that there was a state in the US with the same name. I told her about how my dad used to do a big puzzle on the floor with my help, with the fifty states as puzzle pieces. Dad knew where everything was, and of course he even knew where all the real-life railroad tracks led.

I started to feel like I could learn to like this school. The evenings and weekends were what I found scary and disturbing. The second weekend I was there I felt settled enough to wander around the house like it was my own. I rose very early on Saturday morning, crept as quietly as I could, so I wouldn't wake the other girls, and slipped into the living room. I turned on the television set for the cartoons that had been a secret ritual for me for so long.

Suddenly, after just a few minutes of *Scooby-Doo*, the dad appeared, looking infuriated. He grabbed me by my arm and squeezed tightly. "We do not allow children to touch the television in this house," he hissed. I pleaded with him, saying I was sorry for waking him up, but he said he hadn't been sleeping. Cartoons were just not allowed in this house! This father where I was living seemed downright mean, and he frightened the hell out of me on a regular basis.

At recess time, Virginia and I went sledding down one of the biggest hills I had ever seen, and it was a blast flying down it on our toboggans. The trudge back up the hillside through the deep snow, in a long dress, was a whole other matter. It was also hard to deal with the boys when they would join us. They all pawed at our legs and under our dresses. Virginia helped me stop them, as they were so obviously out to molest me. This place was incredibly sexualized, as I would continue to learn.

With each day, I grew more homesick and less content. The dad drove us girls a long way to school each morning. I always suffered from terrible carsickness on the drive there and back. Though I was used to long car rides, I felt so nauseated on these trips to and from school that I often had to swallow my vomit. Then one day, I got *very* sick and threw up all over their car. They tried not to look upset, but I could tell they were.

When I wrote a letter to Mom explaining that I missed home, I received a package from her with a Mickey Mouse plastic purse. It contained two Canadian dollar bills and a picture of the family. I treasured the gift. I took it to school with me to show Virginia and left it in my desk. Having the purse there gave me a reason to tolerate the ride to school, and I began filling the purse with reminders of home.

One Saturday when Virginia came to visit, she and I explored the trees on the hillside and followed some of the numerous trails like we'd done so many times. But this time when we got back to the house, I encountered a miracle. I saw the familiar gold Chevy Impala.

And when I went in the house, I was astonished to see Mom and Dad together. I ran to them, and they scooped me into their tight hold. Right away, Dad acted frantic to leave. I wasted no time in packing my few belongings. Then I remembered the Mickey Mouse purse in my desk at school. I begged Mom and Dad to drive to the school and get Mickey. But they insisted that it was too far out of their way, and that the school would be closed on a Saturday anyway.

I knew that I should have only been glad that Mom and Dad were taking me home to La Crosse, but it felt like a piece was being ripped out of me. I cried and complained. Dad became really scared, though, and said, "We have to get out of this place, *now*!" I didn't understand his sense of urgency at the time.

Mom was nervous too and wanted to leave the Creston area. We were in a fundamentalist Mormon religious compound. These people didn't let go of girls easily, and had a history of violence. We needed to get out of there fast. Mom and Dad bought me new, flowered underwear in place of my lost treasure, but I still wept silently. It is probably not surprising that new underwear didn't cut it for a six-year-old who'd lost a Mickey purse.

Dad always believed it was Crossfield's scheme to get his hands on me as a wife someday. At the time, I discounted this claim like so many others he would make. But wouldn't you know it? Years later when I was in graduate school, Crossfield tracked me down and left a message on my website asking me to get in contact with him.

On the way home, Mom and Dad repeatedly insisted that once we arrived in Iowa, we were never supposed to talk about Canada. They said we were going to make a new start in Iowa, their home state. In fact, we weren't going to live very far from Grandpa and Grandma MacIntyre, they chirped. And don't forget: *Never mention Canada.*

My exposure to the FLDS began to change my beliefs about religion and churches. When you live through the beginning of a religious sect, meet the leader, and come to realize that he is a fraud, it makes it difficult to believe that any other church leaders from any other place and time are any more truthful. One person's prophecy is another's delusion. Coincidentally, the mass suicide in Jonestown occurred in the same year that Mom married Onias.

Chapter Seven:
Troubles in Denver

D ENVER IS A SMALL town in the northeastern part of Iowa. It boasted a population then of about 1,600 people. In a town of this size, very little business isn't everyone's business. When Mom graduated from Denver High School in 1963, the graduating class consisted of just thirty-two people.

Our Uncle Paul lived outside the limits of this little town in the same farmhouse where Mom grew up—the farmhouse that belonged to Grandpa. We camped on his land until we found more permanent housing. I liked staying on the farm, and I especially enjoyed seeing our cousin, Autumn[44]. Autumn was not Uncle Paul's daughter. She just visited him a lot because her dad, our Uncle Andy, liked to spend time with his brother.

Autumn was nine, two years older than I was, and we were instantly like best friends. We played and hid from my brother David, and all the other younger male cousins. It turned out that Autumn was having a hard time. Her parents were divorced. I asked what divorce was, and Autumn told me in a matter-of-fact manner that it meant her mama and dad would never be together again. She told me about her parents fighting all the time before and after the divorce. "One of the things they fight over most is me," she said in dismay.

I listened carefully to Autumn about her parents fighting and divorcing. It was about to become a word I heard from children all around me. Autumn pointed out several new and confusing concepts to me. For example, I would not have Autumn's mother for an aunt anymore, but her father would still be my uncle since he was a blood relative to my mom. As I listened to Autumn, my head swam with all the information. In the end, Autumn asked me to become a blood buddy with her. That way we would always be close. We pricked our fingers and exchanged small drops of blood.

Before long, our family learned of an immediate vacancy in a new apartment building on the southern outskirts of town, so we moved in. Mom and Dad became the building managers in exchange for a reduction in rent. Dad provided maintenance, while Mom collected rent checks and cleaned the building. The work also allowed her access to household cleaning supplies—a vacuum cleaner, mop, and broom—things we didn't have previously.

A faint scent of smoke always drifted through the building from the apartment downstairs. Since Mom was worried the elderly woman below us would complain about our footsteps if they were too loud, she didn't want to say anything about it, and she was always yelling at us to stop running around "like a herd of elephants."

Dad started a job at Iowa Job Services, which meant he was placed with companies that needed temporary workers. He worked at a grain elevator, as janitorial staff at an office building, and in a lot of other similar jobs. Once, when Dad was working at a lumberyard, he asked his boss if he could take the extra wood pieces left around at the end of the day. He brought home two boxes full of wooden blocks in different shapes. Dad searched through the boxes to throw away any that seemed to have splinters. When he was satisfied the remainder were safe, he gave them to Mama to sand. After she worked strenuously for hours with sandpaper making sure there were no rough edges, she gave them to David and me. We immediately began to decorate them with crayons, turn them into construction projects, and find a thousand other ways to play with the blocks. A few days later, Mama came home with two bags of wooden spools she had purchased at a secondhand store. I used mine to represent little people. David and I played for hours with the small cities we built. We smiled contentedly at our new toys.

Mom decided that she wanted to teach elementary school again, but when she applied for the job, she was shocked to learn that her teaching license had expired. More than ten years had passed since she got it. To renew the license, Mom was going to have to take two classes. She was the smartest woman I knew. She always corrected our English and grammar. "No dear, not *them* toys, it's *those* toys," and, "I'll take your pic-ture, not your pitcher." She seemed to know at least something about every topic imaginable, but at one point when I was looking around for important papers, I saw her college transcript. I was stunned. Her grades were all over the place: a few D's, a lot of C's, and far fewer B's and A's than I expected.

This changed the way I viewed Mom. When I asked her about school, she admitted that when it came to academics, she had always been full of good intentions but little follow-through. She'd bring home an armload of books to study, only to end up carrying them back to school the next day untouched. She would sit in front of a Bunsen burner during labs in science class realizing that she had entirely missed the instructions and didn't know what to do. As a result, she regularly made the B honor roll in high school, but only rarely earned an A.

Nevertheless, she enrolled at State College of Iowa (now the University of Northern Iowa) in 1963 to earn a degree in elementary education. But just because she had an undergraduate degree didn't mean she retained much information, with a memory as poor as hers and as distractible as she could be. Much later on in her life, she was officially diagnosed with attention deficit hyperactivity disor-der, but at the time it just felt like failure She wasn't surprised when she heard the students in her classes identify the trailer home park and the apartment buildings we lived in as the lowest-class places in town. The classes only made her want to move away from Denver.

In the summer I was sometimes allowed to visit Autumn's house. With each visit, it became increasingly uneasy for me. Autumn was beginning to act very strangely. The two of us slept together in the same bed, and Autumn started fingering my vagina. I ignored this as long as I could. Often Autumn didn't even seem to be awake. I never told Mama what was happening on these visits, but I quit asking to visit Autumn. That also meant I wasn't going to be spending time with horses anymore. Autumn was the one who knew all about how to handle horses.

David didn't have anyone to play with, so for a while I stopped avoiding him. Together, we found there were sandy patches in the cornfield behind the apartment where corn would not grow. We made a path out to one of these clearings and declared it our "fort." I'd say it was a nice summer, but I couldn't get my mind off what Crossfield's son or Autumn had done.

Since we had so little furniture, our apartment was virtually empty. The whole family slept in sleeping bags laid across the living room floor in our apartment. Only the dark tan metal heating registers running along the floors broke up the monotony of the walls and carpeting. That is, except for our father's handmade canvas flag of "Zion," loosely resembling the flag of Israel, on one living room wall. We didn't know anything about Zion or Israel yet, so David and I just revered the flag out of deference to Dad.

Samuel, David, and I got sick a lot in Denver. Because of our sleeping arrangement, Mom could always hear us lying not too far away, softly crying out in pain or moaning for hours on end when we did. Though she tried hard to take care of us at these times, and would have made an exceptionally good nurse, all that Mama could offer was liquid vitamin E drops. To no one's surprise but her own, her herbal remedies never seemed to work.

Finally, after a couple of days of crying, David or I would be taken to a doctor. The doctor would make us wait out in the waiting area since we didn't have an appointment and had Medicaid. David could and would scream out in agony for a couple of hours when he was suffering. Other patients with routine appointments frequently offered to let us go first, but the doctor said no.

As we slowly acquired a few pieces of furniture, our apartment became a more comfortable place. Even though we had a couple of places to sit, and eventually beds to sleep in, there still wasn't a TV to watch, and that was what usually provided such a needed distraction from all our troubles. Sure, the family had no money, but it was Mom's fault we couldn't have a TV. She said we were not going to have one even if we could afford one, because it had unholy influences and watching television just taught children to value materialism. When we asked what materialism was, Mom replied it was valuing things and possessions above the love of God. We all promised television would not do that to us, but she was unrelenting.

It was all the more interesting, and always a pleasant surprise, when for a brief period, and usually for a specific reason, Mom would allow a television in the house. Once, it was so she could let us watch *Roots*. I think her experience with racism in Iowa classrooms must have spooked her. She didn't want us to turn out like the rest of her hometown seemingly had. We watched the whole thing, staying up late despite the fact that I was only seven and David just five. It's clear that Samuel, still a toddler, picked nothing up from the series, because he grew up to be a flaming racist. After the series or another targeted show was over, the television was gone as quickly as it had appeared. These long stretches of time without a TV usually ended with Mom giving in, or someone else in our extended clan bringing one by, because one of us kids had so obnoxiously hinted to them that we didn't own one, so they felt they had no choice.

In second grade, I still felt lonely, and the teacher was mean to me. I can't remember what I did to get the pattern started, but I was always getting put into a desk in the corner for talking. Plus, I hated math. There were these timed tests that made me so nervous that I felt as though I had to pee. I guess it was an anxiety reaction. Sometimes I didn't feel like I could hold it much longer. I asked Ms. Zach to allow me to go to the bathroom. Ms. Zach let me, but not without putting me in the corner for using the restroom during class instead of at recess or at lunch.

I had been quick to understand things when I first started school, but now the teachers said I was behind the other children. Mom would come home from a parent-teacher conference with one of those pitying, disappointed looks, and tell me, "It's just because of moving around a lot. Now that we're settled down, you'll catch right back up." But the catching-up process was taking a long time to happen. I was labeled "remedial" at this point.

Things were not going well at home either. Dad kept finding only part-time work for minimum wage. He couldn't find a solid job that supported the family or that even came close. Mom was in school. There was just no money.

Mom was constantly calling Dad a pessimist, which was true. He was one. But that didn't mean he lacked a sense of humor. Once, when Mom told Dad to start a Pessimist's Club, like the Optimist's Club, he grumbled, "Ah, probably no one would come anyway."

Chapter Eight: Merry Christmas

THERE IS, IN FACT, a special, crippling quality to poverty in the modern Western world. For the penalty of . . . destitution is not just the absence of things; it is also the absence of meaning, the exclusion from participating in the essential socializing events of modern life.
—James Twitchell, 2011[45]

Moving around so often had taken its toll on our celebration of Christmas, and any other holidays or special occasions for that matter. But I felt it more around Christmas. We'd never had the chance to develop any of our own family rituals for these occasions. In Denver, we finally had time to think about giving gifts and having Santa Claus come by. Dad had lots of long woolen socks, and we nailed these to the wall with tiny nails. We decorated a small Christmas tree that we picked out at a farmer's stand along the highway. We used popcorn to make a garland and made several decorations by hand.

Finally, the big day arrived. Santa had filled our socks with apples, oranges, peanuts in the shell, and a few candies. There were even gifts under the tree. I tried to hide my disappointment when my presents were a can of chicken noodle soup and a can of creamed style corn. David got green beans and vegetable beef soup, because those were his favorites. What I earnestly wanted was a red sled. The best option would be a toboggan, which you could sit in with your legs extended in front of you. But there was also a small round sled in which you sat cross-legged and held onto two handles. Either sled would have thrilled me, and neither would have cost more than twenty dollars, but that was more than our parents had. I thanked them for the food.

The only reason there was even food to give as gifts was because Mom and Dad had finally applied for food stamps. The food stamps were necessary as a replacement for a portion (just some) of the money Dad couldn't earn working a part-time job for minimum wage—which was $3.10 per hour at the time.

It was all right until school started again, and everyone began asking what I'd been given for presents. I'd invariably hear the girls in my class, talking about Barbie dolls, Atari gaming systems, Simon games, or a whole host of other popular games and toys they had received. When it was my turn to share, instead of confessing to my soup, corn, and peanuts, I would make up stories about the presents I received, including most of the ones I heard the others talking about. Everyone was suitably impressed until recess, when a girl asked me over to play Barbies. I was caught lying. I had nothing to bring to her house.

During lunch hour at school, I always ate a lot of food, since I usually didn't have anyone to talk to. The food was comforting. Maybe it made up for all the other things I was missing. Plus, Mom didn't prepare things at home very often without getting angry, because she resented how Dad isolated himself from the family at dinnertime. Before and after dinnertime too.

When David was an infant, Dad walked away from his first family meal. He ate cold food out of a can in another room pretty much from then on. Mom cooked candlelight dinners made up nicely for him, and the family, but Dad refused to join us. She set up interactions between us during the day, like bicycle rides with David and me strapped to child seats on the back. He went once.

We continued with our short weekend trips in the car. They were still a family pastime. I loved Dad's small collection of eight-track cassettes (e.g., Three Dog Night, the Carpenters, the Eagles), which alternated with his favorite radio station, but now I was out of tune as the family sang together. These trips were the secret to keeping Mom and Dad happy and harmonious, while avoiding the prohibitive cost of marriage counseling or court proceedings.

Chapter Nine: Yo-Yo Mood

I USED TO DREAD seeing Mom at her timeworn black manual typewriter. She could never see the pattern she followed, whereas I could describe it for her in detail. She would start to feel some energy, and then make a grocery store run that involved filling at least one bag with candy bars and other sugary or salty treats. It wasn't uncommon to see her buy huge bags of M&Ms, six-packs of Reese's peanut butter cups, the extra-large bar of Hershey's chocolate with almonds, and several kinds of Shasta pop, including cream soda, root beer, lemon-lime, orange, and grape.

If we didn't think it through each time, it was easy to get caught up in the couple of days of energy and positive mood. She shared her goodies, she was happy, and often she would break into song. When she was in this good mood, she would write on her typewriter for hours. But we dreaded the rest of the cycle. Usually within a day or two, she would be in a deep depression, unable to get out of bed. She would cry, refusing to speak to anyone, and generally became inconsolable.

Her use of the typewriter wasn't the only clue signifying her good moods though. There were times when she cleaned the whole apartment in a way that could be truly frightening. This involved scrubbing *every* surface, using an old toothbrush for the faucets and the tighter spots. None of us kids cared for these spells, because we were the frontlines of these cleaning brigades, regardless of the time of day or night she ordered them.

There were also moods in which she decided that we should only eat natural, healthy foods from a local co-op. To our childlike minds, these were some of the worst good moods she could have. Thankfully, they usually only lasted a couple of weeks. We would eat foods like tofu, carob, and dried fruit. More than once, we had a gallon tub of peanut butter divided neatly between its concrete-like peanut mass and the two-to-three inches of oil that sloshed above it. Sometimes you simply couldn't mix the two.

Like a pendulum dictated by money and mood, our nutrition was either all junk or all organic food from the health food store. As economic troubles continued, Mom had less and less choice about what to serve. Many meals came out of cans. We began to eat the same meals night after night. Macaroni and cheese, grilled cheese sandwiches, and soup became constant suppers.

The carbohydrate-heavy meals rarely included meat. Meat was just too expensive. The starchy options soon began to take their toll on everyone's weight. We all began to have puffy faces and round bellies. It was cheaper to eat junk than healthy options. The things that should have made us lose weight, like a restricted food budget, did not. We still gained weight.

Eventually, Mom and Dad sought the assistance of the Department of Social Services for the second time after their experience in Wisconsin, but only because they "had to." There were lots of people who applied for welfare even when they "didn't have to." This hypocrisy runs rampant among poor, conservative white people. Uncle Paul used welfare, too, before looking down on everyone who still had to be on it once he got off. Dad made it clear that going on welfare made him feel lousy and didn't jibe with his principles. After a lengthy application process, we began receiving Aid to Dependent Children of Unemployed Parents, food stamps, and Medicaid.

As a result of our new, heavily stigmatized status as welfare recipients, Mom's new ritual was to make us clean the city streets with trash bags in the morning. This was well before anyone ever heard of Adopt-A-Highway. She started doing this for two reasons. One, the town's motto was, "Cleanest Little City in Iowa," and she felt it had too much litter lately to justify that claim. And two, she felt that since our family had to make use of government assistance, cleaning up roads and highways could become a good way to pay the public back.

Mom and Dad didn't take us to church for a long time, maybe because they were still unsure of what to do spiritually after the salvation supposedly offered by polygamy—oops, plural marriage—failed to materialize. But more importantly, the nearest mainstream LDS Church was twenty miles away, and they couldn't afford the rather strict tithing practice. They were lost spiritually because they were lost financially.

Strict tithing meant the church pressured its members into giving ten percent of their income to the church, and tracked the congregation's generosity as they gave. The church elders *counted what came in from whom*. Our parents were too embarrassed by their income to participate in the process, even if they felt they could have afforded it. They couldn't have afforded it.

The family regularly gathered on Sunday for a private worship service led by Mom. As a prelude to these religious meetings, Mom and Dad assigned Bible readings. There was a family church "school" with drawing, reading, and discussions about Jesus and God. Once when we were learning about the Book of Acts, Mom asked us who Theophilus was in the Bible. Our brother Samuel answered, "The awfulest in the Bible is the Devil." He didn't understand why the rest of us were laughing. If you say Theophilus's name out loud, it really does sound like "the awfulest." The time our family spent praying to God was peaceful, and it brought us closer. I loved God as much as ever and carefully thanked Him for any happiness I felt.

I pictured that He had a soft voice and that He loved to sing. Mama told us God loved all children. She was careful to stress that this included *all* children, whether they were Black, red, yellow, or white. After a close examination of my skin, I determined that I must be yellow, or, since I had recently gotten plenty of sun, brown.

Our dad was definitely a shade of yellow. The damage hepatitis had done to his liver was still evident. It didn't occur to me to pick white.

During one worship service, Mama said she was not getting enough help cleaning the house. She decided that the TV had to go again. It was a negative influence, and it kept us from doing what we were supposed to do. I begged alongside David and Samuel for the TV to stay. We didn't want to be different from other kids. We wanted to be able to talk about the same cartoons and shows as all the other kids. Somehow, the very idea of constantly losing the TV made it seem invaluable. Sure enough, like all the other times, Mom determinedly carried away our portable, black-and-white TV, this time the one that required a pair of pliers to switch between channels.

During another of our family worship meetings, Mom made an announcement. She had a "vision" of three "spirits" yet to be born, including the order of their birth. She was going to have three more babies, she said ecstatically—a boy, then a girl, then another boy. Mom's "visions" and other intuitions were unassailable, of course, because they were divinely inspired. In other words, she *felt* the voice of God. Dad also regularly received "prophesies," but it was too late for him to hear a different plan from God regarding more children.

This impractical vision put me in a great dilemma as a strong believer in God, Jesus, and prophesies—just as our parents taught me. Either God wanted Mom to have three more children, which was absurd if He were all-knowing and all-wise, or God didn't want Mama to want more children, and she was getting her wires crossed. I didn't know what to believe. Something wasn't right. I went for honesty. "I think it's a bad idea to have more kids when we don't have any money," I stated. Her eyes narrowed. The tension level rose. I might as well have suggested an abortion. As far as she was concerned, life began before conception.

She always had answers for us. "Well, what if your father and I had believed something like that when we had you? Don't you love your little brothers? If everyone waited until they had enough time or enough money, no one would ever have children."

Little did I know, Mom had *had* an abortion. She had become pregnant in Canada by the Prophet Onias. She had quietly gone to get an abortion as soon as she got back to the United States. Her Holy Ghost told her this child was not meant to be. She only told my sister of this years later, and then, when I was somewhat shocked to have heard the story, Mom confirmed it with me. Onias probably would have killed her for having an abortion. Literally, given the violence and murder that he participated in seven years later.

How can you argue with a vision from God? All you have are human appeals to reason. We took her "intuition"—as she also called it—as a revelation, and when we could least afford it, plans were made for three more children to be born. In late summer, Mom told Dad and me that she was pregnant with her fourth child, whom she knew would be a boy; it was God's plan.

Dad and I remained silent, exchanging a quick glance. On her bad days, we were already doing most of the household management and childcare. There were many bad days.

Mama was sensitive, able to detect even subtle disapproval in body language. We never bothered with noncommittal but supportive comments about the pregnancy, because she could spot insincerity a mile away.

Dad never tried to argue against the idea of expanding the family. He just seemed resigned to it. Though he obviously had some say about whether they would have more children, Mom had a habit of "disappearing" for days to give Dad time to think about his "lack of support," and this seemed to work pretty well to subdue any objection. This was terrifying to experience as a child. You didn't know if she was going to come back. You didn't know where she was. It left me much more responsible for taking care of my younger brothers.

But there it was. We had almost no furniture. We slept on old army-issue sleeping bags in the living room. Dad worked temporary jobs for minimum wage. But Mama had a vision, and the family would double in size.

I'd been going to work with Dad for years. The first time I remember, he was working for Kelly Services, a company that provides temporary workers to various businesses. Kelly Services couldn't find Dad temporary employment, so they assigned him to work as the janitor for the Chalet Center, the office complex where Kelly Services was located.

He worked in the evenings after the business closed. He'd rustle my hair or gently jab my shoulder with his fist, "Whaddya say, wanna come to work with me?" I hated babysitting by now, and this was an out from that. It was also a guaranteed chance to read or get some sleep after waking up at 4:00 a.m. to deliver newspapers, going to school, and then heading straight home after school for chores.

At some point, Dad started to ask me if I wanted to help him at work, not just keep him company. My preference, of course, was to sit and read while he worked, but if he was running behind, Dad would tell me I had to help him. We cleaned everywhere in every way: bathrooms, the employee kitchen, the break room, offices, the grounds, hallways, you name it. One night, Dad got an assignment to paint the interior of the building. He told me to paint along the wood trim near the floor. I told him that didn't sound right. I told him I was confused. He didn't seem to understand I had a lifelong issue with prepositions. However, I went ahead and followed his order, or so I thought, and painted the wood trim along the carpet.

Dad came back screaming in horror. "What did you do? You've ruined this wood! You weren't supposed to paint the wood trim! You got paint on the carpet in a couple of places. This isn't what I told you to do at all!"

I'm pretty sure he got fired for that. Kelly Services didn't want their wood trim painted. They wanted their walls painted. It was a stupid mistake—one an eight-year-old might make.

Mrs. Eskridge, a teacher from my elementary years, was pivotal in my life, the first of a set of inspirational teachers and mentors I would be blessed with in my years of going to school. When they looked at me, other teachers saw a low-income child with few skills. What she saw was potential, and it was just what I needed. I had started the year still labeled as below-average at reading and math. But when Mrs. Eskridge assigned each student to do a report on the state of Iowa, plus one other state, I did a report on all fifty of them. I wanted to please *this* teacher because she cared about me and saw me as an individual.

Mrs. Eskridge made every afternoon spectacular. Every day she read a chapter from a novel written for children. It usually took her less than a month to get to the end of each book. I woke in the morning, anxious to get to the classroom where Mrs. Eskridge shared intrigue and fantasy. She had a trick. She wouldn't finish reading the book. Children had to check the book out from the library or buy a copy of the book to see how it ended. Sometimes it was getting us hooked on one book from a series, leading at least some of us scrambling to read the rest of the series. Brilliant.

We heard about the lives of the Boxcar Children.[46] They were orphaned siblings who made a home in an old railroad car. Spoiler alert: A wealthy man eventually adopted the children, and they went on to solve mysteries. She read to us about the world of The Great Brain,[47] about a boy who lived among Mormons. I could relate. It was my favorite book series for a long time. She read to us from some of the most incredible, award-winning children's books written, Newberry Award winners.

Now, I was a voracious reader. I learned to walk and read at the same time so that I could read while walking to and from school. I read so many books at the school library—and later, the town's tiny public library—that I ended up openly afraid that I would read all the books in the world at the rate I was going. I thought I had better slow down. Mrs. Eskridge reassured me that there would always be at least one more book ready for me whenever I finished them all because someone was writing a new one each day. I felt much better and began to dig back in.

Mrs. Eskridge was so nurturing that there were always a few children who would linger in her classroom to talk to her at the end of the school day. She didn't mind having students help her clean up the classroom by erasing the chalkboards and taking the erasers outside to beat the chalk out of them. At the end of each school day, I began offering to do extra chores for Mrs. Eskridge, and it became a regular habit for me to stay with her for up to an hour after school ended.

And she loved music. After most of the other students left, Mrs. Eskridge would take out her record player and put on 45s of Elton John songs, and we'd all sing and dance to "Crocodile Rock." She also had a song by Jimmy Dean called, "Big Bad John," about a giant heroic man who saved his fellow miners by holding up a timber while they escaped, only to die himself when the mine collapsed. Everyone, including Mrs. Eskridge, would cry a little when she played this song.

Aside from letting me become her after-school shadow, Mrs. Eskridge did something else magnificent to boost my educational trajectory. She said that rather than being behind academically, I should be placed in the Talented and Gifted Program. She changed the way future teachers looked at me. She changed the way I looked at myself. She changed the way I spent my time. I no longer lacked direction or got bored.

I couldn't stop reading. When Mama said to turn off the lights and go to sleep, I would go into one of the empty bedrooms instead, pushing my book under the door and into the sliver of light from the hallway. I would read for hours and hours. Sometimes daylight would come through the windows, and I would realize that I had stayed awake all night.

Best friends? Who needed best friends when there were books? There were hundreds of people to meet in books. There were junior detectives of both genders solving crimes. There were talking animals sacrificing themselves for the good of others. There were all of

Judy Blume's books. Pippi Longstocking particularly appealed to me for some reason.

Reading was an excellent escape, and I was beginning to need to escape more and more. Mom was still regularly cycling between can't-think-straight and can't-leave-bed modes. Then she started insisting that it would be a good idea for David and me to be home-schooled. I was horrified! I loved going to school at this point. It was a safe haven. But as her next delivery date approached—for my brother John—she forgot about homeschooling. I was *so* relieved. Later in life, when my niece and nephews would have to endure online school during the COVID pandemic, I thought of them often with serious concern.

The year was 1979 and Mom was cranky—probably owing to her extended labor pains. She wanted the whole family to be present for the birth of her fourth child, but Dad wanted to go to work. She kept David and me home from school as soon as she felt labor pains. I was grouchy about missing school. Of course, the last thing she wanted to do was have her baby in a hospital, and we all knew it. You could tell by the way she angrily bundled up and demanded our dad drive her to the hospital that she wanted to maximize our guilt. She returned with a baby boy the next day.

It didn't matter how cold it was, we had to walk to and from school because Dad had to take the car to work. It was an icy, blustery day when keeping one's head down was the only way to stay warm. Something green caught my eye. Frozen in the ice were not one but two twenty-dollar bills. I stopped and began to chip them from the ice with my fists. When that didn't work, I covered the bills with some snow, and I ran home to get Mom. She got a hammer and a hot water bottle before following me back to the curbside spot where I found the money.

We all went to the store and bought groceries after she helped me chip the money free. Mom told me how proud she was of me but asked me if I remembered to thank God for helping us in our time of need. Of course, she was silly to ask me that because I'd already done so, probably out loud. That night we ate hamburgers, the first meat we'd had at home in a long time.

In early spring that year, Mom dressed up like a widow in all black clothing for three days, and she wouldn't speak to anyone except baby John. I don't think she even moved from her rocking chair except when nature called. When she finally did speak, she said she was trying to send everyone a message that she was a "widow of life," and that her family didn't love her. She said her actions were modeled after Martin Luther's wife, who dressed in black to draw attention to the fact God must be dead with the way her husband was acting.

David and I asked each other what a widow of life was, but neither one of us had any idea. We decided not to worry because we knew she would soon be happy and typing again. Still, it was hard not to feel guilty for causing Mom to feel like she was widowed. Always fixated on mother-child relationships, Mom would carry around a picture of Madonna and child. She never mentioned to us that she felt permanently distant from her own mother. It turns out Mom had always felt responsible for the fact that her mother never became a chiropractor. Many years later, she would admit she never felt she deserved her own mother's affection, on the rare times it was given. I didn't feel that way. Even if our mom seemed broken down sometimes, I still felt she loved me. Even when she'd abandoned me.

Mom made a pact with God. In exchange for having John, she asked God to look out for her family financially. This would be a substantial challenge to His omnipotence. With Dad becoming more and more withdrawn, isolated, and barely able to do anything but report to work, she worried that soon he wouldn't be able to work either. This would be a violation of their pact, and she would be upset with Him for it. If Mom wasn't on speaking terms with God, who was left for her to talk to?

When she finally got out of the rocking chair, took off the black clothes, and began speaking again, she was infuriated with everyone. She insisted that we were going to have to help her with John. She was exhausted. If we didn't help, she was leaving. This assignment began my many miserable nights of shaking John's crib back and forth, carrying him around the living room with a small bouncy motion, and trying to rock him in the rocking chair. As a seven-year-old, just two months shy of eight, I was about to start a cycle of poor sleep habits that would never go away. If I wasn't already up all night reading, sometime between 11:00 p.m. and 5:00 a.m., John's high-pitched scream would cut through the silence, and my mother would plead with me to take care of him. I was exhausted in school. My eyelids drooped heavily every day. I just didn't want Mom to leave.

When she got in these moods, she was always angry at us. If she thought we weren't keeping the house clean enough, we were liable to get a "clunking," which was when we were either rapped by her knuckles or fingernails against our heads. She also pulled hair, always seemingly focused on punishing our heads. Eventually I learned that her parents had done this to her.

Chapter Ten: Marginal Parents

I DON'T REMEMBER WHAT I said to myself to justify my first theft of candy from the store at the gas station. I remember that it was a rainbow-colored sucker and, as usual, I didn't have any money. I picked up the candy and put it in my pocket before going back to get the gallon of milk I was sent to the store to pick up.

After paying for the milk, I walked outside and put a couple of blocks between myself and the store. The milk was too cold to carry anyway, so I set it down and took the sucker from my pocket. It was so pretty I didn't want to eat it. I just stood there and stared at my contraband.

I didn't feel excited about getting away with stealing. I also didn't feel guilty about stealing, since I thought of my prize as candy that God wanted me to have. I wonder where that came from. I surmised that if God didn't want me to have it, then I would have been caught. When I got home, I showed my brother David and told him what I had done. Instead of telling our parents, he volunteered to help me with my next escapade. It wasn't long before small pieces of candy were disappearing from stores all over Denver, the culprits less than ten years old.

Our alliance could never last long. I started going to war with David shortly after he begged our parents for a chance to be the "responsible" child. He didn't like having me as a babysitter when I was only a couple of years older than he was. He felt he could be just as responsible as I was. For a change in routine, Mom and Dad took me along with them to the Weathervane, the local diner, where they spent all their time then, leaving David to watch Samuel.

We left for about an hour, but David found a way to use the short time to get into trouble. He took Samuel to our cornfield fort to play with matches. David probably just planned to show Samuel how easy it was to light the dry, harvest-ready corn on fire. In the process, he managed to light a small part of the field on fire. Firefighters were called to the scene. David didn't earn back babysitting privileges for years.

Life in Denver, Iowa, for my parents, became about subsistence and the constant search for jobs that turned out to be temporary. Dad worked at the Waterloo airport and in many other businesses doing physical labor or maintenance. He worked, he always worked, but his earnings were so inadequate. Many of the jobs meant he came home dirty and coughing up disgusting things that worried our mom. She didn't want him getting sick again.

Mom took work as a substitute teacher after she renewed her teaching certificate. Later, she obtained a job as a supervisor at a daycare center. Still, she continually cycled between depression and shades of mania. She regularly wrote letters to her family about her moods:

"I have been taking L-Tryptophan (an essential amino acid, written up in the National Enquirer) for depression. It's amazing the difference in the ability to cope. I can't explain the technicalities, but having a little thing like a flat tire would be completely devastating before. Now, it can be kept in perspective, and even be enjoyed as a break in the routine. Now, I still have depression I've noticed, but I can fight it. Before, I had no weapons to fight with"

It could be that the L-Tryptophan was slightly useful. It does have known effects on the serotonin levels of people who take it.[48] Or, it could have acted as a placebo. Nonetheless, Mom experienced a crash again, and was soon feeling depressed, after L-Tryptophan was temporarily taken off the market when a bad batch was linked to a serious medical disorder.[49] The fact that Mom and the rest of her immediate family were regular consumers of the National Enquirer or other tabloids as a source of medical information, but distrusted medical doctors, gave them no pause.

Hypomania—Mama's overactive and excited behavior—is a symptom that some mistake as a sign of happiness. It just means that a person has a lot of energy, but they can still be irritable, frustrated, and impulsive. In fact, they tend to be. For example, Mom would just take off to get away for a day or two. Sometimes she went alone, and sometimes she took us kids with her. Her trips away were usually in response to an argument with Dad, and those arguments seemed to trigger her hypomania, or vice versa.

Patriarchy had driven my parents crazy. My mom hated the actual tasks demanded of a housewife, which is why she so often brushed them off herself and onto me, or even Dad. Mostly, she demanded that Dad take his role as head of the household very seriously, but he could never meet her expectations.

One afternoon, Dad came in the door after looking for work, and Mom threw a cup of coffee at him. The cup shattered against the window, breaking it, and sending streaks of cream-lightened coffee running down the wall.

"How dare you! After we've talked about this?" Mom said, glaring at him.

"What did I do?" he asked.

She couldn't have been more furious. "You think I can't smell it? You reek of cigarettes. You know they make me sick! I feel like I'm going to throw up right now. It's not like we haven't talked about this!"

They had. I'd heard them talk about Dad sneaking cigarettes many times. I thought they smelled bad too, but Mom made such a big deal out of it that sometimes I would secretly take his side. Near the end of what now seemed like scripted arguments rehearsed for a show, Dad would say, "I didn't want to get married, but the damn church plagued me with this 'blessing.'"

To which Mom would say something like, "It wasn't a psychic reading. It was a blessing suggesting the path to your spiritual future. If you didn't want to be married or you don't, then end it!"

The fight typically ended in silence, and never progressed to the point where the D-word was mentioned. After this particular argument, Mom took us kids to Nauvoo, Illinois, to see where Joseph Smith had built a great temple that nonbelievers had burnt to the ground, and then to Carthage, Illinois, where Smith and his brother were killed by vigilantes after Smith was charged with treason following his declaration of martial law in Nauvoo.[50] This wasn't our first trip to Nauvoo and Carthage. Before John was born, Mom and Dad took David, Samuel, and me for a trip there to better understand Mormon history. Dad also wanted to visit a place called Adam-Ondi-Ahman.[51] It was supposed to be the gathering place in the Latter Days. We'd driven forever to reach this secluded area deep in the woods of northwestern Missouri. We just stood there in this grove of trees and prayed. It was supposed to be deeply spiritual, but it seemed so very ordinary. Without Dad along, we didn't have to go out to the Adam place. I hear that nowadays, it's an End Times tourist attraction for Mormons.[52]

After two days, we finally returned home in time for family Sabbath services. Mama had not called or checked in during our absence, and we found Dad apprehensive and fearful that she had taken us back to Canada. He was very relieved to hear that we only went to see where the Latter-day Saints had built their first temple, and where Joseph Smith, their leader, had been violently taken from his people.

Over the summer, with school out, Mom and Dad started what became a long-term habit of going to a diner, café, or fast-food restaurant for coffee, and leaving me to babysit David and Samuel, sometimes for hours at a time. They almost always took baby John with them. They explained that they needed some peaceful, quiet time to talk about family issues and problems. They were going to try to repair their marriage. They asked me if I was willing to be responsible for helping them spend some time together, which would assist the whole family. At first, I eagerly agreed to be the extra-grown-up childcare provider. It felt like such a compliment. I was eight, but "so responsible."

If anyone wanted to know where our folks were, the Weathervane was one of the first places to check. They spent so much time at their booth that the restaurant staff started to get to know Mom and Dad. The owners were kind people, but they got assertive enough to tell my parents to leave during the rush for they rarely purchased more than two cups of coffee. The residents of Denver regularly observed a group of kids, ranging in age from infancy to eight, walking together with a stroller, and crossing the busy Highway 63 to find their parents.

Mom and Dad never touched a drug other than caffeine. Instead, they would indulge themselves in delusional thoughts about prophecies of the Lord, and what to do about employment and financial woes. They talked about passages from the New Testament, Old Testament, Book of Mormon, Doctrine and Covenants, and other sources as well. Their focus was on the End Times. They were also busy reading books like *The Late Great Planet Earth*,[53] which influenced millions in their generation to believe that Armageddon was coming very shortly, and *None Dare Call It Treason*,[54] which claimed there was a conspiracy of government officials involved in manipulating ordinary citizens.

Astrology was another fervent interest of theirs, particularly of Dad's. He continued to insist that he had been to another planet, and he loved to examine star charts. Looking to the sky always made him happy. Sometimes, he would take us outside at night to point at Orion's Belt, Ursa Major, and Ursa Minor. Mom would tell stories about the sky, where she'd been able to point out the Southern Cross.

Mom would also convert full names into numbers and then use those numbers to create numerological charts. These homemade charts became my parents' tool for decision-making in a host of life areas, such as career and parenthood.

My siblings and I have each received a personalized numerological assessment of more than twenty pages in length. Mom and Dad thought that these charts, and astrology and numerology generally, were tools given to humanity by God as a means for guiding one's life plans, or as clues to God's wishes. All things under heaven belonged to God, and that meant He had developed astrology to be used as a guide to the future. In fact, understanding what God wanted for them was the purpose of their lives, a necessity for them in large part because they so lacked a sense of purpose of their own.

My parents' quest for knowledge meant an exploration of faiths, tapping into one's intuitive spiritual discernment, and perpetually seeking the one true religion. I've often said their mental illnesses combined to make a new religion just for the two of them. A lot of people would say they were "possessed by demons" because of "spiritual mapping," because they believed in astrology, or because they were Mormons. They weren't possessed by demons. They were mentally ill, and irrational, and living in Fantasyland.

My mother touted the services of a chiropractor who could determine what was best for your body by asking you to hold different herbal pills in one hand, while testing your strength in the other arm, as not only plausibly scientific but having "the studies to prove it." Yes, but what kind of studies? Had she known science, she would have realized they weren't scientific.[55] Kurt Andersen explained that our parents' generation was taught to question everything, from science to government to medicine. Mom's family already had those kinds of views. Dad was more than willing to listen.

No matter how it started, their life on the edges of society reinforced negative beliefs about the medical establishment, the government, and the public school system. Meanwhile, their faith in the paranormal, and the occult, in addition to the pyramid schemes, and charlatans was unwavering. With the help of *Fantasyland, I* realize they were 100 percent a product of their generation; their delusions, loose associations, and other strange beliefs very much shaped by the currents around them, just like the rest of us were influenced by those currents. They weren't the walking anachronisms I thought they were for most of my life. While other modern nations have embraced rationalism, our nation has "rushed headlong back toward magic and miracles, crazifying some legacy churches, filling up the already crazy ones, inventing all kinds of crazy new ones."[56]

Most everyone I know can tell you their birth Zodiac sun sign. I'm an Aries. A smaller percentage of people, such as my mother, know moon signs, rising signs, and many other signs. She could tell you where each of the twelve signs of the Zodiac were located in the sky at the time of your birth, and furthermore, what that meant about your personality and life path.

Out on in the fringes of society, Mom and Dad found friendships with people who shared and shaped their belief systems. The quest for truth transpired while they sat at a diner having conversations with all kinds of people who drove through town on the busy highway. Those diner friendships only made them odder, magnifying their delusions and reinforcing negative beliefs about the government, conspiracy theories,[57] and the decay of humanity.

Mom and Dad didn't realize people in Denver were talking about how unsupervised their children were as we wandered across town now and then looking for them. The stage was set for an intervention by the government that would finally justify Mom and Dad's paranoia. There would indeed be an Armageddon-like event coming at the family level.

Slowly, our family began to curtail our already minimal spending on things such as clothing, heat, and—finally—food. Mom and Dad approached me one afternoon after our worship time and asked me if I would be willing to take a paper route to help with family expenses. I was not eager to get up every morning before sunrise to deliver papers, but I said I would do it if it would help the family.

At about the same time I started my fourth-grade year, I started my first job. I was nine years old when I became a *Des Moines Register* newspaper carrier for half the town of Denver, Iowa.

Chapter Eleven: Looking Up at the Poverty Line

TOWARD THE END OF the school year, a new family moved into the apartment complex across the parking lot from us. The teenage girl in their family had an incredible ten-speed bike. I didn't have any bike, let alone one as cool as a ten-speed. I gradually gathered the courage to ask the girl if I could ride her bike. When she said yes, I couldn't believe it: my first shot at riding a big bike! It was red, white, and blue, like the flag. So patriotic. So cool.

I pedaled up a small hill, rounded a corner onto a flat road, and then turned down a steeper hill to round the block toward home. I built up speed as I flew down the road. A growing sense of dread started to overpower me. It intensified when the corner at the end of the block drew near. I knew what was going to happen and was filled with the paralyzing fear that I was going too fast to turn onto the street that led back home. I tried anyway, and the tires slid on the gravel of the unfinished road.

The ten-speed and I traveled on our sides over the small rocks until coming to a stop at the curb. I was scraped and bleeding, and my mouth had forcefully hit the curb, but I didn't feel anything as I jumped up and inspected the bicycle. Just as I feared, the frame was bent, and one of the tires was flat. Pain shot through my body, but I picked up the bike and ran home.

Mama was in the parking lot talking to the mother of the girl who owned the bike. I gasped in short sentences that I knew we didn't have the money to pay for the bicycle, and I couldn't stop apologizing to both Mom and the girl for ruining the bike. They just stood perfectly still for a split second and then began separating me from the twisted metal.

I was a mess, with blood coming fast from my mouth, arms, and legs. Mama and the neighbor pulled me into the bathroom of our apartment and put me in the bathtub. They poured water over the wounds to clean them out, but Mom decided that she would have to drive me to the emergency room. The doctors there had to remove lots of tiny rocks from the muscle in my arm, before putting stitches in the large, gaping hole. Mama stood at my head and combed through my hair with her fingers as she reassured me in a whisper that it would be all right.

By evening, my fever climbed until Mama took me back to the hospital, where they confirmed I had an infection in my arm and admitted me. Since they placed me in isolation, I got my own room. Everyone who visited me had to wear a mask and gloves. I hated hospital life because I was alone in the room with no way to visit the playroom. I was also in a lot of pain but too fearful to push the call button to ask them for help, a tendency that became a lifelong issue for me. I couldn't even ask a nurse for the popsicle they promised me and that I desperately wanted. The cold would have made my burning and throbbing mouth feel better.

Something good came out of the bike accident though. While I was in the hospital, Mom was hired as a bed-maker there. Along with being a substitute teacher, which would always be unpredictable financially, she now had a job with more stability and a consistent schedule.

When Dawn moved to town, I finally had two girls I could talk to in school, including Carmen who supported me when I crashed the bike. I couldn't stop the gush of information, emotions, and experiences I had stored up, waiting to share them with a friend. So that I could fit in better with the girls and possibly make some more friends, Mom allowed me to join the Girl Scouts. I became a Brownie. Mama showed me the picture of herself when she was little in her Brownie uniform, smiling broadly. I felt honored to continue a tradition that she had started.

To show my gratefulness, I thanked God and read Bible verses just like Mom told me to do. She didn't need to remind me though. I was way ahead of her. I was starting to make friends, and we even had a TV again. I felt blessed.

Things went sour between Mom and me when all the other Brownies decided to go trick-or-treating together. Halloween sure seemed like it would be a fun holiday, but Mom said it was over-shadowed by the Devil, and she didn't want Satan's influence in her family. We had never been allowed to dress up or go trick-or-treating. It was the same attitude she had about listening to rock music.

Mom wasn't going to change her mind just because my Girl Scout troop was going trick-or-treating. Her answer was a stiff "No," just when things had been going better. My heart sank and I begged her to change her mind. I already felt different from other kids in many ways. We didn't have a sled, a bicycle, furniture, or until recently, a television (and I knew it wouldn't last long). If I couldn't go with the Brownies, I wondered, couldn't we just make simple costumes and walk around the neighborhood? Mom refused. She took all of us to the public library on Halloween night instead. The librarians had bowls of candy out and allowed us to take two pieces each. We picked out books and drove home. I stared stone-faced out the window of our car watching the groups of children walking together in their costumes. I wasn't going to cry; I didn't want to get a headache.

By the time Mom announced she was pregnant again, I had started to buy into her "vision" of having three more children, a boy, a girl, and then another boy. I was hopeful that after three boys, this baby was finally going to be a girl. Once again, Mom planned a home birth. I was nine years old now and could assist with the delivery. I was good at taking on responsibilities.

The truth is I was fatigued every morning from reading books until way too late and then getting up at 4 a.m. to deliver papers. This meant walking down to the spot where the papers were dropped off, preparing all the papers by folding them with or without protective rain sleeves, depending on the weather, and loading the delivery bag. The whole process of delivering the *Des Moines Register* took about two-and-a-half hours each morning in the summer. It took up to an hour longer in winter.

I found a couple of ways to pass the time while I delivered papers in the darkness. For one thing, I read the paper. I needed the streetlights to see, and after I reached each new light, I had a small window of opportunity to read more words before I was cast back into darkness and the words faded away. I could only read the front page since I didn't want to unfold any papers, but my love affair with current events began by reading the front page of the *Des Moines Register*. One of the more unhelpful stories I read was about a paper carrier, a boy named Johnny Gosch, who'd been kidnapped while delivering the *Des Moines Register*.[58]

The paper route had been okay in the summer, but as the mornings got steadily colder, two-and-a-half hours delivering papers became nearly unbearable. This would begin my lifelong fear of winter. I'd bundle in several layers of sweaters, put on heavy boots, and pull on a parka. Each day, I walked about three miles to deliver the route.

Denver bragged that it was a mile wide, and I traversed it hundreds of times. The exertion from lugging so many pounds of newspapers taxed my lungs as I struggled to breathe the bitterly cold air. The exhaled moisture of my breath made my scarf damp and frozen. My mittens never kept my fingers from freezing, and my multiple layers of socks didn't save my toes. When it was extra cold, my eyelashes froze together as my eyes watered in the wind. I had to pull my mittens off and gently pry my lashes apart to see.

Around Christmas that year, Mom joined the Metropolitan Chorale, a local choir group. They were putting on a performance of Handel's *Messiah* for Christmas, and she went to practice faithfully. This put her in a good mood, to be sure. Grandma MacIntyre even sewed her a choral dress big enough for a pregnant woman. Mom borrowed a box set of the *Messiah* from the library and played it continuously. When she took David to practice with her once, he sang along in an empty seat in the auditorium. People were impressed a child of his age could sing along with the complicated score. They suggested he try playing violin.

Mom told Grandma MacIntyre about this feedback, and somehow convinced her to pay for a couple of violin lessons for David. But there was no way Mom and Dad could afford to continue with them, so David didn't get to play the violin for long. Mom and Dad were to face more financial challenges right away in the new year.

Mama was crabby about her extended labor pains. She again wanted the family to be present for the birth of her fifth child. Dad grumbled something about getting extra hours at work. I complained throughout the day about missing school.

But this time, when Mom was ready to have her baby, she didn't have to get angry at us, or feel compelled to go to the hospital to make us feel guilty. Everybody had a role in the delivery, and my job was to cut the umbilical cord. We gathered all the towels in the house, made ice to crush, and then waited. Dad was mostly in charge of helping to deliver the baby, but the rest of us squeezed in around Mama to put cool, wet washcloths on her forehead or to pat her shoulders for support. Then Dad got impatient and left the room, leaving Mom alone with us kids.

Just as she had predicted from her revelation, Mom had a baby girl. We all had gotten impatient waiting for John, but this time we didn't mind so much. It was worth it, as Mom's long-prophesied baby girl came just like she said; she was named Senja[59] after our Finnish grandma, the one I had known only a short time before she died, when I was four.

After cleaning Senja up and wrapping her in a large beach towel with red lobsters on it, we tied her umbilical cord tightly in two places with dental floss. Next, I had to cut the cord, which was hard to do even with sharp scissors, but I was determined. With a snap, the last strand of sinewy tissue gave way, and I disconnected my little sister from the placenta. I was ten years old at the time.

After Senja was born, the family outgrew our two-bedroom apartment in Denver. It was also too expensive, with the additional mouth to feed, because money was that tight. As school let out for the summer, Mom and Dad announced that we were moving to the farm outside of town where Mom grew up. They asked grandfather for permission to move there when we could no longer afford the rent. On the farm, we were going to plant three huge gardens and try to grow enough food to get us through the next winter.

Mom had a habit of saying some particular idea, thing, or person was "providence." She would recite clichés such as, "God always opens a door when he closes a window." We ended up "living like they did on *Little House on the Prairie*" when she decided the abandoned house she grew up in would be our new home. Yep, it was "providence" all right.

There were no more government benefits either. Our new president, Ronald Reagan, the one our parents helped elect,[60] cut the benefit programs. Laws were passed to restrict Aid to Dependent Children of Unemployed Parents to single-parent families. Food stamps were also cut. Mental health services were put into block grants, lump sums that allowed too much discretion to states around how to administer and fund the programs. This meant that states like Iowa could enact cuts. A lot of Americans are convinced that block grants are good because they mean freedom, or something like that. But they are horrible for poor and vulnerable people.

Our parents weren't too worried at first. They were confident Reagan's "trickle-down economics" would actually start to work—an expectation that later became a running joke across the country when it never happened. As time passed, though, it became clear that our situation was more ominous. Mom called the welfare office to see if our family could receive additional aid now that she had another baby. The answer was no. Welfare was only available to single parents now. In fact, every kind of aid that had been available to us was slashed under Reagan's economic plan.

Then Mom got laid off from her job at the hospital. It turned out they were only hiring bed-makers for the summer to replace those who went on vacation. She could be called to substitute teach from time to time, but it was often too treacherous on the roads for her to accept a job when winter came. Dad was laid off from his job not too much later. Going into my fifth-grade year, the only person in the house with a steady job was me, with my paper route. David soon had a paper route as well, when he applied to be a paperboy for the other half of the town.

The farmhouse used to be white, but gray fit it better now. When we moved into it, the paint had peeled in large patches to reveal a grayed wood. The house was half of a hotel that had been moved from three miles north of the town to almost two miles south of it by my grandfather back when he had money. The entrance was still majestic. At the southeast corner of the house, a thick, ornate wooden door stood bordered by two giant windows. In the walls of the house, expanding out to the left and right of the door, these massive windows seemed better suited to a downtown department store with mannequins posed under lights.

One of those windows had what looked like a bullet hole in it, but Mom said it had been punctured by a truck making a delivery to Grandpa's business. The porch that stretched along two full sides of the house in front of these show windows was missing a good many of its wooden slats It had deteriorated to the point where walking on portions of it would surely mean falling through to the ground four feet below.

"Ahhhhhhh, get it out! Get it out!" Mom shrieked to Dad. She was pointing to a rat lying dead on the floor of the living room; then, it was more maggot than rat. These vermin didn't get her spirits down, however. She was excited about the possibility of being able to live independently without any help from the government. We just needed to do an awful lot of work to make this place livable. We worked day and night with scrub brushes, paint brushes, and hammers.

The row of connected small barns that used to house horses, wagons, and supplies was deteriorated. Many barns were leaning over. The barn farthest from the house held several dozen tins of nuclear raid supplies left from the peak of the Cold War. Mom let us pry one open, and there were crackers inside just as the label said. Some of them had been eaten away by some kind of critter. The rest had long become inedible. We loaded up multiple carloads full of tin cans and took them to the county dump.

Old, rusted implements and tools peppered the landscape of the farm. The three burned barns that had served as work buildings for Grandpa's business now sat as gaping pits with years' worth of garbage thrown in. An old pink-and-white RV our grandpa had worked on, with some of his patented advances built in, sat on the property. It wasn't locked, so it was fun to play in. It had held up surprisingly well over the decades since it was built in the mid-1950s. It wouldn't drive anymore, but someone could have lived in it if the weather was just right about half the year. Of course, those were also times of the year when bees, wasps, and hornets were active and lived in and around the RV.

At first, moving to the farmhouse was exciting. David, Samuel, and I explored all the land where our mom had grown up. The driveway felt at least as long as a football field. When our uncle and aunt had lived in the farmhouse with their sons for a short while, our uncle had built an enormous tree house for them. We were warned to stay away from it because it was no longer safe. After climbing part way up to examine it, we decided the deteriorated wood was indeed hazardous, so we stayed away.

There was a large grove of trees where honeysuckle, wild strawberries, and blackberries grew along the fence line of the property.

Here, we found trees with long branches we could run to, grab hold, and swing ourselves twenty feet through the air to land like Tarzan. There was even a small creek at the back edge of the property. I pretended I was with the characters from *Bridge to Terabithia*,[61] calling a small patch of land in the middle of the creek my Terabithia.

The gardens needed regular tending. David and I had to hoe every day for hours to keep the weeds from taking over the acre-plus of land we had planted. We were most excited about harvesting the popcorn. Unfortunately, David didn't listen to Mom or Dad when they told him to always wear shoes while you're gardening, and he hoed the nail right off his big toe. He screamed so loudly he might have been heard on one of the neighboring farms. But no one came, so I was alone and frantic in helping him that day.

We ran to the hose and sprayed ice-cold water on his toe until the blood seemed to stop running so fast and most of the dirt was cleared away. Then we wrapped it tightly in a towel. I knew he needed to have hydrogen peroxide on his toe, but I didn't want to be the one to pour it on. He was so glad when Mama got home because she could hold him. I just couldn't comfort him like she could.

There is no question that our family was living a few decades, and sometimes even a century, out of step with our surrounding community. We used an old-fashioned wringer washing machine. We listened to an AM radio for the programming. Without television, radio soap operas from the 1930s and 1940s became a chief source of entertainment for me while I did chores. My favorites were "*The Life of Riley*" and "*Fibber McGee and Molly*." We also checked out records from the public library to listen to as a family, including Newberry Award–winning children's books in audio form. While the rest of America was admiring the special effects in *Star Wars*, and beginning to buy personal computers, our family was living as though in the Great Depression, huddled around a radio or record player for nightly entertainment.

Mom had no relief from her mood, which was cycling between desperately depressed and excited and hypomanic. When she was feeling better, she pointed out brightly that we were making it on our own without the government. They were so proud we were doing it. The family was no longer receiving welfare to supplement their earnings. It wasn't by choice, yet they didn't get upset with Reagan and his welfare cuts. Instead, they thanked him. We had our own place. We were canning our own food now that fall had come, and we had harvested our gardens. When Mom was down, though, she wouldn't get out of bed, in a room that stayed dark. Mom knew we were living on vegetables, with little protein.

The house was a dangerous wreck. Sometimes Mom blamed us kids. Sometimes she blamed herself. Sometimes I blamed myself. Either way, I was consumed by guilt that somehow Mom was miserable because I wasn't keeping the house clean or the boys well behaved. I went on endless missions to give the place a makeover, trying to enlist the help of my younger brothers through pleading, manipulation, and fighting.

Mom said poetic things about not suckling at the government teat anymore, as if we had been dependent piglets. Dad grumbled that he had earned his government's help. Mom reassured him that he was entitled to benefits, but we didn't need them. She was wrong. What they didn't understand was that the tri-county area was having an economic meltdown. Reagan's lower taxes didn't help our state. There were no full-time jobs for my parents to get. No one in our family understood macroeconomics, so they naively believed in Reagan's trickle-down theory.[62]

The only other program our family was on was free school lunches. In those days, you were given a bright-pink lunch card if the government was subsidizing your lunch, and a mint-green card if you could self-pay. I was hyper-aware we were using that government program because everyone in our small cafeteria could see my pink card. Some kids made snide comments about our eating on the taxpayer's dime. Those comments must have been channeled from their parents. I had struggled to make friends since coming to Denver, and this added shame didn't help.

Otherwise, Mom and Dad considered themselves self-sufficient. We heated the main bathroom of the farmhouse with a kerosene heater, which also lit the area. There was a wood stove where we could cook when we got a fire going. At least there was electricity. We used it to run an ancient wringer washing machine, a radio, and a fan. But that was over the summer, and things became increasingly dire financially soon after. The washing machine broke shortly after Thanksgiving, meaning Mom had to either wash clothes in the bathtub or go into town to use the laundromat when she had extra money.

Mom and Dad had canned the food from our summer gardens, so we mostly didn't need a refrigerator. They had a Conoco Gas credit card that paid for gas and a few groceries. The Conoco station where our parents shopped was in the nearby city of Waterloo. It was a tiny store built in the 1950s, nothing like the fully stocked convenience stores of modern gas stations. But it sold milk, hot dogs, and snack food.

Speaking of food, I can't forget to include the government subsidies program, so I guess that represents another government service we used when we were "self-sufficient." The government subsidies program meant having large bricks of cheese and powdered milk delivered once a month. The powdered milk was disgusting no matter how much Mom tried to mix it in with real milk to cut the taste. But the cheese was heavenly, and we devoured it at almost every meal. It's my understanding that other people got other varieties of commodities from the government depending on what surpluses farmers had.

When I turned ten, Mom's brothers and sisters gathered for Easter, which was on my birthday. To me, it seemed like everybody was there for a big party for me. We went to the roller-skating rink for the first time. I strapped on the skates. They were so easy to use compared to ice skates. I asked for a pair of roller skates for my birthday or Christmas or any reason at all. Mom said we couldn't afford them, but if I saved up my tips from my paper route, maybe I could buy them myself. I frowned. I hadn't been able to keep my tips from the paper route almost since I started it two years ago. I guessed that I wasn't going to see roller skates anytime soon.

Mom and Dad were in such dire straits financially they approached their parents for help, two wells that had been tapped dry already. Grandpa Meyer recommended that Mom turn to the Lutheran Church to which he had donated thousands of dollars "for the poor" to over the years. "Well," he said, "if you don't qualify as poor, I don't know who does." And Mom had gone on a mission for them after all. The pastor of the largest congregation of Lutherans in Denver asked how he could best help. My parents considered the offer and decided that a $600 loan until Dad could get a job would be most helpful.

They were quickly blown off. They weren't even told there was nothing the church would do. Church members did bring by Easter baskets for us kids though. It was embarrassing to see kids from school handing us baskets of candy with looks of pity on their faces. They felt they had done their duty. Their charity was consumed by the end of the day.

People in town believed things were horrid at our house. I found out later they literally were taking notes which would be used in court documents. Meanwhile, Mom wrote to her family about the citizens of Denver, and she nailed it. She could be so sharp and cogent sometimes:

"Their acts of charity become just fluffy, feel-good ways to pretend to care without having to tamper with any real inequities in a corrupt system that breeds poverty, like mosquitoes in stagnant water. And this practice has skyrocketed astronomically since the faith-based constituents have gained political power.

"They applaud their political and religious leaders when they claim to focus on Jesus' words, 'The poor you will always have with you'—but they've twisted it into some perverted mandate for keeping it that way!

"They are increasing the suffering of the poor, somehow blaming them for their 'choice' to be poor; never mind the host of Bible references in which God wants us to help the poor . . . [not] judge and condemn them."

Chapter Twelve: When We Were at Your Mercy

T HIS CHRISTMAS WAS LOOKING a lot like last Christmas. No presents. No tree. Wool stockings hung up on nails on the wall. Christmas was the least of our parents' worries. On December 16, 1981, my younger brother and I rode the school bus home at the end of the day. The ride home was short. Our house was the second stop along Highway 63. People near the front of the bus began loudly chattering as we neared our home. I strained to see what was causing the commotion. Two police cars were parked at the end of our long driveway.

One of the cars belonged to Terry, the deputy sheriff who came to our elementary school to talk about bicycle safety and not taking candy from strangers. He had a popular police dog, a German shepherd named Smokey. Sitting next to one of the police cars was a calm but panting Smokey. The police cars may have drawn the attention of the kids on my bus, but it became apparent that all eyes were on Smokey. That dog had a following.

I followed David down the steps of the bus. We immediately walked up to Smokey and ran our hands along his furry head. I decided the kids on the bus probably wished they could be us. The deputy sheriff stepped forward and smiled broadly. "Hi there. Are you the MacIntyre children?"

"Yes, I'm Deborah, and this is David. Where are my mom and dad? Is everything okay?"

"Oh yes, everything is just fine," the deputy said soothingly. "I think you know me from school. Is that right?"

I nodded in agreement and slowly raised my hand to slip my arm around David's shoulder. The sense that something was horribly wrong became intense.

"I just came by to tell you two that it is all right to ride with this police officer. He's going to take you to Waterloo."

David and I said nothing. Stunned, we crawled into the back seat of the other officer's car, following the direction of his outstretched hand. Riding in silence, David and I had a nonverbal conversation of shrugs and head shaking. I gathered the courage to speak and leaned into the wire mesh dividing the officer from us. I softly asked where we were going.

"We are going to St. Francis Hospital. But don't you worry, everything will be all right."

During the eighteen-mile drive, a horrible thought crossed my mind. Obviously, Mom and Dad were dead. How had this happened? The only logical answer was a car crash. I stared straight ahead and began wondering how my siblings and I would take care of ourselves. I squeezed my brother's hand and whispered that I would take care of him. Inside, I was petrified.

The ride seemed to take an hour. We passed the small man-made pond on the outskirts of Waterloo, and I was certain we were about to begin our newly orphaned lives. I wondered where Samuel, John, and Senja were. A fleeting thought became an unsettling conviction. My youngest siblings were obviously in the car; they had died along with my parents.

We arrived at the hospital, where the deputy ushered us into the emergency entrance. A bearded man with long hair approached us. "Are these the MacIntyre children?" he asked. The deputy confirmed that we were.

"Come with me, kids," the bearded man commanded.

Oh, no, this is it. He's going to tell us that our entire family has died, I thought. I was guided into a small room, where a woman with blonde hair took my hand. David was taken somewhere else.

As I entered the room, I was relieved to see Mom and Dad seated at a small table. They were alive! I rushed to my mom's side and threw my arms around her. It was evident she had been crying. Since my parents were living, I thought it was obvious that my little brothers and sister were the ones who were dead.

"Mr. and Mrs. MacIntyre, we need to talk to your daughter privately. The officer outside will bring you to the lobby area." My parents were not recognizable because they behaved like obedient children. I was unaccustomed to seeing my parents following orders. The bearded man told me to take the seat my mother had vacated. He settled across from me with a clipboard. I noticed it was a female police officer who sat in a corner of the room.

"Did you eat breakfast today?" the bearded man asked quickly.

What a weird question, I thought. Experience told me that I should answer yes. Grandma and Grandpa would also ask this question whenever I went to stay with them. Mom and Dad told me to always answer yes. I was getting overly warm in my winter clothes, but my feet were wet and cold. I curled my toes tightly together as I considered his question.

"Yes, I had cereal, and eggs, and bacon," I said, lying.

"Does your family have a refrigerator?"

"Lots of them. They all stopped working. We keep things outside to keep them cold." That was true. We did store food outside in a metal container. It had been snowing outside for at least a month. We packed snow around the container.

"Where do you sleep?"

"I have a sleeping bag in the basement. Why are you asking me these questions?"

"Your parents left your sister and brothers alone at home. They can't do that. I want you to tell me honestly about how they take care of you."

I didn't like this man with a full mane of dark hair around his face, from his unkempt hair to his thick beard. He scared me, and I resented how he talked about Mom and Dad. I said nothing, staring at him.

"Okay, you told me you had bacon and eggs this morning. How did your Mama cook these for you?"

"We have a hot plate. It's like a mini stove."

"Hmm, well, your house does not have heat."

I could only glare in response. If he was at our house, didn't he see the wood-burning stove in the basement where we plainly warmed food, and the coolers outside where we kept cold food? At that point, a man wearing a white coat opened the door. He was obviously a doctor.

"I can examine her now," he told the hairy man.

He held my hands in his, carefully looking at my fingertips. He then asked me to remove my boots and socks. I did so unhappily because I was worried my toes would never warm up. He looked worried about a burn I had on my thigh from an ember that had flown out of the stove several days earlier. It was not healing well.

At the end of the day, I can say, fortunately, I had been wrong. My entire family was alive. They just were not going to live together anymore. Child welfare workers had responded to reports that my siblings and I were being neglected. The workers from the county Community Action Program (CAP) had come by to assess what our energy assistance needs were. When they arrived, the temperature in our house was thirty-eight degrees, except in one room where we all lived across from the wood-burning stove. They found our food supply consisted only of canned vegetables taken from our garden that previous summer.

Years later, when I read the child abuse report, I thought about how the child abuse investigator failed to see my parents were American heroes for getting off welfare. Everyone likes people who do not take welfare. The child welfare report even noted my parents "stood self-righteously" by their statement that they had accepted Ronald Reagan's call to "get off the welfare wagon," and "stop being dependent on the government."

I also didn't realize until I was an adult that my ultra-conservative, fundamentalist parents' views might have prompted their liberal social worker to look for evidence of child abuse.

We were living independently, and if that meant living like folks did a hundred years ago, then what was the issue? Well, apparently, doctors claimed they recorded frostbite on John's and Senja's toes. Mom responded in the margins of the abuse report in orange, highlighting that she didn't see how this could be true because Samuel didn't take the kids outside and it wasn't cold enough inside.

The investigator penned a report that reflected his complete ignorance of the structural problems that caused and maintained their poverty, all of which Mom and Dad tried to bring up during the interview. He made them seem like lazy, poor people who were also not using the system enough—an interesting, paradoxical perspective to take. We could have "made better use of the Community Action Program," the report read, without specifying how.

We actually had used CAP quite a bit, it being a new program put in place to help poor people. The farmhouse had a wood-burning stove, but it only kept the basement warm. It turned out that the wood stove came from the CAP. If you came down the staircase, the stove was on your right. On your left, all seven of us huddled for heat in a small cement room, the floor covered with a bed and sleeping bags. The stove served as an actual stove as well. CAP also got us five refrigerators over time (all of which broke), three cribs, and boxes and boxes of clothes. Mama didn't know what to do with all the stuff. It was clutter. My parents were trying to get CAP to fix the roof of my grandpa's farmhouse, and then insulate it.

Now that it was winter, produce from the gardens was supposed to hold us over until next summer. We had canned the yield from the three enormous gardens we had planted. It was this food we warmed on the wood-burning stove from CAP. Since CAP didn't deliver any wood for the stove, Mom and Dad were slowly burning the porch of the farmhouse to keep us warm and to cook. It wasn't enough food, though, as evidenced by the fact that the teachers were taking notes about my brothers and I receiving leftover food from other students at lunch.

When Child Protective Services inspected the farmhouse, things went downhill. There was no heat in most of the house. Not only was it structurally unsound, with a roof in bad need of repair, the staircase and flooring were precarious in places, and the electrical wiring was badly in need of being brought up to code.

Also, the house was not clean. Well, that's not fair, because we didn't have a washing machine, only the old ring washer. The child abuse investigator described the bathroom as filthy, due to seeing

Mom in the process of washing out cloth diapers in the bathtub. Still, there was no question that my parents were in denial about conditions at the house. I was too.

In other respects, the child abuse report was simply misleading. The investigator made all kinds of unfounded allegations against our parents that made no sense. For example, he put easily discredited innuendo into the report suggesting they did drugs. He reasoned that if these Mormons were willing to break the rule on drinking coffee or smoking, why not other rules? They, of course, didn't understand they were dealing with fundamentalist Mormons, who *could* drink coffee or smoke. The report revealed that gossip was a factor in the probe, using phrases such as, "Rumors in town were . . ."

The investigator dug deeper into a few things. He collected the notes from teachers about how dirty we were. That was David and I covered in newspaper ink after finishing our delivery routes. He interviewed the principal, who said my dad was turned down for a custodian job at the elementary school because he had a bad reference from a cemetery. My dad had never applied to or worked for a cemetery. He had applied to work at our school and been turned down *by the principal* who now made up this story.

David and Samuel each had a teacher taking down her observations of their appearance and behavior. They recorded everything from a duct-taped shoe to dirty clothes. The teachers didn't know we had to wait and save gas money to make a big trip to the laundromat. During their drug awareness education unit, one of my little brothers said he'd "seen something that looks like marijuana in his mom's pills."

Almost everybody should have found the idea that mom had a marijuana pill mixed in with the ones that were just popped in her mouth is completely absurd. In 1981, that was just a joke. This was long before it was legal, of course, in some places (still not Iowa) so it didn't come in edible forms near us either. The teachers recorded this "highly reliable" information in their notes. No one in our family was aware of this surveillance, or that they used mindless comments—sorry, "information"—from David or Samuel.

Mom and Dad *could* say some strange things, make bizarre interpretations, and isolate themselves in suspicious ways. For example, when my third-grade teacher wanted to put me in the Talented and Gifted program, my parents thought it was a conspiracy, and they refused at first. That could have been interpreted as drug-induced paranoia instead of as a symptom of their respective mental illnesses, along with their obsession with persecuted religions. Of course, the officials weren't aware of their conditions, but they did very little to find out.

The State never figured out—or, really, cared—that these two people were clearly mentally ill. As they phrased it in their reports, Mom and Dad "had strange social opinions," and they thought Dad was simply irresponsible, knowing nothing about schizophrenia or the disorders related to it. In the report, Mom and Dad were instead subjected to cruel indifference. It was common for child-welfare workers on the front lines to be poorly trained in mental health well into the twenty-first century. In 1981, in Iowa, they couldn't even recognize psychosis.

As a preteen, I knew nothing about mental health either. I blamed our father in just the way they did. Wasn't he stupid? Wasn't he a bad father? He left a six-year-old to babysit a two-year-old and a baby!

Mom highlighted about 90 percent of the original child abuse report in orange when she got her copy. Orange signified that something was inaccurate. I saw her point in numerous places, but when I read it, there were places where I simply had to shake my head in disagreement and wonderment with her.

The child protection worker didn't know a lot of things that they could have, and which would have been mentioned in the report. They didn't know that Mom and Dad, due to their nerves, consistently left us alone to go have coffee. They couldn't handle the noise we made, so they put me in charge.

Dad may have treated all of his children like mini adults simply because he didn't want to be involved in parenting. Once we could talk, Dad expected us to be mature enough to be responsible. You weren't supposed to need punishments. Maybe that's why he felt comfortable leaving six-year-old Samuel to babysit two-year-old

John and nine-month-old Senja for more than two hours on the very day the authorities showed up. Or maybe he felt it was safer to travel without the children because his car was unreliable. Mom vehemently defended Dad's decision to let Samuel babysit, arguing that he was "very mature" for his age.

Still, the fact was that county workers were there waiting for Dad to return. He had gone into town to call about a job. Time got away from him. He was seen sitting in the Weathervane reading the newspaper and drinking coffee. "Yes," Dad protested to child welfare investigators, "so I could look at the help-wanted section and make some phone calls. Our phone at home wasn't working. Someone was on the phone here at the Weathervane, so I sat down with a cup of coffee to warm up and look at job ads."

Even so, the child welfare people handled things very poorly. If you're going to help a couple of mentally ill, poor people, you have to use a kid-glove approach, not a hammer. They threatened Mom and Dad and scared them even more than usual. Even though the State very quickly assumed long-term custody of us, they strung Mom and Dad along, letting them believe that when they voluntarily signed over custody, they could easily get us back. They just had "to complete a list of tasks."

The night of December 16, 1981, they told my parents they could keep us, but that they had to find some place besides the farmhouse to stay. This time, Mom asked Uncle Paul for shelter. In my eyes, he seemed to agree only begrudgingly. When we came running in the door, David looked at the Christmas tree brimming with wrapped presents underneath and asked, "Which of these presents is for me?" I overheard Uncle Paul saying that his sister had selfish children. We weren't the kids getting presents.

Mom was keenly aware what an imposition her large family was on her brother, especially since he and his wife were about to throw an office party, so she went to Child Protective Services and voluntarily signed papers allowing the State to take "temporary" custody of us. The next day, child protection workers came to the school to get David, Samuel, and me. The babies were taken to another foster home.

They took us to a foster care home a few miles outside Denver. The family had a mother, father, and a son who was in my class in fifth grade at the elementary school. The foster mother had the custodian job at the elementary school that my dad had applied for. She broadcasted that she got the job because she was bored and needed something to do. The boy told everyone in class that I was living with him. Starting the first night I was there, the mother didn't tuck me in or give me a hug. I told Mama about this in a phone call, and she asked our foster mother, "Why don't you give my children hugs?" She said that it wasn't her job.

David was spanked for turning on the bathroom light when he went to pee in the middle of the night. Later, he became obsessed with the foster care family, prank-calling them for years after we lived there. Samuel wasn't taking the separation too well either. He kept hiding under the dining room table, softly crying. I started crawling under there with him.

Mom was most worried about Senja living in foster care while she was still nursing. Senja was not even a year old, and Mom had research from La Leche League that showed separation between a mother and her child during that age period could negatively affect attachment. She went to the library, got articles about the harm of disrupted attachment, and gave copies to the guardian ad litem chosen to represent us kids in court proceedings. No one appeared to read what she brought.

Court proceedings never went well for my parents. Everybody—the child abuse investigator, a new social worker called in to assess the situation, the judge, the guardian ad litem, and the court-appointed lawyer for my parents—thought we should be taken away from my parents. Then they asked us kids.

When they put me on the stand, I fiercely, defiantly, and obnoxiously defended my parents. Mom had an emotional meltdown with her court-appointed lawyer. Finally, the social worker hammered out a plan. Our parents had to stabilize their housing situation before we could come back. That wasn't a problem because they had already gotten into housing in Waterloo. They secured an apartment in a subsidized townhouse that had just been built.

Due to the shortage of affordable housing, small government housing developments with about thirty units each were built in a few communities on the West Side to move at least a few African American families out of their segregated community.[63] The protests were so massive in those white neighborhoods, the largest petition created in the city's history was signed to prevent the housing. Luckily, it didn't work.

Placating those white residents, the housing authority kept the racial composition of the units at less than 25 percent African American. Local white residents were still unhappy. They became part of the 12,000 people who made the exodus from out of Waterloo and into the nearby counties following the integration of schools and neighborhoods in the 1970s and 1980s.[64] We moved into those government housing projects in 1981 and immediately faced neighborhood hostility and racial animus.[65]

The Department of Social Services required Dad to get a job, but he'd already found one working part-time as a janitor, once again at minimum wage. It was still the best he could find in that economy. They also mandated parenting classes and family counseling. Theoretically, once their situation was settled, Mom and Dad could have their children back. But they completed the list, and the State still wouldn't give us back.

Mom and Dad went to the media and told them we had been "kidnapped" by the State because they were poor. The *Des Moines Register* ran an article with the headline, "Jobless Pair Fear Kids Will Be Snatched Away." A radio station carried a question-and-answer with Mom; and the local TV news showed footage of our dilapidated farmhouse and of my siblings crying as a result of being taken by the State.

After a three- and then a six-month period of assessment, the State ended up letting Mom and Dad keep us. The family counseling assessment team did one session with the family and declared that we were "fine" and didn't need any help. The team may have told our parents this to make them feel better, because we definitely needed help. In that respect, the assessment team was just as wrong as Child Protective Services had been. However, they recognized that Mom and Dad were not being treated well by Protective Services. As one worker put it, "I see a lot of good in your family; you guys just got the shaft."

Forty years later, both Mom and Senja, say that their attachment to each other was forever affected by the foster care separation. Mom says she was permanently distant from her own mother, and Senja says she feels the same way about herself and Mom. It's true. Senja's capacity for attachment in relationships is damaged. She was at just the age developmentally to be affected in this way by the separation.

Sometime during the foster care period, before she got her kids back, Mom randomly went into a Catholic Church and asked to speak with a priest. Father Kelly came out to talk with her. She was so distressed that she vomited in front of him in anxiety. He listened to her try to tell her story, and he referred her to Dr. Nestor Pangilinan, a Filipino psychiatrist. Mama was grateful to Dr. Pangilinan because he knew she didn't have any money to pay him. He sat and kindly listened to her talk for a long time. He started the process to have Mom officially declared disabled. This meant that the family would be entitled to income support from the government again. It was also the first time that anyone had recognized that Mom was mentally ill. The child welfare office should have long ago done what these two men did, almost reflexively

Long after the incident at the farmhouse, Child Protective Services monitored our parents with regular check-ins. They could have helped a lot if they had done things right by, for example, setting our parents up with psychiatric medication and psychiatric rehabilitation that could lead to full-time jobs. But they didn't seem to know *how* to help. They would end up only making things worse.

The clash between our parents and Child Protective Services was like a hurricane to our family. Just a few months without their children had traumatized Mom and Dad. They were more paranoid than ever. Everyone was out to get them. Their fear only grew when the property managers of our housing complex kept making surprise inspections, which Mom and Dad thought was part of a plot to target our family in coordination with Child Protective Services.

My parents' strategy of getting us back by using the media had worked—but at a cost. Many awful things were said about our family publicly, and a lot of it was just plain wrong. *Our parents were on drugs. Our parents were welfare bums.* That one really hurt, considering that they had been so proud to be off welfare.

I had been subjected to public humiliation in school when our foster brother told everyone about our situation. Keep in mind that Mom's graduating class in Denver was thirty-two people. There were probably just a few more than that in my fifth-grade class. I felt humiliated when our family's story was represented in the media as one of degradation and filth.

But I thought Mom must have shown the *Des Moines Register* article to my next fifth-grade teacher when we transferred to the Waterloo School District, because my teacher was so sweet to me on the first day I started school at Blackhawk Elementary. Mrs. Farmer was special to me. We hung around a few kids in the apartments who were Black, but Mrs. Farmer was the first adult Black person I knew. She was smart, kind, and beautiful. She wore her hair in a big Afro, and she loved to wear large hoop earrings.

The thing I needed most when I was eleven years old was sleep, and I wasn't getting it. I was so tired one day that I came to school without a shirt on. I started to take my coat off, and there I was, completely naked under my spring jacket. Embarrassed that someone might have seen me, I slinked to the front of the room and told my teacher about my predicament. Mrs. Farmer let me run home and finish getting dressed, since the apartments we had moved into were right next to the school.

My eating and sleeping habits continued to be unhealthy, and very hard on my body. I was reading late into the night as an escape from life. I spent my afternoons babysitting the kids. I continued to spend my mornings delivering newspapers. They had transferred me to a route close to where we lived. Around then, I somehow got a bicycle for my paper route. The route still took quite a while, but it cut a lot of time off to be able to ride between addresses.

The only guaranteed food was school lunch. The Special Supplemental Nutrition Program for Women, Infants, Children (WIC) program bought cereal and milk for breakfast. Otherwise, it was macaroni and cheese, or grilled cheese sandwiches, or hot dogs, or nothing for supper, alternating with Mom's manic junk food.

Unlike the teachers in Denver, Mrs. Farmer seemed to understand our family's poverty. But Waterloo is a city with deep racial rifts. It didn't take long for me to run into racial conflict that caused me to worry about trusting people of a different race. I vaguely understood that white people had created this problem with slavery, but not how that directly impacted me now.

In sixth grade, one of the apartment kids was messing with me after school. His name was Marcus[66]. He bullied our brothers too. Finally, I confronted him directly. I told him I was telling the principal what he was doing. He pulled his arms back and thrust his chest forward. "You want a piece of me? Let's go."

I told him, "I don't fight. I just want you to leave my family alone."

"You fought Kevin Lowd and you lost," he said, snickering. Yeah, because bullies seemed attracted to me.

"But I didn't want to," I said.

Marcus punched my chest. It hurt, but I could take it.

"Come on," he said. Finally, I hit him back. We fought for a minute or so, and then Marcus's friend pulled on his arm and said, "I think you've made your point. Let's roll."

The next day I was shocked when I was called to the principal's office. Marcus reported me for being a bully, and he said I called him the N-word. There was no way on this green Earth I would have called him that. I was furious that he was lying and getting me in trouble.

When I told my side of the story, I wasn't sure if the principal believed me or not, but he suspended both of us for three days for fighting. Actually, as bad as racism was in our area then, I'm kind of proud of our principal for believing Marcus, even if he did lie. This was my first negative interaction with a Black person. Now, I was a little bit afraid despite my positive relationship with Mrs. Farmer. I didn't know at the time about the history of racism against Black people in Waterloo.[3] I only understood that we were on the receiving end of the backlash. I'm not happy Marcus targeted me, of course, but it did lead to the beginning of my awareness of the racism problem.

As poor people, we often ate at free dinners provided in the community. One day, Mom and Dad brought a man named Patrick Adams[67] home because it was "providence" that they happened to meet him at the Catholic Worker House, where homeless people stayed and poor people came to eat.

After leaving the free supper that night, they all went to Hardee's. Our parents said they had talked "about everything under the sun" from the "time we got there until dawn. We just had "so much in common." They were explaining to me why I had been babysitting around the clock again, something I didn't feel I could handle any more.

Patrick Adams was as Anglo-Saxon as his name suggested, from his rusty, auburn hair and freckles to his light, blue eyes. He didn't have to be much of a con man to fool my parents, but he did have to read them. Patrick extracted enough information from our folks to know what to feed back to them. That's how he learned he needed to say he was a Native American prophet.

For more than a decade, the Church of Latter-day Saints (LDS) and the fundamentalist Mormons (FLDS) had played a significant role in Mom and Dad's lives. Mormons believe they have a special relationship with indigenous Americans. Their "prophet" Joseph Smith, who started the Mormon Church, proclaimed he "divined" that Jesus, despite having been born in the Middle East, visited North and South America. Smith told his followers the proof that Jesus went to the Americas was the acceptance of the Spanish in South America by natives who expected the "return of a white God."

It was laughable stuff, then as now, but that's what my parents would say. My formal education on how to be a Mormon was limited to two years belonging to a Ward—a ward being a local Mormon congregation. Most of our church sessions were spent meeting as a family in our living room. The facts that Jesus would have appeared Middle Eastern, or at least not white, and that the Spanish quickly slaughtered South Americans, never seemed to baffle Smith's followers.

Anyway, Pat Adams surmised that Mom and Dad thought Mormons were expecting a white, Native American savior, or had once had one, or something like that. He stood in for somebody Mom and Dad had primed themselves to cherish and trust: a twenty-something impersonator who, as we found out later, was posing as an eighteen-year-old holy man. He said he had recently lived in the local orphanage called Brentwood, which, conveniently, was a county away.

Patrick Adams had to find a place to live among the many products our parents had purchased in the past couple of years of their underemployment. Each was an attempt to earn money when jobs were scarce. These products included mini trampolines, Amway, Willard Water, Slick 50 fuel enhancer, and a couple of boxed-up kerosene heaters. In each case, a persuasive salesman had sized up our parents as easy pickings. Anyone pained with a conscience would never have taken advantage of their gullibility in response to any sales claim..

The companies that sold these products used pyramid schemes or multi-level marketing campaigns. The people at the bottom of the pyramid, like our parents, ended up with a lot of unsold product. Therefore, Mom and Dad came out worse off financially than when they started, just as these companies had planned. Besides, sales work depends on building a network of customers, being able to run a business, and understanding that you have to manipulate people. Our parents were struggling to get the laundry done.

Again, when I read Kurt Andersen's, *Fantasyland*, I understood our parents better. They were part of the conservative social networks that were flush with these kinds of pyramid schemes. Why does God let you get conned?

Prophet Pat wasn't supposed to be there, living among the boxed products that were carefully hidden under blankets to look like furniture. Government housing rules specified a certain number of occupants, and they all had to be family. The people who lived on the other side of our duplex were both nosy and cozy with the managers/overseers. As things stood, we were already barely passing inspections. Pat kept a cagey presence. He had only a suitcase of belongings, which he could quickly pack when inspectors were coming.

Pat only came in and out of the back door. He managed to evade the manager by only going out at night. He slept on the sofa, which Mom always called a davenport. (Other kids seemed to have no idea where she got that name for it, but she had me calling it that too. These same kids would laugh at me, so it didn't take me long to switch my language to say sofa. Mama seemed to have a lot of funny words like that for things.)

I could see right away from his dirty clothes, scruffy beard, and a duct-taped suitcase that Pat Adams had been homeless. Fair enough; prophets are often homeless. He also started giving me lascivious looks not long after moving into our apartment. It was a curse to have developed substantial breasts by age eleven. It made me look sixteen. It shaves off a good portion of your youth when men start looking at you in "that way" when you're still just a child. He was a full-blown adult leering at a child who looked like a teen. Gross.

Pat had to keep his "prophet" mystique alive, so he must have caught an idea from a book he was reading — *The Amityville Horror*[68] by Jay Anson. The idea no doubt occurred to him after hearing my parents talk about how our former house in Denver was possessed by the Devil. He told us he would stage an exorcism. A lot of things had gone very wrong in that farmhouse. Mom and Dad went to war with each other. The State of Iowa took us. Many years before, our grandfather's American Dream had died tragically, his bipolar disorder as disabling to him as it later was to his daughter. There were many reasons for our family to think the place was possessed.

Pat Adams made us go back to the house at night, because "that's when the spirits dwell there." Our parents believed everything he told them. We had to pair up to share the flashlights necessary in a farmhouse with no electricity. The light they provided was otherworldly. Slowly, he had us creep up to the second floor, where he deemed the level "spirit-free," and pushed the family upward to the attic. He performed several rituals with ridiculous chants he'd conjured, exaggerated shaking and twisting, and terrifying screams. Mama appeared to be totally captivated. David grabbed my hand, squeezing it to the point of both comfort and pain.

My eyes widened both to accommodate the darkness and from fright. David's breathing was heavy and ragged. I was having a hard time catching my breath too. The attic was stuffy, full of cobwebs, dust, and darkness, except for the thin points of light aimed from our flashlights.

Pat Adams read to us from *The Amityville Horror* despite the fact none of us was old enough to handle it. The stories of ghosts with evil intent brought to mind the Devil, and I thought God seemed far away when he read us the book. I had just started to read *The Amityville Horror* at his urging, and I believed him when he said we were in a real haunted house. His frenetic gyrations, babbling, and frequent use of total darkness when he had us switch off the flashlights convinced me he had rid the house of demons.

After the big exorcism, I kept reading *The Amityville Horror*, and I began to have the same feelings of skepticism as when our parents fell for huckster salesmen in pyramid schemes. Later, I learned that Pat Adams hadn't performed an exorcism.

Even before Pat admitted he stole the exorcism idea from the book, I didn't trust him. After all, there were clues everywhere that this man was not indigenous and not a prophet, but rather was taking advantage of our parents to have his room and board covered, while being flagrantly sexually inappropriate with me, their eleven-year-old daughter. I'd always believed in our parents and stood up for them at every turn. Only eighteen months earlier, when child abuse investigators had interviewed me about how our family lived, I had covered for them. I had said we got enough to eat when we really didn't. I had stated that they never hit us. It was when Pat Adams came to stay that I saw our parents for who they were. They were crazy.

One night, Mom was having one of her episodes. She'd been working hard all week proofreading at the Cedar Falls newspaper, so she hadn't been getting enough sleep. She was eating a quarter-pound bag of M&Ms, drinking a heavy volume of Shasta Crème Soda, and nibbling on a giant Hershey's chocolate with almond candy bar while she sat at the kitchen table.

She had taken out the old typewriter. By old, I mean it was vintage 1940s or something, with ivory keys that needed to be pounded down an inch or more to generate a letter. Naturally, these typewriters became valuable after Mom didn't have hers anymore. Her fingers flew on the machine while she insisted humbly, "Oh, I don't type that fast." It was all that piano playing she did. It made her long fingers nimble and quick. When Mama typed too fast, the old typewriter's hammers would tangle with each other. She would have to stop and put the hammers back in their proper place before continuing.

On this particular day, she said she finally had enough energy to go through our mail. It often built up during the many days she spent without energy and in a dark, moody state. Today, one of the items in the mail was a notification that we were going to have an inspection of the apartment outside of the standard, scheduled inspection each quarter.

It wasn't clear which level of government had implemented the Gestapo-like standards to which apartments had to be kept in order, but this particular government housing came with inspections of the duplex to see if you were keeping it clean and maintained. They occurred at three-month intervals or less, emphasis on less. It was public property, so management had a right to ensure the apartments weren't being trashed. However, they used this right excessively. One of the rules Mom broke was that she stored her pots and pans in the oven, so she was written up for that.

According to the letter Mom opened that night, the apartment overseers had given us three days warning, but Mom had just gotten the notice because she was behind on the mail. The inspection was happening tomorrow. The inspection turned out to be the result of "information from reliable sources" that "the apartment was not being maintained to standards." This probably meant our nosy neighbors were reporting that Pat Adams was staying with us, or they were saying our apartment wasn't clean. Both were true.

Mom had been going through the mail since she got home from work at 5:00 p.m. For her, this also meant writing letters to all manner of people to update them about the family. It could be her father, her brothers, her sisters, a friend, or some other extended family. I started to receive a steady stream of these letters, often daily, once I moved out years later. This made doing the bills and answering mail take hours. It was 2:00 a.m. when she opened the envelope with the notification. She panicked. She woke up Dad, and he panicked even more.

Soon, Mom was shaking everyone awake, and not gently. If you didn't get up quickly, she pulled you out of bed until you were either standing up or you hit the floor. "I want this apartment cleaned from one corner to the next. This is toothbrush time, people. We are getting inspected tomorrow. We could lose our housing."

We hurried as fast as we could in our sleepy, irritable states. The toilets were cleaned. Check. The pans beneath the stove's burners were cleaned. Check. The lint from the dryer filter had to be removed. Check. Our dad was so paranoid he would lose custody of his children again that he even required that the wires of our bed springs be dusted. It was to be another sleepy day at school, but we passed the inspection. Pat Adams hid out at Hardee's for hours.

If there's anything Mom would not abide, it was making her house dirty. That's not to say her house wasn't something to hide behind the curtains over 70 percent, maybe upwards of 80 percent, of the time. It was. She did not appreciate that fact one bit. She would pick up items from the floor or the furniture one by one, calling out who it belonged to, then she'd hurl whatever it was toward the correct bedroom with a force liable to cause injury to anyone who got in the way. As you retrieved your offensive item, she gave you a look that let you know you had taken a piece of her soul.

When she was using manipulation, it was not, "Get your room cleaned or we're taking away your TV privileges." It was, "Clean it, or we're taking you to the county children's home (i.e. Brentwood)." That last one sometimes came with a ride past the home for orphans in the family car.

Set against this maternal power and the emotional abuse Mom inflicted on her kids was the immovable fact that Pat Adams was a slob. He left his dirty clothes everywhere. He wouldn't do the dishes no matter how many times he was asked. Mom considered clean dishes his payment for living in our crowded apartment rent-free. Still, he wouldn't do the dishes.

Mom couldn't pick up on the signs the guy was a lecherous fraud, but she finally sent him packing when he still wouldn't help. Not that he had much to pack. She just gathered his things and put them on the little back patio. Then she told him to get out or she'd call the police. She pointed to the door and repeated, "Get out," until he was finally gone.

Pat Adams leered suggestively, but that was all he ever did. At the same time he was living with us, there were threats from people who weren't strangers at all. I guess what I remember was considered "sexual experimentation." Authorities don't count it as sexual abuse unless the children are five years apart in age. It hurts when I remember what cousin Autumn did when I was younger, so I guess her experiment was a failure, at least for me. But then, when she was thirteen and I was eleven, we spent a day at the carnival and in the backyard that was worse.

We were supposed to hang out at the city's annual "Cattle Congress." She spent all her time hitting on a scruffy carnie, and when I finally did get her attention, she insisted we go on a ride. I told her it would make me sick. After hoping throughout the circular motions that I could make it until it ended, I threw up for many miserably long minutes in a trash can.

That same weekend, Autumn gave the next-door neighbor, a boy I disliked for being one of the nosy backstabbers, a hand job right on our back patio. Any number of other neighbors could have seen it. Whenever I wince at the memory, I cannot get the picture out of my mind of all of them staring out their windows seeing through me. I was supposed to stand in front of Autumn and the teen to block the view of the neighbors, but I knew Autumn could be seen from any number of angles.

I know now that she *had* to have been sexually abused. I know what that can do to a girl.

Chapter Thirteen: Guilty of Child Neglect

WHERE AND WHEN IT started, I'm not sure. Was it his music on the radio? A video? Did I see a picture of him? Peer influence? It's hard to say, but I developed a huge crush on Michael Jackson sometime in 1983 after Pat Adams moved out. I shushed my brothers and sister when they tried to talk as the radio played MJ's songs. I used cassette tapes to record his songs from the radio, always unhappy when the deejay would cut into the end of the song with nonsense.

I volunteered to babysit for a neighbor's kids as much as I could so I could glue myself to MTV, in hopes of catching a view of a Michael Jackson video. I wrote "Deborah loves Michael" all over my schoolbooks and notepads. I also wrote it in permanent marker on the brand-new desk Mom and Dad bought for my room. Mom was furious. My diary gushed with my desire to marry Michael and my conviction that if I willed it hard enough, it would happen.

Running late one day, I rushed into math class. I started to grab a chair next to Chris, a boy whose crush on me wasn't well hidden. I might have been known all over school to be wild about MJ, but that hadn't stopped Chris from noticing the breasts I wasn't supposed to have yet. He thought it would be funny to tease me by pulling the chair out from under me. Instead of taking a seat, I went crashing down to the floor, tailbone first. Pain shot through my spine. I didn't want to cry, but tears came to my eyes anyway.

When I got home from school, I announced to Mom, "I hurt my scrotum today." She burst into a hearty laugh. I wasn't amused by her apparent lack of concern. I was holding my hand to my lower back, so she knew what I meant. "Do you mean you hurt your sacrum?" I realized my mistake, and my cheeks reddened in embarrassment.

"I think I need to see a doctor. It hasn't stopped hurting since it happened." I should have known what she was going to say. She was the daughter of a chiropractor for goodness' sake. "I'll make an appointment with Dr. Wright, and he can fix you right up." Of course, Dr. Wright was one of the many chiropractors she had seen over the years. She didn't seem to notice how kooky some of them were. Some of them were really crooked, forcing clients to buy into "plans" that costs thousands of dollars to get services.

We didn't have a car, so we took the pitiable city bus system[69] from Waterloo to Cedar Falls. the twin city west of us. What would have taken fifteen minutes in a car took almost an hour by bus. With the way Reagan cut back on all public services, we were probably lucky to have public transportation at all.

After the initial appointment, when Mom filled the waiting room with conversation and kept Dr. Wright busy answering questions during my adjustment, follow-up appointments were scheduled for the next year. Dr. Wright claimed it would take that long to correct the damage to my sacrum and spine.

Mom didn't have the time to escort me to weekly appointments that took more than three hours to accomplish if you included transportation time. This meant I was on my own. It didn't take long for Randy, the bus driver, to figure out that I was a regular. He told me he was eighteen years old, but looking back with an adult's eye, I estimate he was probably twenty-five at least.

Over time, Randy's conversations with me took on a creepy tone. As a twelve-year-old, I was clearly a child, but he constantly talked to me in sexually suggestive ways. I should have moved to the back of the bus, but I tended to get carsick when bounced around the back. I sat within earshot of Randy and carried on light banter. Eventually, he asked me out. I told him I had a boyfriend. That was a lie.

Unfortunately, Randy wasn't the only adult who had been hitting on me. Sometimes it felt like I was surrounded by them. Uncle Rick[70], married to Mom's oldest sister, Cleo, tried to come onto me.

Later, everyone found out he'd molested his daughters. He had tried to get Mom and Dad to let him bring me on a trip to Arizona with Cleo. Ostensibly, this was to meet our cousins. Luckily, Mom and Dad said no. It was my paper route that saved me. We needed the money.

Another time, Mom and Dad drove the family to visit this uncle and aunt in Illinois. While there, Uncle Rick again tried to molest me. I got up right away and went to Mom and Dad. I was too wise to perverts now, but I sadly didn't tell them about it.

During these bus trips to the chiropractor, though, I was soon up to no good. After the brief adjustment to my lower spine and neck by Dr. Wright, I had a forty-five-minute wait for the bus home. I began to go into the nearby Osco drugstore to kill the time. At first, I just read the magazines. They had everything: *Mad, Tiger Beat, Seventeen, Teen Beat, 16.*

The walls of my bedroom were covered in pictures of Michael Jackson cut out from magazines like these. Every teen magazine had a story about Michael in every issue. We couldn't afford to buy magazines though. Slowly, I went from browsing through the magazines at Osco to slipping them into my backpack. The employees had gotten used to seeing me there, and they didn't seem to suspect me. Eventually, my conscience screamed at me, but it was the kindness of the Osco employees that changed my behavior. What if they were getting in trouble for stolen magazines? What if they started to suspect me? As a white person with an innocent face, though, I got away with stealing. I went back to reading, instead of taking the magazines.

My back problems seemed to subside for a while, though they never really got better. I asked Mom if I could quit going to the appointments. She agreed, and thankfully that ended the time with Randy the creepy bus driver, although I still saw him when we took the bus for other things. It also ended my time at Osco, and I almost never read a teen magazine again.

With Pat Adams gone, Mom and Dad were back to relying on me all the time to watch the kids when they were at work or having coffee for hours at Hardee's. As a newly minted twelve-year-old, I wasn't always good at managing four children. Sure, I'd been doing this work for years, but it kept getting more complicated.

The full story of what went wrong one day in 1983 started when a young neighbor who lived in the same complex pounded on our front door. Breathlessly, he sputtered out the words like he'd been running: "Your brother is getting beat up in the church parking lot by some of the neighborhood boys!"

This wasn't surprising. The kids who lived outside our fenced-in duplexes had parents who'd protested the building of low-income housing in their community. There was a trailer court on the other side of the back fence of our property, so they must have felt they had enough poor people in their area even before the housing project went up. These kids were just reflecting their parents' hostility.

I reacted without thinking. Or maybe I reacted the way I did because I was already so used to babysitting at that point. Either way, I turned to Samuel, just eight at the time, and asked him to stay with four-year-old John and toddler Senja while I went to help. I told him I would be right back.

I have to give a little background about what I was wearing, because it goes to evidence, as they say. I need to establish that I was not just roller skating for pleasure that day. I took off from our apartment toward the church, wearing my roller skates, because I always wore my roller skates, just like the character, Tootie, on the sitcom, *The Facts of Life*. This was 1983, in the days before in-line skates. Mine looked like sneakers on four fat wheels. They had red, yellow, and blue stripes down the side. Dad saw them at a warehouse sale a few months after we got back from foster care and made the rare luxury purchase to make me happy. These skates were an enormous source of pride for me. I only took them off for school.

The fight occurring in the church parking lot was across the street from Blackhawk Elementary school, which bordered our duplexes to the west. It took me only a couple of minutes to skate there. About five boys were gathered around David and the bully, who were dancing around each other in a circle, and throwing punch-es—alternating as they swung their arms wildly. I broke through the circle and yelled, "Hey, David, you have to come home! Mom and Dad said so!" I wanted to get him out of the fight without making him seem like a coward or like he needed to be rescued. That would only make his social situation in the neighborhood worse. I pulled at his arm. "Seriously, you'll get beaten with a belt by Dad if you don't get home."

I wished our dad was home, but he had to work. So did Mom. Suddenly, I was shoved from behind, and one of my skates hit a tiny rock on the parking lot cement. I flew forward, knocking my brother over. Two of the boys who'd been watching the fight started helping David's adversary by kicking David as he lay on the ground. They kicked me as well.

I really shouldn't have tried to break up a fight in my skates. However, I simply never took them off, except for school, baths, and sleep—many times not even for sleep. These boys were smaller than me, and I was pretty sure I could fight them off, but I couldn't get to my feet. Then, to my horror, I saw Samuel start punching the boy that David had been fighting. I got to my feet, punched at one boy, and screamed with blood-curdling seriousness, "David and Samuel, it's time to go home!" The scream echoed off the walls of the church.

All the neighborhood boys ran off.

Turning to Samuel, I hissed, "What are you doing here!? Didn't I tell you to stay with Senja and John? I told you I would take care of this!" Samuel's loyalty to David was absolute. Samuel followed me there because he thought he needed to defend his best friend, his brother.

"I left John with Senja. He was watching her."

I asked him if he was nuts. John was too young. There was established precedent for letting six-year-olds babysit in our family, but four was outside the range of acceptable.

As we walked home wincing in pain, we assessed our injuries. There were bruises, swelling bumps, some cuts, a bloody nose, and a general state of filthiness. Mom and Dad weren't due back for a couple of hours, so we would have time to clean up. They would be sympathetic anyway because they knew none of us were the type to start a fight.

When we got to our duplex, there were two police cars outside with their red lights reflecting off every apartment in the cul-de-sac. I couldn't believe those boys had the nerve to call the cops on us. We were the victims of their bullying. Besides, the police didn't do anything about bullies, or else we would have tried to call them ourselves. When I stepped into the duplex, two officers immediately started to search me. One of the officers was in a regular police uniform. The other one was a blonde woman in a pantsuit with a badge pinned to her jacket.

Pantsuit asked all the questions, while the man in the uniform stood next to her frowning. "Where have you been? The sun has just set, and you've been off roller skating when your brother, John, says you are supposed to be babysitting him."

She didn't seem to notice how disheveled, dirty, and injured we all were, or maybe she did, and she made the wrong assumption. Her tone was sharp and angry.

"That's true, officer. I am babysitting. But I wasn't out roller skating. I was trying to rescue my brother from being beaten up by some boys over at the church parking lot."

She had wrinkles from too much time in the sun. Her hair was light blonde with what appeared to be gray streaks. Her eyes were narrow, and her lips were pursed tightly in a scowl. "You can't come in here on roller skates and tell me you haven't been roller skating. Do you realize you've been gone for twenty minutes?"

Twenty minutes? How did that happen? I thought it was ten at most.

"I asked Samuel to watch John and Senja, but he just came down to the fight. I know eight isn't very old, but I was looking after my little brothers when I was eight for short amounts of time. I thought it would be okay. I thought I'd be right back." I was puzzled. How could that have taken twenty whole minutes? It must have though.

I felt so ashamed I cast my eyes to the floor. She knew she had gotten to me. Her angry lips curled into a smile. She seemed pleased I was so upset. "Well, one of your neighbors heard your sister crying at the top of her lungs, and she called us. So, your judgment in leaving your eight-year-old brother to babysit was very poor. Where is your mother? Typical government housing resident, I suppose—at the bar?"

Okay, now I was upset with her, and not thinking about what I was about to do. My consciousness of poverty-bashing had been keen ever since our family was featured in the newspaper by that reporter who expressed such a damaging attitude toward poor people. Many people, including kids in my class at school, had responded to the article negatively, with ridicule and shaming comments.

I defended Mom and Dad to Pantsuit. "My mom and dad are both at work. My mother works as a proofreader at a newspaper in Cedar Falls. My dad is a janitor for Operation Threshold. Dad works until midnight, but my mom should be getting home anytime now."

"How old are you? Pantsuit snapped. "If you are not fourteen, you need to be certified to be a babysitter in the state of Iowa!"

I had gone through the weeklong training at one of the local hospitals to get the certificate. "I'm twelve, and I am certified. I babysit other people's children besides my brothers and sister. I'm very sorry about what happened. I just didn't know what to do with this situation, I guess."

Pantsuit gave a derisive snort of agreement. "You certainly didn't. They should take your babysitting certificate away from you."

Anger shot through me; I couldn't control myself. "Why are you being such a bitch!? What would you have done in this situation?" Pantsuit looked shocked, immediately turning red. "You'll pay for that!" She opened our screen door and left. The other officers milled around our living room.

Our apartment manager showed up, and pretty soon, the police officers and our manager were searching our apartment. During this chaos, Mom came home. She started to cry hysterically right away, scared that a child protection worker would be called in and she would lose custody of her children again. The police and the apartment manager finished searching the apartment. They left with nothing. The building manager cornered Mom to tell her that she would be written up for storing her pots and pans in the oven again. Eventually, everyone was gone. I finally had the chance to tell Mom what happened. She believed me. She knew I wore my roller skates all the time. She knew about the bullies in the neighborhood. She forgave me for not knowing what to do.

A few days later, a child abuse investigator scheduled a visit with Mom and Dad while I was at school. He never spoke to me. The investigator filed his report, and a copy was sent to us in the mail. The report said that there was an "incident of child neglect perpetrated by the child Debra MacIntyre." He couldn't even spell my name right. I was a twelve-year-old child abuser, only eleven a month before. According to the babysitting certification law, I couldn't babysit anymore. What a disaster.

After I'd been branded a neglectful caregiver, I decided to go looking for the child abuse investigator's report about me. As I read it, I saw none of my side of the story was included. No explanation of what happened was given. Just a comment about our parents needing to find better childcare. I also went looking for my parents' copies of the child protection reports created when we were taken away by the State of Iowa and put into foster care. (I read all of these again when writing this book).

In the child abuse investigator's report, I learned that when the county checked into Senja's birth information, they discovered that she had not been registered with a birth certificate in the nine month after she was born. As far as the State of Iowa was concerned, Senja didn't exist, because Mom and Dad never reported her birth. Their anti-government views led them to hide the birth—distrustful views that stemmed primarily from their conspiratorial thinking and their religious beliefs.

When I added it all up, there were plenty of truths to agree with in the child neglect report, but I couldn't tell Mom and Dad that. To admit this to them would be no less abhorrent to Mom than it would be to confess having stolen her children. But I somewhat agreed with the people who decided to take temporary custody of us over a year ago. I didn't agree with their plan to keep us permanently, though. That was nasty and underhanded. They should have helped our parents. But that's just it. We needed help.

When you can't afford childcare, you fall back on what you can manage. It may not have been legal, but Mom and Dad still needed me to watch the kids a lot. Managing middle school as an outcast girl was taking all my time and energy, but I still needed to be a mother to my brothers and my sister for long periods after school or into the evening. Finally, one weekend night, I was in my bedroom crying from what felt like an overwhelming amount of stress.

I didn't think I could handle being such a bad sister, a bad friend, and—since I could keep going forever—a bad daughter, etc. I went to the kitchen, got a knife, and sliced twice across my left wrist so that I might die. The cuts weren't very deep, and they ran across my wrist, not down, which was, of course, less effective. After I didn't seem to be dying, I gave up and decided God wanted me to live. I perked up and started a campaign to change my life. I complained more loudly with each passing day about my responsibilities. This led to the decision to find alternatives. This meant that Mom would find a family friend, neighbor, or relative to watch one or more of us for an extended period.

Our neighbor Bob and his wife became caretakers for Samuel and David. Another neighbor, Sue, was always willing to take Senja, who was a charming two-year-old rather than a terror. John frequently went to stay at Sue's or at Grandma and Grandpa MacIntyre's house. That left me. From the start, there was almost no question where I was heading; I was going to work with Dad.

He let the employers know I was there. He had me doing a minimal amount of work. He was a custodian for Operation Threshold now. They had something to do with helping low-income people find housing. He was making $3.25 an hour and never got a raise in the three years he worked there. During my visits there, I became more and more uncomfortable. Dad was saying suspicious and paranoid things. He believed that one of his co-workers was out to get him and that other workers were conspiring to take over the agency. He turned what must have been office politics into a game of intrigue with cloak and dagger tactics that could potentially turn deadly.

His on-time record was often determined by his ability to get transportation. After the car died, he had to rely on the city's slow and limited bus system. This erratic means of transportation made him incredibly afraid he would lose his job. It was around then, when our need for stable transportation was at its most desperate, that we began to see a lot more of Dad's friend, Loris, who would pick Dad up from our house and take him to and from work.

It was a good thing for Dad to have a friend. Suddenly, he was having vibrant conversations with Loris as if they'd been close for years. It was never clear to me how they met. You knew when Loris was coming because his booming voice preceded him. Loris had a round face, but his frazzled hair obscured it. His hair was everywhere. On his chin, over his lips, on his cheeks, visible along the collar of his shirt, on his fingers. His long, black-and-gray hair was unkempt and often full of crumbs.

He traveled in a van filled with some of the spillover loot from his hoarding affliction. He didn't have room to give people rides unless he left his wife, Fran, at home. We all liked Fran, so it was a shame when he had to leave her behind. On the other hand, maybe that was okay. It was also hard to watch how Loris treated Fran, barking orders and loudly shouting his displeasure with things he thought she did wrong.

When Loris was around, our dad's beliefs became clearer than they'd ever been before. For years, Dad had gone mostly silent without a best friend. After he'd been sick and in the hospital for over three months when I was five, he'd isolated himself. In the last two places we'd lived, he was too paranoid to speak to other people. He took jobs where he worked alone at night. Now, finally, when I was almost a teenager, Dad had someone to talk to about his "epistematics," or, in other words, his Theory of Everything. Don't bother looking for his definition of "epistematics."

Dad was seeking a mathematical equation to describe his Theory of Everything. He described his theory as a "*new revolution in science and theology that would bring them . . . back together again.*" He was able to pinpoint the origins of his ideas to the visions he had when he was a child. Loris was enthralled and hung on his every word.

Dad would say his ideas were best represented by pictures and symbols rather than words. His two most-prized possessions, besides his Bible and *Strong's Exhaustive Concordance of the Bible,* were his colored pencils, stored lovingly in a wooden box with a metal latch, and his Spirograph set. The Spirograph set had plastic gears with interlocking teeth around their edges, some shaped like circles, some like rods, and others like triangles.

He used his pencil to spin the gears around, creating beautiful shapes that looked like colorful daisies. Some of his designs were pastel, some were bright, vivid colors, but they all made a lovely pattern. They were essential to his Theory of Everything: *"These will be the language of my theory,"* he said. *"My theory is an eclectic combination of sacred and secular wisdom. It has very ancient roots and futuristic elements that make it world-class in its character."*

Dad showed Loris his creations. Loris was fascinated. I'm not sure how many other people Dad told about his Theory of Everything and his history of space travel, or how they reacted to the information. Dad could talk for hours with just the right person. I'd seen him do it at Hardee's with random strangers. Talking at the restaurant like this never seemed to result in any friendships for Dad, but here was Loris, seemingly out of nowhere.

Loris did give Dad practical information, like the local church schedules for soup suppers around the twin cities of Cedar Falls and Waterloo. But what Loris mainly gave Dad was a chance to pontificate on the heavens, how they are connected to God, and how science relates to both. Every day, Dad studied maps of space. He had a keen knowledge of the stars and planets. When I was younger, he seemed brilliant to me. He seemed to know all about the sky, the Earth, and the Bible. Listening to him talk to Loris, though, he sounded out of his mind.

Chapter Fourteen: So Many Churches

*C*LEARLY WHAT THE POOR *are after is what we all want: association, affiliation, inclusion, magical purpose. While they are bombarded, as we all are, by the commercial imprecations of being cool, of experimenting with various presentations of the disposable self, they lack the wherewithal to even enter the loop.*

—James Twitchell, 2011[71]

Our family's solitary Sunday worship services were about to end. David and Samuel ran inside one day and yelled together, "There's a big blue bus outside, and it's taking people to church!"

"They said they have video games. Can we go?" David asked.

"Video games in a church?" Mom called back from the kitchen. "Seems inappropriate. You can go if Deborah goes with you to supervise." Looking up from my book, nonplussed, I faced a barrage of begging from the boys.

"Fine, fine, if the bus is still there by the time I put on something that's worthy of church, you win," I said. After I changed and we headed to the bus and sat with a few other apartment kids we knew, teasing each other until the bus driver apparently decided enough of us had been recruited.

Once we got to the Sunnyside Temple, the youth group leader took our bus of kids on a tour of the church building. We had to wait our turn to start the tour because there were other buses of kids coming from other parts of the city. The church was massive, with the best part being the particularly enormous youth lounge. It had a beverage bar, cable TV, three video game machines, an ice cream and popcorn station, and comfy chairs.

Most people seemed to be working hard to get a seat up close to the minister. This arrangement made it easy to hug the end of a row of chairs at the back near the vestibule. I grabbed both a hymnal and a Bible to bury my face in. This would allow me to avoid any unsolicited conversations.

Mama always taught us God wanted us to be poor. She showed us the verse in the Bible.

It is easier for a camel to go through the eye of a needle, than for a rich man to enter into the kingdom of God. (Mark 10:25)[72]

There were such verses all over the Old and New Testament. I clung to them to feel better about being poor. It was in part what they were intended for after all. The minister preached, "Jesus taught us that the poor will always be with us. There will always be some people who cannot or will not work hard enough to earn the riches this Earth provides as a gift from God. Amen." (The congregation repeated, "Amen.") "You can always find the strength to work through our Lord by coming here on the Lord's Sabbath day for restoration and healing."

He kept going, but I heard nothing else that he said.

A sharp pain tore through my abdomen, doubling me over. Although starved with a growling stomach, rather than needing to eat, it felt as though I needed to expel everything from my body. My cheeks were on fire. I now knew there was nowhere safe for me to go. Even in the house of the Lord, being poor meant being degraded and insulted. *There will always be some poor folks who are simply too lazy to get the Lord's riches.* Okay, not his exact words, but his meaning. Here in church, they were perpetuating stereotypes.

On the bus ride home, someone from the church announced that we should invite our parents to come to church but could just keep coming on the bus ourselves. Amid the noisy whirlwind of children running into the apartment, Mom asked us how it went. The boys told her how much they loved playing with the video games. They begged her to start making this our regular Sunday church. Mama agreed to give it a try.

The bus that came to pick up kids in the apartments to take them to Sunnyside Temple didn't pick up adults. And city buses didn't run on Sundays. So, Mom got the brilliant idea to walk as a family to the church. She pointed out that it would be good exercise. As usual, Dad declined to be any part of it. About half of the two miles to the church didn't have a sidewalk, so we trudged along a four-lane street with relatively steady traffic. That made the miles seem longer, especially if it rained, because the ground would be wet and muddy, or cars going by would splash the pools of water onto us.

Mom eventually learned this was one of those new megachurches popping up all over the United States that pushed what folks recognize now as a "prosperity gospel."[73] Mom didn't care for a church associating Jesus in any way with money. She said she wanted to live a life of poverty if the Lord would assure her we wouldn't starve. Her mother had grown up as poor as can be because her grandfather had died in the 1918 flu pandemic. So, her grandmother had to raise her mother pretty much by selling eggs from their chicken coop. When Mom listened to her mother talk about her childhood, she could hear how loved her Mama had been. Her mother also painted a vivid picture of life in northern Minnesota with crunchy footfalls in the snow.

Everything about growing up as poor as her mother Senja[74], Grandma Helja, and Uncle Arvo sounded romantic to Mom. On the other hand, Mom had nothing but negative impressions of her father's side of the family. Yes, they had substantial amounts of wealth, but they were always accusing each other of trying to take it. They were like vultures when anybody died, swooping down on the deceased's assets. These pitiless people didn't seem to care about each other at all. It was just money, money, money with them.

Then, Mom saw a TV exposé of Sunnyside Temple in which a whistleblower from within the church had shared a memo talking about "recruiting 'inferior' children to the church through a busing program." The memo didn't specify why the church was doing this, nor did it define inferior kids, but they were trolling around government housing looking for kids like us. Mom was disgusted. Were they expecting to make money off these kids somehow?[75]

The megachurch seemed to give Mama an idea. Maybe she had been at the wrong church. Maybe God had not healed her mental anguish, physical pains, and marital problems because she was in the wrong faith. This "revelation" began a years-long tour of chu rches.[76] The next one on the list was very different from Sunnyside Temple. It was an activist church. I don't remember the Methodist denomination. They participated in political protests like fighting for Central Americans enduring abuse and assassination from their US-backed government. The whole family, even Dad, walked in a city parade with the church members, carrying signs for the people of El Salvador. We left this church because Mom had a crying spell while singing in the choir, and she vowed never to put herself in that situation again. She didn't want to be seen breaking down.

Inevitably, one of two things would happen. Either Mom would continue to have problems with her mood—pretty much a given—or, she would leave a church having decided it was not the one true church. It was the small-minded people in a church who would drive her away the quickest. Mom would catch them talking about each other behind their backs. Or perhaps talking about her. Sometimes she would get the "sense we just aren't welcome."

I gave Mom a lot of pushback about the three-spirit "vision" of children she claimed to have had back before we went to foster care. She had an intuition of the spirits of her three yet unborn children. I loudly protested when she'd said she was having three more. I grumbled, "I already have enough trouble handling the children I've got! We can't afford it! Where will they fit?"

Of course, I loved each child as he or she was born, but there were so many long nights when the babies needed tending. Mom said she had to rock her sister's crib when *she* was a little girl, so even if it was making me miserable, I had to take a turn.

"Yeah, I'm guessing you didn't have so many younger brothers and sisters," I grumbled to myself. That's when Mama announced that it was time for her last child to be born, Isaiah[77]. After the foster care incident, Mom predicted the arrival of a boy within two years. She wanted to have a child who wasn't tainted by the "awful taste of the DSS [Department of Social Services]."[78]

Sometime after she told Dad and me that she was pregnant, they got into the worst blowout they'd ever had. Worse than the night Mom threatened to burn the house down; worse than the time she threw the coffee cup at the window, clipping our father's head. This time, Dad hit Mama with a bottle. She later said he was angry that the "*sexist government*" required him to go to work and didn't allow him to go to school while she was allowed to go to school. He didn't seem to understand that as a "disabled parent" now, Mom no longer faced the same requirements, thanks to Dr. Pangilinan. If only Dad could have seen or identified himself as a disabled parent too. If someone had only suggested or even required an assessment, maybe he could have.

Violence was becoming more commonplace in our household. Mom was still knocking our heads all the time. I was hurting David and sometimes Samuel. The boys were not going to listen to my authority. It didn't matter that Mom and Dad held me largely responsible for the care of the kids and the state of the household. David had stabbed me with a pencil twice by this time, breaking off their tips in my palms. The gray-blue graphite remnants were embedded in my skin for decades. Then he broke my right wrist, and I had to wear a cast for six weeks. It was cool, though, because it was a removable cast.

Mom and Dad had another nasty argument and Mom decided to walk out on Dad, taking us kids along. There weren't too many places to go without a car, but Happy Chef Restaurant was open twenty-four hours a day. A few hours after midnight, the manager, or maybe the waitress, decided they didn't like the fact that we had been sitting there for hours on end.

Mom probably stayed awake, but the rest of us had fallen asleep. Someone tapped me on the shoulder. I opened my eyes to see a policeman standing over me. I panicked. Were they arresting Mom!? Oh my God, are they arresting *me*!? Instead, the officers escorted us to the homeless shelter. The sun was starting to come up, but I was ready for sleep in an actual bed. The staff at the shelter let us sleep late but woke us up after a couple of hours to eat lunch with the other residents. The Catholic Worker House assigned chores such as kitchen duties and bathroom cleanup. I helped do dishes, which was no small task with a packed house of people.

Dorothy Day started the Catholic Worker House network, representing charity for the poor at its most benevolent. The staff at this shelter were supportive. The other residents were not dangerous the way people everywhere who *have* shelter say they are. Instead, it felt comfortable to be around them because nobody seemed to be judging anybody else for what they were wearing or where they'd come from.

Right away, there went Mom, volunteering our place as a place to stay. "We'll put them up!" Mom repeatedly chimed in. "That's what Jesus would want us to do." She came by this habit righteously. Grandpa Meyer, her father, is said to have suffered from "Dented Can Syndrome," in which the afflicted is overly sensitive to people, animals, and objects that appear to be hurting, left out, or misshapen. He bought the can with no label, deformed into shapes a can opener would never open. He brought home wandering hitchhikers, homeless people, crooked Christmas trees, and injured squirrels. He married our grandma, widely described as having grown up in a chicken coop.

I brought our neighbor, Sue, and her five children into our lives because Mom asked around the apartments to see if anyone could watch her kids. Sue became Mom's "if-I-can-manage-it" babysitter. When she agreed to have us over, she had ten children running around her duplex. Her one weapon of calm and distraction was cable TV, which she insisted on having no matter how much she couldn't afford it. Sue had a daughter who was just a year or so younger than I was.

I liked Daphne[79], but she had to be an at-home friend. Daphne was not popular in school. Just like me, she had out-of-style, run-down clothes. Just like me, she lived in government hous-ing. Just like me, she had a differently-colored lunch card. Those three things alone were enough to get you bullied. It was worse for Daphne though. She had a boyish face and body. She wore her hair in what looked like a boy's mullet. This brought down the rain of gender-related abuse. "Hey, you, are you a boy or a girl?" some idiot would sneer. Daphne just kept her head faced straight forward, but not down like I would have done. I always went up to her after an incident to see if she was okay. Daphne never outright cried, but she could get very red-faced and teary. She would curse and throw her things around.

I should have been a better friend. I tried to walk home from school with her. She had gotten into fistfights, and I was afraid the same thing would happen to me—again. I had traded blows with two boys already. But I also didn't want to see my social status lowered further in school; it was just starting to climb up from rock bottom.

Not long before this, I had a terrible experience. I had been feeling good about myself because I had some new clothes. During recess, some of the popular girls approached me. For a second, I was exhilarated; apparently, they were coming to include me in their clique, because I had new clothes. I was so immature about this sort of thing at the time.

"Where did you get that outfit?" Missy Metzger[80] sneered. "It is so ugly, and it doesn't match." She was wearing expensive jeans with a pink polo shirt. Her light-blonde hair was feathered back from her face.

Kim Fagen chimed in to say, "You need to tell your mom to buy you a bra because you are totally drooping." Finally, another member of the group pointed to my shoes. I don't remember who she was because I couldn't lift my eyes to their faces, and I wasn't processing what they were saying.

But that was no excuse. I wasn't a good friend to Daphne. I was a coward.

Mom was trying hard. She was spending more money on my clothes and junior high trappings than she was on my younger brothers. It was more money than the family could afford, especially because I was finally making plans to quit my paper route. Mom was trying to help me "fit in" to the best of her ability.

Not long after that, we had a major household epidemic of lice. I can't remember if the school alerted Mom to the problem or if she discovered it herself, but each of us contracted lice as if the pests were playing dominoes.

At the time, you needed a prescription to get the shampoo that killed them, but Mom was afraid Child Protective Services would be notified by the doctor if she took us in for treatment. Her alternative cure was old fashioned nit-picking, as the term was originally intended. She would hand pick every lice egg, (or nit), and bug out of every single child's head. When she called me over for inspection of my scalp, I thought she was just casually feeling around to make sure no bugs were crawling all over me, but to my horror, the nasty little things had gotten onto me too. I ended up getting good at nit-picking, lice removal by hand, like Mom was. I was utterly disgusted the entire time we did it, and I felt queasy most of the time, but I did it. We were so obsessive, we got them all.

A few weeks later, Kim Fagen was laughing at me in the gym locker room as we changed. The locker room was the place you practiced some form of Zen meditation, or you suffered. I carried extra pounds from ongoing bingeing episodes, and of course this was most evident when I couldn't hide behind clothes. To play off her ridicule, Kim walked up to me and said, "Listen, my friends and I were thinking that we'd like to hang out with you. Would you like to meet us at the roller rink this Friday night? Let's say at 7:30 for open skate?"

I almost forgot my self-consciousness over being half into a swimming suit. That weekend, I eagerly grabbed my skates and took off for the rink. Luckily, it was within walking distance from the apartment. After paying my way in, I saw no one I recognized. At 8:30, I decided to give up and go home. I had obviously been played. A couple of kids from school had seen me sitting there waiting for the popular girls from school to show up, but I never put on my skates. I had to do something about my reputation at school.

I was still babysitting, but now I had some fraction of nine children to watch. Sue and our mom went shopping at garage sales. They were going to get a cup of coffee at Hardee's. Half of the kids wanted to go to the public swimming pool, so would I watch the other half? It wasn't so bad because I had Daphne to help me maintain authority. The kids often ran loose in the house playing together, allowing Daphne and me a chance to turn on MTV. The all-music, all-the-time video station was only a year old.

I was still notorious for my absurdly intense crush on Michael Jackson. I had even purchased one of his trademark jackets with zippers all over it, like in the *Thriller* video. My decision to buy this coat made Mom furious. The day I spent wearing the red, zippered jacket to school at least drew me the attention of Michael Pryor[81], a boy one grade up from me. He became the first boy I ever dated. He was kind to me, flirted with me, and I invited him over to our place. He was the boy who gave me my first kiss.

The jacket with all the zippers had to be returned after being worn only one day. We didn't have the money for it, and I was supposed to buy something "reasonable." Another girl named Deborah, who seemed to be able to get along with the popular kids, also wanted to hang around me. She had been my friend in elementary school for a couple of months, so I guess she must have liked me from the time we spent together back then. Her social circle included people who seemed to be accepted by popular kids without being popular themselves. I slipped into their group.

I don't know what you do to qualify for Mensa, the group for people with high IQs, but Dad became a member. He attended a few meetings and then decided to bring me along. The host lived on the West Side in a nice house. I felt underdressed and uncomfortable.

Despite being only twelve, the man running the meeting offered me liquor. I drank a few sips and began to feel warm sensations in my body. The host was very proud of his car. It was a Jaguar. I could understand why he was individually pulling guests into the garage to look at it. After he had more to drink, he began turning his attention to me. He rubbed up against me, brushed my hair back from my face, and touched my arms.

His son came home from somewhere and he changed his behavior briefly. Then he came up with a brilliant idea. He was going to take me out for a ride in the Jaguar. He asked Dad, who distractedly said yes for some reason. Dad clearly wasn't thinking, because the man he gave permission to was drunk. Soon, I was out in the night air sitting in a Jaguar convertible with a forty-something man pawing my thigh. When we got back to his house, Dad said it was time to go. I was glad to get out of there. This man did give me a copy of *The Princess Bride*,[82] though, which I still treasure only because it's such a great book.

Chapter Fifteen: To the East Side

ISAIAH WAS BORN IN 1984 in a hospital, rather than at home, because Mom was thirty-nine years old. Shortly afterward, we moved out of government housing. School had just ended, so I was going to spend the summer before eighth grade settling into a new neighborhood.

Moving was always so hard, especially because of Mom's rule that you must thoroughly clean both the place you are moving into and the place you are leaving. This meant down-on-the-floor with a scrub brush or behind-every-cranny with a toothbrush kind of cleaning.

I was sad, eager, dismayed, and bigoted about moving, because Mom found housing in the part of town where African American people mostly lived, that was called "Smokey Row."[83] There were a few white folks, like our family, that either lived there for political reasons (to integrate the city) or for economic reasons because they couldn't afford better. We lived there for financial reasons, although I think Mom would have done it for political reasons, too. We didn't know the city's racial history, the struggle for integration, the fight against racism.

I later learned that government policies helped *create* ghettos. The Federal Housing Administration (FHA), established in 1934 refused to insure home mortgages in or near African American neighborhoods. This policy, known as "redlining," thus reinforced and even created poverty centers in many U.S. cities. At the same time, the FHA was subsidizing builders who were mass producing entire subdivisions for whites-often with the requirement that none of the homes were sold to African Americans. Insurance companies used the lines drawn by the FHA as an excuse for denying policies to business owners in Black communities.

Mom knew much more about the racist past of Waterloo since she learned about it in the class she took to recertify for teaching. The first big groups of African American migrants to arrive in the Waterloo-Cedar Falls metropolitan area came from Mississippi. They were recruited by railroad companies as strikebreakers in 19 10.[84] The strikers met them at their trains with pitchforks. Eventually, the white workers allowed the Black workers off the train, but they segregated them into twenty square blocks of Waterloo right next to the train yards. This section of town remains a low-income African American community called the "Black Triangle" to this day.[85] In 2018, Waterloo was ranked the worst city for African Americans in the USA by 24/7 Wall Street.[86]

One of the biggest employers of Black people in Waterloo was Rath Packing Company, a large meatpacking plant. On some of our many car rides, Dad would drive past the massive buildings on the Rath site and remind us that *his* father worked there when Dad was a child. By the company's fiftieth anniversary in 1941, the Rath complex included 150 buildings and spanned forty acres. With nearly two hundred buildings on site by 1950, the plant was the "largest single unit packinghouse in the world."[87] It was the Titanic of packinghouses.

When Rath closed, it resulted in job losses that would be added to the unemployment from massive layoffs at John Deere Tractor Works, now Deere & Company. Altogether, Waterloo lost an estimated 10,545 jobs as a direct result. Job losses would continue to strangle Waterloo right into the middle of the 1980s farm crisis. By the time the doors at Rath permanently closed, the lines to get free commodities, such as government cheese, powdered milk, and peanut butter, were blocks long.[88]

Suddenly, the city of Waterloo and the state of Iowa were on the hook to take care of communities like the "Black Triangle." They had to pool resources and try to absorb the damage to actual lives from the job losses. Social services had to be provided to counteract the effects of economic hardship. Reagan was elected president after touring the country talking about welfare queens, so it was clear that the federal government wasn't going to help poor people in Waterloo any time soon. The white community took a hit, but eventually it mostly recovered. Black residents suffered, and that didn't change. The middle-class livelihoods many had attained were wiped out. The exodus of the remaining professional and middle-class African Americans from Waterloo since 1980 on has been described as "contagious."[89]

In short, we were moving to the most economically wrecked part of an economically ruined city with a long history of racial strife. We couldn't afford to move away from the ghetto. Black people were expressing their anger. Race relations were getting thorny.

A few days after moving in, a friendly, light-skinned Black girl approached me as I hung our family's laundry on the backyard clothesline. She was striking. She had large dark eyes, long, thick, wavy black hair, and smooth, tan skin.

"Hi," she said, "My name is Annette[90]. My next-door neighbor Brenda told me you just moved into the neighborhood. Where did you live before?"

Guardedly, I responded, "I used to live on the West Side, over by the high school."

"I know someone who lived over there. Those are nice places. How come you moved to the East Side?"

She continued the conversation, a surprising development. I wasn't used to being truthful about my background without the other person losing interest in me.

"My mom didn't like the monthly inspections," I said. "The managers yelled at her for storing pots and pans in the oven. She wanted to get our own place before they found a reason to kick us out."

"Well, are you going to be done with the laundry soon? I want to introduce you to my friend. By the way, your house has bats." She was right about this, as I found out later when I found one whipping around my bedroom.

Before I went over to talk with Annette and meet her friend, I looked hard at my appearance in the panel of mirrors on our living room wall. It was time for my extreme self-consciousness to take over. A wave of nauseous anxiety passed over me as I realized I had on Goodwill-odd, red polyester shorts and a see-through blue cotton shirt. My hair was uncombed and old eyeliner rebelliously blackened the area under my eyes. I quickly changed into a denim mini skirt and a polo shirt and ran a comb through my hair. After using a tissue to rub away the eye makeup, I was barely presentable, but it would do.

Annette and a brawny Black girl sat on the concrete steps leading to Annette's front porch. I took in the unfamiliar girl's glistening Jheri curl hair style with envy. The wet curls made perfect spirals. That was the way I wanted my hair to look. I had had one perm, and it transformed my plain, boring strands into a mane framing my face.

"I'm glad you decided to come over. This is Erica[91], my friend from around the block."

"Who do you know from Edison Middle School?" I asked. She named some people that I knew, but I wasn't friends with any of them. But Erica knew two boys I knew, Mike Pryor and Ricky, his best friend. They were both cousins of hers. I had dated Mike a little. This would turn out to be a fateful connection with Erica and Annette.

Mom promised that I would outgrow my baby fat. Wishful thinking. I slapped at my tummy and then headed to the living room for my daily ritual of self-degradation in front of the mirror. Mom said that the mirrors made our otherwise small home look bigger. She was right. Without these mirrors, the cramped space would have been more confining. Maybe that was why the mirrors seemed to make me look bigger as well. But maybe not.

I started bingeing in about third grade to deal with stress. Five years later, I desperately needed to control the effects of my binge-eating disorder. Examining each of my body parts in the mirror, I decided that my legs were satisfactory, nice even. They were muscular from the past couple of years spent riding my bicycle in the morning for my paper route, and the couple of years spent walking around delivering papers before that.

On the other hand, I could barely stand to evaluate my abdominal area stretching from just under my breasts to the swell of my hips—round, curving well beyond the width of my thighs. It looked like I had swallowed a life preserver. I pushed the fat on my hips in to get a sense of my potential, but it simply crept between my widespread fingers. Maybe if my thighs were also large, I wouldn't look so funny.[92]

My hair was straight, thin, and limp, and sweat melted it onto my scalp. The perm was long gone. On another day, I had taken brown construction paper and cut it into several skinny strips. Next, I held the paper behind my head to estimate what I would look like with longer hair. Not bad.

Instead, my hair was shorn following an incident at the beginning of the summer. I thought bleaching your hair meant using chlorine bleach, the same kind you put in your laundry. Allowing the bleach to soak into my hair while absorbing the sun resulted in a straw-like texture. The strands were dead, and short of shaving my head altogether, I begged a beauty school student to rescue what she could. Now, all I had left was short, frizzy hair I badly wished to regrow. As penance for my unattractive appearance, I obsessively went through the motions of several hundred jumping jacks every day. My breasts hurt from the jarring motion.

Thus, I spent the summer before eighth grade exercising as often as possible, living on grapefruit slices and Crystal Light lemonade. It worked though. By the time school started, I had accomplished two things. I had lost a lot of weight, including the bubble around my belly, and I had solidified my eating disorder.

Starting in eighth grade, Erica became my protector in our neighborhood, where bullies sometimes targeted me because I was white. She also instigated trouble for me. She joined with Annette in nudging me to have sex with another of her cousins when I was thirteen years old. I'm not blaming Erica and Annette for getting me to start having sex. Julius[93] may not even have liked me, but I had a crush on him, and I was plenty eager to sleep with my crush. That's what I thought everyone did.

I liked him in a melodramatic, middle-school-girl kind of way, with all the intensity of emotion that entails, and no hint of rational thought, especially because he looked like Michael on the cover of *Thriller*. Watching him cut across the front lawn of the school building, I was astonished that a star was living among ordinary people. For a few days, I told no one about what I was experiencing when I saw him.

After school one day, I spotted Julius just as I was grabbing a bus seat next to Erica. In an embarrassed whisper, I pointed out the window.

"Do you know who that is?"

"Why? He's my cousin. He thinks he's something else. Trust me, he's not."

"I think he's totally fine. Do you talk to him?" I was excited to be so lucky. His cousin was my friend.

"Ah, we exchange words now and then. He's a cousin somewhere on my daddy's side. We ain't that close."

Just then the bus driver turned up the volume on KBBG, the only radio station in town dedicated to music for Black people. Morris Day and the Time sang *Ice Cream Castles* at a volume that made further conversation difficult. Miss Edie, the bus driver, didn't like listening to teen gossip, and the radio tuned us out. For some reason, teen music was preferable.

When the bus arrived at our stop, I walked Erica to her house. Erica asked me to wait inside the doorway while she went to ask her mom for permission to hang out at Annette's house. Erica and I knew that Annette would be home from school soon. We just had to wait for the high school bus to arrive. We sat on Annette's front step, and I began asking questions about Julius.

What happened next filled me with humiliation. *I had the warped belief in my head that when two people have sex that means they are married.* That idea no doubt came from the times I spent with fundamentalist Mormons, or Bible study with Mama and Dad. Or maybe catching Mama in bed with Onias. Annette and Erica suggested that I could have sex with Julius. They said they'd heard he was interested.

Hot damn. It was going to be just like romance books I had read. The Harlequins, with a man who rescued a woman from her terrible life circumstances, had made an impression on me. I was already a love addict. Now, Julius would save me from my family.

Annette had never had sex and she said she wanted to wait until she was an adult. Erica had never had sex but said she was curious. If I took up Julius on what they said was his offer, I would be the first girl in our social circle to have sex. Erica and Annette talked me out of any of my worries. Plans were made.

I went over to Julius's place with Erica after school one day. Following our plan, she left and walked over to her friend's house and waited for me. Julius's father had a good job at John Deere. That was a union job at the biggest manufacturer in town. My eyes widened with awe, not able to believe my luck that my prince charming was rich as well as gorgeous.

On September 19, 1984, I lost my virginity—a thirteen-year-old girl with a fourteen-year-old boy. It hurt a great deal, and I couldn't wait for it to be over. When it was, I thought we were husband and wife, or at the very least a committed boyfriend and girlfriend. Since we had "lain together," we were married in the eyes of the Lord as far as I knew. Then he told me harshly that it was time for me to leave, seemingly outraged that I was still there. I was confused. And hurt. I had gotten blood on his father's sheets. He didn't know what a virgin was, or that I had been one. I never knew there would be blood. The next day in school, instead of holding hands, walking down the halls between classes, he spread humiliating rumors about me as he bragged about "popping my cherry." He also said I was "a lousy lay." This was no Harlequin romance.

With my self-esteem in the gutter, I still pursued him because I believed we shared a sacred bond, and he obliged me a few more times so I could "practice with him and get better at sex." This pursuit of a boy who didn't love me, or even like or respect me, clearly mirrored Mom's actions with Dad. She was always chasing his love, and he was never going to give it. But knowing I got the habit from Mom didn't stop by feelings of being worthless.

To punctuate the sense of being used, Julius came downstairs after the second or third time and slugged me across the jaw. He had just remembered I'd gotten him in trouble with his father for staining his sheets when I hadn't warned him it was my first time having sex. I cried and tried to explain again that I hadn't known there was going to be blood.

Once, Julius took turns having sex with me and then another of my friends, Chyrell[94], each of us going upstairs for some time in his bed. I convinced Chyrell it was normal based on what I had learned from my polygamist background. But as I sat downstairs listening to the sounds from upstairs, I felt I'd been punched in the gut. I reached into my memory to understand the situation. If I had to share him, wasn't it just like when Mom had taken us to Canada?

Some kids were having sex for the sake of having sex, but a lot of them were naively intent on establishing a long-term connection to the person they were pursuing. That just never happened. Most of the boys were just going for the sex. Among the girls, many of us talked about marriage the way we talked about Barbie getting her dream house. It was time to start finding a mate. Everything about it was teenaged and almost never touched by adult thoughtfulness. Some girls believed getting pregnant would get a boy to marry them. If nothing else, getting pregnant tied a man to her for life. Maybe that was better. I thought having sex meant you *were* officially married. I once had a "poverty expert" tell me that Black women rejected marriage—that that's what the data told him. But marriage, or at least lifelong partnership, was all my friends and I talked about.

Annette's father was messed up. He drank. Even though that wasn't Dad's problem, we could relate, and talked about everything. My dad was messed up too. Just like mine, her parents were later separated but couldn't afford to divorce. It felt so comforting to have a best friend who understood me. We could wield, "You so poor . . ." or, "Your mama so poor . . ." jokes at the other's expense. Samuel listened to us and couldn't stop walking around saying, "You so poor you have to put french fries on layaway at McDonalds."

Annette and I talked very little about race, but a few specific subjects did come up. How people treated interracial couples like her parents, for example. When I first met her, I assumed she was Latina. I had no clue what it meant politically, socially, culturally, or racially when she described herself as *mulatto*. In retrospect, it makes me sad that she used that term because it meant she had internalized others' racism.

Mulatto is a categorization for a half-Black and half-white person that came from the time of slavery.[95] After all, white people had to be able to define what makes a person Black if they were going to enslave Black people. Another offensive term from that era was *octoroon*, which meant a white person who was one-eighth Black, which was considered the minimum definition of a Black person in some states.[96] I don't know how many people were aghast hearing me call my best friend mulatto when I described her that way, completely out of ignorance.

One time, when Chyrell and I were at a West Side McDonald's only a few weeks earlier, two blatant racists harassed us, threatening Chyrell to get back over to her side of town. I started to mouth off to them, but Chyrell looked genuinely frightened, and she asked the cashier to call the police. I thought about it later and realized how stupid I had been for not realizing how dangerous situations like that were for her. It made me feel sick to my stomach.

Chapter Sixteen: Rape

I T WAS THE LATTER half of my eighth-grade year, and I went to visit Chyrell after school. I knocked on her door, and her older brother, Andre[97], answered. He told me Chyrell was out running an errand. "Would you like to come in and wait?"

I hesitated. Chyrell's mom didn't like white people, which you could tell by her side-eyed looks and sarcastic comments, and she might be home. I decided to chance it. I sat down in the dining room, and Andre asked if I wanted to see his brother's latest art-work. Chyrell and Andre's brother, Darius, was a budding artist, and he made the walls of his bedroom into his canvases. His specialty was to draw women's eyes in intricate detail. I was relieved to have something to do while I waited. I was shy and just a no-name eighth grader. Andre was a senior in high school and a deejay at KBBG.

I followed Andre up the stairs to Darius's room. Moments after I got there and began admiring the artwork, Andre pushed me onto the bed and pulled my shorts and underwear off. I struggled against him, trying to push him off. I was in shock and frightened, and with his body on my chest, I was struggling to breathe. "Get off me!" I implored.

"Don't you like me?" he asked. He was the brother of one of my best friends. I said yes. Once I said yes, I felt I had consented to this attack, and for the rest of the painful rape, I fixated on how I had just given him permission. But I wasn't interested in him and hadn't expected this from him. I yelled at him to stop, but, of course, he didn't. When he was done and finally got off me, I grabbed my underwear and shorts, pulled them on, raced down the stairs and out the door. I sprinted home, desperately wanting Mama to hug me and tell me I would be all right. But no one was home.

Eventually, I just decided not to tell her. I told almost no one, in fact, but one person I did end up telling was Chyrell. Chyrell didn't believe me, couldn't see her brother in that light, and our friendship was over from that point forward.

It only hurt physically for as long as it took him to finish his attack. He gave me crabs, which I knew how to get rid of by hand because of the family's previous lice infestation. But the psychological and emotional effects lasted a lifetime. At the time, losing Chyrell's friendship hurt most of all.

The friends whom I trusted, Annette and Erica, had encouraged me to have sex with a boy who didn't like me. This was not exactly a marker of good or wise friends, but at least they stood by me when I was raped. Erica also went with me to Planned Parenthood to get birth control pills. I got the pills because somewhere in my muddled thirteen-year-old mind after the rape, I at least figured out what a disaster it would be to get pregnant. Even though I had no intention of being sexually active after that, I realized then that a girl didn't always have a choice about whether or not there's a penis inside her. In that way, it worked the same way as the hands that had already helped themselves to various parts of my body.

Planned Parenthood was supposed to be such a *liberal* organization, but they didn't come off that way at all. One of the nurses was downright mean. She kept bringing up my age, and she acted disgusted. By coming in I was being responsible, but she lectured me, and it seemed to take all day to get the pills. Erica had decided to get a prescription too. The nurse's tone of voice clearly suggested she thought we were horrible little girls with terrible parents for seeking birth control at thirteen. We left with the pills. Erica said she didn't get any flack for them at home. There were so many other teens having sex without any protection, but we were at least showing common sense.

Erica sat next to me in orchestra class for six years. We were both second violins. I'll always have this warm association with Erica from listening to the notes of her violin in my ear. One night, Erica and I had an orchestra concert at West Middle School. We didn't have a car, she couldn't give me a ride because her family filled their car, and the buses didn't run that late in our neighborhood. I finally decided our family would have to walk to the school for the concert. This concert was several miles away, and round-trip, carefully carrying an instrument, it was a hike. But somehow, I got something additional out of the night that way, more than just the pleasure of having pride in my performance.

After the concert, I got into a conversation with my science teacher, Mr. Fetner. He found out how far away I lived, and that we had all walked to the show. He was very impressed. He treated me like I was special from that point forward.

Later in the year, I received a form in the mail saying I had been anonymously nominated to the Iowa Girls' Leadership Camp. That meant I got to spend a week for free at a camp in Backbone State Park, where all kinds of workshops and trainings were held to help a group of mysteriously selected girls learn to become leaders. I think Mr. Fetner did that, and it was invaluable in shaping my life goals. I'd already wanted to focus on a career as a meteorologist or a judge, but let's just say I was a tad unfocused. Now, though, I was sure I was going to college.

When school wasn't in session, we spent part of every weekday, except Wednesday, at the Salvation Army lunchroom. On holidays, the local news stations came down to talk to the people who ate there. When we were preteens, we were excited to be on television. When adolescence began, we hid from cameras, scared to appear in such a shameful place. Stephen Moreland[98], one of the kids who used to live in the apartments next door to our duplex, saw us there and told *everyone* in school.

Every few months, our family would become even more desperate for food, perhaps in part because of our increasing need to buy nonfood items like soap or Band-Aids. During these times, I skipped school and rode the city bus with our mom to the county food bank. Together we carried two boxes of food home, which was the bimonthly allotment for a family of seven. My siblings would tackle us at the door, grabbing at boxes of Kraft Macaroni & Cheese or pulling out the Pop-Tarts. The food from the food bank was high in carbohydrates, and highly craveable, but not very nutritious. Nowadays, food banks have much better additional nutrition.

I made the mistake of being prejudiced. Of course, white people do this all the time, but I really blew it. Since Andre was Black and he attacked me, I trusted that white boys were safe. It only took one more sexual assault, the summer after eighth grade, to disabuse me of that idea. This time it was Tony, a boy I thought was my new boyfriend. I was babysitting my cousins when he called and asked if he could stop by. I was reluctant but I agreed. Once he arrived, he forced himself on me in the den. He didn't have my consent. I didn't want to look at his face as he ignored my firm refusal to have sex. It was painful and grueling to handle because I was completely unready to have sex and it burned. I kept pushing him off to no avail. Showing where my priorities were, my biggest concern was that he not make noise because I didn't want to wake up my cousins. I didn't tell anyone this happened.

Suffice it to say, there was no phone call from a "prophet" the second time Mom felt she'd reached her limit with Dad. In the past, before the State took custody of us, she'd taken us on trips to get away, like to see her old friend who was a pastor, or to Nauvoo, or camping in a downpour on the Mississippi River. Mom had worn down the tires driving throughout Iowa, Wisconsin, and Illinois. Now, we were trapped in a little house without a car, so Mom had no way to get away from Dad when they fought.

In late summer, Mom asked Dad why he was living with his family if he refused to participate in it. His response? *Convenience.* Mom had been making some money under the table cleaning apartments. Through this job, she saw a basement apartment with lots of bookshelves that he would like, and she advised him to take it. They still had little clue that he had schizoaffective disorder, which made participating in normal relationships next to impossible for him, to say nothing of what it took for him to be a husband and father.[99] No one had ever given him proper treatment. It was easy to see Dad as the ogre. I thought kicking Dad out was the best decision Mom had ever made.

Mom thought it was Loris's ideas that hurt her relationship with Dad. Loris started planting the bug in Dad's ear about how terrible women were generally. Over time, he started to say negative things about Mom. He likely told Dad that she was cheating after she moved to a new home. Once, after they had separated, she caught Loris driving Dad past the house slowly as if they were scoping out the joint. But, let's face it, how well was this marriage working from the start?

Dad eventually wrote to me regularly. At this point, I was well past the age when explaining himself would have been helpful to me. But it continued to be necessary for him:

"I was offered $1 million back in 1968 but turned it down because nobody gives away money without a hitch. I was right. I know too much, and some prefer me dead. That is why I have stayed clear of the family, after all the troubles, to prevent any more evils to arise. You kids don't appreciate this right now, but I hope to clear the air as you get older and are more mature in life to understand and appreciate the wiles and evils of life."

Dad had woven a story about having to leave his family that sounded like something out of a bad spy novel. He left town a little over a year later, and I didn't see him for ten years. I did continue to get letters, and these displayed Dad's continuing bizarre thoughts. While other people lamented their absent fathers, I was too embarrassed by mine to want him around. I pitied him and worried I might become like him.

During my eighth grade year, Mom told me I should end one of my friendships, just as she was about to end her best friendship, because matching rising signs in our horoscopes indicated we were going to be betrayed by a close friend. This was no horoscope from the daily newspaper though. This personalized horoscope was a star chart carefully crafted by Mom, following meticulous research. "Oh, those are just silly—*much* too generic to be of use to anyone," Mom would declare when asked about the horoscopes in magazines and newspapers. Dad likewise had been no slouch when it came to building astrological charts from scratch. In fact, he was the one who taught her how to do it.

After Mom described her plans for us, I had to sidestep her for more than a week to prevent questions about how my relationship with Annette was going. Mom temporarily ended her friendship with Sweetie[100], her best friend. Mom met Sweetie through another friend, Liz, whom Mom met in the Mother's Chorus, or the Metropolitan Chorale, or one of the singing groups she joined as a stress release. Liz was a genuine hippie who spent half her time in Costa Rica doing community service work. I just loved Liz and still do.

Sweetie was a spitfire, no-nonsense boss of a woman. She felt that since she had a car and could give us rides, she was allowed to haul Mama anywhere she wanted. This was often to bingo, where she regularly trapped Mom for hours. Mom would put her head down on the table and sleep until the games were over. She was with Sweetie when I was raped.

Sweetie was the only woman working on the factory floor in a sector of John Deere & Company in the 1970s, and she fit right in. This served her poorly one night when she was playing poker with some coworkers after work. Everyone stayed late into the night, leaving behind one seemingly average white guy, Michael Moses.[101] He was the son of a prominent dentist in the community. After everyone else was gone, he attacked Sweetie with a liquor bottle. Blood ran down her face and back. She was not a small woman, and she fought him off. During the struggle, her screams brought down the neighbors from the upstairs apartment, and he ran out the door. She went to the hospital, got more than two hundred stitches, and told police what happened to her.

Unfortunately, though she knew the name of the man who attacked her and although she gave a description of him, his status in the community meant that none of the officers took her seriously. She swore to the police he was a serial attacker. She could just tell. Eventually, police caught up with him after he killed two women. He now sits in a cell in an Iowa prison for life. She always felt that if the police had listened to her, those two women would still be alive.

Sweetie was orphaned as a child and grew up in the Soldiers' and Sailors' Home in Illinois. It's a little like Boys Town. Her attachment issues with her sons were hard to watch. She just yelled at them. All the time. Then, she'd apologize. She'd do the same thing with Mom. She also openly smoked marijuana in front of Mom and her own sons. Mom was taken aback by such behavior, but she did end up learning that the child abuse investigator who falsely accused her and Dad of being drug abusers was someone Sweetie smoked marijuana with at the time. This was years after either my mom or Sweetie had anything to do with him.

Mom broke up with Sweetie over the horoscope, but Sweetie came back to her pleading to renew their friendship. Mom's devout belief in forgiveness as one of the fundamental Christian principles renewed their friendship. Sweetie was thus forgiven for the ominous horoscope—sorry, *star chart*— that Mom herself had developed. They had their bad days, but they never stopped being friends again. Not even when Sweetie got arrested for drug possession. Not even when Sweetie was caught dealing drugs. Not even after Sweetie tried to get us kids taken away from Mom again. They only drifted apart when Sweetie got a serious boyfriend. Then, they would make contact again when Sweetie came up for air. Sweetie spent her shortened life with us, and I loved her, too.

Mom did have people trying to look out for her. Senja told me she was extremely embarrassed once when she came home to see the principal of her elementary school standing in the kitchen. The principal had apparently brought Isaiah home from school, and for some reason, wanted to come inside our house.

Senja said, *"My protective instinct kicked in, and I asked [the principal] if I could help her with something. She replied, quite pleasantly, that she was intent on helping us. . . . –she said it looked like we needed a little help cleaning up our kitchen. . . . –Her approach to enthusiastic teamwork appealed to me, and soon I found myself scrubbing the dishes while she wiped them clean and Isaiah put them all away."*

Afterward, Senja's principal took the kids out for pizza, declaring that good workers deserve a good meal. She talked to them out of interest, not to pry for information. It turned out she'd met Isaiah and liked him. She saw that the family was probably struggling and had stopped by just to check on them and offer her help.

There *are* a few angels on this Earth.

Monthly food stamps went quickly in our household. Initially, a large grocery trip was made. That food was usually gone in a matter of days. We kids would overeat, knowing that food would be scarce later on. During the rest of the month, we were able to eat once each day in school.

Whatever food stamps were left following our grocery trip were used to purchase household supplies. Mom would send my siblings and me on individual trips into the store. We were told to make a purchase that totaled just over one dollar. The change from this purchase would hopefully be near 99 cents. Then, we all pooled our coins together, often gathering nearly five dollars. This money went to buy laundry soap, shampoo, or light bulbs. Of course, this strategy for getting coins from food stamps wouldn't work with today's electronic card system. It makes me wonder what poor people do now to get those other basics.

It was around this time that my big toe got infected, swelling with pus, and it hurt like hell. It turned out to be an ingrown toenail that required a doctor to cut off half the nail. Mom had Medicaid to cover her children, so I was going to be able to see a doctor. However, there were copays with most doctors, and we couldn't afford those. We went to the People's Community Health Clinic, where poor people went for health care. It didn't require a copay, but you had to complete a lot of paperwork to sign up for their services. Paperwork was not a problem for Mom. She was used to filling out paperwork as a means of getting help.[102]

After they called me back to see the doctor, he put anesthesia into a needle and injected it into my toe. Then he started to cut my toenail in half and pull it off. I screamed and shrieked, "It's not numb enough!" The pain was piercing from my toe throughout my body. It felt like he had decided to torture me. I couldn't breathe; the pain was so great. He replied, I kid you not, "Well, you're not paying anything for this visit, so just deal with it." He continued to cut my toenail off as I screamed.

Chapter Seventeen: Corn Rash

"THERE IS NOTHING TO your hair, but it is soft."

Patrice, another one of my Black friends, laughed as she played with strands of my hair.

We were sitting on the bleachers at the side of the school's pool, about to hear something Mr. Johnson was announcing only to the girls. Mr. Johnson came out and—in a flash— announced, "Girls may be excused from swimming during their menstrual cycles if they have a note from a parent or the school nurse." Then, he sent us into the girls' locker room to change into our suits, while allowing the boys to come out of their locker room and jump in the pool.

In our locker room, as we were talking and exchanging glances while changing clothes, I couldn't help noticing an enormous scar on Patrice's breast. I must have been staring because Patrice said, "Go on girl, go 'head and get a good look. It's nasty. I'd be staring too."

In a neighborhood where it was essential to be tough, Patrice had a reputation for being among the toughest. Patrice had pulled such a large patch of hair and skin off a girl's scalp that she needed stitches. She had been in a fight with two girls at once and won. Now, she told me proudly, "It was an all-out fight. She came away messed up too." Then she added, "But, I'm not proud of myself."

Patrice's injury happened during a fight with a grown woman. Patrice was fourteen, but she looked like she was twenty. She went to a bar folks just called the Motorcycle Club, but it had some other official name. She went without even getting carded. This woman had been drunk and started the fight with her that mauled her breast.

For me, it was strange to think of Patrice as anything but sweet, funny, and loving. She was quick to laugh, with a beautiful smile that showed off bright white, perfectly spaced teeth.

After school, Patrice smooth-talked the bus driver into letting her ride my bus home. When she said she was going to my house, the driver finally shrugged and let her on. She giggled as she slipped into the seat next to me like she had gotten away with something. She had. There were policies against doing this. It was that adult look of hers.

Patrice liked our family. She said complimentary things to our brothers, and they started following her around, eager for positive attention. The first place she headed was for my clothes. I didn't have a closet. Instead, the clothes hung on a rod that separated the bedrooms from the rest of the house. They served as a sort of curtain between my room and the living room. She flipped through each choice, pulling out a few now and then and throwing them on a chair. She left a few garments still hanging, but there were a lot fewer when she was done.

"These are no good. You can give them away or throw them away or something, but they make you look like a nerd." I wasn't offended that she was telling me most of my clothes were terrible. It felt she was taking care of me. I craved this kind of nurturing from anywhere I could get it. Listening to her talk, I went into a trance-like state, feeling the warmth of friendship.

"I can't find anything for you to wear to the Boy's & Girl's Club dance. We're about the same size. I have a pair of gray leather pants you could borrow. Then we can use this black-and-white print shirt to go with it," she said, holding out one of the few shirts that had been purchased by my grandma.

The next day, I wore the leather pants to school with my stylish shirt. Of course, the collar was pulled up to show I knew that was the fashion. I was wearing one of my cheap jelly shoes. Probably, the black ones. It was uncanny how many more people smiled at me. In fact, everything seemed to be going my way, building my confidence throughout the day.

It was Friday. It was sunny with fat, puffy clouds drifting by every so often. School was almost out, and I couldn't force myself to listen to Mr. Fetner talk about Earth science. Instead, I fussed with my fingernails, repeatedly checked the clocks, looked around at my classmates, and tried to slow my heart rate by taking deep breaths.

When the bell finally rang, I just sat there and waited for all the other students to leave so I could catch my breath. I was so excited about the dance that night. Julius was supposed to be there. I was still stuck on him in a sick and masochistic way, which led only to misery and feeling rejected.

At the school buses, Patrice waved to me and yelled, "I'm coming to your house," before she got onto her bus. About an hour later, she was on our porch knocking on the screen door. I came outside, and we both sat down on the top step of the three that led to our screened-in porch.

We started dancing to practice for the club. I blurted out, "This dance is going to be so much fun! I've never been to a dance." Suddenly, my shoe slipped on an acorn or rock, and my leg went out from under me. I fell to the cement and heard the ghastly sound of fabric ripping. Patrice's leather pants were torn at the knee. There was no way to sew them. The gash was huge. I panicked, thinking, "That's it, our friendship is over." I knew it would take me a long time to pay her back for the pants, and Mom wouldn't have the money to give her.

"I'm so sorry. I can't believe that happened. I'll babysit for the next three months to buy you new pants." I pled for her forgiveness. Patrice looked panicked too. But after a moment, she bent over and exclaimed, "Your knee is bleeding something awful. We need to clean that out and get a bandage on it."

Okay, so she wasn't saying anything about the pants. I knew they cost about forty-five dollars. I earned $1.50 an hour babysitting, so it would take me . . . Oh crap, I couldn't do math in my head. I felt so awful for doing this to her. I think the pants actually belonged to her mother. We went inside and tended to the wound, and I changed into some off-brand jeans. It was painful to walk the five blocks to the Boy's & Girl's Club because my knee throbbed and stung. At the door to the club, a staff member was checking IDs to verify membership. She pulled me aside and said, "I'm afraid your ID says you are ten years old. This dance is for teens thirteen and up." I was stunned because it meant there was an error on my ID. I wasn't sure how it happened, but I was definitely thirteen; nobody knows they are thirteen more than someone about to turn fourteen

I was downcast but still hopeful. I had some things going for me—my appearance for one. Not only did I still generally look three to five years older than my age but I had powerful evidence of my teenage status in my pocket — my West Junior High School ID declaring I was in eighth grade. It convinced her that the club had, in fact, made an error with my ID.

My injured knee provided me with an excuse not to dance. I was feeling stiff and in pain. But the powerful need to belong kept me out on the floor dancing in a circle with the group. I accepted gentle ribbing about my poor dancing skills and kept trying to get better. The music they were playing had such an enticing bass beat. I recognized Prince, Morris Day and the Time, and Sheila E, but I didn't know the other artists.

If my friends hadn't been there, I would have felt fearful because of my creeping sense of vulnerability about being one of the only white people in a room of 300 people. I was anxious at social gatherings anyway, but I usually felt like I was invisible without belonging. Here, where I stood out, I could feel people staring at me. They weren't necessarily hostile, but they did seem curious. I felt pings in my chest from standing out and not belonging.

My friends brought my attention back to the group. We were dancing, scoping the room for "fine" boys, and laughing — typical eighth-grade-girl stuff. There were a lot of high school boys to admire. Then I saw Erica pointing at my backside and whispering to Tonya. They both burst out laughing. I knew what it was about, so I joked with Erica, "Okay, you might as well say it."

"Girrrrl, you have a flaaaat booty!"

The whole group whooped and wiped their eyes. They knew I could take it. It was an established reason for ribbing. I belonged to this group. We were close enough to tease each other, just like in my family. I belonged to a group for the first time. Of course, I would also obsess about this physical flaw, anyway.

Other white girls showed up, but most of them lived on the west side of the river. Just like every other white girl who spent time with Black people, they were called N-word-lovers the way I was. One, Beth, was older than we were by a couple of years and had already dropped out of high school. She dated much older boys. Through her, I eventually met Franklin[103], who was a senior in high school. Franklin had a stripped-1975 Dodge Charger. He'd worked on the car, painting it his own unique colors and putting silver hubcaps on the tires. Most importantly, when I got into Franklin's car, I saw the handle of a phone receiver from a pay phone hanging from the ash tray.

The steel cord attached to the phone could be seen dangling behind the console toward the floor. It appeared Franklin had driven up to a pay phone at a gas station, placed the hand receiver in his car window, rolled it up, and then driven away, ripping the vital part of the phone away from the stand. The part of me who had depended on pay phones throughout my life was perturbed, and I told him so.

"You're not going to ask me if it works?" he said, laughing.

"Of course not, don't be ridiculous," I said, laughing in return. We had no concept of the cellular or satellite phones that were only a decade away.

"Can I please date you? I am charmed by intelligent women, and every other woman who has gotten into my car has asked me if that phone worked. Please?"

We drove around town, stopping in the park to talk for hours. I learned he lived with his sister because he was an orphan. He was about to graduate from high school, and he had decided to join the Army. He asked me if I would be willing to continue being his girlfriend while he went to basic training. I blushed my agreement and kissed him. I was nearly a child myself, but I was seeking out a mate to start a family with at the age of fourteen. My boyfriend was a full four years older than I was. He was pretty upset about that when he found out. He thought I was sixteen.

Not that we didn't fool around a little at times, but Franklin made me feel respected because we never had sex. He didn't break up with me when I gently turned him down, saying that I had been traumatized. Franklin laughed, saying he had to worry about the law now that he'd learned I was a minor anyway. Franklin got up early in the morning to drive me to school, because he knew that I didn't like waiting in the freezing cold at the bus stop when winter came. He started to show me what love was, which would allow me to recognize it much later in life.

One day, Franklin and I were driving around in Waterloo's twin city, Cedar Falls. We were going through residential neighborhoods, and taking it nice and slow, to avoid a speeding charge. It didn't work, at least the part about avoiding the police. Soon there were cherries in the rearview mirror. The first police officer to the car asked Franklin what he was doing in that part of town. He then asked what we were doing together. His voice was thick with disapproval.

"Are you two doing drugs? I'm going to need to search this car." I started to mouth off and tell him what an ass he was. I told him what he was doing was illegal, but Franklin begged me to be silent. His urgency convinced me to remain mute, even as I wanted to try to get the officer to give a good reason for stopping us. Eventually, he let us go after a lengthy, illegal search. I didn't think about the long history of violence between law enforcement and Black people in this country, or about how my confrontational attitude with the cop had put Franklin at risk. If I had escalated the situation more than I did, there's no telling what might have happened.

Franklin must have wanted to fix his wounded pride regarding law enforcement. Not too much later, we were driving past the Taco John's, and it was apparent right away it was being robbed, which was not uncommon at this particular location. We could see people were lying on the floor. Franklin parked in the small lot behind the fast-food joint. He slowly approached the door.

After what seemed like way too long, he came back to tell me that he learned the people were on the floor because they were counting to one hundred as the robber had instructed. Franklin told them the robber was not around, and they could call the police. I hit him on the arm repeatedly but softly for being so reckless, while secretly admiring his heroism.

Just about the same time Franklin and I came upon the robbery, Mom was acting like a hero too. In the middle of the night, two burglars crawled in through the front door, in complete darkness. Mom was sleeping on the sofa as usual. One of the men must have bumped into something and made a noise because it woke her up. She crept to the kitchen, grabbed a broom, and started hitting the men with it while yelling, "Get out of my house!" over and over at the top of her lungs. They ran out the door and under a streetlight with Mama chasing them down the road. She could see they were two teenagers in hoodies. By then, we were all awake, and soon she was getting pats on the back for chasing off the would-be robbers.

Franklin may have courageously taken on the robbery situation, but he became another source of conflict between my parents and me. As a fourteen-year-old, Mom decided I was too young to date an eighteen-year-old. That's true. I was. But it seemed to me that this was more about his race than his age. When David riffled through my dresser and found the contraceptives I'd barely ever used, naturally he told Mom. Dad was also told about it, and from his roach-infested apartment near downtown he started visiting, giving lectures. I was attacked by both parents.

One night during one of our fights, Mom threw the television set at me. Franklin was waiting outside, so I picked up a knife and pointed it at her as I backed my way out of the house, dropping the knife at the door. As I jumped in his car, I slammed the door on my finger. The wound almost certainly needed stitches, but we never went to the hospital. A deep scar with some long-lasting nerve damage was the result.

I stayed with Franklin for a few days without calling either parent or showing up to school. From my perspective, I was protesting their racism. When I returned, Mom required that I start seeing a counselor. I was identified as having a mental health problem, major depression.

When I continued to act out, Mom and Dad took me to see Rabbi Sol Serber at the synagogue in town. I met with the rabbi twice for about two hours each time. He listened to me speak in depth and at length about my history. He wanted me to understand that I had learned a lot of confusing messages about male-female relationships. He said my sex education was not good and that the choices I made were putting me at risk. He said it wasn't my decision to date interracially that concerned him; it was my decision to tie up my whole life in a boy at my age. I believed him. He introduced me to the notion of feminism, which I'd certainly never gotten at home. He finally said, "Some people succeed because of their parents, and some people succeed *in spite* of their parents. I think you know which you are. Just don't forget to succeed."

There really are a few angels living among us here.

Luckily, having a temporary job working in the cornfields broke up the summer a little bit. Otherwise, it was just the monotony of babysitting for three straight months, which I still seemed to do nearly every day as it was. I worked for a woman just down the street from us who had three children. And there was another woman who had two children and let me hide at her place when I ran away from home. I was tired of kids though. My siblings wore me down.

Beginning in 1985, I spent my summers detasseling corn for several years.[104] It was field work for minimum wage, but you didn't have to be sixteen, like with most jobs. You could start working at age fourteen because it was considered farm labor. In the summer, Grandma and Grandpa MacIntyre let me stay with them for two to three weeks during the detasseling season. They lived closer to the location where laborers were picked up and dropped off, and they could use their car to pick me up.

In the early evening, Grandma put me on a daybed in their enclosed front porch. As a child with chronic insomnia, I lay awake listening to the sounds of my grandparents getting ready for bed. First, Grandpa told "Mother," as he called Grandma, that it was time for him to go to sleep. Grandma was a bit of a night owl, and she continued to move around the living room cleaning up. Eventually, I heard the ten o'clock evening news covering agricultural and farm markets, weather, sports, and local stories about petty crime. Afterward, Grandma always watched an episode of *M*A*S*H*. She chuckled softly from time to time, but I never understood the humor at that age. It became one of my favorite shows as an adult.

After the television had been switched off, the silence was disturbed only by the ticking of their grandfather clock and by the trains that periodically rumbled by a few hundred feet away. Between those two things, I struggled to sleep most of the night in Grandma and Grandpa's house. The clock not only ticked loudly but it also rang its chimes on the quarter hour. Then, on the hour, a full cacophony of bells made my heart race all over again. Even if I managed to drift off, the midnight hour startled me back to full consciousness. After the chimes had quieted, there were twelve loud dongs. Panic set in because I realized how exhausted I would be the next day. Panic never helps with falling back to sleep.

Above me on all sides were bookshelves. I was afraid to turn on a light and wake up my grandparents. But I could read the titles of their book collection using the streetlight that filtered through the sheer curtains. There were books on archaeology, nature, and science. I chose a guide to identifying North American birds and found a sliver of light near the foot of the bed to read under. I liked to read about owls because I liked how they were associated with wisdom. At some point, I finally drifted off.

On my first day of work, Grandma woke me up at 4:00 a.m., and I stumbled into work clothes. It was hard to feel hungry before feeling awake, but I choked down a bowl of cereal. I couldn't imagine a day in the fields with the heaviness in my arms and legs. Grandma took me to the site where workers were picked up. At 4:30, two refurbished old school buses that had been painted gray pulled into the large strip mall parking lot. Grandma made sure I had my lunch box and gloves and wished me a good day. I was glad we got there early because I was able to grab a seat near the front. I knew I could quickly become carsick if I tried to endure the bouncing and lurching that occurs when traveling down dirt roads in the back of a bus.

I shivered even though it was summer. I was wearing a T-shirt and shorts, usually appropriate for a day in the hot sun, but, as it turns out, not one in the fields. The mornings could be chilly, so I made a mental note to bring a jacket along in the future. The buses loaded slowly with arriving workers until it was time to go, no matter who was missing. The trip to the fields took forty-five minutes, maybe as much as an hour. By the time the buses pulled into the field, the sky had lightened, but the sun was still not visible.

Two brothers, Don and Dick Briggs, ran our crew. They were local celebrities because each coached college wrestling. They invited a couple of the star wrestlers to serve as supervisors. The men asked us all to sit on the grass in a semicircle around them. The grass was wet with morning dew. Some people pulled out a sheet of plastic and sat down. I continued to stand, along with a few others, confused that people had plastic. I certainly didn't want wet shorts to start my day.

The bosses pulled out a giant box of garbage bags and walked over to those of us awkwardly looking around.

"First-timer, huh?" one of the wrestler-supervisor asked as he handed me one of the bags.

"Yes, sir," I admitted, wishing that I didn't have to be called out as inexperienced. I took my bag and made my way through seated people toward the back of the group.

The Briggs brothers each tore a full stalk of corn out of the ground. "You see this," Don asked as he held up the stalk. "This here is a breed of corn that grows tall with a lot of ears. But this plant is weak and vulnerable to being damaged by winds. See how its ears of corn are tiny?"

Dick Briggs stepped forward, holding up his stalk, and shaking the dirt from the roots. "On the other hand, this breed of corn is short and sturdy. It has fat ears of corn, but not very many of them. So, basically, both strains of corn have faults; but if we help these plants reproduce together, they'll create seeds that can grow into corn with all the best characteristics and none of the faults. We have to do this every year because the corn that's made from these seeds can't reproduce."

When he pulled away the leaves from the tight spindle, immature tassel silks appeared. "We need to give you a little lesson in corn anatomy and reproduction," he said. "Corn stalks each have leaves, ears, and when they get old enough, they develop tassels. Tassels are the yellow tops of corn that appear when the corn is becoming mature. The tassels contain the pollen that corn uses to fertilize other plants.

"We are trying to make hybrid corn. This means we are removing the tassels from all the short grain so that only the tall corn is fertilizing the field. A machine has gone through these areas and cut off most of the tassels, but if even a single tassel is missed, it can fertilize an acre of corn and ruin thousands of dollars', maybe even millions of dollars' worth of corn. That's why the seed company is willing to pay our crew to walk through and remove any remaining tassels."

"Now, the tassels don't look like what you are used to seeing," Dick Briggs said, interrupting. "Right now, they look like this."

He held up his stalk of corn and pulled the top bundle of leaves out. He handed the tassel to a worker and asked that it be passed around. When it got to me, I examined it carefully. It looked like a tall flower that hadn't opened, because it was wrapped in a thin spike of tightly wound, green leaves. The bottom of the tassel was a pale green, almost white, and it was smooth as if it had been cut from the stalk by scissors. It was also wet.

We had to locate these tassels, pull them out, and throw them on the ground. I felt sure I could do this job well. The Briggs brothers began assigning each worker to a row of corn.

"Put on your garbage bags," barked the brothers.

I watched the workers on either side of me punch three holes in their trash bags and then pull them over their clothes. I whispered to a girl with a raincoat in the next row, "Why are we wearing these garbage bags like raincoats?"

"The corn is wet until about midmorning, so you'll be soaked to the bone if you don't wear it," she responded. "You'll get wet anyway with only a garbage bag. Also, you should have longer sleeves for your arms. You're going to get eaten alive."

Horrified, I exclaimed, "By *what*?"

"Oh, don't worry. If you're thinking about bugs, you'll see them, but they don't usually bite. It's the corn leaves. They give you corn rash."

She was wearing a gray, long-sleeved T-shirt under her raincoat.

"What is corn rash?" I asked, but before she could answer, the supervisors yelled for our attention. A moment later, they blew a whistle, indicating that it was time to begin. I started walking along my row, pushing aside the thick cover of leaves, scanning for hidden tassels. The rough surface of the corn leaves was immediately noticeable as they brushed against my uncovered arms, legs, and face. Every once in a while, a leaf would get you at just the wrong angle and make a small slice into your skin with its sharp edge.

After about fifteen feet, I found my first errant tassel. I gripped two gloved fists around the underdeveloped top of the corn stalk and pulled with all my strength. With a "plup" sound, the tassel flew out, sending me back a step. I looked inside at the space and saw a small perfectly round hole where the tassel had been. It had pulled out cleanly. You had to make sure it pulled out cleanly. My first success. I continued along the row, picking up speed as I became more confident.

The corn was tall enough that it was only possible to see the people in the rows on either side of my own. The two individuals in the rows next to mine were experienced workers, and they had pulled way ahead of me. I had been hoping for a little conversation. I heard them laughing in the distance and tried to work faster to catch up. Moving faster resulted in more minor corn-related injuries. Who knew the hazards of corn? Almost everyone I was working with, apparently.

Just as my coworker suggested, the leaves were coated with both droplets of water and what seemed like a coarse dust. Their edges were razor-thin and sliced at my skin, leaving behind a small smear of wet, grainy corn dust. Sometimes the cuts were deeper, drawing a thin line of blood. It didn't take long to collect scratches along my cheeks, but most were in the crook of my arm, on the fatty skin near my elbows. In no time, my skin reddened and swelled. This was corn rash, and it both itched and burned. My second mental note: wear longer sleeves.

Meanwhile, I tried to ignore the discomfort by focusing on the corn. I learned to scan with quick intensity for the long, thick tassel bundles, because the supervisor had said that just one tassel could cost a million dollars. It didn't take long to become soaking wet from dew, even with the garbage bag on. I would have to try and get a raincoat from our grandma. Wet as I was, I was becoming thirstier and thirstier. I realized that my water bottle was on the bus. I would have to wait for a drink until we had cleaned a row that ended near the bus. Rows were approximately a quarter mile, and it took a while to scan the corn as you walked.

By midmorning, the corn was dry, and the sun burned hot on the black plastic of my garbage bag. It began to feel as though I was being cooked. I tore off the garbage bag and stuffed it in the back pocket of my jean shorts. Most noticeably, the top of my head, my nose, and my ears were becoming hot in the sun. A novice to the fields, I had not worn a hat or even brought along sunscreen. My thin, blonde hair provided little protection to my scalp. I managed to borrow some sunscreen for my face and arms because sunburn was beginning to set in on top of the irritating corn rash. I also got permission to fetch my water bottle from the bus. I nearly finished drinking my water supply on the walk back, and it was not even lunchtime. When I returned to the site where workers were resting, I realized that some had placed a milk jug filled with water at the end of their row. Most had names written on them. There were a lot of little secrets to field work.

The rest of the day was exhausting. The sun continued to burn my scalp, and when I reached up to touch it, I could feel blisters, which easily popped, seeping fluid. If the corn leaves had seemed sharp in the morning, the afternoon sun dried them into perfect blades. The corn produced "corn sweat" or extra humidity that made the heat seem worse.[105] I was so relieved to see the sun beginning to set. The Briggs brothers ran ahead of the work crew and drove the buses closer to us. The forty-five-minute ride home was relaxing, but muscles throughout my body began to stiffen. I asked the girl with the raincoat to sit by me.

"What's your name?" I asked as I thanked her for her advice during the day.

"Sonya," she responded. "Where do you go to school?"

"I go to West Junior, but I live on the East Side."

"Really? Where?"

As I described where I lived, Sonya became excited.

"I don't live too far from you. Maybe I could get a ride from you to the parking lot where we meet the buses?"

I felt immediately sorry and cast my eyes to the floor. "Oh, I am staying at my grandma's, and she lives really close to the strip mall parking lot. I'm sorry."

"It's okay, I understand. Hey, when you put your head down just now, I saw some nasty blisters on your scalp." She was right. All the fat, fluid-filled bubbles had popped, crusted over, and taken on a nasty appearance. It was a good thing I couldn't see them.

Once Grandma had collected me from the parking lot, I told her that I needed a list of items for work. It took a few moments to build my courage because Grandma could be cross when confronted with unexpected stress or demands. I showed her my scalp, and she gasped. She noticed that my ears were also blistered. By now, it was evident I had sustained third-degree burns. Instead of going straight home, we drove to a discount store and bought a baseball cap, a bandana, two gallons of water, and strong sunscreen.

I was filthy, so Grandma recommended a bath. My skin was burnt, scratched, cut, and covered in corn rash, so I used cooler bath water than usual. It felt so good to be clean even as my whole body seemed to sting. Grandma told me she would wash my hair, and afterward, she put first aid cream on my scalp. Painful heat pulsed throughout my body.

After dinner, I watched Grandma sew the new bandana around the baseball cap so it would cover my ears and neck. She placed it on my head and laughed, pulling me toward the mirror. We both thought I oddly looked like Muammar Gaddafi, the Libyan dictator. Grandma gave me some aspirin, and soon I couldn't keep my eyes open. That night, I fell asleep without a problem.

The next two days, it rained and the soil grew into a thick, sticky mud. As I trudged down row after row of corn stalks, my shoes became caked with mud and my feet became harder to lift. Much harder. Still, you had to move quickly down the row. Falling behind could mean a reprimand. Eventually, the mud sucked one of my shoes entirely off my foot. I couldn't pull the shoe out, so I just left it. Behind me, the field supervisor broke through a row of corn and stood in the dirt pathway. His walkie-talkie crackled loudly, and I jumped.

"Good job, MacIntyre," he stated. "I've been periodically checking your row, and you haven't missed any tassels." He had no idea that my obsessive-compulsive tendencies would never have allowed me to miss a tassel.

"Thank you, sir." I was sheepish, embarrassed by the attention from authority but more worried that he would notice my bare foot. He didn't, and he pushed through the corn row to check on the next worker.

It went on and on like this, day after day. Two more weeks of this job and I would earn $500. Doing this job was supposed to be a rite of passage for an Iowa teen. I wasn't navigating it very well, as one could see in the wear and tear on my body, but I did earn the money. I used the cash to buy the family a banana-yellow station wagon with large brown rust spots. We finally had a car again for the first time in two years.

Chapter Eighteen: Meeting Phyllis

MOM TOOK US TO a Black church, where we sat in the back. Everyone was very welcoming when services were over, and we all just mingled amongst the crowd. For the first few months, there was a visiting pastor from Minneapolis, and he was fiery.

The choir made me love gospel music. It was so much better than the dreary, tuneless hymnal music I was used to. Mom volunteered to help organize the clothes closet, run by the church. They had donations coming in from everywhere, but they sat in boxes. Mom got them sized, put on hangers, or folded onto shelves and put in the right places over a relatively short period of time, and she continued to volunteer there semi-regularly. I'm not sure why we stopped going to that church, but I suspect it was because Mom didn't know how to assertively say she didn't have the wherewithal to keep maintaining the clothes closet.

Plenty of people just didn't understand that our mother had a mental illness. She didn't talk about UFOs like Dad did, but she was just as impaired. Everyone from me to Ronald Reagan was expecting her to just get a job and support her children, not realizing how serious her issues with executive functioning were. What is executive functioning?[106] In part, it's the capacity to see your problems, determine a solution, and then take the appropriate steps to get from point A, where you are, to point B, where you want to be. Mom didn't have that ability, for a couple of reasons. She had bipolar disorder II, but it was her serious attention deficit disorder that most affected her planning and follow-through, or executive functioning, day to day.[107] Without the right help, her mind was scattered, and her energy level weak and uneven. Mom kept seeking answers in God and in churches, but no answers came. She was much more like a dependent child who needed to be guided through her troubles, but there was no one there to help her. No one, except for me.

Dad moved to Wisconsin around the time I bought the family the banana car. He wasn't there to give Mom emotional or financial support beyond the $50 in child support we received each month (he paid more, but the State collected the rest). Even at his best, though, he wasn't very good at supporting Mom, due to his own mental illness. But Mom was now totally on her own. Grandma and Grandpa MacIntyre did provide a kind of safety net. A few times when Mom was desperate to pay a bill, she would go with hat in hand to our grandparents.

It was a pretty awful experience to ask them for money. They made you feel like you were stealing it from orphans. I know because I asked them a couple of times myself. They didn't always say yes, either, or provide explanations. Grandma and Grandpa could be hard to relate to. They were rigid about their Catholicism, sometimes making you feel guilty that you weren't Catholic too. When you talked to them, you had to think carefully about everything you were going to say so that it conformed to their expectations for proper thoughts and behavior. That made begging all the more soul-crushing. But even if it was psychologically torturous to rely on them as a last resort, it was good to have a last resort to go to in the worst moments.

I was better at this than my brothers or my sister, so Grandma liked to spend more time with me than the others. She also took a particular liking for John. Since spending time with the grandparents was not pleasant, most of my brothers and sister were mostly relieved that they weren't asked to come over to Grandma and Grandpa's more often. However, they were also jealous.

I can't say I really enjoyed being with Grandma, because she was so particular, although I attempted to make the best of it. She wanted me to learn to sew, so she tried to teach me. I wasn't good at it. I cut a pattern incorrectly, and she yelled at me, causing me to cry.

I couldn't thread a needle quickly, so she'd snap at me, also causing me to cry. It did seem like she felt bad for making me cry, but I could see why Dad had a hard time growing up with Grandma. She would have been hard to please, hard to live with.

Once, Grandma took me on a trip to Chicago, where she attended a conference with other professors in her field. I gave a dollar to a homeless man begging on the street as we walked around downtown. She chastised me. I cried. But two things came out of that trip. I wanted to be a professor like her so I could take trips to major cities. And I knew I disagreed with her about charity because she didn't understand what it was like to be poor.

I loved Grandma, and I told her so. All she said in response was, "Mm-hmm." She was wholly uncomfortable with saying, "I love you" to me. I assume that was true for her generally. It made me sad for her. I just kept telling her I loved her, even if it made her uncomfortable. At least Mom said, "I love you" to us on a regular basis and was more easygoing.

The Waterloo School District had been busing Black children to predominantly white schools to increase integration after decades of segregation in the city.[108] Desegregation happened quickly despite the protest from racist parents. Waterloo Schools are racially balanced for the most part today, although the schools on the East Side still under-perform those on the historically and predominantly white West Side.

Through this desegregation effort, a few of us poor white kids were also sent across town. This integrated schooling was moving me into a district with completely different people—people who had money. I didn't like them.

They appeared to dislike me as well, casting disparaging looks at my secondhand clothes. When they saw me with Black kids, they would roll their eyes. I kept my distance from the rich kids. I tended to hang around my own kind—folks who came from families with nothing to live on but pathetic jobs supplemented by welfare when needed.

Our neighborhood friends were a diverse mix of poor and working-class African Americans and poor whites. We were listening to rap while other students were listening to pop music. I hated most of the music white people were creating in the 1980s. But this is not the place to mock A Flock of Seagulls.

In 1985, the fall of my first year of high school, I was spending a lot of time with my best friend, Annette. On freezing mornings, Annette and I sipped on peppermint schnapps at the school bus stop; she got it from her mother's liquor cabinet. We usually had to trudge through a couple of feet of snow for many blocks, and the walk left us dancing in place, attempting to get warm. The alcohol went immediately to our frozen fingers and toes and left our mouths feeling tingly. There was no concern about the legality of alcohol consumption, and we were never caught. We were exceptionally lucky.

Because of her attractiveness, Annette was highly esteemed among the hormonally charged boys in the neighborhood. She caught the eye of a boy who was considered the sole claim Minova,[109] a girl who was quick-to-fight and had a reputation for seriously hurting other girls. She pulled out huge chunks of hair. She once pulled a girl out of a car window to fight her.

Still, Annette didn't discourage the boy's advances. He was a starting basketball player for East High, and Annette thought he was "so fine." Consequently, Minova had a serious vendetta against Annette, and I was unfortunate enough to be there when it all went down.

When we got off the school bus one day, Minova was waiting in a car with her sister. When she saw us, she hopped out and pointed a long butcher knife in our direction from about five feet away. She said something like, "I'll take the pretty out of your little whore face." I didn't catch it all.

Suddenly, Minova was screaming and waving her hands in the air. She was madder than hell, and Annette was running down the street. I froze and observed the scene in a confused, disassociated state. Minova turned to me, her eyes crimson red and watering, her knife-wielding arm waving, and, "My quarrel ain't with you," she said quickly as she spat over and over. "You lucky this time, but you keep hanging with that whore, and you may get hurt." She got into the car with her sister, and as they drove away, I heard her say, "Damn bitch maced me."

I couldn't breathe. Everything in my chest had been sucked into a tiny ball, and my heart hammered two steps ahead of me as I rushed home to what I hoped would be Mama's waiting arms. The helicopter seeds that had fallen from the trees above crunched under my feet. I didn't know Annette had the mace. What if she hadn't had it? What if Minova had taken out her anger on me? Mom wasn't home. I just curled up on my bed with a stuffed animal. I needed someone older than me to be at home that day. When I faced a knife, I froze.

The violence in our household mirrored the violence in the neighborhood. Brothers hitting brothers, sisters beating brothers. I hit David with a crowbar when he found my birth control pills and told our mom about them. David hit me. Samuel, John, and David fought with each other almost daily. Not only would I go on to cause two brothers to need stitches but I would also go on to be suspended three times from high school for fighting. I fought with my own best friend, with her avenger, and with a girl who said I looked at her funny.

On January 12, 1986, a woman I didn't know from the neighborhood pounded on our door more frantically than I had ever heard. I ran to the front door and flung it open, I knew something was wrong, but I was scared, because I was at home babysitting alone. "Your brother's been hit by a car! He was hit hard! He went flying over the top of the car. You need to get to Allen Hospital!"

I didn't have the means to get to the hospital, or a way of contacting Mom to tell her what happened. She may have been at Hardee's, but the restaurant had long ago instituted a policy of refusing to take calls from us for Mom and Dad. I called Annette and asked if she would drive us to find Mom. Sure enough, Annette and I found Mom at Hardee's, and I told her the news. She left right away for the hospital with John, and I was sent back home with the kids.

It turned out that David had darted out from behind a snowbank to cross a busy, four-lane street, heading for the 7-Eleven, when he was hit by a car. He landed directly on his head. The woman who hit him was mortified. David was in a coma, though he continued to cry out. The doctors drilled a hole in his skull to allow his brain to swell.

When I went to visit him for his breakfast meal once he was awake, he was dealing with short-term memory problems. Later that day, after lunch, I dropped by again, and David asked me why I hadn't visited him. He'd totally forgotten I had been there.

David also drove the nurses nuts because he kept forgetting he had pushed his call button, so he would do it repeatedly. Eventually, he seemed to function better, but he'd had a serious traumatic brain injury,[110] and he had all the risk factors of a person with one.

David still wasn't okay when he finally got out of the hospital. He had insomnia and brain fatigue from having to relearn things. The hyperactive boy was gone and in his place was an inactive one. At West Middle School, David was allowed to take a daily nap in the nurse's office for the rest of seventh grade. His dream of playing football in high school was destroyed.

Remarkably, David was hit by a car again. This time he was sitting on his bike talking to friends on the sidewalk over on Riehl Street. A car jumped the curb and hit him. As I tried to get a ride to the hospital to see David, John was jumping up and down, and I hit him with the telephone receiver to get him to stop. This was back in the days when phone receivers were big and hard. Suddenly, in addition to whatever David's injuries were, John needed stitches. I felt awful about it afterward, but at the time, all I could focus on was the fact that he wouldn't stop interrupting the phone call when I was so distressed about David. John and I were both scarred by the incident.

Once I got to the hospital, I was holding David's hand while he got stitches, when suddenly, the doctor directed a nurse to get me out of the room immediately. I was going to faint. Apparently, I had turned green and started to collapse as I watched the doctor sew parts of my brother's arm back together. I didn't end up getting sick, but it did convince me a career in the medical field was not in the cards for me. Nonetheless, I immediately became a young volunteer—a candy striper— at Allen Hospital for a hundred hours. My apron was red, my shirt was white.

Mom's next church was the Christian Scientists, where she got a job playing the piano. The congregation in Waterloo was so small that it rented a room in the YWCA for its Sunday services. When our family of seven showed up for our first service, we doubled the size of the regular congregation. Two of the devout Christian Scientists who attended weekly were Vern and Mamie, who had a van.

They realized the Bananamobile was not comfortable for seating seven on the ride to church, so they offered to stop by in their van in the morning and pick half of us up. Then, they offered to do things like take us on picnics at Hartman Reserve Nature Center. They couldn't get enough of the MacIntyre children. I'm not sure why they loved us so much, but they were full of hugs and kisses, and it felt good.

Unfortunately, that wasn't the case with Ted, another of the congregants, who was about eight years younger than Mom, and single. She asked him out on a date or perhaps just asked him to coffee or something like that. They ended up seeing each other a few more times. It was pretty clear that Mama was smitten with him. At some point, however, he let her know that her six children were too much for him. When things got awkward for them, we ended up quitting that church. But not before it had affected our family negatively by pushing a fundamentalist prayer-over-medicine philosophy. David needed professional help, and he wasn't getting it.

One figure stands out in my miserable youth of fundamentalist evangelical repression, Nicky, Mom's sister was the embodiment of feminism, modernity, and humanism—. She was really named after her father, Henry (remember, that's not his real name). They stuck an "ita" at the end of his masculine name and thought that would do. It just made for an odd name in the Midwest. Since she hated it, too, she always went by Nicky.

Nicky was the first woman deputy sheriff in my home county, Black Hawk County, Iowa. She let me hold her gun once when I was young. Our parents were not into guns, so this was a big deal. It was heavy and foreboding. It made her seem like a badass. Identifying with her is no doubt the reason I initially chose a career in criminal justice.

From that point forward, I was all about our Aunt Nicky, the cop. I was the good girl. The law-abiding child, while my brothers not only got caught committing petty crimes but became deeply intertwined with the justice system, intensifying their adverse outcomes.

Nicky eventually moved away to Las Vegas. She decided to become a corrections officer instead. She worked in the jail. For the next fifteen-plus years, Nicky continued to move prostitutes, addicts, and dealers through the Clark County jail. She came back to Iowa with war stories. So many people were hooked on drugs. Her stories kept me away from all drugs despite their ready availability in my neighborhood.

One of the things I admired most about Aunt Nicky was her concern for the inmates. She spoke about how many of the other guards were sadistic or cruel to them. Many times, an inmate would come to the jail addicted to heroin, so they would go into withdrawal while incarcerated. This is obviously very painful. The other guards often laughed at these inmates in detox, but Aunt Nicky would sneak them spoonfuls of sugar, which helped reduce their misery.

Even as I believed our aunt was the wisest woman in the world, she was poisoning me. She subscribed to every women's magazine you could imagine, from *Cosmo* to *New Woman* to *Vogue*. In addition to sending me her sophisticated hand-me-down clothes, she sent me heavy boxes of old magazines that must have cost her tons in postage.

I thought thumbing through hours of columns on dieting, relationships, and "having it all" was turning me into a feminist woman. Instead, it was aggravating an eating disorder. When I glance through those magazines now, I immediately feel the pressures that triggered my symptoms. I won't blame the magazines for starting my eating problems, which already existed. But the way they were written and advertised made my disorder infinitely worse.[111]

I had seen Phyllis Gray walking through the hallways of our high school pulling a wheeled briefcase behind her. She looked like the kind of person you'd want to hug for a long time. She was not skin and bones where you feel like you might break the person if you squeezed too hard, but round and fleshy with broad shoulders. She wasn't very tall, but she held her head high, and her hair added a couple of inches. She had it pulled back from her face in a bun that sat at the top of her head, near the back. The bun fluffed out into an Afro puff.

You could tell she worked hard because she had small bags under her eyes from lack of sleep. Sometimes, her radiant, caramel skin looked a little too pale. Other days, she must have gotten a few hours of extra shut-eye, because her eyes would shine more brightly, and her skin would glow. I didn't know why she came to the school once a week and sat in the commons area where we had lunch and study hall. She was always talking to students at a table she claimed as her own.

Earlier in the year, during the summer before I started high school, my best friend, Annette, went away for six weeks to an educational program she called Upward Bound.[112] I didn't know what that was, and since I didn't get to go, I was jealous of the stories she told when she returned. She had met many new friends from all over northeastern Iowa. She had taken fascinating summer classes taught by college students and teachers who had won awards for being so good at teaching. As she showed me picture after picture of people I didn't know, my eyes eventually glazed over. Seeing I was no longer interested, she was downcast but agreed to talk about local gossip she had missed while away. People she knew. People I knew. It just seemed fairer.

When the 1985–86 school year started, Annette met with the unfamiliar woman who came to the school once a week. She told me her name was Phyllis Gray, and she was the director of the Upward Bound program. I see, I thought to myself, another experience Annette was having without me. I felt left out. Feeling left out was nothing new to me. In fact, Annette was tapping into an old insecurity that stemmed from elementary school. At least there was no bullying now.

Annette told me not to pout. Once, when I wasn't taking the bus home and didn't have to rush out of the school building, I joined Annette as she meandered around the high school socializing with boys. We ran across Phyllis in the commons area starting to pack up her things. Annette introduced us. Then she burst out, "Hey, maybe you are eligible for Upward Bound too!?"

Phyllis sat back down and looked through her briefcase. She pulled out a lengthy application and said, "I'd be happy to see if you qualify." The application had a long explanation of Upward Bound, a section for our mom to complete about our income and our parents' education, an essay section for me to complete, and numerous questions about my educational status.

I sat down with the essay and tried to think of something better to say about my motives for wanting to join Upward Bound than, "I want to spend time with my best friend," but I was on the fence about attending college. I was worried I would have to take care of my brothers and sister. Eventually, I wrote an essay that talked about my love of education, my desire to go to college, and my worries about not getting to go. We must have completed everything correctly because, within two weeks, Phyllis sent our family a fat, yellow envelope announcing my acceptance to the program.

Suddenly, during study hall, I was no longer chitchatting with my fellow nerds at the outcast table. Phyllis had me sitting at her table. She expected me to be doing homework. She was there to help if I needed her.

There were other expectations as well. I had to come to a two-hour group tutoring session held every Wednesday night at another high school. If I stayed on the A honor roll and attended all the tutoring sessions, I could earn a stipend of $30 a month. This was incredibly motivating since that stipend covered the expenses to get me to the tutoring sessions.

At home, this was turning out to be an awful year overall— not that "awful" stood out relative to other years. On top of David's terrible accident, Annette was getting jealous of the time I was spending with Franklin, so I was about to lose my best friend.

She decided to make up a story about how he was cheating on me by dating another girl at the same time. The other girl's name was Kim, and she was his ex-girlfriend. The story had a ring of plausibility. I believed Annette and refused to talk to Franklin. He came by the house repeatedly. I told my many brothers to turn him away. He was devastated, unable to understand why I suddenly wasn't speaking to him.

Eventually, I ran into Kim, and she told me none of it was true. I called him to apologize, but he was fairly hurt. We continued to stay broken up. Franklin did write a nice letter from Army Advanced Individual Training (AIT) in Georgia, though.

Chapter Nineteen: Upward Bound

T HE PREVIOUS SUMMER, ANNETTE had gone away for the summer to my idea of utopia. I felt left behind. When ninth grade ended, and summer came, it was my turn to go away for six weeks in the summer. The paradise Annette had described was Luther College, a small, private college in Decorah, Iowa. Low-income students lived in the college dorms, learning study skills while being tutored by expert teachers with whom we took classes in the afternoon.

Kicking off the Upward Bound program, Phyllis had a commanding voice, an attitude that brought fear to most delinquent students, and a warmth that healed the hurt among us. She was a fearless leader, took no guff, and didn't hesitate to send students home for infractions. I respected her so much as an example of a strong woman. There were other strong women at Upward Bound, women who were showing me that you could rise above a rough background to get a college education. One of the most influential was Melanie Hoffner. She seemed to understand that my problems in life weren't academic as much as social. She went on a campaign to raise my self-esteem in increments. She mainly wanted me to know that being a little bit overweight did not mean I was worthless. She was the first person to challenge my eating disorder, which was about to get a whole lot worse.

The weight I had gained from bingeing after the sexual traumas I experienced hung heavily on me psychologically.[113] I felt powerless. Also, being fat meant being excluded from the attention of most boys.[114] I very much wanted to meet a rescuer.[115] A rescuer could take me away from my family.

Upward Bound saved my life! It helped me make better decisions, and it educated me. Old notes I read from my file say, "She is actually coming out of her shell." I didn't really know many people except Phyllis, and as an introvert, I wasn't quick to make friends. Nonetheless, just like Annette, I started to form relationships with other students from cities all over northeast Iowa.

Upward Bound always had something interesting planned for evening recreation and weekends. At the end of the first week of Upward Bound, the schedule shifted to weekend activities. We had a dance on Friday night. Someone introduced me to Adam[116], a tall, thin boy with thick, dirty blond hair hanging just to his shoulders. He was from a rural town in northeast Iowa. He seemed rebellious, perhaps due to his expert handling of a cigarette. As he spoke with me, he looked intently into my eyes and expressed a genuine interest in meeting me. My own sense of worthlessness prevented me from believing his apparent sentiment.

Toward the end of the night, Adam asked me why I was content to sit alone in a corner. I admitted I was not skilled at dancing, so he suggested I try slow dancing with him. He added that it did not take a lot of coordination. I responded with anger, telling him I did not need his charity. He did not reply, and he left me sitting there alone. What the hell was wrong with me?

When the Upward Bound talent show began recruiting acts, I wanted to be on stage. I hinted to Adam that I would like to sing a song but that I was cursed with a wretched voice. He expressed a similar thought about his own voice. One of us suggested that we do a lip-syncing duet as a joke, and the other took it seriously.

To be chosen for the variety show, we needed to practice our carefully choreographed moves. The words to the song created feelings of hope and possibility in my mind.

Eventually, Melanie Hoffner offered to let me wear her bridesmaid dress. The night of the show, I was overwhelmed with a sense of belonging. My new friends were the most respected in the program, and they liked me enough to offer their best wishes. Adam squeezed my hands and with confidence said, "We're going to kick butt." I was nervous as the introduction to our song began, but when I concentrated, my fears disappeared.

The Upward Bound summer was supposed to last for six weeks. My family desperately needed money, and the middle weeks of July offered the promise of those jobs detasseling corn. With the chance to make money, I left Upward Bound for two weeks, regretting intensely my need to leave.

The day before I was to return to Upward Bound, my brother told me that Grandpa had died. I admired Grandpa MacIntyre, but I also silently felt distressed about the added time away from Upward Bound. It took the funeral itself to tear me out of my self-absorbed despondency. I felt guilty for missing the chance to know the charity of my grandpa's acts of kindness, which the priest listed at length. The priest didn't mention his son's family as one of those charities.

I returned to Upward Bound in time to join the annual trip to a large city. We went to Chicago, and I claimed the seat across from Adam and his girlfriend. I stifled jealousy and justified the happy couple by noticing how his beautiful girlfriend was better suited to him. Nevertheless, Adam mentioned that he missed me.

When I got home from Upward Bound, I began a starvation diet, which limited daily my food intake to a grapefruit, a Diet Pepsi, and a convenience store bag of Planters cashews. I also eagerly joined the YWCA, where Mom had been attending water aerobics periodically, and where we had all attended the Christian Science Church.

I joined two of their regular aerobics classes, attended the water aerobics classes with Mom, and was in the weight room daily. My eating disorder symptoms were a means to an end. I wanted to be thin so I could attract a rescuer.[117]

Chapter Twenty: More Violence

THINGS WERE GETTING TROUBLESOME in the neighbor-hood. I was never a fighter at heart, but I lived in a neigh-borhood where being a combatant was a necessity. I was suspended for fighting twice in middle school and three times in high school. Annette and I got into a physical fight over what happened with Franklin. It happened in front of her house. I was half a foot taller than her and quite a few pounds heavier too. It didn't take much to win that fight. We both got suspensions from school because the fight was on the way home from school. I thought I was done fighting then, but I should have known she would want revenge. There was at least one more fight coming as a result of the fallout from my relationship with Franklin.

On the other hand, Latisha[118] was never a friend. She was a serious enemy. Latisha told everyone that she was going to give me a beatdown because I spread the rumor that her brother was in jail. This was not true. The real reason was that I had thrown down with Annette a couple weeks before, and I had gotten the upper hand. It was ninth grade, full of ridiculous stuff like this.

From behind a row of bushes, Latisha dove at my chest. I fell backward onto the concrete sidewalk. Grabbing my legs, she dragged me to the gravel alley and began pounding on my stomach and face. I didn't fight back but instead pulled my arms in front of my face. Latisha grabbed my hands and scraped my knuckles against sharp rocks. Torn skin hung from the bony parts of my finger.

"You ain't never gonna call my brother a jailbird again, ya hear?" Latisha repeatedly yelled. Her assault was unrelenting, and her strength clearly dominated my own to the point that fighting back was pointless.

"I didn't even know you had a brother," I protested.

Actually, I had only recently learned she had a brother, but I had never said anything about him because I didn't know him. I certainly never would have said a bad word about him. As far as I knew, he had never been to jail.

In the background, I saw Annette for the first time. She was watching my beating intently. Latisha punched me until she tired, occasionally daring me to hit her back. I ignored her taunting and fought back tears. Eventually, Latisha kicked my abdomen a few times and walked with Annette to her house.

I hobbled to my house, overcome with shame, anger, and shock. Pain and intense emotion made it impossible for me to hold back tears. The stinging pain made me aware that Latisha had also given me numerous deep scratches. The mirrors at home revealed that my face was a mess. I called out to see if any of my family was home, but I heard only silence. I curled up on the sofa, praying that Mom would be home soon. I needed her comfort. When Mom arrived home, I could barely choke out an explanation to her questions about my terrible condition. I couldn't answer her. She wrapped her arms around me and made soothing noises. After I had regained my voice, I told her about Latisha's ambush.

"You're going to have scarring on your face if we don't clean those scratches. You know, I think aloe would help. Brenda's family has a live aloe plant. Let's clean your face and ask for some aloe vera leaves." I didn't care what she did. I just wanted her to make me feel better.

The next day, Phyllis asked me what happened when I got to school. I started to cry, and she hugged me. She told me it would all be okay. Even if I didn't have Annette as a best friend anymore, I was still in Upward Bound.

At about this time, Ormond Gardiner[119] asked me out on a date. We were supposed to go to the movies. Instead, when he picked me up, he drove straight to a large municipal park a few miles from our house. Ormond surprised me by kissing me almost right away.

"Let's get in the back seat," Ormond said, looking at me intently. But I was starting to get a little bit scared. Everything was moving too fast. We got into the back seat, and I tried to start a conversation, but Ormond immediately started kissing me again. I was wearing a jean skirt, so it was easy for him to reach up and pull down my panties. He managed to do this as he pushed me back on the seat. When he started to push himself inside me, I screamed so loud that he smacked me. After he was done, he said, "Get out!"

I walked home in a cold, windy rain. Once again, I was in shock, and found ways to blame myself for what happened.

In response to this latest sexual assault, I began bingeing on junk food again regularly. My weight climbed thirty pounds over a short period of time. Without the paper route, I became more sedentary. My self-esteem was steadily declining. However, I was also participating in Young Leaders in Action, another group I'd been mysteriously nominated for. Through this group, I met the governor for the second time, and there is a picture with me posed next to him smiling. I didn't care for him, but it was the governor. I didn't feel like a leader, though.

Chapter Twenty-One: The Era of the Devil

S CHOOL HAD ENDED, AND during the summer before tenth grade, my family was moving again. We moved to a relatively decent-looking house on the west side of Waterloo. This house was a step up for us, so I was happy about that. Best of all, I didn't have to change schools. Then, a few weeks later, Mom announced, "We're being evicted."

"What happened!?!" I screamed at her. My frenzied mind did a mental review of everything involved in being evicted. Homelessness was a given. What about our stuff? We didn't have a lot, but there were clothes, dishes, and household supplies. I paced the floor. My heart raced.

"They refused to grant us two months' rent," she sighed.

That was a standoff between the landlord and Mom that she was bound to lose. The house we were renting was in a working-class neighborhood a few blocks from the middle school. It was two stories with a basement. The basement was the reason our mom wouldn't pay the rent for two months. It had flooded. It was only about two inches of water on the floor, but Mom had trusted the landlords when they said the basement never flooded.

She was angry at the landlords because we had only been in the house for about a week. When we moved in, she made us carry all our moving boxes to the basement so we could give the house the scrubbing Mom always insisted on before putting everything away. Now, everyone's clothes had to be rewashed. Mom was especially angry, though, because the dirty water saturated everything from paperwork to old letters, to family photos—all damaged or destroyed.

Mom's anger was amplified further by the fact that Uncle Lowell[120] was one of the landlords. Aunt Cleo had married him a year earlier, after divorcing her first husband, the child molester. Uncle Lowell seemed jolly and looked like Santa without the beard. The betrayal by a family member was too much for Mom to bear. In her typically ineffective way, she decided she would demand that the landlords pay her back for misleading her about the basement. She was nice about it at first. They were never nice about it.

The night of the eviction, Mom relied on a friend with a car to load the belongings we couldn't get into the Bananamobile. She was fortunate, and another friend of hers found us another place to rent, over on the East Side again. The house was charming enough. All the previous tenants' belongings were still there, so we had no choice but to move our things into the small garage at first. These residents had used house plants, curtains, and lots of decorations to make the house look nicer than it really was. Once they moved everything of theirs out, and we moved in, the house no longer had the previous appeal.

I had my own room on the second floor, but to get to *their* room, the rest of the kids had to walk through mine. In other words, there were no doors on my room. The kids' room fit four comfortably as an open studio-type layout with wooden desks built into the wall posts, drawers integrated into the wall, and spaces in the wall just big enough for a bed. Mom had her own room downstairs. It was the nicest home we had ever lived in outside of government housing.

Unfortunately, the house came with a "neighbor," a sociopath that no one had told Mom about. Charles[121] went out of his way to make trouble for other people, and still does, and Mom might as well have had a target pasted on her back. Senja's most prized companion in the world, her cat, Toonces, disappeared, having last been seen playing near Charles's garden.

Charles also leered at neighborhood women and, to support himself, filed frivolous lawsuits against all manner of people, including our family on two occasions, and Mom most recently. His teenage son told us that his father played Russian roulette with him, which helped explain why his son seemed so fragile or traumatized. The boy came over to our house and spent all his time there from the moment we moved in, and Charles, of course, hated that. It was a risky move to let him stay, but Mom wanted to give the kid some love.

With my detasseling money as a start, it took me less than a year to save up enough money for a used car of my own. I bought a 1974 red Mercury Comet with white wall tires. I was going to be sixteen soon, and this car would allow me to drive to a part-time job if I got lucky enough to find one.

After so much positive intervention from Upward Bound, I was ready to become a model student. I wanted to participate in extracurricular activities, start thinking about college, and figure out how I might get a scholarship. Phyllis was providing me with ongoing, invaluable support.

I wanted to be the perfect profile of a college applicant. I ran for student council twice. The first time, I made the mistake of running for class treasurer against a popular girl. I thought maybe if all the unpopular people voted in a bloc, I stood a chance. They didn't, and I didn't win. The second time, I tried for something less ambitious—student council representative. I won that election in my junior year. As one of our duties, we selected four families at Thanksgiving time for the student senate to sponsor. A family was chosen from each class year in high school.

The administration office provided the student senate with helpful information about which families were the poorest and most in need, providing profiles of families without their names associated. The Student Senate leadership made its selection and we were told to contact the family to see if they were willing to go on the "shopping trip" to the local grocery store. It was awkward as I learned that my family had been selected by leadership. I mean, I was supposed to go on the shopping trip as a representative of the student senate *and* as a part of the selected family. When I went to the store, having the Student Senate paying for our groceries was humiliating. Charity is lovely, but it can be so shameful.

Our nightly tour of churches offering free suppers stands out as another example. I always wondered what these people who came every week on Wednesday night or Friday night to volunteer for the food service really thought of us. We were there each week, so they might have thought we were very needy. But I already knew from experience that they might have thought we were parasites.

I had started to be very conscious of how society, and the people I encountered, talked about poor people, and as a result, it felt like we were pests. Each visit to a church—Concordia Lutheran and Saint Patrick Catholic Church among them—felt more embarrassing than the last. We encountered *good* people putting in their time, but with more than enough self-satisfaction and classism to go around. For *way* too many people, we were so poor we didn't deserve to eat, or even to live. It was the Reagan years, and he *hated* poor people.[122]

My German class was going to visit Germany for ten days over spring break, and I really wanted to go. I looked at the cost of the trip. There was no way. I couldn't earn enough money for it. I couldn't ask anyone for it, and I couldn't pray for it because I had learned a long time ago that praying for things didn't work. I told myself that one day I would go to Germany and visit the cities where my great-great-grandparents had lived.

Almost every other evening, I made Mom sit at the kitchen table with our stack of bills. She didn't have a checkbook because she lost her account following a series of overdrawn checks. So, making budget after budget, Mom and I juggled the monthly welfare check to cover bills. Some months we could pay the heating bill, and other months we chose the water. I used to stare desperately at the numbers of our credits and debits, praying we could find the money to pay them all. Eventually, as part of the almost nightly bill ritual, I added a lecture to Mom, and I could be insufferable about it. It was arrogant to think I knew better than her how to solve our money problems. But she was so frail and weak. Knowledge wasn't the problem. In this way and a few others, our roles were reversed, and it was like I was her mother.

It seemed like she was just waiting for a decent husband because she had no hope with six kids. I pleaded with her to get a job. I helped her complete resumes and applications, but I also tried to insult her into working. Over a ten-year period, Mom worked as a housekeeper at a hospital, a substitute teacher, a daycare worker, a temp for a secretarial service, a housecleaner, a proofreader, a receptionist, and a graduate student.

She could never keep up with her work while also trying to keep her children from running wild. I knew that Mom struggled to care for our family without my help. Yet for some reason I expected she could manage both a family *and* a job. Most people can do this, but Mama isn't one of them.

When we moved into our new place back on the East Side, we didn't realize it was infested with mice. While I slowly got used to the mice as cohabitants of the house, I was awakened by a tickling, scratching sensation on my back one night while I was sleeping. I screamed at the top of my lungs. The mice had eaten through the top layer of my mattress. I woke Mom and David up and screamed until they forced the mattress out of the upstairs window onto the upper part of our garage roof. Living in the same house was one thing. Their organized takeover of my mattress was quite another and left me without a place to sleep.

I covered the metal bed frame and springs with a sheet and tried to get back to sleep. No one could have held more contempt for

Mom than I did that evening. I had been making jokes about how the mice were getting into the private chocolate supply in my dresser. I'd kept a positive attitude, a sense of humor, but not that night. I went to her room, demanding a bed. I told her that she had to get a job, or I would take my siblings and leave.

The next day, Mom found another temporary job. She desperately wanted to move our family out of poverty, but there were always competing needs. Either she worked, brought in small amounts of money, and let her children roam unsupervised, or she parented us reasonably well while falling far short on providing basic needs, and we still roamed unsupervised. It was poverty due to mental illness more than anything else. There seemed to be no way out.

Rows of empty chairs separated me from the gaggle of students gathered around our high school theater teacher. I lingered pensively in the back of the auditorium. It was tryouts for the school play, something I hadn't attempted before. I didn't know a soul, but they all seemed to know each other. A few minutes later, an attractive, heavyset girl came bounding up the stairs toward me. "Come down and sit with us. My name is Linda[123]," she said, beaming. Her kindness radiated from her and calmed my nerves. She spoke with me for a few minutes about the process of auditioning for plays. Linda told me I would be meeting the drama teacher who was beloved by all the students. They called her "Ma."

Ma was famous for only selecting actors for her plays from among students who knew her. Linda seemed to know her well. She introduced me enthusiastically, despite having met me only moments earlier. No doubt, it was her influence that led Ma to choose me for a part. On the day the play opened, however, there was trouble.

An announcement came over the intercom that Deborah MacIntyre had someone waiting on the phone for her. Ma sent another student to transfer the call to the phone backstage. I took the call minutes before we went on. I had expected the purpose of the phone call was for Mom to wish me luck and tell me she was going to be late to the show. Instead, I learned she was blaming me for the state of depression she was in. The phone call was an icy rant. I was shaken and crying, but dramatically, in a lame attempt at humor, I told my fellow actors who had seen me on the phone, "The show must go on." This, despite my minor role in it.

I had friends from Upward Bound who lived in small towns such as New Hampton and Cresco. However, it was good to have a best friend in Waterloo again. Linda's home was a safe haven. She was a good listener, and Linda helped me talk about some of what I had dealt with in my past.

Linda was also the friend who talked me and Mom into going to see a bellicose speaker who claimed to have been a Devil worshipper. The arena was filled with eager listeners. He told everyone that the entire country was teeming with Satanists who performed animal sacrifices and recruited children to take part. Everyone was terrified when they left. Afterward, Linda drove out to the park in Waterloo where rumor had it that Devil worshippers sacrificed animals. She seemed to want to catch them in the act. I'm not sure what she thought we were going to do at that point. Of course, we never ran into any Satanists no matter how many times we looked. Nobody else in the country did either.[124]

Chapter Twenty-Two: A New Dad?

MOM WAS STILL EARNESTLY trying to find a man to replace Dad after she made him leave. I had to exercise my veto power against potential new dads over and over. "No, Mama, I think he's just trying to find someone to take care of him," I would say, or "No, Mama, he's just so smelly. If he has access to a shower or a bathtub, he's not using them. I'm just saying."

There were men who stayed for weeks, and men who just stayed a few days. I don't remember all of them, but three of them stood out because they put in more than a six-month stint. Carl could rig a car even when mechanics said it was dead. He could repair them all, at least up to a certain degree of difficulty. Beyond that, he had a buddy who ran a used car lot in a particularly poor part of the city. This man could fix up your car if Carl couldn't.

In keeping with the reputation of used car lots, the quality of used cars, and the principle of, "You get what you pay for," I ended up buying three cars in three years from Carl's buddy. Mom bought more than six over a longer period of time. Carl's friend's cars went for far less than a thousand dollars, and he took payments in installments. As a teenager, I didn't have a lot of other options.

Carl talked funny, in a way that made him seem slow. Mom said he'd been in special education classes in high school. He might have talked that way because he had been in a motorcycle accident though. He'd had a head injury at some point in his life. Once, famously, he rode his bike through the doors of his high school, down the hallway, and out through the other end. This got him a reputation around the city as "that idiot." Either way, Carl swore he was a lot more mature now that he was well over thirty. He was at least ten years younger than Mom.

The best thing I remember about Carl was that he taught me how to drive a stick shift. We were living on a hill with a near-forty-degree angle to it. People with automatic transmissions heard their cars groan, grind, and rattle when trying to accelerate up our street, so it is easy to imagine how challenging it would be to get a manual transmission to run without stalling on it. To Carl, it was the perfect place to teach me how to shift gears. He had me stop in the middle of the slope numerous times, and then told me to drive forward from neutral to first gear. Once I stopped getting frustrated with repeated failure, I noticed I was getting better at it. Carl was patient but tenacious about teaching me how to drive a stick shift, and it worked well. When my Comet bit the dust, Carl found me a car with a smashed-in front end, a manual transmission, and no radio, promising to put in a stereo with a tape deck.

Carl was around when Mom decided to go back to the Mormons full time. Considering that her brother Paul had been attending the "Cedarloo" ward services for years, Mom thought: "Why not try it out ourselves?" I can think of a million reasons now, but at the time I was happy to see Mom get moving again. Paul had a salesman's personality, persistent and annoying. He'd been giving the church 10 percent of his income for decades, and he was becoming a big wig there. We began taking the Bananamobile and my smashed, white Toyota to LDS services. I was put into the young woman's group, where we used a workbook called *My Personal Progress*[125] to complete goals like learning to sew or cook. We needed to master *all* the skills of being a good Mormon wife, in fact. I dutifully tried to work through the book to make "progress" too, although my ultimate progress differed from the intended course.

Everybody's favorite man for Mom wasn't picked up at the Salvation Army where we ate for lunch so often. Mom was reading the *Enquirer,* the *Sun,* or the *Globe,* one of those tabloids. She said she'd been scanning the personal ads "on a lark," when she "happened upon the most enticing ad" in the men seeking women section. Mom was always pretty sappy and regularly fell for tortured metaphors, so who knows what fantasy Prince Charming was selling? Whatever it was, she wrote to him. He wrote back. She sent him more letters. He responded, often from postmarks all over the country, a fact most people would have taken as a bad sign. He grew up in New York City, where his thick accent came from, but he said he'd been living in California for years. This exchange of letters, interspersed with a couple of collect calls, went on for more than two years before they decided he should come to live with us because they were soulmates.

Things weren't easy for Robert when it was his turn with "these hellions," as we kids were called. He was a hippie, and still said things like, "Far out, man." He had a "Whoa, whoa . . . --easy there, baby" attitude toward life, and played up a sort of "smooth Italian" schtick that could be entertaining. He drank too much wine but always did the dishes, so he was invaluable to Mom.

Robert liked us. At least he said he did. Individually, he treated each of us with respect. That didn't stop him from having the same reaction Dad did once he came to grips with the totality of managing six rowdy kids. He said we were a nightmare, in so many words. Difficult to handle. Disobedient. Manipulative. He stuck it out for several months though. After he left, Robert kept in touch with Mom for years. She always said she was in love with him. Eventually, his responses just stopped coming.

An announcement came over the intercom at school for Deborah MacIntyre to come to the central office. It was a message from Mom telling me not to go to after-school activities that day. Instead, I was supposed to go home to watch the kids.

After continuing to worry during the last two periods of the day, I drove home to find a note for me on the kitchen table. Mom wrote,

"I met the most delightful people. They wanted to go to Cedar Rapids overnight to see if we can talk to Diane and Eddie." Beyond that, there was no explanation given. Unbelievable.

Except that it wasn't. She was manic again, and just taking off without thinking was practically her brand when it came to mania. I was immediately perturbed. I would miss rehearsal, and the curtain was going up soon. We really needed to go through our lines.

I turned to David and pleaded, "Can you please watch the kids until I get back from rehearsal for the play?" He reluctantly agreed. I drove back to school, rushed through my lines, and quickly got home, where I found David passed out on the sofa with a bottle of vodka in his hand. The children were running loose. I was so angry with him that I couldn't see straight.

I yelled at him that he had no common sense. I didn't consider how his judgment had been impaired by his head injury. I didn't have compassion for things like that because I didn't understand them. I didn't realize that it was probably a bad idea to leave the children with him in the first place. Even with his poor decision-making, David somehow managed to escape most legal entanglements. When he was caught doing things like breaking into a vending machine with Samuel, prosecutors were quick to recommend residential placement for him. He went to rehabilitation programs for traumatic brain injuries, where he started to make progress.

It was heartbreaking to see a boy who blew away academic aptitude tests struggle to use skills like organization, self-control, and goal planning. He was sent to the Job Corps as another intervention and learned welding there.[126] He was proud of his welding skills, but he was sent home early from the program for drinking.

I redirected my anger from David back at Mom when I thought about how she had left me in the position she had with David. I knew Sweetie was going to call Child Protective Services about Mom's decision that night, but I didn't say anything to her. Maybe she needed a reminder from CPS to stop making me parent all the time.

Isaiah was incredibly hyperactive. His bouncing-off-the-walls behavior made him accident prone, and he was frequently getting hurt.

Beginning in Head Start, teachers reported Mom left and right for abuse, but she didn't use any physical punishments on Isaiah whatsoever. She was petrified to do so. The rest of us were envious, as we thought back on our days with injured asses and knocked heads. But Isaiah would keep getting himself hurt in ways that looked like he was being harmed at home, so child protective services just kept coming. They freaked Mom out, but their checks and balances on her poor parenting were comforting to me.

Chapter
Twenty-Three:
Suicidal Mama

I T STARTED OUT AS an ordinary day. I was running late to school. Mom was scrambling to round up the boys, and that meant yelling orders to get dressed and grab their things. I was on my own. I didn't always groom adequately. One of my friend's laughingly referred to me as "the girl with the washed-every-other-day hair." I think it was said lovingly, but she sometimes had a streak of snark that made you wonder. I don't think she realized the futility of trying to shower daily amid our chaos.

Before we moved to this house, we'd lived in a couple of apartments that had modern bathrooms with nice showers. In those days, I almost always took a morning shower to wash away the sleepiness. However, this house had a stand-alone shower in the basement with either a gush or a trickle, depending on your ability to turn the overly sensitive knobs just so, coming from the pipe that served as a shower head.

When you got out of the shower, there was about a foot of concrete that was not freezing from where the water had run down to the drain in the floor. If you made a dash for it, you could make it to a patch of floor rug without touching too much of the wet, icy cold part of the concrete floor. Then, you would shiver as you dried off and got dressed in clothes that got stuck as you tried to pull them over your still-overly-moist skin. This morning was more of a fall-out-of-bed and commandeer-the-family's-only-bathroom day. Since there were six children, I didn't get it for long before someone was banging on the door with one thing or another. My family has a noticeable lack of boundaries.

I was at play practice. We were kicking back in auditorium seats and running through our lines when a woman from the central office came in and whispered something to Ma, the theater teacher. She pulled me out of the group and told me to go to the central office. There, I learned from emergency officials that Mom had attempted suicide and was in critical condition at Saint Francis Hospital. Stunned, I turned to Linda with frozen emotions. She hugged me tightly and asked what I wanted to do. I was suddenly angry with Mom for doing this to her children. I knew immediately that I was now in charge of the household, so I sprang into action.

First, there was getting my brothers and sister home from school safely. I drove from Head Start to Lincoln Elementary School to Logan Middle School, at each point finding children who were confused and angry about why they hadn't been picked up yet. I told each child what happened, and we all rode home.

I made mac and cheese for dinner. Everyone had to have tiny amounts of milk in their cups to make the gallon last, and that drew grumbles. Mom had run out of food stamps a few days earlier. I asked David if he thought he could manage to watch the kids after I put them to bed, so I could go and visit Mom, or at least show her some support. He insisted he should come along with me. However, someone had to stay with the kids, and I was the only one who could legally drive. I believed I knew what I was facing, whereas he did not. After convincing him to stay, I drove across the city to the hospital.

I thought I knew what I would be up against, but I wasn't psychologically prepared to see Mom hooked up to intubation, pumps, and IVs. It didn't help that it had gotten dark, and the curtained area she was in kept her in a shadow, broken only by the lights of the medical equipment. I had assumed I would be overwhelmed with grief and sympathy for her. I wasn't.

There was nothing but a rush of rage. How could she abandon us? I wanted her to wake up so I could scream at her. Instead, after staring for quite a while, I turned around and started to go, but ran immediately into Uncle Paul. He didn't seem too impressed by Mom's behavior either. He made some negative comments, and then finally asked if I could call his sister, Cleo, to work out some arrangement for the kids and me. He came across as stiff and cold, not the least bit comforting. I told him everything was taken care of and got out of the hospital as quickly as possible. I drove to Linda's house. She had been a good friend, but she was about to become a great friend. We talked for quite a while before I felt guilty about leaving David alone with the kids so long.

In the morning, my first concern was with keeping the Department of Social Services out of the picture. With our family's history in the system, I didn't want them getting wind that there were unattended minors. To avoid losing custody of us again, Mom had to find places for all of us to stay while she was hospitalized for six weeks.

David went to Mom's friend, Liz. Samuel went to our grandparents. A teacher named Mrs. Navarro, who had both Senja and John in her classes, said she would take care of them. Isaiah was taken in by Sue Smith, who agreed to make sure he got back and forth to Head Start. Linda convinced her parents that I should stay at their house. Soon, I was living in a nicer home. It was a stark contrast to the years I had spent living with Mom, whose poverty-level income was dependent on disability payments and welfare. They had a steady supply of food, household items, three functioning cars, and room for casual spending. They seemed rich.

As soon as Mom was moved to the psychiatric ward on the fifth floor of the hospital, she was able to have visitors. I drove the kids with me to see her. I wasn't sure how I was going to react to our now-conscious mother. She looked vulnerable and pale when they finally brought her around the corner from her room to the visitor's lounge. I had no more anger, just worry.

I quickly told her how I handled the living arrangements for the kids, and how she didn't need to worry about the child welfare investigators coming around as far as I knew. I asked her how long she was going to be there, and she started to cry. "I don't know. I'm not sure when I'll be better."

Chapter Twenty-Four: Overcoming Adversity

I FOUND OLD LETTERS Mom had written before I went to college. In March 1988, she wrote to a friend:

"I called Uncle Andy—upbeat. He's on Pamelor for depression and Trixalene for circular thinking. I think I could use that. You met Ruth. She's back out at MHI [Mental Health Institute, a State Hospital]. *I wonder how long she'll be out there. Was so paranoid lately. Was arrested for public intoxication early Monday a.m. Got back on those drugs. Was a space case. Too bad. She has so much to offer. I think a lot was her family that made her feel of no value—the black sheep, sort of."*

Mom identified with black sheep everywhere. She was talking in this case about Ruth, a friend of hers with schizophrenia. Mom made a lot of friends during her inpatient psychiatric stays. This provided her with social support she sorely needed. It had its drawbacks though. We got attached to Mom's friends, like Ruth. Because of her symptoms, her son had been removed from her home by either her family or the state. Having her son gone broke Ruth's heart. We tried to cheer her up by visiting frequently.

Mom's letter continued,

"David living with his Dad now. Samuel is Student of the Month but has a rotten probation officer. Got to court again on the 7th. Wish he'd get off probation. It's getting me depressed. They like to rule your life. Very real problem."

David's stay with Dad was short-lived. He thought it would be life changing, but instead it was a painful disappointment. David never specifically said how his time living with Dad went, but let's just say he never wanted to live with Dad again. He must have learned very quickly that Dad was not all there.

I don't know what force of nature got me up in the morning. I still existed on next-to-no-sleep, and the Mormons had a morning Bible study for teens, a class I felt heavily pressured to attend. At first, I was aghast at what we were doing. We took our Bibles, crinkled up individual pages with relevant Bible passages on them, and then colored their edges with colored pencils. This was in preparation for a contest the study group leaders conducted each morning. They would call out a random passage, and you could win small prizes by being the first one to locate the Bible verse. We turned our Bibles to the side, pushed on the Bible's spine so the pages would fan out, and then shuffled quickly through the colored edges to find the one that matched the Bible verse that was called out. It felt like we were defacing Bibles to me.

The time spent in Bible study made me want to try a fresh start, *spiritually*. I wanted to wash away all the sexual attacks, the bad decisions, and every other sin the church loudly condemned. I decided to have my adult immersion baptism, and I was going to have Uncle Paul be the one to baptize me. Maybe it would bring us closer. Nothing else had.

Adult baptism was a glorified day for Mormons. They showed everyone a video about a little boy who was asked to give some blood to his dying sister to save her life. The little boy looked panicked and scared, but he did it anyway. A little while later, the little boy asked the doctor when he was going to die. He believed he was giving his life to save his sister because he thought they would have to take all his blood. Everyone was teary-eyed in the room, and the metaphor for Jesus was pointed out to those who hadn't gotten it already.

They had me dress in all white robes. I was led from an area resembling a locker-room into something that looked like a tiny swimming pool. Paul dunked me, and I was once again a Mormon.

It wasn't long before I recognized that I didn't feel any closer to my relatives though. The church felt creepier the longer I stayed, and I stopped going after a couple years.

Dad was happy about that. He never stopped being angry at the Mormons for influencing him to get married and have a family. Nonetheless, Dad was faithful about paying child support. The State took all the money he paid, except $50, because Mom was receiving welfare. He couldn't pay that much anyway, because even after he moved back to Sheboygan, Wisconsin, a year after they separated, he still didn't have jobs that paid more than $3.35 per hour, the minimum wage there at the time. Dad worked for Kohler, the company that makes toilets and sinks. Then, he worked for more than ten years for Walmart as a stockman. In 2014, Walmart workers cost taxpayers $6.2 billion in public assistance.[127] My dad worked for Walmart for all those years as America supplemented his wages by paying welfare to his family.

Dad's favoritism toward me lasted past when he was living with us. He kept in touch with me regularly by writing letters and sending birthday cards, but he didn't do the same with the others. Mom was discreet about giving me his letters, and I kept them hidden from my siblings so as not to hurt them. In many ways, they were lucky they weren't getting these missives. They were regular reminders that Dad was mentally ill because he wrote some really bizarre things in them. He also wrote Mom, and, of course, she would pass on his greetings to the other kids. In this way, they never really had to know that he was mentally ill.

My junior year of high school was my best year, because the influence of Upward Bound was really starting to take hold. I participated in theater, speech team, drill team or color guard, tennis, powder puff football, and the student senate. I had been playing violin poorly in the orchestra since sixth grade. I started to dig deep and learned a piece to try at district competitions.

My efforts got me the Most Improved ribbon from the orchestra teacher, which was more embarrassing than anything. Still, I had to work hard for that ribbon. I also kept up my rigorous workout schedule. I tried to make myself the kind of all-star applicant who would receive scholarship offers from colleges.

I continued to participate in Young Leaders in Action, a community-funded program to train future—drumroll—leaders! I jockeyed between that and my training from the Iowa Girls' Leadership Camp. I got "student of the month" from the local Rotary Club and I had to give a short speech.

I looked around the club's grand ballroom, the site of the honors day luncheon. I had never been to a catered event before, and I felt anxious around all those people in nice suits. I sensed I didn't belong with these people, like they were better than me. Everybody there seemed fake, I wasn't so sure I wanted to raise my social class above where it was, and certainly didn't want to belong to theirs. I found engaging in chitchat with phony people loathsome.

I found anything they talked about *shallow*, and they would have found anything I said *depressing*. If I had been honest, that is. But I faked it.

Being part of the speech team at school was challenging, given that Ma didn't consider me one of her favorites. She seemed to like students in accordance with their popularity. She also appeared to like them for how much they kissed her ass, and I didn't have it in me to brownnose her. Therefore, she gave me the worst assignments for the speech team—extemporaneous speaking and book review. Other students got to do choral readings, dramatic readings, or oratory, which were all considered categories for professional speakers with potential talent as actors.

Extemporaneous speaking had me lugging around large boxes of *Newsweek* and *Time* magazines in hopes they would contain articles on a topic I would draw from a hat later at the competition. Sometimes, they would let us know what the potential thirty or more issues would be in advance. We used the magazines we brought to prepare our speeches in a very short amount of time. Most times, though, we had no idea about possible issues in advance. Once you pulled a topic, you had thirty, or sometimes sixty, minutes to write a five-to-ten- minute speech on the subject.

One time I drew the question, "Should teenagers be allowed to get abortions without their parents' consent?" It was a hot-button issue in the media. I combed through my magazines, found a couple of articles on the topic, and jotted down facts and opinions as quickly as possible. Next, I used the notes I made to formulate the outline for a short speech. The whole process made me so anxious I had to pee.

I really disliked Ma for making me do this category. But it was helping me to get better at thinking and speaking on my feet. It was also getting me more and more comfortable in front of groups. Two local organizations held speech contests. One of them was the Optimist Club.

Entering the Optimist Club contest turned out to be a bit of a mistake. I didn't realize that Ma's daughter had also entered the competition. I told Ma I was entering the contest, and I asked her if she could listen to my speech, but she turned me down, calling it a conflict of interest. When the day came, I was certain they were going to pick Ma's beloved daughter as the winner. She was the sort of girl who'd always gotten that kind of recognition. She tried out for community theater, and got a part. Her looks and popularity had me convinced I would be shooting for second place.

When they announced that I had won, I was stunned. It meant I was going to regionals to represent the Waterloo-Cedar Falls metro area. Ma took a long time to stop scowling at me each time I saw her after that.

I also participated in traditional school events like homecoming and prom during my junior year, which was really like a senior year because they were closing my high school. I had been crash-dieting, and it was wreaking havoc on my body. My standard lunch was a Diet Pepsi and a small snack bag of Planters cashews from a gas station across town from my high school that Dawn and I would go to at lunchtime every day. I reasoned I was getting my protein from the nuts. They also sold cigarettes to underage kids there, which was actually the original reason we would go there.

Now my body was starting to rebel. I had a mysterious stomach condition that woke me from my sleep screaming in pain. I thought I was dying. I cried the whole time Mama drove me to the hospital. I screamed at the hospital throughout the X-ray and the prodding and poking. Finally, the doctors decided to do an enema to help fix my system.

Another time I developed a serious case of thrush, which involves having your entire mouth full of something like canker sores. It's a fungus that is usually kept in check by a healthy immune system. If you've ever had one canker sore, you can imagine what it would be like to have thirty or so at once. I couldn't eat anything without severe pain. My body as reacting to the lack of food. It was showing signs of anorexia.

All my dieting and exercising may have been keeping my weight down, but it wasn't making me less clumsy or more athletic. When the Presidential Fitness Tests[128] came around again, I knew I wasn't going to pass most of the exercises, but I did want to run the mile within the timeframe they established as "passing." It would be the first and only time I ever managed to meet the minimum on one of those fitness tests, which I think just puts you in the top 50 percent of students, for whatever that's worth.

Underpinning all this unhealthy eating and physical activity was a bad body image. I believed my picture was next to the definition of ugly in the dictionary.[129]

Figure 6. Junior Prom

But I was most proud of my appearance at prom. Nobody needed to know my date, another Upward Bound teen, suffered from paralyzing social anxiety that made it excruciating to try to talk to him all night, whether on the bus ride from Waterloo to the Mississippi River or on the ferry boat ride and dinner cruise that followed.

This poor soul was capable of yes or no answers, so if I worked very hard, I could keep things going. But by this time in my eating-disordered mind, I was meeting societal body norms, and that was what made me happy. I had starved myself to the point where I had an hourglass figure. I was no longer shaped like an apple.

A postcard sent to Mom's family in November 1988 read:

"Samuel's 13 and acts like it, mouthy little brat sometimes. Very poor grades. Starts counseling Dec. 13 because of it. Real attitude problem. I'm back on antidepressants for 2 to 5 years. Worked overnight through the holidays. Got sick."

I was excited she was going to be taking medications steadily for the first time in her life.

Because of my good grades, Upward Bound rewarded me with the chance to take college prep English in the summer after my junior year of high school. This meant I would have six college credits for free, an especially nice gift in my situation.

Students in the class got to live in dorms separate from other Upward Bound students, with only a resident teaching assistant there to supervise our behavior. The course was extraordinarily challenging. The professor assigned each of us a different book to read, maybe to discourage cheating or working together too much.

I was assigned *Native Son* by Richard Wright.[130] I learned about how destructive ostensibly well-meaning white people could be when trying, often condescendingly, to help Black people. My dear friend Roxanne[131] wasn't so lucky and was lost in the unfamiliar language and dialect in *Dubliners* by James Joyce.[132]

I thought I was a solid writer, but this class alarmed me by showing me that I wasn't. I didn't even know how to use a semicolon, and I still don't like them. Were my high school teachers just giving me good grades because they liked me? Was my high school education inadequate? Yes, it was. I earned an A in college prep English by the end of the summer, but I had so much to learn that it was dizzying.

To celebrate completing the class, we students got our hands on some alcohol. I'd never liked beer because of its bitterness. Most of my liquor consumption was limited to sips of schnapps at the bus stop on freezing cold days. I'd certainly never been sick from drinking.

But they brought wine coolers, and they tasted so good. One wine cooler is not particularly intoxicating. Five of them, when one has no tolerance for alcohol, was a disaster. When the party ended, I went straight back to my dorm room and passed out. Sometime later, I threw up in my sleep.

My friends saw what had happened and immediately carried me into the girls' shower and turned on the water. It was dangerous that I had gotten sick on myself in the way I had. I worried the whole next day that I would stink of alcohol when I got near the Upward Bound staff. If they noticed, they gave me a break and didn't kick me out of the program for it.

Upward Bound's whole mission was to get poor, at-risk, and first-generation students to college. Phyllis took us to a few different schools for campus visits that would help us decide where we might like to go. We visited Iowa State, the University of Iowa, and Drake University. I became aware of an ROTC scholarship from the Navy. It would pay for my entire college education, but there was a hitch. I would have to major in mechanical engineering.

I was reasonably good at math but had done poorly in geometry. An engineering degree might be a stretch, I thought. When I had the same teacher for trigonometry my senior year that I had in tenth grade for geometry, he lowered his glasses down his nose, peeked over them to get a better look at me, and announced, "MacIntyre, I didn't expect to have you back here." We both laughed.

I went in front of the commanding officer at the University of Iowa's ROTC program for an interview. He was all business, with a military crispness to his questions during his brisk interactions with me. I didn't expect to get the scholarship, but a letter came in the mail a few weeks later announcing that I had indeed gotten the award. I would go to Drake University in Des Moines, with a full-ride scholarship—if I agreed to dedicate my life to mechanical engineering.

I thought about it for days. I didn't have much time before I had to let them know my decision. Finally, I decided that I couldn't dedicate myself to engineering for the rest of my life. It just didn't interest me that much—full-ride scholarship or not. (Missed opportunity alert: two recent favorites of mine on TV, as an aging adult, are *Impossible Engineering* and *Engineering Catastrophes*.)

After that I made no further movement toward prepping for college for some time. Phyllis implored me to tell her what was getting in the way of sending out applications, and I finally admitted I was scared to leave my brothers and my sister alone with Mom, who had been particularly symptomatic lately. The next week, Phyllis arrived at my school with an application to Luther College. She pushed it toward me and said, "Please fill this out." She then spent time helping me write the essay.

Within a week, she took the completed application back north with her. When I was accepted to the school, she sat me down and said, "Deborah, don't you worry about your little brothers and your sister. I will take care of making sure they are all right. You can never really help them if you don't escape this situation yourself." I cried and got one of her amazing hugs. Phyllis Gray saved my life. I'll probably say that again before the end of the book.

Waterloo closed my high school after my junior year, so I had to go to East High for my senior year. Going to East High came with a certain aura of toughness and attitude that other kids in town just expected. When someone asked you where you went to school, and you said, "East," their eyes would get big, and they might take a step back and make some comment like, "Aww, yeah, I know better than to mess with you then." David and I attended school together for the first time in a long time.

Except for his propensity to run late in the morning, which had gotten worse due to the sleepy stupor he always seemed be in after his head injury, I enjoyed driving David to school. We joked around with each other, until the day he played the ultimate joke on me. Just as we were getting out of the car in the school parking lot in the morning, he pushed my stick shift into neutral. He then quietly unlocked his door. We both walked into the school building laughing as usual. David's lunch hour was always one hour before mine, which was kind of a bummer for me because I would have enjoyed eating lunch with him. I was finally at an age when I appreciated having David in my life.

Instead, I hung around two girls I had met smoking. We'd get in my car and drive around with smokes at lunchtime, cranking Guns & Roses on the car's tape deck, sometimes stopping at a convenience store or a fast-food restaurant for something to eat.

On this day, though, when I got to the parking lot, my car was gone. I looked around in a panic. Who would steal my piece of junk, 1970s, brown, Toyota stick-shift? It turned out David had rolled it to another spot in the parking lot to put one over on me. The first time he got me with this trick, I was furious with him. Then, it became something he did on a regular basis, so I knew to hunt around for my car, and I'd just laugh about it.

Chapter Twenty-Five: With Help from My Friends

I N THE WORDS OF Booker T. Washington, *Success is to be measured not so much by the position one has reached in life as by the obstacles one has overcome while trying to succeed.*[133] And the process of overcoming requires a lot of assistance from friends.

One of my best friends from school, Dawn and I started working at Nino's Steakhouse when we were sixteen. Dawn first, and then she got me in the door. It wasn't easy to find a job that paid above minimum wage as a teenager in Waterloo. The unemployment rate was high in the area during the 1980s from the loss of a lot of industrial and agricultural jobs.

Dawn shifted her car into third gear, turned down the radio, and said, "I just need to make a quick stop at work. Want to come in with me?"

We each spent hours and hours at Nino's: fixing salads, cutting onions, peeling shrimp, and chopping lettuce. The staff at Nino's kept things interesting. In our job as prep cooks, we spent time with full-time workers who included ex-cons who'd become chefs, waitresses who had made serving a career, and lifelong bartenders who drank slowly too much of their own stock. Most of the staff had a story about wiping out on a motorcycle, drinking until they almost died, or an ex who was making their life hell.

I was every bit from that same kind of background. But for my whole life, the strong impression I made as some kind of nerd or religious freak had kept me slightly alienated from other poor people. Was it the words I used? They spilled over from the books I read. The chef took to calling me "Bookworm," and it stuck. After a couple of years, everyone at the restaurant knew that I wanted to go to college. They also knew that doing so was going to be a financial struggle.

On this particular day, Dawn and I were supposed to go see *Cocktail*, the movie with Tom Cruise. It wasn't unusual for Dawn to want to stop by work. I followed her in the door.

"We have to talk to Cheryl," she said. "Cheryl's counting tips in the party room." When they yelled "Surprise!" I initially worried that I had just walked in on someone else's surprise party. My coworkers had organized a party to help me afford some of the expenses that were still standing between me and college. They helped me out with my remaining tuition payment. They also helped me with the supplies needed to live on campus in another city, everything from a laundry basket to toothpaste. I couldn't have been more grateful.

In January 1989, I packed up all my belongings, and drove my 1971 Plymouth Valliant to Luther College in Decorah, a beautiful town in the northeast part of the Iowa, nestled among tree-covered bluffs. A river runs through the city near the quaint downtown. I had gone there in summer with Upward Bound for a few years, so it was familiar to me. To me, Luther represented freedom—from poverty, from pain, from welfare, from fundamentalist churches, and from being at the mercy of my damaged family.

Chapter Twenty-Six: Adjusting to College

I ARRIVED ON CAMPUS as a student from what "poverty experts" call the "underclass." It was supposed to be the second semester of my senior year of high school, but I had graduated early because I was so eager to get to college. Unfortunately, this meant that when I arrived on campus, there was no freshman orientation. In fact, no one was there. The campus was deserted for the short January term.

Fortunately, I had Phyllis. A product of the South Side of Chicago,[134] Phyllis had thrived in nearly all-white Decorah, in part because her sister was there too, and in part because the campus climate at Luther had been warmer and more welcoming to minority students once, in the 1960s and '70s, than was the case during my years there.[135] Phyllis was originally from Mississippi, so she had experience in the rural South that helped prepare her for rural Iowa. Phyllis got me to college and kept me in it. I was about to get a solid education, but I felt isolated from my family, worried about my mother's mental health, and anxious about how my brothers and sister were doing. Things had not been well at home.

David struggled in high school to the point of dropping out. Phyllis, who by then was a mentor to the whole family, invited David to rejoin Upward Bound so he could finish high school. He would be doing so with Samuel, who had also dropped out of school, but in the eighth grade. Since they would both be going to an alternative high school, they stood a better chance of finishing. John would enter Upward Bound as well.

Phyllis was keeping her promise to help me with the family, but there was still a risk my brothers would use drugs. I suppose, at one time, there was a risk that I could have taken that route myself, say, around the time in eighth grade I was riding around in the back seat with someone who offered me a line of cocaine. I'd made it to college, though, where I was assigned an essay authored by a man who said that poverty was not bad.

Senja began to send me a letter nearly every day, and I wanted to write her back just as often, but college was so time-consuming and demanding. One of her first letters arrived in March of that first semester. It began, "*I want you to come back home. I miss you. Everyone misses you. Do you want to come home yet?*"

Sometimes when I called home, Mom guilted me about being at college and not helping her. This tore at me. The thing I treasured most about escaping deep poverty was escaping the heavy co-parenting responsibilities heaped on me as a child. I was almost two hours away now and couldn't help her parent anymore.

I got a job at the campus café, where students and faculty hung out together. I also had a job off campus as a waitress at Country Kitchen. By this time, I was well on the way to rejecting my fundamentalist Christian background. My boss at Country Kitchen was reluctant to come out to me as gay. He was worried that I would reject him because of my religious background, but I told him I accepted him completely since I already liked him. We became fast friends. Despite my upbringing, I had just never picked up the anti-gay beliefs of the church. Ok, that's not quite true. I have a form from tenth grade on which I circled gay people as a group I would be uncomfortable with in public office. I still remember that. It was when I was regularly going to Mormon Bible study. By college, my attitude had changed. Maybe Mom prevented us from being exposed to the homophobia and other hate that fundamentalists spew. It wasn't her style to reject or discriminate against anyone, in large part because she felt so misunderstood and judged herself.

My Paideia class was focused on Russian history, literature, and current events. *Paideia* is a Greek word for "learning," and it was where I learned how to write while incorporating my education on larger topics. I wrote a paper on the ways psychiatry was used against political dissidents in the Soviet Union. It made me aware of how psychiatry had been used against women in our own culture, locking them up just to prevent their independence or to block them from power.

I never read anything written by Karl Marx, despite the focus of my Paideia, and having studied the collapse of communism in the Soviet Union around that time. The notion that college professors were turning students into Marxists always struck me as ridiculous. Not one of them ever tried. I can't tell you how many times I have been told by clueless people that I must have learned "that Marxism" in college.

My most challenging class was Biology, which played a role at Luther as a killer weed-out class for premed students. Unfortunately, no one had given me a heads-up about that beforehand. I never studied so hard for anything in my life. Because I had two jobs and other classes, though, I didn't study particularly well.

I took Biology because I wanted to be a Psychobiology major to study schizophrenia. I wanted to understand my dad. Another class that first semester was Introduction to Psychology. My advisor, Dr. David Bishop, would become one of my biggest supporters and cheerleaders in college.

I still appreciate the foundation in psychology that Dr. Bishop provided. The topic of personality was most relevant to me because I believed that my personality was formed in part by poverty, but not in the way that Charles Murray suggested. I thought poverty virtually guaranteed trauma, repeated trauma. And I knew that trauma could shape personality.

It was about this time that I received the assignment to read Murray's essay, "What's So Bad about Being Poor?" and respond to the professor's questions about it.[136] I didn't do the assignment the professor requested. Instead, I got off work late and pounded out an essay on the typewriter explaining to my professor exactly what was so bad about being poor. I told him about being too cold, too hot, too hungry, too dirty, too pained, too overworked, and too stigmatized. I told him about having to go to foster care, because my parents were too poor to take care of my siblings and me. I told him about the chaos in my family, having to be a parent since I was six years old, and the violence in my neighborhood growing up. I wrote about having been sexually abused by the son of my mother's polygamist husband when we were part of a fundamentalist Mormon cult, and how grooming had led to my repeated sexual vulnerability.[137]

Professor Lund didn't grade the assignment. He just gave me credit for it. Instead, he told me he didn't know what to say. He didn't realize Murray's essay would upset any student so much. I couldn't help but give him an "Are you an idiot?" glower. This was in 1989, long before trigger warnings, but I would have appreciated one. I was furious. I couldn't sleep for days. Imagine you've been through a war, and someone says, "Let's imagine it was a slice of paradise." It's hard to express the level of anger you would feel. I almost dropped out of college that night. If these evil people truly thought poverty was no big deal, I didn't want anything to do with them. I went into a state of depression over Murray's opinions, which were presented as "facts" both by Murray and my professor.

Thankfully, Phyllis talked me down and kept me in college. She told me there were many other experts on poverty that I would learn about, and she was right. They knew more about poverty, though rarely directly. Many of them (unlike Murray) had good ideas, but at the time, none mentioned fundamentalist religion or mental illness or repeated trauma as reasons why people slipped into poverty or had trouble getting out of it.

Most leading economists who publish academic papers are more liberal than Murray,[138] but I didn't know that as an undergraduate, when my professors were teaching me Milton Friedman and neoli beralism.[139] This was the end of Reagan's two terms, which were so catastrophic to anti-poverty efforts, and to the socioeconomic leveling that had been achieved after World War II. The ideological drift was definitely to the right.

The poverty experts that I first encountered at Luther, and at the University of Michigan where I went to graduate school, were more knowledgeable about poverty than I was when I started college, but only in a book sense. There might have been one or two who had actually experienced poverty, but most of them were decidedly upper- or upper middle-class. So, they had no idea about poverty in any real sense, and it showed. I still learned a great deal by reading their books. I understood better how my family's poverty fit into the bigger picture. I understood why it happened the way it did, and when it did. Still, these "experts" often made sweeping generalizations that were inaccurate, because they had never directly experienced what they were talking about. Murray was at least right about that, but it was the *only* thing he was right about.

Despite the specter of Charles Murray, my first semester of college went well. I got As, except for a B in killer Biology.

When summer arrived, I stayed on campus to take a class, work my jobs, and hopefully see my brothers, who would be there as part of the Upward Bound program. Phyllis hung up a piece of David's art on her wall that showed blocks falling. Phyllis told me its title was *Off Balance*. Mom worked for the Census Bureau that summer, as she did during many census summers. It was one of the few times she would get full-time work. She was good at it, and it gave her a sense of pride to participate in this massive civic project for America.

The class I took was Sleep and Dreams. I was very invested in it, because I never got much sleep and I never seemed to remember any dreams. As part of the class, I was allowed to hook Roxanne (who was also attending Luther from Upward Bound) up to machines and monitor her for a night of sleep. I have to tell you that it is agony to be a sleep researcher around 4:00 a.m. when you're watching someone sleep and all you want to do is fall asleep yourself.

Roxanne worked in the school cafeteria for her work study. She worked with a boy nicknamed Beagle, who was tall and lanky with piercing blue eyes. I fell for his eyes, sadly unable to see the danger behind them. This is no love story, even though my brain wanted to tell it that way for a long time. It is not romantic. It's manipulative. He stares into my eyes, I fall for them, and the whole narcissistic abuse cycle kicks in.

He took advantage of my feelings for him. By asking me the right questions, he figured out I believed in grand notions of romantic rescue and marriage, or something. I hate gender conditioning.

Beagle got me high on marijuana for the first time. He also roofied me, because I passed out. For years, I just assumed I passed out from the marijuana, but after talking to more and more marijuana users, and then becoming one myself, I realized that the notion that weed made me pass out was far-fetched. So again, I say he roofied me in the half a beer I drank.

From this one encounter, I became tangled up in an embarrassing, three-year, on-and-off affair with Beagle. The only thing I got out of it was a job where he worked, Mabe's Pizza Place. My income doubled and my social life improved. But I never received love, friendship, or even warmth. He used me. In fact, he even choked me one night when he was drunk.

Campus Greek culture is noxious, regardless of the campus or the era. By the 1990s at Luther, it took a noticeable turn for the worse. There was too much toxic masculinity in fraternities[140] and too much toxic femininity in sororities. Substance abuse was rampant and played a role in Beagle's taking advantage of me. One of my introductions to Luther College campus life was a story of a freshman woman who was suing the university for steering her away from reporting her gang rape by some fraternity members to the police. Beagle ended up hanging around the men who did it. Beagle was the first college-based distraction from my life plan. But Phyllis kept encouraging me to focus on my studies.

My new roommate the next fall was Roxanne, whom I'd been close to since Upward Bound. We even got a credit card together, which wasn't wise at all. It later became a bit of a problem, but that's what our level of trust was. We moved into a cockroach-infested apartment in the Winneshiek Hotel Apartments in downtown Decorah. Since then, the building has been completely renovated back into an elegant and expensive hotel. But in 1989, cockroaches scurried everywhere, including once into the face of my clock radio, where it died. Every day, when the alarm clock went off, we had to see its carcass staring back at us.

Roxanne and I had pledged to the coed service fraternity Alpha Phi Omega during the spring. We were eager participants who volunteered for as many service projects as we had time for, and Alpha Phi Omega soon began to take up almost all our free time. In the fall, Roxanne and I volunteered to co-chair the biggest volunteer event Alpha Phi Omega would have on campus that year, Cool-Aid. It was an all-day festival with several bands held on the lawn of the campus library. It was a fundraiser, so we had to design a T-shirt for sale. We may have come close to infringing on the copyright for Bart Simpson with our image, but it was for charity. The day of the festival was sunny with picture-perfect. For the most part, the day went off without a hitch. Students enjoyed themselves, and we were relieved to have such an enormous task behind us. Neither of us had counted on how much work it would be.

Life in Decorah was starting to take my attention away from my family in Waterloo, but I tried to focus on them whenever I could. As the semester passed, I bought Christmas presents and wrapped them for weeks. I was going to come home as Santa Claus with a trunk full of gifts for my brothers and sister. We were going to have a good Christmas. Finally. We'd never had a Christmas full of presents.

Life for the family had continued to be as challenging as ever, although there was some hope. In a letter to her sister Cleo that September, Mom wrote:

"Samuel had to have a rabies shot when a dog bit him on his paper route. They used to be worse. So expensive, though. One of the Census takers got bitten this summer, too. Have more energy on

Prozac—that's what helped our brother, Andy. Samuel is adamant he wants to quit school. Someone stole the tiny TV right out of my bedroom."

Mom was commenting on one of the first times she'd been on a prescribed medication for her depression. Would she take it?

Everyone seemed to enjoy Christmas for the first time in my memory. I was able to take earnings from my job and use my first credit card to get lots of gifts. We were going to have a better decade, right? Right? Not a chance. Despite my best efforts, things were going to get dramatically worse.

Chapter
Twenty-Seven:
Raisins and Peanuts

S INCE I ENROLLED IN college a semester early, my sophomore year awkwardly began in January 1990. I decided to add a Social Work major after talking to a student named Gretchen who worked with me at Oneota, the student café. She was a Social Work major, and she said social work professors focused on the poor. They cared about values. This seemed right up my alley. I went to talk to her advisors and immediately added the major. I was young.

I don't think Dr. Bishop appreciated my decision to drop Psychobiology and study just Psychology along with my Social Work major. My new co-advisor, Lee Zook, was a better fit in terms of values and background. He would serve as a strong support to me while I tried to navigate higher education as a person from poverty. He grew up Amish, so he understood strict religious communities. I'm not sure how much I ever told him about my background with fundamentalist Latter-day Saints. I tended to keep that history buried. But he told me about being Amish, and that gave me important perspective on my situation.

A social work major meant I had to have an internship in the social work field for a month during our January term, or "J-term." I picked an internship that allowed me to stay home in Waterloo after winter break and live with my family for the month.

It was good to be with them again. Everyone seemed happy to have me home, for a while at least. But I was busy with my internship. I was placed at an agency for people with serious mental illness, sort of like a drop-in center. Our clients were mostly diagnosed with schizophrenia. It turned out that some of the people were friends of my mom's. I found out after I left the program that one of the clients who was her friend jumped off a tall building in downtown Waterloo. We were both so saddened by his passing, but it wouldn't be the last time someone we cared about with schizophrenia was lost to suicide.

Tuition for a private college was not cheap, and I started to feel its weight. While I paid some tuition costs through work-study funds and other job earnings, I mostly relied on subsidized and unsubsidized loans.[141] This was the dawn of the student loan debt era. Moreover, my general ignorance of financial matters led me unthinkingly to build credit card debt, with the family Christmas celebration being a major source.

I was also becoming alienated from my peers. They were upper-class and didn't have to work. I was constantly having to wait on them at my jobs. I wanted to drop out of college to help Mom, who was calling regularly, making me feel guilty. I was getting letters from Senja saying she missed me. It was overwhelming.

Phyllis met with me and told me a story about raisins and peanuts and how they go great together even though they aren't alike. I was a raisin in a peanut world at school, and I was going to have to get along with the peanuts, but I could excel because raisins have value, even to peanuts. The metaphor doesn't sound as impressive as I write it now, but it worked, and I agreed not to quit college. It must have been her caring delivery that made the difference.

Samuel was not doing well. Around that time, Mom sent a postcard to Cleo:

"It looks like I'll be teaching Samuel at home. Refuses school. How are you doing on Prozac? How long were you on it? That's 4 out of 6 of us. Sure must be hereditary, huh?"

Mom was still trying to sort out her treatment, and what medications to use. It would have been nice if her siblings had been a consistent source of good medical information, but they weren't. Most of them were similarly struggling to figure themselves out and having trouble accepting the truth of their own mental health problems. They grew up with the same more-or-less crazy father, in a family which nonetheless strongly stigmatized mental illness. And Mom had long been identified as the "crazy one," in supposed contrast with them. None of them suffered as significantly as Mom did, and that fact made it easier for them to think their situation was completely different from hers. They were inconsistent at best in their supportiveness toward Mom.

The issues with Samuel and school were long-standing and ongoing. It's a shame there weren't apprenticeships anymore, because Samuel might have been responsive to a system of that kind. Mom wrote her sister again: *"Went to Toughlove last night. They're going to go to court with me on Friday. They talk of in-home detention."*

ToughLove was a misguided, damaging intervention[142] that Mom tried with most of my brothers. It was practically a parenting fad at the time. It was good that Mom had other parents for support and didn't feel alone. While some of the ideas of ToughLove weren't bad, as a whole it was precisely the wrong approach for my brothers, and she delivered it in a consistently inartful way. The strategy involved getting too harsh with sensitive and vulnerable kids. My brothers hated it. If anything, it led them to rebel further.[143]

Waterloo is a small city surrounded by a hundred miles of farmland in every direction, peppered with only small towns. It is an oasis of sorts where rural folks can go to a shopping mall and ethnic restaurants. Charles Murray is from Newton, Iowa, about ninety miles southwest of where I grew up. Folks there were probably afraid of Waterloo.

The Cedar River divides Waterloo, not only geographically but also into the economic haves and have-nots. Samuel entered adolescence on the wrong side of the river. At twelve, he was consumed by the need to get a head start on adulthood and move to the other side. He probably questioned whether there would be a place for him, a way out of welfare. Samuel took a job at the Gold Card Club, a golf course for people from the west side, the better side, of the river.

Without a father at home, Samuel sought out someone to show him how to be an adult man. Samuel chose the owner of the Gold Card Club to be that role model. This man seemed to have lots of money and what resembled wisdom about the world of Waterloo. He told Samuel, of course, that a boy needed to work hard to succeed, and in fact that it was the *only* thing a boy needed to do. When Mom wouldn't allow him to work instead of going to school, Samuel stole a van and took it on a high-speed chase across state lines into Nebraska, where he crashed. He didn't know how to drive yet.

Mom sent another postcard to Cleo in May of 1990:

"Did you hear about Samuel running off twice? Stole van, in accident after high-speed chase with police in N. Platte, Nebraska. Then hopped off the plane at unscheduled stop in Lincoln. Caught hitchhiking on I-80 Westbound. Both boys were in detention center here. Now, Samuel's in Stillpoint Adolescent Psychiatric—evaluation program at St. Francis psych ward (the same place where I was). Samuel has upside down cross etched into his ankle by rubbing pencil eraser on it until it burns. Permanent. Also has inverted 3-prong pitchfork on his forearm . . . It's the symbol of the BGD. The Black Gangster Disciples gang. To invert it shows contempt. Just what you need when you run into a gang member, huh? David has two assault charges on him out at the detention center. One more and he automatically goes to Eldora. Both times were fights with kids out there. John's teacher called and recommended a Big Brother. On waiting list. Isaiah's teacher called and was not to report progress either. Had a migraine Monday. I'm going to ToughLove."

There were so many things going on with my family at this point. My brother had engaged in a runaway attempt that involved grand theft auto and a high-speed police chase. Samuel was also making it part of his identity to act out against the Black people in our neighborhood. This was coming out of my brothers' encounters with the juvenile justice system. Samuel had been a fan of rap and hip hop for months, so I thought he'd be different. He was meeting the worst people in jail, of course, regardless of their race, but the experience led him to be a racist, as he tried to protect David and protect himself in there.

Fortunately, Samuel was going to benefit from restorative justice, a progressive form of intervention[144] that included an opportunity for alternative sentencing almost never offered to Black offenders at the time. He never acknowledged the immense break this gave him compared with how a Black offender was routinely treated for similar charges.

I was studying German as a minor, and my professors were planting the idea in my head that I could go to study in Germany in my junior year. It was a preposterous notion to me. Where would I get the money? But it was Germany. And they were making it seem like I could borrow the funds. I had wanted to go there so badly since high school. I investigated the possibilities and went to talk to Phyllis.

She got back to me a short time later. The dean would help pay for my trip to Germany. I could go. I had to earn the rest through waitressing at Mabe's. No problem. I knew how to get good tips with a bright smile and good service.

Starting in 1989, and throughout the four years of my college education, I worked at Mabe's, and every Wednesday night, the Winneshiek County Republicans would come in to strategize winning political campaigns from the local to the national level. I checked around to see where the county Democrats met each week. I was told they only met right before elections. I knew that Republicans were going to own Iowa in no time. If you could get Winneshiek County to turn Republican, then you were taking down the pillars of liberal thought in the Midwest.[145]

I was now far enough out of high school that I could begin working for Upward Bound. I was hired as a tutor during the school year, when students were assisted at their schools, and a residential counselor during the summer, when they came to campus for two months of instruction. I had a group of girls in the dorm I supervised; I cherished my position.

I put hours and hours into photoshopping the girls' images in my "cluster" onto feminist role models. I wanted to avoid the classic Disney princess themes that had been present during my high school summers at Luther College. I instinctively knew encouraging love addiction[146] was unhealthy. I wanted to be a good influence. Then, when the girls came, I sat with them through suicide watches and eating disorders and trauma. I hope they learned things too.

Upward Bound was always measured for academic outcomes; sometimes it did well and sometimes it didn't. But that wasn't all Upward Bound was doing. It was treating trauma—poverty-related trauma—and trying to educate teens at the same time. I don't know how many times Phyllis talked about the "poverty brain," but she was an expert on it, lectured on it. Unfortunately, I never saw the concept make its way into academia the way it could have. I would later see an article which described children in poverty having brains that looked similar to those of stroke victims.[147] Okay, that's close. But was anyone really taking those findings to heart?

My Social Work classes were opening my eyes. Increasingly, I wanted to go to graduate school. When I first read the books of Sheldon Danziger, I thought he was a hero. He introduced me to the concept of structural poverty. He helped me understand that my parents didn't just lose everything because of their mental illnesses. My dad couldn't get a job because jobs had disappeared. And my parents couldn't get help, because help had disappeared. Dr. Danziger wrote in *Confronting Poverty:*[148]

"By the late 1970s, . . . a pessimistic view had emerged. It held that government was incapable of dealing with the major issues confronting U.S. society. Although a decade earlier government could do 'almost anything,' now it could do 'almost nothing.' Proponents of this view argued that social welfare programs had grown too large

and had become a drag on economic growth, that work incentives had eroded for both the poor and the rich, and that the incentive to work had been weakened ... [and that] 'these programs should therefore be scaled back or eliminated' (Murray, 1984)."

Charles Murray had not only been responsible for telling Americans that poverty wasn't that bad, but he was also one of the "experts" selling people on the idea that social programs were too large and were eroding incentives. He was part of the reason my parents were struggling so badly in their attempts to leave poverty in the 1980s. This man was deliberately worsening the lives of poor people with his policy recommendations, and then writing papers asking shit questions like, "What's so bad about being poor?"

I thought about how my classmates in fifth grade had caught me picking food from the garbage to eat, and then later how they talked about me behind my back because my foster brother told everyone in our small town that I was in foster care. I wanted to be a voice speaking out against Charles Murray's lies about poverty and helping Sheldon Danziger talk about poverty in an accurate way. But it still seemed like a pipe dream.

By this time, David and Samuel were starting to date. Unfortunately, they were dating the same girls, and the resulting jealousy was predictable. They were both experimenting with drugs, and both were in Upward Bound. Phyllis had ensured that John would be in Upward Bound too. But Phyllis could only do so much.

Over the summer of my sophomore year, in 1990, Adam suddenly reappeared in my life. He was the boy from Upward Bound who had shown some romantic interest in me back then. While on leave from the Navy, he visited Luther College on his motorcycle and indicated he was interested in spending time together. I arranged to go to his aircraft carrier's decommissioning ceremony in Virginia.

We then left Virginia Beach to travel toward Nashville, Tennessee, to visit his parents. He talked to me like we were a serious couple. It's silly, but during one of our motorcycle rides in Nashville, Adam scrawled our initials into the drying concrete of an overpass under construction. I took that seriously, as if it meant we were permanently together. It was immature of me. I still lived in a world of Disney fairy tales.

On June 3, 1990, Dad wrote:

"I hear by the grapevine you plan to get married one of these fine days. Well, good. Let me know ... One bright spot: I got a 4-volume set on artificial intelligence and found out that I had worked out the rudiments much on my own. The expression $\Delta o23/\partial K$, $S_{12}C_{10}$ is like what $E=mc^2$ is to physics and math. So that was quite a surprise. In some instances, I am ahead of the state of the art."

Oh, Dad. His equation was not the equivalent of $E=mc^2$ or anything else. I'd tried to follow his thinking long enough to know that his equations didn't solve any long-standing problems in science, no matter how convoluted he made them look.

But Adam *was* acting like my serious boyfriend. For a short while. We met in Florida next, but he couldn't sustain the act, and broke up with me outside a bar in Clearwater without really giving me a reason. He just let me guess that it wasn't working out.

I went home in autumn of 1990 bracing for loneliness, overwhelming homework, guilt from Mom about helping with my siblings, and more feelings of wanting to drop out of college. I felt suicidal.

The letters weren't helping. Mom wrote in July:

"Got another child abuse 'deal.' Long story. Won't bore you. David's coming back by here in August. I don't think he likes the group home. He has a second job at KFC. Guess not much else you'd be interested in. **Can't shake the feeling that you're ashamed**

of your family. I analyzed why I was so depressed before and after and while you were here. I was surprised to learn I had a great deal of resentment towards you [emphasis in original], *and by not cleaning house, it was my subconscious way of getting back at you. Not on a conscious level, mind you, but the truth is that was a real feeling and it's best to deal with reality?"*

Mom sent me messages like this regularly, that, as intended, produced guilt and made me feel I should drop out to help her with the kids. She always found ways to blame her depression on me, some of them quite creative. This time I was ashamed of my family, so that's why she was depressed. I wasn't ashamed of my family. I was frustrated with our poverty. I had to work *so* much because of our poverty. I was frustrated about *why* we were still poor.

It was about then I watched Pink Floyd's *The Wall* for the first time. It is an excellent movie, but one which at the time only seemed to further encourage or reinforce my feelings of alienation. Feeling more suicidal than usual, I went to the college counseling center. I was told I would be limited to eight to twelve sessions with the social worker.

It seemed like not enough to handle my problems, but it was better than nothing. I felt like dying, and furthermore, though I'd yet to be diagnosed with them, I had complex post-traumatic stress disorder, bipolar disorder II, binge eating disorder, and who knows what else? I had more issues than a college counselor could handle in eight to twelve sessions.

The counselor I had referred me to the local Adult Children of Alcoholics[149] (ACA) weekly meeting for free and reliable support. I found out that by sending me there, he had to stop attending himself. I understand now that he sacrificed that for me. It was deeply appreciated and necessary.

I attended the Decorah ACA[150] steadily for two years, except for when I was in Germany. I needed the group's love and support. Even though I really can't stand twelve-step models, I took what I could use and left the rest, just like they say, and it was good. The people who attended were golden, and I appreciated the weekly meeting so much. They helped me heal for a period of time from the pain in my heart. They helped me graduate from college. For the rest of my time there, my weekly meetings with ACA were as crucial as my education.

Around this time, I also read *Healing the Child Within: Discovery and Recovery for Adult Children of Dysfunctional Families* by Charles Whitfield.[151] From this, I was introduced to the idea that I could have post-traumatic stress disorder from traumas I had experienced growing up. But I couldn't afford to treat it professionally. I was lucky the self-help option was available. I tried to extend the same magic to the Overeater's Anonymous group, but like I said, I can't stand twelve-step programs, and this group put a lot of stress on Step One, which deals with God or a Higher Power. I made it through Step Five before I had to quit.

Actually, it wasn't the Higher Power and God stuff that did me in. It was Step Four: Make a fearless and searching moral inventory of yourself. My sponsor was completely incompetent, making me embarrassed about my relationship with my parents. Worse than that, she made me feel shameful about the abusive sexual relationships and rapes I had experienced as a confused young teen. That was enough to ruin the entire recovery process for my eating disorder. And there was much that I needed, and would need, to recover from on that front.

Chapter Twenty-Eight: Family Troubles

D AD WROTE ME ON August 28, 1990:

"*I profoundly apologize for not being in Decorah on Father's Day. It would take a dozen letters to explain 'why' I have not been in touch . . . I've made a lot of progress on development of an idea that has taken over 26 years to get established. There was very little to draw on. No library books or texts. So I had to pioneer in the raw, which has held me back. But a breakthrough has occurred! Some of the simplest inventions took a great deal of work to get to a workable, refined state they are today. So, if you feel ashamed of the family, well, we're under development right now. No one can take away the experiences we have individually and collectively . . . I've made a discovery, too. A Big One. If you're interested, I'll discuss later. I'd like to build a niche business, ideally, on all this . . . But I've discovered, I've invented, I've conquered.*"

I felt let down and disappointed by Dad not coming to visit me as he had promised. He had missed high school graduation. Now, he had missed this Father's Day visit, and I found his "reason" annoying, though I was used to his personality by now. I would rather have seen him than listened to his delusions.

The next month, Mom wrote:

"*Samuel's being a jerk. Has a real attitude. Goes to court on Monday and to be honest, I want him to go elsewhere . . . He won't help with housework [so] . . . when the house went to crap while I was working on my resume, and he wouldn't let John go over to Lurch's with him . . . I couldn't go to my women's retreat. I let down the other group members, and the people who paid for me to go, and offered to babysit . . .*

"*Samuel seems to crave disruption and chaos. Like a sick, twisted mind that smiles at his victims. He really could be a cold-blooded killer or master criminal. I don't want him around. He's like Ruth in a way. She was great when she was okay, but when she got psychotic, you didn't want to be around her. He said, 'Forget it!' When I asked for his cooperation to get ToughLove into schools. A real jerk!! David even seems mild now [in comparison]. Your dad always figured there would be more trouble with Samuel than David.*"

Ruth was Mom's friend with schizophrenia who ended up killing herself.[152] I felt terrible that Mom had to handle my brothers by herself, while also trying to get a job. Samuel was acting horribly, but I understood why he resented the ToughLove program and refused to help her with it. Mom rightly characterized Samuel's behavior as pathological, but clearly implied he was a psychopath. That idea came from ToughLove.[153]

While Samuel was assuredly being a punk, he was a teenager, so his rebellion also seemed developmental. Either way, it was being handled poorly. This was all after running away and stealing a van. He would end up staying out of major criminal trouble. He was trying to cover the scars he had from growing up poor as he put together a first draft of his identity, and the result was his angry, rebellious behavior. He was extremely lucky to get into a program with a philosophy of rehabilitation in an era when long sentences and condemnation were much more in fashion.

Unsurprisingly, Samuel didn't and doesn't appreciate the privileges he experienced in the criminal justice system. If he had been Black and committed the same crimes, he would have been in juvenile prison until he was eighteen. Instead, he was released early and was able to continue trying to escape the facts of his childhood in poverty. Sadly, he still has a long way to go.

The next month, Mom wrote again: "*Still working for Paul.*" He had a pickup truck accessory business just as pickup trucks were about to explode in popularity. Mom did all kinds of bookkeeping work for him sporadically for many years.

Uncle Paul spent years arguing politics with Mom, and starting when I was about fourteen, she would put me on the phone to argue with him on her behalf. It was through these arguments that I came to understand that my uncle was cruel to poor people, and a racist. He voted for the cuts to welfare that contributed substantially to Mom and Dad losing custody of us to foster care. Of course, I knew they had voted the same way, but for a completely different set of reasons than Paul did. Sad reasons, in Mom and Dad's case. These were the very politicians who literally made their life together all but impossible.

Given that Uncle Paul had once been on food stamps himself, I saw him as the self-serving hypocrite that he was on the subject. His attitude toward people on welfare, people like his sister, mind you, was that they were lazy parasites . . . and overwhelmingly Black. I tried to explain the *reality* of welfare and the people on it—you know, people like his *own sister*—and how his views had directly hurt us, but he was uneducable on the subject. Racism is a powerful force. He took his political orders pretty much directly from the Mormon Church.

He was also under the heavy influence of the burgeoning right-wing media ecosystem of the time, a pox that has shaped conservative reality and conservative talking points for more than forty years. The effect has been enormous. How many liberals have politically noxious relatives who were once reasonable people, until they turned on Rush Limbaugh for their commute home, or ran across Fox as they flipped through their cable channels?[154]

Suddenly, Grandpa Meyer was using terms like "feminazi" in his letters to me, which arrived frequently. Since letters had always been his primary means of contact with me, I can line them up in chronological order to see my conservative but hitherto evenhanded, grandfather go from a supportive man with empathy for the less fortunate, animal or human, to one who began to constantly degrade poor people, even his own family, who had the misfortune to need government assistance. It was hurtful, and I told him so. He relented for a bit but forgot his emotional impact, and then started in again with another Limbaugh-inspired rant:

"Rush L. is not the ogre you visualize him to be. He just happens to be opposed to the few real feminazis out there who wish to speak for all women. The true feminazis hate him and this is what has to be understood."

Dishearteningly, Grandpa became a lesser person, a meaner person, and his hours of listening to Limbaugh were directly to blame. At least Grandpa softened his tone when I reminded him that his daughter and his granddaughter were *female* and might deserve a place in the world outside the kitchen or the bedroom. But he was enraged and bitter about "those" people, and "those" people were irresponsible women and pretty much everyone not employed by a defense contractor (the one group who deserved to benefit from the taxes he paid). My other relatives didn't treat us much better.

Grandpa cast his vote for the Republican candidate every time he could. Then he went to the Salvation Army for lunch, just as he did every day. Social Security was his only income, and it didn't pay him enough to live on. He never acknowledged the contradiction between his voting preferences and the reality of his life.[155]

Eventually, Grandpa Meyer decided to try to humiliate me. During my sophomore year, he invited me down from Luther to give a speech at his Lions Club about "what college kids were being taught nowadays." He was sure I was going to arrive full of liberal claptrap and that his fellow Lions would tear me apart.

Instead, I arrived and gave a speech about Charles Murray and his essay, "What's So Bad about Being Poor?" It was truly a piece of conservative nonsense, and as a poor person, I was going to tell the Lions Club all about why that was so. I shut them all down in stunned silence for a moment, leading Grandpa to laugh and say, "I guess I prepared you for a liberal." They didn't know how to respond to my case against bad conservative arguments. Grandpa didn't expect to be proud of me, but the Lions Club members liked me.

Contrary to Grandpa's conspiratorial assumptions, I was in fact being taught conservative social welfare policy in my economics and political science classes. What I learned didn't explain my parents' poverty whatsoever. I didn't see any theorists talking about religious fundamentalism spawning overly large families that needed welfare to support them. They only talked about Black and Brown families and their alleged social pathologies. That's it. I wanted to scream at the racism demonstrated by my professors.

But some of my professors did mention macro-economic conditions, such as the ways the job market had changed. They also offered theories about lower wages over time. They were teaching me about structural causes of poverty.

Chapter Twenty-Nine: The Dream of Germany

M Y DREAM OF STUDYING in Germany soon came true. In January 1991, we left for Muenster, Germany. There were thirteen of us, led by Professor Liermann, who had grown up in Nazi-era Germany. But, in my mind, I was there with my friend Deborah MacGregor[156], who I knew from working at the café. We were required to take three classes during our semester abroad: Paideia II, which was on the Rise of Nazism; our Religion requirement, which was the History of Protestantism; and, German, of course.

Both of the history classes broadened my horizons significantly. It was news to me how much division there had been within Christianity over fundamental tenants of the faith. Mom and Dad had tested the water of many of the faiths that we surveyed, especially the modern Protestant sects. I was relieved that the Waldensians were not around much anymore, because they really took that vow of poverty seriously. Mom would have wanted to join them.

However, the class in Germany that had the most impact on me was Professor Liermann's Rise of Nazism. He began with the history of antisemitism within Christianity. Among the first things early Christians had to address was how their new faith, born of Judaism and centered around the claimed resurrection of a Jewish man, was different from Judaism. They spoke of a blood atonement, or a debt owed by the Jewish people for Christ's death.[157] Blood atonement was something my parents' strange cult had talked about, and it never disappeared from Christian thought. Instead, it sat and festered, ready to be cited by the next narcissist looking for a scapegoat. Someone like Hitler.

Charging any interest whatsoever on loans was called usury, and only Jews did it, because Christians considered it a sin. Christians also considered Jews sinners for handling money. Therefore, since they were persecuted, Jews were only allowed to work in banking professions Christians wouldn't touch. This can be connected to the parts of the Bible condemning money changers.

Our class took a brief but deep dive into the psychology of the guy with a bad moustache.[158] He was angry at the very people who were patrons of his art. I learned how mentally unstable the guy really was. Hitler had an experience during World War I in which he escaped death, and he is said to have believed he was divinely inspired from that point forward. He was said to believe he had a special mission. But he was not a well man. He had no regard for others and a deep desire to create scapegoats. In the wake of World War I, Germany craved scapegoats.

Professor Liermann had grown up praying for Hitler in his nightly prayers. He had gone to youth activities organized by the Nazis, even though his parents were part of the resistance movement. He explained how scared his parents were to be caught as resistors; they had him participate in all the pro-Hitler activities to hide their resistance work. He talked about how American GIs liberated his city; they gave him bubble gum, so he liked them.

The Nazis loved to be sickeningly methodical. He spoke about how enthusiastically SS men signed up for their jobs. *There were no Nazis forced to do what they did. He told us this again and again.*

The next thing Herr Liermann did when we were in Germany was have us listen to Hitler's speeches, which had been played incessantly in venues ranging from barrooms to stadiums. Hitler started small and got bigger. His crowds responded uproariously to his barking tirades. Professor Liermann would point at the screen, almost apoplectic, and say, "See, see, what a bad speaker he is, yet they cheer madly!" He'd remind us time and again, "He was a lousy speaker! He didn't even speak German well, as an Austrian man with a dialect. But mainly, he was prone to ranting and self-aggrandizement!" At the time, I had shrugged and figured Herr Lierrmann was exaggerating. Hitler's speeches must have been decent enough to draw such crowds, right?

Then, in 2015, Donald Trump happened, and I saw how naïve I'd been. I recognized the ranting, self-aggrandizing style in his speeches. Like you can't understand how this guy is popular. He's a rodeo clown. He's vomiting racist tropes. He plays the ultimate victim. And for a large segment of the population, that's exactly why he's popular.[159]

Herr Liermann wanted those of us in the classroom to understand on a visceral level how jaw-dropping it was that a ranting, raving sociopath was so popular with crowds, but I don't think we students ever demonstrated the full understanding he desired. If Herr Liermann were still alive, I'd tell him I get it now. I completely get it. Donald Trump made me understand.

Professor Liermann described how Hitler stood in bars and beer halls, and just created rallies of people who were angered by and riled up about Jewish people. Next, his rallies started to get violent. The violence spread out from there into street violence in which hate crimes occurred constantly.

Everybody thought this was a phase in the 1920s. Most Germans expected the hate crimes to go away when the economy improved. Looking over Hitler's speeches, Herr Liermann described how he formed a political party, but it wasn't that popular. In fact, most people don't realize the Nazi Party never received a majority of German votes. Ever. They were just a minority political party that knew socialism was very popular at the time, so they cynically pasted the label "Socialist" in their title, then they wrote antisemitic, white supremacist legislation that had nothing to do with socialism. In fact, Hitler eventually tried to kill most of the communists and socialists in his country.

Hitler spoke to ordinary, uneducated citizens. And not that many of them, overall. Less than 40% of Germans *ever* voted for a Nazi. The rest of the population was either determined to call themselves apolitical or was part of an ineffective resistance.

Hitler used a state of emergency to seize power from a democracy. It was a democracy with a constitution that had flaws in it, not unlike ours. Working within the system to defeat him failed. Working with violence outside the system didn't penetrate his defenses. Economic inflation among the masses seemed to be the spark that lit the fire in the 1930s.[160]

While in Germany, I lived with the Lohmann family, who had graciously opened their home to students for years. Mr. Lohmann was a police commissioner, and his wife was a psychiatric nurse. Since the Berlin Wall had only fallen a year or so earlier, Herr Lohmann was asked to go to East Germany regularly to help retrain the East German police. He said it was a challenging job. Changing a culture always is.

I went out on the weekends to an Irish pub with Deborah. There was an Irish folk band called Franey's Well that played there almost every weekend; they were terrifically popular and for good reason. The whole pub would dance on tables and sing along to the music.

It was spring break time. We had an entire month off, so we all planned to travel during March of 1991. As college students with a lot of free time, many of us had purchased a Eurorail pass to tour Europe. Four of us women took off together, traveling first to Austria. As a bunch of Mozart lovers, we headed to Salzburg.

Next, we traveled south through Italy to make our way toward the ferry to Greece. Once we arrived in Greece, we were dismayed to discover that the trains only sometimes ran when they said they did. They also warned us we would have to find a place to spend the night, because no train to Athens was expected for the rest of the day. At first, we were so tired and upset. But the Greek hostel owners gave us *ouzo* to drink. Even though I hate black licorice, I drank it; we all got a little drunk and a lot happier.

The next day we made it to Athens. It was so crowded, so polluted, and so amazing. It was Athens after all. It was my first time in an ancient city, let alone a city that wasn't really in the most advanced part of the world anymore. There were animals hanging outside with blood dripping from them, flies drawn to their carcasses. It all looked so unsanitary, and I felt blessed for our health standards. Thank you, government regulation.

Just as we arrived at Hotel Rio and got settled in, there was a loud explosion. We asked the front desk man, George, if he knew what happened. He said a terrorist attack had occurred just down the block. The Turkish ambassador was visiting, and the bombing we'd heard was an assassination attempt. It had to do with Greece's relationship with Turkey and the fight they had over Cyprus. He explained the whole story to us. We didn't even recognize what kind of danger we could be in there.

But we saw so much. The markets were dazzling with color. Then, we made it up to the top of the Acropolis and we saw the ancient grounds. That was mesmerizing. I could not believe where I was standing. Democracy had its infancy here. It was like getting to meet your hero, but without the disappointment.

I had been collecting souvenirs all along the trip, little items for the kids at home: pieces of the Berlin Wall (which were authentic, since I got them from the Berlin Wall myself), Russian soldiers' pins for Dad, and other collectibles.

Our next stop after Athens was Rome. We had been warned about the children who try to mug you at the train station when you arrive in Rome. All the Germans tell you about them. And they did almost get us, but we snatched the children's hands from our purses and scolded them.

We had *not* been warned about the muggers on the bus to the Vatican that two of the four of us would encounter. Let me start by telling you that these buses are fantastically crowded; everyone is squeezed together. The muggers would work in pairs. One of them was a man with an erect penis who would grab your hand and try to make you touch it. While you were busy trying to wrestle your hand away, and of course, distracted by that serious task, his partner would reach up under your coat where your purse was hidden and then either cut it or snatch your wallet.

They got two of us using this exact method. One of them was me. We had gotten separated from one another on the bus. I discovered the mugging right away and reported it to my friends. We then all had to go to the Italian police station.

Once we arrived, the Italian police scolded us as American women for not screaming. They said that American women were vulnerable to this kind of attack because we always tried to fight off the attacker on our own rather than crying out for a rescuer. I had never screamed during an assault but thought maybe their focus should be on addressing a crime problem, if they apparently knew about it.

My souvenirs had been stolen. My credit cards were missing. My cash was gone. But the traveler's checks were replaceable, thank goodness. We also called our credit card companies, who promised to have cards available to us by the next day. Our trip was not ruined. But the souvenirs I had so meticulously collected for my family were gone.

We made our way back to the Vatican, where Deborah jumped on my back to take a picture of the Pope, who walked right by us only a foot away. Unfortunately, the picture didn't turn out.

We traveled to Paris next. The people were, just as everyone said they would be, impatient with us. But we were dumb tourists asking annoying questions and so were exactly what Parisians hate. We saw the major sites, and I was sufficiently awed. My favorite was the Sacré-Cœur Basilica. The white walls shone in the sun and looked so stunning. We snuck down to Versailles to see that historic landmark as well. Then, exhausted and filthy from sleeping mostly on trains to save money, our dirty troop headed back to Muenster, Germany.

We were back to learning about the rise of Nazism. Now, we'd moved onto the 1930s. Professor Liermann described propaganda and how it works.

We read a book called *Damals war es Friedrich* (*This Time It Was Frederick*).[161] It was powerful to read in German about the Kristallnacht, when Germans terrorized Jews, breaking the windows of their businesses and looting them. The Nazis had seized power through claiming there was a terrorist attack that justified martial law. This wasn't so, but Hitler used the mechanism to suspend democracy. The German Constitution was weak and allowed for this type of maneuver. Professor Liermann warned that the US Constitution showed alarming weaknesses as well. I shivered but didn't know how right he was. Trump and the January 6, 2021, insurrection in the United States were still far in the future, but they exposed many of these weaknesses.[162]

My brother Samuel wrote me a letter in April 1991. He was going to be in Upward Bound that summer, and the city trip was to Washington, DC. He said, "*Waterloo was in the national news for some economic thing. Guess it's all negative, but I didn't see it. The mayor is really upset.*"

Looking back, I thought for certain this had been when Charles Murray published, "The Coming White Underclass,"[163] because Waterloo had been identified as a city with a big white underclass problem. But that article didn't come out until 1993, and *The Bell Curve*[164] didn't come out until 1994. My poor hometown, always drawing bad headlines.

After I was back from Germany, Dad sent me a letter, warning me, "*Be careful! I read about the Red Brigade and the Stasi of the Eastern sector.*" Germany had been unified six months earlier. I had traveled through the former East Germany to get to Berlin, and I had seen East Berlin, but I was now safely back in the west. My host father was one of the people retraining the Stasi.

Dad wrote:

"We are sorry to hear about your misadventures in Roma. I felt something even before you went over. At least you're safe, I hope. I'm glad you visited Dachau. Back in high school, I met an Army officer who was at the liberation of this place. To hear his story was an experience—it affected him thoroughly. I'm glad you're getting your life values and perspective molded by their reality and not on the word of others. It will be more meaningful in the long run. And you can see why I am very opposed to militarism—of its ideology and dangers of power unrestrained by moral circumspection. It shocks me to have learned about Roman history, it's stormy times from Caesar down to now and realize my daughter got robbed there!"

Dad's sense of doom before my trip was no indicator that anything would happen. He had that anxiety regardless. It was genetic to the family. But I had the same sense of history my father had. I had done a paper in high school for Upward Bound on Roman law. It took me all summer to research. I developed a certain awe for their civilization. But I also had this rather nasty experience to remember there. Such is life.

Overall, I learned a great deal about authoritarianism and right-wing movements thanks to Professor Liermann. I ended up wanting to study the topic independently, so I focused my senior paper on it.

Chapter Thirty: My Mentally Ill Family

A RISTOTLE IS MISQUOTED AS having said, *"There was never a genius without a tincture of madness."* My editor thought Aristotle or whoever said this was romanticizing mental illness, but I don't think so. I think it may have been appreciating that one place to look for genius is among those who have mental illness.

At the end of the spring semester of 1991, Roxanne decided to leave Luther College and move to Charlotte, North Carolina, to be closer to her sister and her nephew. I was upset that she was leaving, so I decided to follow her there for the summer. I moved in with Roxanne and her sister's family, including Brandy, Roxanne's miniature, long-haired dachshund. I worked at Burger King and Olive Garden. My sole purpose was to make lots of money in order to buy a quality used car.

Mom wrote almost as soon as I got there. She was in love with a man named Larry. He was a hillbilly. He was kind and gentle. He was a family man. He wrote so well. He believed in communication. He loved her jokes. Okay, this all sounded good—but with my mom I knew there was a hitch.

In July, Mom sent a list of nineteen things to do to keep busy if I was dealing with boredom. On her list she included writing to her new love, Larry. The enclosed address made it clear he was in prison.

His sentence must have been too long, or someone better must have come along, because Larry didn't last long enough for me to worry about writing a letter to him.

In the same letter, Mom expressed how proud she was of my brother David. He'd been working regularly at IBP (Iowa Beef Producers, except they butchered hogs, too), the meat packing plant, sometimes pulling double shifts. He had a better attitude now, and he had even defused a bad situation at work a few nights prior. Later that month, Mom announced she was $37 overdrawn at the bank as well.[165] Home was chaotic and that was unfortunate. I didn't know how to help.

For the fall semester of 1991—the start of my junior year—I found a new roommate named Kim, who remains a good friend to this day. She was a friend from my Psychology classes, and it seemed like we would get along well. We did. She joined me as a member of Delta Alpha Delta, by then an anti-sorority sorority.

They sponsored things like Safe Sex Night at the local hookup place, where we handed out condoms as our public service, or Polyester Prom, which was our satirical formal. Perhaps the best thing was "I am Woman" fests where we randomly gathered to sing Helen Reddy's song and celebrate feminism.

Phyllis from Upward Bound had never stopped mentoring me. But she also understood when she needed to delegate her responsibilities. She asked a woman named Carol from Student Support Services (SSS) to work with me. SSS is another federal program for first-generation and low-income college students designed to enhance successful educational outcomes.[166] Like Upward Bound, SSS came out of the War on Poverty. During my junior and senior years of college, I received aid from SSS. They began helping me prepare for entering graduate school.

That fall, I started a job that had been recommended to me by a Social Work professor. I worked for C.L.A.S.S., or Community Living and Social Support. It was a program designed to help people with serious mental illnesses who were living in nursing homes to move into their own homes. Now I had four jobs. I was working in the café, at the restaurant, for Upward Bound, and for C.L.A.S.S.

I was getting valuable, hands-on experience working with people who had serious mental illnesses. I also made a lifelong friend in my boss, Matt. He shared that he had bipolar disorder, and this really gave me hope regarding what people with mental illness could achieve. It was eye-opening to meet someone with a serious mental illness who was functioning well and holding down a professional job. Furthermore, Matt encouraged the staff to help our residents become as independent as possible. Instead of warehousing the mentally ill in nursing homes, we were helping them to move back into the community.[167] Our clients were successful too.

Matt took me to Independence, Iowa, to the state mental hospital, the Mental Health Institute, the place where my grandfather had been taken. It was an antiquated building that looked like a spooky castle, like where Frankenstein would have lived. We toured the top-floor museum, which exhibited many historical treatments for mental illness like ice baths and lobotomies.

Matt also gave me the opportunity to hear Joel Slack, an advocate for the treatment of the mentally ill. He had once been in a catatonic state for many years, and during that time he was hospitalized for catatonic schizophrenia.[168] Mr. Slack had been treated like a piece of furniture by most people, and he could bring tears to your eyes describing how he felt about it.

My parents were two seriously mentally ill people who were never really offered proper treatment for their conditions while I was growing up and entering adulthood. Instead, they were treated like criminals and child abusers. I felt bad for them. They didn't get the chance to become like Matt. My grandfather probably gave up his business when his mental health faltered.

Mom was now writing another prisoner, Jerry. This wasn't Larry—that was the previous prisoner. In August 1991, I got a letter from her that was really just a long letter from Jerry to her. I didn't appreciate getting her mail. I was never going to like her prison pen pals. It was all part of the prison ministry she volunteered for, but I didn't think it should become a love connection.

She also sent along a letter written in what we call "Germlish," which is a lot of made-up words that mix English and German. It was partly her eccentricity and partly her desire to practice the German she had been speaking since childhood, when my grandfather spoke it with her. She'd had to talk to Isaiah's teacher. Isaiah had been acting out in school.

"Isaiah had two bad notes the first week. Focus on the Family had a radio show about kids' learning styles. Some are visual, some are auditory, and some are kinesthetic. The last group are most likely to get in trouble at school. That's Isaiah!! Good old touchy-feely Isaiah. David missed school, because he didn't want to miss one day of work, and he was exhausted. Has his 90 days in."

I was losing my patience with her prison puppy love (or maybe I was just upset to know that she was listening to *Focus on the Family*). Upward Bound had taught us the same learning-style information.[169] I hadn't approved of one prison pen pal yet. I just didn't like how naïve she was compared to how streetwise these men were. It bothered me how much she sounded like a teenage girl regarding men she had never actually met. Not just one, but several at this point. I wished she'd seek men who weren't potential predators. Especially because I'd already taken after her in that way more than once. Her example had not been a helpful one.

Meanwhile, I learned that conservatives were now selling marriage as a cure for poverty.[170] *I rolled my eyes.*

Senja wrote me a letter in November 1991 in which she announced:

"I got 5 As, 4 Bs, and 2 Cs. On the Iowa Tests of Basic Skills, I am in the top 3 percent. Get this. I am getting a math and science award, but

the ITBS says I am not so good at those. Our 'guinea pigs' are doing fine, except they're gerbils." I smiled sheepishly at my mistake from a letter I wrote home. I needed to get it straight that they had gerbils. I liked the little guys.

Another letter from the same month said, "*David got into an accident. Someone smashed his car majorly!*" My brother having yet another accident where he potentially hit his head wasn't good.[171]

In January 1992, I wanted my senior year Social Work internship to be in the juvenile justice system, specifically doing restorative justice,[172] because of the transformational work they seemed to have done with Samuel. And to a lesser extent, the good work they were doing with David and John. When I applied, I was told that my brothers' involvement in the juvenile justice system disqualified me from working with juveniles but that they would let me work with adults.

I was very hesitant to be part of the adult criminal justice system. But I finally agreed because I needed to fulfill the internship requirement. This meant I spent my senior year as a probation officer working all over northeast Iowa. I was involved in writing pre-sentence investigations, figuring out how to lead the sex offender treatment group (a book of its own), and tailing a lot of seasoned probation officers to learn the ropes.

I found a letter from David that seemed like it was written around this time. It referred to his missing a Valentine's Day date and not getting to tell the girl he was sorry. Then he wrote, "*I'm just slowly getting depressed. The only thing keeping me straight is the thought of independent living. One more week.*"

This was the first time I began to worry about David's mental health. I wanted him to be able to get his own place as he wanted but worried that in the end he wouldn't be able to handle it. For example, David struggled a great deal just with waking up after being asleep. Without outside help, I worried he would miss any goals that required him to be somewhere at a certain time.

Mom sent a letter in February 1992:

"Dave leaves for Job Corps Tuesday. Life should calm down after that. Want to go to Toastmasters tonight. Good program you might enjoy. By the way, I talked to Legal Services about Gold Card Club. We're waiting to see about the statute of limitations. Lawyers saw the wrongdoing clearly."

Mom wanted David to be at Job Corps as much as he did. I hoped it really did mean life was going to calm down. Gold Card Club was where Samuel had worked underage. Mom may have wanted to pursue something against the owner of the Gold Card Club for turning her son against her regarding the goal of completing high school, but she couldn't afford to. Legal services or Legal Aid, the lawyers for poor people, told her that it sounded like she had a case, but they couldn't help her pursue it. Of course, she never did.

At the beginning of April 1992, Mom wrote:

"I'm waiting for David at the Plasma Center. David's home for the weekend and coming next weekend too. Enjoys welding—got burned in the arm. Isaiah's still sick. Fever since Thursday. It's Sunday. Goes to the doctor tomorrow if he's not better."

It was disheartening to know David was selling his blood plasma just as Mom had done for years. In fact, Mom couldn't sell her blood plasma anymore because her veins had collapsed, and the staff could no longer get a blood draw.[173] At least David was enjoying the welding.

Mom wrote to me again in Germlish. She told me she'd been in a significant car accident and had whiplash, and the other person's car was totaled. Then she said the fire inspector had been by the house, and there were $900 worth of repairs that had to be made or they'd have to move out. She had no idea where she was going to get the money for these repairs. I sent as much money home as I could to help.

David had received his GED. She pointed out that David had had nine accidents with his head across his life.[174]

I graduated with the May 1992 class, even though I wouldn't complete my degree until December. Dad sent me a letter about my graduation:

"Our profoundest apologies—on the birthday and graduation. I had planned 1) time off to attend (shortage of help), 2) purchase of Wal-mart stock on your behalf (a bimbo failed to inform me on the proper application forms). But my hopes and plans fell through as circumstances dictated events these past four months . . . the reason I chose the "funny" graduation card is a) humorous relief—life is too serious! b) at one point in 1988 the reality of travel to other worlds was very real. An intelligence contact was experienced about 4 times so there is a reality of this despite . . ."

He didn't even finish the sentence. He just told me to stay in touch. Love, Dad. Naturally, his letter was more disturbing than supportive and loving. Now, he was telling me he'd been visited by aliens. I didn't want to know about my dad's contacts with alien beings. I didn't want to be told that I could have had stock in a company, but "Oh well, life doesn't work out and plans fall through." Over and over. Right, I gotcha.

Mom also wrote in May, once again in Germlish. She shared that she was playing the organ at church on the Sabbath, and she was also attending Bible study at a Seventh-day Adventist Church. I was happy she was in a community she liked again. It felt like the hundredth church she'd tried out in my life. There was an aimlessness to it, a sense of having no rhyme or reason to it, at least theologically. Theologically speaking, it was completely absurd.

In fall 1992, both Samuel and David attended Expo High School, which was the alternative high school in Waterloo for students with academic or behavioral problems. They both seemed to thrive there, so much so that the *Waterloo Courier* wrote an article about the success of the two of them in order to showcase Expo. They were both able to earn high school degrees from Expo instead of getting GEDs.

I was a temporary probation officer right after college graduation for three months in the summer of 1992 while my internship supervisor went on maternity leave. I had finished my degree, so I was considered a full-fledged probation officer. It was somewhat hilarious to have me in this role, because my appearance is not at all intimidating. I have been described as "sweet, kind, understanding", etc., by people in interactions. It's not the disposition typically associated with probation work.

This dispositional mismatch was clear to me during my year-long internship my senior year of college. But I now needed the money, I knew it was only for three months, and I didn't realize what one of my duties would be. One of the duties always given to the lowest probation officer on the ladder was to co-lead the sex offender treatment group.

Worse than that, I had to drive two hours to do it once a week. One of those sex offenders later murdered a woman. There was nothing I'd picked up about the guy that told me he would do that.[175] He has driven my amateur study of psychopaths.

In October, Senja shared that she and John had to walk all the way to Logan Middle School every day because Mom's car didn't work. It was a long walk, far too long and tiring to do before school.

In another letter from the same time, Senja wrote:

"Today, after school, a whole bunch of Black kids beat up a white kid. There was a whole bunch of them, too. One or two followed me and John home till we turned into a junkyard. That stopped them. I mean I have nothing against blacks, but they shouldn't beat anybody up. Black or white."

Why mention it at all? To give some background on family experiences that may explain why Samuel is so racist in the present day, I suppose. However, because she is highly educated, Senja is not racist.

Finally, Senja updated me on her pets, and also, importantly, on her "cop card" collection. How many police officers could she collect from the local police force? Despite my brothers' involvement in the criminal justice system, her attitude toward the police was still positive; she wanted each of the local police officer's cards. To be sure, though, the police treated my brothers well compared to how Black or Brown people were and are treated.

⚜

In the November 1992 general election, it was only the fluke of a popular third-party candidate that year that gave Bill Clinton his victory. I voted for Clinton, but he was not a liberal. He was a neoliberal, which might sound similar, but is worlds apart.[176] One assumes he still believed in democracy, but he adopted most of the economic policies of austerity, or cuts to social welfare, while privatizing government services. There was no candidate in the election representing traditional liberalism.

Somehow, I also voted for Republican Chuck Grassley, because I thought he was a moderate Republican, and that reflected my values at the time. It's the only vote that I've ever regretted.

Samuel had a steady job at the meatpacking plant, as did David. But David didn't like the job, and he had welding skills, so he applied to do that instead. He got the job and started welding for some time. However, he struggled on an ongoing basis with waking up for work. Waking up in general had been extremely difficult for him ever since his head injuries.

Mom wanted David to go back to the rehabilitation program that had served him so well when he was seventeen. But now that he was an adult, he had to pay for the program out of pocket, so they would garnish his wages if he participated. He could not be persuaded to agree to this. Samuel was turning out to be a model citizen rather than a master criminal.

Senja informed me that she was entering a math and spelling bee on January 9, 1993. She was an academic star, so I wasn't worrying as much about her. She told me she dreamed I came and took away her still missing cat. I should have seen it as an omen that Senja was going to have problems. I got my sister a new cat.

⚜

Abracadabra! Phyllis Gray worked some more of her Upward Bound magic, and David was going to go to college. He picked Iowa State University. I was so happy for him. I drove three hours from Decorah to Ames to visit him. I was living in Decorah for eight months to work before starting graduate school in Michigan.

Mom wrote in February 1993, focusing on David and Iowa State:

"Poor kid . . . called 3x yesterday. Bored silly. Said he has no money even for a pop. Can't party with everyone else, doesn't really know anyone yet and he didn't get that security job. Said, 'I'm ready to come home.' I gulped and was glad he clarified, 'for the weekend.' I told him Spring Break wasn't that far off, and gave him several suggestions for things to do, none of which held any immediate appeal. Said he's burning out with study. He sure could use a letter, if you have any free time."

I was immediately alarmed when I visited David. His dorm room was filled with empty liquor bottles and beer cans. He was knocked out on his bed in the middle of the day, clearly suffering from a hangover. I asked him how classes were going. He admitted that he had been struggling. I confessed to him that I had partied a bit when I first went to college. I may have even come close to getting myself killed from drinking too much, but passing out saves a person. I tried not to judge him but instead to empathize with him.

When I got back to Luther, I sent David a letter of support meant to encourage him in his studies. I included the story about raisins and peanuts that Phyllis had told me. He probably wasn't dealing with the kind of issues with social class that I had to contend with because Iowa State is a public university, but it had to be a factor.

On February 17, 1993, Dad wrote:

"A lot of problems up here—a lot of adjustments in the works, and a lot of uncertainties. We've written David encouraging his schooling. Please continue to support him. I understand your money troubles. I don't have any immediate solutions. Everyone is in a bind these days and I suspect it'll get worse. I have misgivings about Clintonomics."

My father was right not to trust Clintonomics. As I said, Clinton was not really a liberal. In 1994, during his tenure, so-called welfare "reform" was passed, which made even further cuts in aid to the poor.[177] A crime bill was passed that incarcerated more people of color in the subsequent thirty years than at any point in history.[178] Trade deals were made that eviscerated the power of unions.[179]

Needless to say, David dropped out of Iowa State after only one semester. His grades did not reflect his abilities. Of course, after his head injury, his abilities were not what they once were. He once scored off the charts on aptitude tests.

Mom's letter from February 1993 had continued:

"Well, Marv and I talked on the phone for a while. I'm gonna meet him again at the Cedar Falls Happy Chef after soup supper on Tuesday. I'm going to take Senja (he's met Isaiah who really was well behaved). Isaiah called him mellow. He is I guess—looks older than 42 (is an Aries). Sharon asked what he thought of me (curiosity, you know) and he said he really liked me. The waitress (owner's wife) really liked Isaiah. Marv likes to fish. Just what John needs, er? Isaiah, too, but mostly John. By the way, when you write next, be sure to rave a little about the superior job he did in cleaning his room. It sparkles. Operation Threshold weatherized so it's warmer up there now. Sorry it couldn't have been done when you were here."

Okay, well at least Mom was seeing someone who wasn't in prison. It sounded like things were going decently at home. Maybe we all were. I'll spare you the suspense: the relationship with Marv didn't last either. Perhaps it was the fact Mom had five kids at home with her. Maybe after she'd introduced them one by one, he'd seen the light. I don't know.

Meanwhile, she had to live on welfare, as it had been "reformed." Historian Lily Geismer wrote an article arguing that Bill Clinton did more to sell neoliberalism than Milton Friedman, the economist, had.[180] To summarize her point, Clinton provided liberal cover for a Charles Murray-style approach to poverty. The Democrats were doing exactly what the Republicans do. We were not going to benefit from Clintonomics.

I spent more time studying authoritarianism my senior year. In fact, my undergraduate thesis focused on the moral aspects of authoritarianism and dictatorships. I was interested in moral development, political orientation, and something called the Defining Issues Test, which measured moral reasoning.[181] I tested to see if liberals could think like conservatives, and vice versa, about moral issues. As I predicted, conservatives could not reason about liberal morality, but liberals could reason like a conservative on a morality test.

My senior thesis won an award, but I never pursued publishing the study, which I regret. Now that I think about it, my thesis was probably about empathy rather than moral reasoning. The liberals I surveyed just had a greater capacity for empathy than the conservatives—a finding that has been replicated in multiple ways[182]. Unfortunately for my family, this was a political era when empathy was in short supply.

Chapter Thirty-One: Dreams Come True or Not?

I T SEEMED AT THE time like March 16, 1993, was the happiest day of my life. It was the day my acceptance letter arrived in the mail from the University of Michigan. I got into graduate school, where I'd dreamed of going!

My dear friend Beth Seibert, who tragically passed away shortly afterward of cancer, rode with me from Iowa to Michigan to visit the campus. I wasn't invited to the New Student Weekend they offer to PhD candidates in the spring of their acceptance to University of Michigan, because I wasn't accepted as a first-round student. At the time, I didn't know I was accepted as a second choice. What I didn't know didn't hurt me though, for the most part. I was missing a lot of the orientation information the students got in the New Student Weekend, but I managed to piece together what I needed to do. I scrambled a bit for housing and whatnot, but otherwise, I was okay.

I visited campus during the summer of 1993. The weather was perfect. Ann Arbor, Michigan, was and is idyllic as a classic university town. That summer was also special because John and Senja were on Luther's campus with me for Upward Bound. It was some rare family time together.

In August 1993, Dad got remarried to a woman named Charlene in Wisconsin. Senja and I were in the wedding ceremony. Samuel and his girlfriend Yvette drove up from Iowa to attend too. I liked my stepmom, and I hoped that my father would be happy with her.

In late August, I let the university match me with a roommate, Kyla[183]. I thought her name sounded Norwegian, but I was far off. She was Nigerian. She was a beautiful soul inside and out. I couldn't have been luckier to find her as a friend.

I started graduate school in the fall of 1993. When I looked around the introductory class at my cohort of twelve incoming doctoral students, I immediately felt out of place. Then, Professor Garvin told us to look to our left and then to our right, and to expect that only half of us would finish the program. He was right. Only six of us got our PhDs from that cohort. It feels like a miracle to be one of the six.

Senja wrote me in September to say, "*Mom is writing to prison guys, and I fear for her safety. But she says that she doesn't give them her home address or her phone number.*"

Meanwhile, Mom sent me a postcard that didn't mention the prison letters. She told me she had a weeklong headache. She said David was doing well working at IBP as a red hat, which is a safety officer. She told me that John liked being at East High School.

In mid-September, Mom informed me:

"*That darned guy never came through with Dave's $200. But we got him a neat lil 'ol Dodge Aspen for $175. Runs, well cared for, '78, gray. Samuel and Yvette plan to move back in at the end of October.*"

Mom's birthday is in September and her present from the family that year was a massage. So, she got it. In response, she said:

"*I still say a good massage when I was in the hospital in 77 would have done more than pills and therapy combined. And a lot cheaper, too . . . Had a 1 ½ week headache, off and on. Here are some Isaiahisms or things that Isaiah has been saying incorrectly about the Bible. Daniel in the Lion's bin. Jesus was God's only forgotten son. Who tends the other sheep when Jesus is out getting the Lost sheep?*"

Whoa, this was news to me. She hadn't mentioned before that she went to the hospital in 1977, but she had many unexplained absences during that year, so I could imagine that was another one. Now, I can't deny my mother's theory about the healing power of massages. I could easily get more out of massage than a therapy session, but since it's considered a luxury, insurance never covers them.

At the end of September, Mom told me she "applied at McKinstry—actually got interview. Went well. ½ time. Chapter 1. Position. Kindergarten." She didn't get that position either. But she also said that Samuel and Yvette were interested in going to school. They wanted to take classes at the community college to get their associate's degrees.

Mom and Senja wrote together in October. Senja said the usual stuff about school being okay. Mom wrote:

"Samuel and Yvette have moved back. Saw Phyllis on Wednesday. John's having trouble with one of his teachers. I think it's the same teacher David had troubles with. Phyllis sympathized. I told John to bring his Algebra book home and we'd muscle through it together. David's always at work nowadays. He's taking double shifts lately. Sweetie has a job at IBP. I'm with R. L. Polk. Door-to-door. Br-r-r now—record cold this weekend. Samuel's talking about Hawkeye [Community College]."

This was a miracle. Samuel, who had dropped out of seventh grade because school was "unnecessary," was now going to community college. I thought about the influence of Phyllis. Still, in October, Mom wrote to tell me that John had been beaten up by a group of kids on the way home from school. She finally took him into the doctor after he reinjured himself playing around with Lurch. It turned out he had a broken arm. Race relations in our town were at a point of open hostility, a phenomenon Frances Fox Piven and Richard Cloward had described as characteristic of ghetto life.[184] It was unfortunate that John was targeted, because he was so quiet and inoffensive.

We couldn't afford to move away from the ghetto. We lived there at a time when Black people were expressing their anger. Race relations were getting thorny. Mom said John still liked East High.

She continued:

"This murder, right next to Logan School, has Senja upset. Keeps talking about future concerns . . . Don't flash your lights at anyone driving with parking lights on!! It's a gang thing—they'll attack. Lurch, Dave, Dan, and another friend were on Franklin & 63 late Wednesday nite after Dave got off work. Car behind them flashed lights, threw a bottle, passed them, then stopped, and started to get out, just two Black guys, so they figured they must have had a gun. Lurch jumped the median and headed toward the police station—wants to get gun for protection. Coulda been tragic? Lurch says ya let em run things by staying in, etc., so they'll take over. Any wisdom to offer?"

Yes, stop acting like you're trolling for enemies.[185] I could picture this car full of white boys with long hair becoming targets for gang members on the East Side. It wasn't out of the question. Because they didn't exactly act cool. They acted just like racist white boys. Acting scared in your own neighborhood was a good way to end up a target. The odds were that the flashing lights were a rumor going around town. I had been cruising around those same neighborhoods with my Black friends, and we would have noticed a carful of racist-looking white boys on Franklin and 63. It wasn't a white neighborhood. The notion that Black people would be "taking over a block" where they had lived for generations perplexed me.

I didn't like how Mom sounded in the letter, so I wrote her back and told her to be neighborly. Be friendly. Stop acting suspicious. Behave as we had always behaved, because she was getting caught up in some racism and it concerned me.

She had included in the letter:

"On the positive side, two University of Northern Iowa Black students are putting on a play in November to decrease violence. I'll bring it up at the next police liaison mtg. Oh, they were interviewing kids near the police station when two more walked by carrying an AK assault rifle. It was the talk of Hardee's this morning."

Mom said that she was trying Overeaters Anonymous for her eating issues. She said she liked it. She also announced that she was starting work for the next ten weeks for R. L. Polk Directory. It was a short-term job at least. Just as Clinton's welfare reform required, Mom was going to try working, undertreated mental illness or not.

She mentioned that her car required a few hundred dollars to fix up and would need a few hundred more to continue running, but she could pay that down the road with this new job. Sigh. The family never gets ahead.

Around Thanksgiving 1993, Mom wrote:

"John gets [his]cast off tomorrow a.m. Was supposed to get it off yesterday, but the doctor cancelled. John's getting into trouble with our neighbor, Richard, and a 20-year-old boy named Heath. A 14-year-old has no business running with a 20-year-old! There's money involved. Heath may be paying John for stuff he steals. Lied last night-said he was at Richard's house, when I had already learned from his mother he'd left with Richard. Still insists he was there. Stubborn boy!"

Mom was supposed to be capable of working and parenting her five children because other single women were capable of doing so. It was a neoliberal assumption. If you use neoliberal values to judge the value of a person, you judge them based on how they perform in the marketplace.

Mom wasn't able to compete in the labor marketplace because she is disabled. She had *officially* been found to be disabled, but it was still assumed that a significantly impaired person could earn enough money on top of the now comically inadequate welfare check to support six children. And that if she had a husband she wouldn't need help at all, never mind her husband's own disability. My mentor in graduate school, Carol Mowbray, was working on programs for people with serious mental illness, like Supported Education[186] and Supported Employment,[187] that would have been effective with Mom.

Dr. Mowbray also studied the meaning of motherhood to women with serious mental illness.[188] It's worth reflecting on why exactly Mom had six children. She had been both Mormon and fundamentalist Mormon for major chunks of her life. Her religion pushed her to get married, specifically to Dad, a man with a serious and persistent mental illness of his own, a man whose thinking was much further from reality than hers on the average day, and then they were encouraged to have lots of children. Not once did her family (of origin) discourage her from having a large family, despite her known inability to support them. The marketplace was in no way useful in preventing this obvious economic problem, or in helping Mom out of it—but according to neoliberals, marriage is good for reducing poverty. That was Charles Murray's theory.

John eventually got caught stealing, or burgling. This was a serious charge that resulted in a sentence at a detention program in Cedar Rapids, Iowa, called Four Oaks. It was a much more serious intervention than anything my other brothers had gotten from the juvenile justice system. John told me he was scared of the other kids in the program, because some of them were true psychopaths.

A letter from Mom in November was in Germlish, so I can only partially understand it years later. She wanted me to know that Isaiah was playing the cello. She also told me that John was getting two F's in school. That didn't reflect what John was capable of achieving. She said David was living with her friend Sweetie, who was charging him $250 a month for rent. Samuel was living with his friend Lurch, but Lurch was moving out soon. Mom didn't like Lurch's negative attitude, and she wasn't wrong; Lurch abused crack and meth. He was a friend of Samuel's going all the way back to elementary school. Mom also said that Yvette, Samuel's girlfriend, was getting her GED. Sweetie was starting to have a meth problem herself at about this time. A veritable buffet of news, as usual.

Meanwhile, in graduate school, I was reading so many journal articles and book chapters, my eyes blurred. Once again, I had to read articles related to Charles Murray, who had recently written an influential article, "The Coming White Underclass."[189] He told America to be ready for a group of permanently poor white people. He predicted some reasons for their existence, but since I came from the white underclass, I had a lot of ideas of my own about why we existed. I shared them in class, and my fellow students agreed. What about religious fundamentalism? My family was, by definition, a part of this underclass, but we were trying to slowly crawl our way out of poverty, no thanks to conservatives like Murray, who thought cutting benefits would help.

In mid-December, Mom wrote:

"I go to a new Catholic Charities counselor. I really like the atmosphere there. Really friendly. Not money-oriented. The depression has been at bay for a while. But it's always around the corner so to speak. It helps to be organized. It does. I wanna buy Samuel a guitar book, but I don't have any money. We have a new dog. Yvette does."

At Christmas, I traveled back to Iowa to be with my family. While we were gathered together, I accepted a beer to drink. A single beer. At age twenty-two.

Senja sent me a letter written on Christmas Day, in which she huffed:

"I was mad tonight because I guess I was just disappointed in seeing you drinking beer, especially since I always thought you avoided it. So I put water in your beer and I layed [sic] it down. I guess I was just shocked. But I should get used to it. You're not my best friend now though."

Oh boy. I tried to console Senja and point out to her that I only drank a single beer, but she felt thoroughly, irrevocably betrayed. It didn't even matter that I almost never drank. Sadly, Senja later became alcohol dependent and continues to struggle with it. Since my sister ended up with the very issue she was concerned about, I struggle with intense guilt over this exchange. At the same time, I also know that her drinking problem is not my responsibility. It's too much to be expected to be a perfect role model.

In January, Senja wrote indicating she had missed school that day. She said she missed the bus, and Mom's car wasn't working. She described the temperature there as ninety below. The real temperature, not the wind chill. Obviously, that's a healthy exaggeration. It was hard to hear that she had to walk in the freezing cold because of our perennial car issues.

Mom also wrote around then, quoting *Des Moines Register* columnist Donald Kaul from January 12, 1994:

"It's not a question of intelligence ... It's a question of taste. If you have some, Limbaugh is an arrogant, caterwauling, self-promoting, mean-spirited, gaseous, buffoon and bully."[190]

Clearly, Mom had the same reaction to the man that I did. But Grandpa Meyer, her father, and Uncle Paul, her brother, were spending hours listening to Rush. Later, my brother Samuel would also spend hours listening to him. Limbaugh's beliefs would be the beliefs of our family members. My cousin put giant speakers on his truck and drove around blaring what amounted, I guess, to white music, trying to prove a point about white supremacy.

That January, 1994, Mom was cleaning out our front porch room to potentially turn it into a bedroom for David. She was willing to welcome him back home. She wrote: "*I wish David would help John with his Algebra. Not my strong suit. Isaiah has a mentor.*" The next January letter said, "*John quit Algebra II. Insists the teacher hates him. I think you or Dave had him.*"

I panicked over John's problems with achievement. I knew he was intelligent enough to be successful in these classes, so why was he clashing with these teachers? I think the teachers might have been stereotyping him based on his looks, his apparent social class. My keen sense of hopelessness about being able to help John led me toward a decision to help Isaiah and Senja down the road.

Mom also wrote, "*Just cleared out whole office and moved Isaiah in there. He doesn't know it yet. What a surprise.*" I guess David wasn't moving back home.

Samuel was working for IBP at this time. He was hoping to apply for a better position within the company, called a "utility." He was a man now and had escaped poverty too. I was desperate to have all my siblings join me in escaping poverty.

In January 1994, I was beginning my Social Work internship at Southwest Detroit Community Mental Health Center. I was assigned to work in the dual diagnosis program. It was exactly what I wanted. I wanted to be working with best practices in the field. Except, when I got there, the man who was running the program, Howard Stanley[191], didn't seem to know anything about dual diagnosis programming.

Worse, Howard Stanley almost immediately asked me for a date at Red Lobster. After I turned him down, he told me he'd been in military intelligence and knew how to track me down. He threatened to get to my information if I tried to cross him. I was scared of him, but I was also not going to take the abuse. I immediately reported him to both the University of Michigan practicum supervisor and the person who supervised the dual diagnosis program, a man named Jorge.

Jorge was as responsive as he could be. He was sympathetic and said he believed me, but the agency was a union shop, and Mr. Stanley was protected by arbitration. Jorge explained that this clause complicated the response of the agency to a claim of sexual harassment.[192] Mr. Stanley wrote a semiliterate letter accusing me of lying about him, and I used the letter as evidence for my point that he wasn't as competent in his job as he claimed. If he couldn't form basic sentences, he likely wasn't knowledgeable about dual diagnosis programming either. I investigated where he got his PhD, and it was from a shady mail-order college.

The agency and the practicum supervisor agreed to move me to the research office, where I did data analysis for the remainder of the internship. I was supposed to be getting hands-on experience counseling people with mental illness and addiction, but I was facing a computer screen instead.

I was so angry. But there didn't seem to be anything I could do about it. I just carpooled back and forth with another Social Work student from Michigan, and I'm sure I annoyed her by complaining about losing the job experience.

That winter, some kids in southeast Michigan were throwing bricks off overpasses onto the road with the intention of hitting cars below. A pregnant woman was killed. A week later, these teenagers hit the corner of my windshield with a brick; luckily, it only shattered the window a little bit.

When the brick hit the window, it scared me enough to almost cause an accident, but—again, luckily—I was in the slow lane, and was able to pull over to the shoulder safely. From then on, I spent the trips to and from Detroit anxious about overpasses and traffic in general. Who am I kidding? I've spent the rest of my life with anxiety around driving.

"Well, my dear, I'll have to tell you about my love life . . . seems to be blossoming again. His name is Wade and he's only a few years older than you are. And yes, he's in prison until November. But I didn't meet him through anyone else, and he is unlike anyone else I've met. Remember when I wrote a Letter to the Editor in the Plain Truth *about depression? Well, he read it in the library there, and wrote. It took me a month or so to even answer it, but there was just something about him that was different . . . Anyway, I figure anyone who's trying to improve himself deserves support. He wants to go into landscaping when he gets out in November. Now I know you're probably having fits about now. But just give it a chance. He's truly unlike anyone else—so thoughtful and sensitive. I am impressed. I mean how many guys read romance novels? Guess what? I'd sent him a family photo and his roommate wanted to write to you. He refused, so he's protective of you. Car in bad shape but using life-prolonging heroics. We're trying to keep up payments, maybe trade. Yvette is taking her GED test soon."*

That was Mom again, obviously. Yes, that's right: conservatives at this time were pushing a marriage agenda for poor women. I wonder which prisoner they wanted my mom to hook up with? As good Christians, they would have to approve of her prison ministry. Were they going to recommend a stepdad better than the father they had recommended? I'm sorry to sound judgmental of criminals, but I'd met psychopaths as a probation officer, and in looking for boyfriends myself, and they're a bad idea when it comes to choosing a life partner. One of them was charged with child sexual abuse, no less.

Mom continued:

"Just read where Prozac helps panic disorder. You might suggest that as an option for your doc. I take 20 mg every other day—seem to do well on that. Isaiah's behavior is downhill again. I have a teacher

conference again tonight. Dave needs prodding. He is stuck in life's cul-de-sac. John's been really pleasant."

She didn't realize that David's "stuck" place was a sign of major mental health problems, and I was only beginning to sense trouble in that area.

"At conference, I learned that Senja's behavior is also 'butt-like' at school. We concluded it has to do with hormones. Got a D- and an A and B. Isaiah's conference today was pretty good. Dave's on days now. I wake him up at 5:30, until he gets acclimated. He wants back on evenings so he can go to Hawkeye for welding. Samuel makes almost $10 an hour now. John is still getting better. This is my bad week—especially tomorrow. So far, so good, except when I went to shower this morning. What a mess all over! Definitely has a depressing effect. Remember that book I was reading on Daniel and the Revelations? I'm almost finished and I want to read it again. It's a commentary on each verse and how it was fulfilling older prophecies. Like Isaiah had prophesied how Cyrus would overthrow Babylon—even giving his name before he was born. Nebuchadnezzar had this dream Daniel interpreted."

Mom continued for another two pages discussing Daniel and the prophecies in the Bible that surround him. She concluded, *"And that's just three pages of that book! It's over 800 pages of historical drama fulfilling prophecies in such detail. See why I was* spellbound?"

Well, to be perfectly honest, these tired old Bible stories had been told to me so many times since I was a child. I used to find them comforting, but by this time, I was starting to find them annoying. I didn't mention that to Mom, of course. But I really was sick of her constant references to the Bible, and my dad's too. I was questioning the nature of a God who would send us riddles and old stories when we needed help.

I was more concerned with what Mom was saying about my brothers and my sister. Now, my sister was having behavior problems in school too? What was going on with our family!?

In April 1994, Mom wrote to me in Germlish. She said that John had been affectionate lately and had actually hugged her. That was pretty good for him. She'd been working for Manpower for a couple weeks, but their computers went down, so she had to go home. She said she'd been going to church choir on Sundays. Nowadays though, Isaiah just sang along so sweetly. She also mentioned that David had been arrested for public intoxication or drunk driving. It was hard to tell which from her Germlish.

My brothers just kept taking turns with arrests and involvement in the criminal justice system. But Mom kept working, doing what President Clinton wanted.

The church Mom had been going to for choir was a Seventh-day Adventist Church. Adventists are vegetarians, so Mom had to change the way she and Isaiah ate. Going to church on Saturday was different, a tradition vitally important to the faith, and an unusual practice within Christianity. Don't even get me started about the Christian Scientists, the LDS, the FLDS . . . It seemed no matter what faith Mom joined, it had to be on the outside, or at least on the margins, of the mainstream. It's tempting to say this was and is all an expression of her self-image, of how she saw herself within her family growing up, of what she thinks of as her place in the world. It's not much of a leap to see her search for a partner among prisoners in the same light. Not a leap at all, in fact.

There were always lots of nice people at the church, as is true of most any church, and this one had a lovely tradition of throwing a potluck after services each week. Mom nearly always brought her famous deviled eggs. She may not have been able to function well enough to cook most of the time, but she could really spice up a hard-boiled egg.

Mom wrote again:

"Worked three days at Manpower. That's three half days. Worked for Uncle Paul yesterday for 7 ½ hours. Possibly he could get us a computer. I'd like John to have one. Dave has a 2ⁿᵈ interview at the blacksmithing shop by Sweetie's. Kids—mostly Isaiah—terrible about messing the house. Awful!! Had to miss a day of work. Got so depressed had to clean house. It was the abyss again. Any suggestions? He's most defiant. Senja's sweet again. I'd like to go to the Seventh Day Adventist Church there [in Michigan]."

That spring, one of the most influential men in the Seventh-day Adventist Church joined a few other men in coming to the front of the pews to speak. Apparently, there had been heavy snow coming down all morning, which was quite unexpected for mid-April. The cars were already under a thick layer of wet crystals. This influential man bellowed so his voice could be heard by everyone: "I'm calling on the single gentlemen to do the honorable thing and help the single ladies dig their cars out, unless, of course, they're on the dole." Mom never went back to the Seventh-day Adventists. With some churches, it wasn't about whether they healed her depression or not. It was about how they treated us.

David loved to work as a welder. Once he was trained to do it, it was his preferred job, so the chance to get on with a blacksmithing shop near where he was living was good news for him. This was going to be his escape from poverty, head injury or no head injury. This was a positive development.

Another April 1994 letter from Mom:

"David quit IBP. He got himself arrested for drunk driving—in the paper. He and I went to Manpower on Tuesday. I go to Goodwill on the 18ᵗʰ for a tour. They've expanded into working with 'people like me.'"

Oh wow, now David had quit his job at the meatpacking plant, and he had gotten arrested for drunk driving. As a former probation officer, I knew what a charge like that meant for him. He would have to get a work permit to get his license to drive to work. Maybe David wasn't getting out of poverty.

Later in May, she wrote again:

"I had to stay home from teaching today—too depressed. No more this year. I get too far behind. I thought the kids would appreciate the computer. Ha. I was so damned busy picking up after their wake, while they played on the computer, I never even got a chance to find out if it was user-friendly or not! So I feel justified! It's going back!"

Mom still substitute taught for K-12 classes in town from time to time, since she'd kept her teaching certificate current. She'd found a way to get a computer, a notable achievement, but thought the kids "didn't appreciate it." I'm not sure what appreciation was supposed to look like, but it sounds like they used it extensively, so I would say that's a kind of appreciation.

If she wanted the kids to be cooperative with the cleaning in return for getting the computer—if that was what appreciation was, well—it was an unrealistic expectation after this length of time. She got rid of their new computer because of an age-old problem of not cleaning, the house being messy, and Mom being depressed about it. Nothing was more predictable. This had been true since 1975.

"Well, Voc Rehab will fund up to $1200 per year. I've got to put together a statement of purpose, have three references. Also applied for a social worker position at Lutheran Social Services. I'll be pissed 'royally' if those stupid child abuse allegations prevent me from getting a job! I rather tactfully handled that . . . 50/50 chance I'll get it. At least I will know how not to treat people. I can't do any worse than Pat M., David D. or Ron K. or Phil D. Boy, there sure are a disproportionate number of assholes in the field, aren't there? Have you heard the figure that 80% of them have their own childhood abuse issues 'to get even with' their abusers via their clients. Sad. My experience is much higher than that. Gene Allison was the only one who ever treated me with respect."

I was dismayed by my mother's lack of self-awareness about her job application. Stunned, really. She didn't understand the nature of the job because she was confusing a social worker with a child abuse investigator, and she very obviously had zero reason to be considering either position. For many years she'd been a client of both agencies, having been referred, as she dismissively said, for "child abuse allegations." She was right that "child abuse" was unfair, or misleading, but "child neglect" was inarguable. It goes without saying she had no degree or license to practice social work.

Mom's reference to Voc Rehab's financing had to do with money for higher education. Mom was going to take classes toward a degree. She hadn't quite been accepted to the Women's Studies program at University of Northern Iowa, but they were provisionally allowing her to take classes. Mom was no feminist. She wanted to enter the program to study the traditional roles of women and how they were starting to get undervalued.

At that point, Mom had never had a neuropsychological examination. When she did get one, she was diagnosed with a cognitive processing disability that was later described as "seizure-like." School was going to be a struggle for her. Work would always be a struggle.

Neoliberals like Milton Friedman disliked professional licensing,[193] such as what social workers have put in place in many states, or what medical doctors have in place across all fifty states. Friedman said that doctors used licenses as a method of gatekeeping not unlike how a trade union functioned, so that other people couldn't enter their field and lower their wages. When I was a Social Work academic, we debated the necessity of having licenses for practice. I saw some issues with licensing, such as the affordability of getting a license for lower income people like me. It would end up being a reason I didn't get licensed personally.

However, I was still in favor of professionals having required licenses. They provided standards of care for clients and guaranteed that social workers had a certain knowledge base. It wasn't a tool for professionals as much as it was a protection for clientele. Otherwise, Mom could have gotten that job with no knowledge base to do it.

She didn't even realize that she didn't have the requisite information needed to do this job.

I was frustrated with Mom and wrote to tell her so:

"You may save this note and read it to your therapist or whatever. The bottom line is this. I am very angry with you. I have been for years, but you seem to have overlooked it. I love you and the things you try to do for me to support me. That remains constant, which may be the reason I stifle my feelings. I want parenting, I want guidance, and I would like to see my other siblings get it, too. Their anger toward you is becoming apparent as well.

"I am also sick of your need to blame me . . . I like getting mail from you, but you send more to prisoners. The kids crave discipline; they need to be told to brush their teeth, to go to bed, to do their homework. They would thrive on consequences, and then I would not have to fill the stupid family role of 'hero.' I don't want it. I want to need things from time to time. I want to be the one who gets to lean on others. In ten years, I have only gotten to cry a few times. I am sick of bearing the brunt of the responsibility and always having to be strong. And if you get all suicidal and start feeling sorry for yourself, so be it. Just don't blame me as is typical. (I have a lot of letters with you saying I cause your depression). Well, you cause mine. Now, grow up, parent. I want to be young."

I had a right to be angry about years of too much responsibility. I had a right to be angry about being blamed for my mom's suicidal feelings. But I wasn't expressing myself very well due to that anger. We needed to sit down and talk out our feelings. Parenting Senja in a couple years would help me have a lot more understanding toward my mom, but I was also finally processing the pent-up anger I felt toward her.

Mom never replied directly to that letter. She sent me a postcard in September:

"New semester, new outlook, same old family. Isaiah's dosage is 10 mg instead of 5mg 2x daily. Senja gets up well. John . . . got up . . .

came home today due to some lunch foul up, but says he wants to go to Expo. Can't for 2 months. Hopefully, he'll go back tomorrow, get homework, and have a 3-day weekend to adjust. Attitude okay. IBP voted to strike."

David and Samuel had successfully finished high school because of the alternative school for troubled students, so maybe Expo would work for John too. If IBP voted to strike, how many of my brothers would it affect at any given time? I think David had quit working there by then, so it was just Samuel maybe? It was hard to keep track. Isaiah hated taking medication for ADHD, but he did much better in school when he did, and his teachers didn't call home reporting behavioral problems as often. It was hard to see him hate the meds.[194]

In October, Senja informed me, *"Dave's still living at home. He drives me crazy. He's always starting things with me. I want him to move out."* Mom included a note on the envelope of Senja's letter. It was written in Germlish. She told me she had a women's history midterm that day. Then she said that John and another boy had broken into East High School at 4:00 a.m., apparently to steal computer equipment. John claimed it was because our computer had a virus. Meanwhile, Senja had been arrested for shoplifting at Target. She had attended the First Offenders program the night before. It had now become a family tradition to attend that First Offenders program. This incident convinced me that I needed to have Senja come live with me.

In November, Senja wrote, *"Everybody says I'm always happy, but I'm not. At least I don't feel happy."* Once again, an early sign of depression. She also described feeling left out. At this point, she was thirteen years old. We should have gotten her counseling right away, but I was still learning about mental health, particularly in kids. Especially in light of the stealing, her comments were a cry for help that is easy to see in retrospect. But none of us reacted then.

Mom sent me another postcard:

"Just want you to know I'm thinking of you. P.O. wants John evaluated for ADHD. Don't be deceived by still waters. Many adult symptoms, too (insomnia, impulsiveness, and procrastination, impatience, temper outbursts, etc.). Your dad and I both scored 20 out of 20 on adult test. Read Driven to Distraction *by Ed Hallowell and John [Ratey][195]—both doctors with ADD. Not always hyperactive, but hyperreactive. Mostly right brain, big picture deficit. (I set my room on fire before age 9, remember). Am on Ritalin 4 days now. Today is the first day I remembered to take my 2nd dose. Isaiah and I gave his 1st dose to school to dispense—we'd both forget!!! Argh. Conferences next week. Senja's cleaned the whole house. You must reinforce that. Hi to Kyla. Josh gets sentenced next month."*

I made a mental note of Senja's unhappiness and worried about it, but I didn't identify my sister as depressed, and I didn't take further steps. My attention was primarily focused on David. Everything I was hearing suggested he wasn't doing well.

In December 1994, David overdosed on his Tegretol prescription. Mom wrote me a letter from the ICU telling me they were giving him a much-needed bath. They were going to test him for sleep apnea, because his snoring made the staff at the ICU sleepy (teasingly). From that point forward, I worried about David's mental health all the time. I didn't know how to get him help.

The reference to Josh being sentenced was to my cousin in Colorado who was just a couple years younger than me. He had to go to prison for a few years for a hate crime against a Jewish person. I didn't know the exact details, but I was ashamed to hear someone in my family could behave this way.[196]

My mother's heavy emphasis on attention deficit hyperactivity disorder was based on the fact that we had known for a while that David and Isaiah were diagnosed with it. Recently, Mom, was given the same diagnosis, and now possibly John had it as well. For Mom, the diagnosis was liberating because it helped her understand many of her struggles. It gave her a language for thinking and talking about her difficulties. It also helped to have the stories of others to relate to.

I had continued to worry about Senja. I was concerned about what might happen to her if she stayed at home. She'd had some difficulties in school and now she'd been to the First Offenders program. This, after all the trouble my brothers had been in. I insisted my sister come live with me in Michigan starting in January 1995.

Chapter Thirty-Two: Inherit the Worst

I N JANUARY 1995, MOM wrote:

"Did I tell you my women's history class is 100% fin-ished—waiting on grade (drum roll . . .). Love my classes this semester. Go to a ♀ welfare and work day seminar on Wednesday. Women from Harvard Women's Economic Policy Council there. I get to go to the First Offenders program again. ☺ Last time."

The truth is, I'd already started to panic about my brothers' life trajectories. David had attempted suicide. Now, Isaiah was being sentenced to a First Offenders program for having committed his first crimes. That meant Mom had gone there for all six kids other than me, and the only reason I didn't have to go is because I was caught shoplifting by Mom, not the store. I didn't know it then, but I had relied mostly on White privilege—being above suspicion—to get away with my other shoplifting, until I finally just stopped doing it on my own.

You'd think we weren't raised with physical discipline. We were. You'd think we weren't raised with religion, but it was heavily forced on each of us. This is why I question these two calling cards of conservative drivel about poverty and crime, among other issues.

We were Charles Murray's "Coming White Underclass." According to Murray, we got there because of our single-parent home. But our parents were married when they had all of us. Religion had everything to do with why we existed, *and* with why our family was split apart. The Mormon Church told my parents to get married, and they did, whether it was a good idea or not. It was not a good idea. This white underclass contained a lot of religious zealots. We knew them.

Murray didn't mention religious fundamentalism as a reason why there are people growing up in poverty, so I'll talk about it. It's a common reason. Poor people and religious fundamentalism go hand in hand, whether because the faithful espouse beliefs of living a life of poverty like Christ did or because they get bilked out of their money by their "saviors."

When Charles Murray wanted us to picture being poor, he never had in mind the poverty of the polygamist, fundamentalist compounds like on the one I lived in for a few months when I was six years old, since they didn't fit *his* mental image of poverty. The poor people there were all married, and they were all white. Lots of marriage up there. No shortage of marriages. They claim to be happy in the way members of a cult say they are happy, with a creepy, Stepford-like smile. Next thing you know, they'll be starring in an escape movie.

I thought Mom might be interested to read a book I'd been assigned called *Unfaithful Angels: How Social Work Has Abandoned Its Mission* by Harry Specht and Mark Courtney.[197] The authors argued that social workers were going into private practice in droves to work with middle- and upper-class people, essentially abandoning their traditional focus on the poor and oppressed. What a shock! They said this was happening during the exact time period when our family most needed social workers on our side, who understood poverty.

Specht and Courtney wrote:

"The United States has been characterized as a 'reluctant' welfare state because Americans have always felt uncertain about the efficacy of providing communal assistance to people in need. In our land of opportunity, Americans tend to believe that anyone who is willing to work can be self-supporting. It is conceded that there are some 'worthy poor' who cannot care for themselves—the frail aged, the orphaned,

and the severely disabled are examples—and help is given to these people, but it is given grudgingly and always under circumstances that make the receipt of assistance as unappealing as possible."

Bingo! My parents were disabled, and the assistance given to them was as unappealing as possible. My aunt then questioned why liberals didn't get people out of poverty. The answer was that they only got to try for a very short time, and then their efforts were cut off. So, they never got to finish their work. Because one of the things the government can't risk doing is providing a life for the poor that is better than how the poorest income taxpayer lives.

The resentment of even the most innocuous hand-up to the poor runs deep in America. For example, my life had been full of trauma and horror, but a charity known as Dorian Music Camps did give me a scholarship to play violin with its summer orchestra in 1987. My uncle couldn't afford to send my cousins to this music camp. Despite the fact that my cousins lived much easier lives and experienced much less trauma than we did, my uncle resented the camp scholarship, so he ranted to me and to Mom that welfare is too generous. This was a private charity that had nothing to do with the government or welfare, but that was how my uncle thought. Narrowly.

Mom wrote in February:

"Deb, you have your grandma's drive and ambition, which helped her overcome polio and accomplish so much (Whenever I run into someone in her classes, they always rave about what a good teacher she was!) Anyway, you both possess that certain ingredient for success, which you are both obviously achieving. However, not everybody can be expected to do as well, and if you recall, I've been achieving a heck of a lot more than I had been previously. Yet, if you think back, I believe most if not all of your comments and observations were on what DIDN'T get done. Sigh. It was an unspoken message that all my efforts were unacceptable and not worthy of note. I'm not saying this to criticize, as you know, and you probably get some of that from

me, too, but just to let you have some feedback as to how those messages affect people. I stressed believing in people and what a powerful factor that is. Now, I don't want you to feel bad. I just think it's kinda neat where we have the kind of relationship that we can talk about things like that. I wanted to bring it up while you were here, but the timing wasn't right and I was indeed depressed, too. Officer Eyestone called Isaiah and told him he couldn't be the same Isaiah he'd met, because that Isaiah had such an attitude. Ha. He just wanted him to know that he'd gotten his letter and wanted him to know he appreciated it, and to keep in touch and call him any time. He really has that 'village spirit.'"

One thing Mom didn't accurately measure was my ambition and drive. My advisor, Carol Mowbray, was the same way. Everyone was treating me like my mental health was good, but I knew better. My eating disorder was out of control. My Complex-PTSD interfered with working on homework. However, I leaned heavily on my doctoral student friends, Kyla, Eri[198], Denise[199], and Tim[200], and I pressed forward.

At the beginning of March, Mom updated me. She said:

"I went to that ADD conference. Your old supervisor and a lot of people I knew were there. It was quite helpful. We're global people, not linear. The speaker, Dr. Lynn Weiss, felt it was not a disorder (just written in the DSM-IV by linear people but if you need the accommodation that it requires to get what you need, then you have to bear that label). They called last night that David snuck out his window. Sigh. Guess whose fault it is—mine. They worked it out."

Mom wrote again a few days later, asking that I send a letter to Grandma, who'd been quite ill. Mom said that David was doing well at a rehabilitation program or a residential program. She said he called it "home" now.

Then, Mom wrote Senja for her birthday:

"Someone could conceivably come and get you if you want to finish the semester in Iowa & take care of that ear. Let me know! In the meantime, here's the card DiLeo sent me with a $20 money order to 'take the gang out for pie.' Nice, huh? I thought when you get to feeling blue, you can just climb right up on my lap in that picture and comfort yourself. We were robbed of that, you know. Dave feels better

now that he's 22. How's 14? We could come and get you Thursday night if you want. Maybe it would be helpful for you to be in on the family counseling. Besides I miss you. But it's entirely up to you."

Mom was trying to comfort Senja after she'd continued showing signs of being depressed. She also missed Senja and probably wanted her home on some level. I wasn't even aware of how Senja was feeling. She wasn't expressing the feelings to me directly. Maybe this wasn't so easy. But this letter clued me in, so I tried to plan a special birthday party for her. We celebrated Senja's birthday in March 1995 by having friends of mine and friends of hers she'd made in Ann Arbor over for a St. Patrick's Day party with games and cake. We decorated the apartment, and I tried to make a special day of it. She seemed happier afterward.

The friends of mine that came over included Kyla, along with Eri, a Social Work doctoral student from Japan; Tim, an African American Social Work doctoral student from the southern US; Denise, an African American Social Work doctoral student from the East Coast; and Anita, an Indian American Psychology doctoral student. These friends became Senja's friends as well.

Mom wrote again at the end of the month:

"I've been engaged in a battle royal with depression all month. Got worse last week. The psychiatrist put me on 4x amount of Xanax—I took only .5 mg and out like a light. Says to double Prozac over weekend now. I was getting way 'out of control.' Doctor says agitation is last stage of all depression. The car's dead. I may get a clunker from a friend of Samuel's for $75. A big rust bucket. Test tomorrow but Uncle Paul has priority proofing tonight."

Mom having to prioritize work over studying the night before a test reminded me of how my life often went. I hoped it would work out to keep Senja, because Mom still seemed overwhelmed at home. Meanwhile, I took Senja home to Iowa for an Easter visit.

Mom wrote on May 1:

"Happy May Day! Well, the car is dead at the post office. No reverse. Sigh. Roosevelt came along just in time—we went to D & T to pick up JaLee while her car is being fixed and then we all went to Hardee's. Sweetie came along, and gave us a lift to the bus station. I'm at UNI—test tomorrow, final in Relationships in Crisis. Speaking

of which, I just wrote to Phyllis for input. Did you know John went out in handcuffs (came back). <u>Lotsa</u> burglaries in our neighborhood. Rumors, too—like Senja and John out Easter morning! It's <u>serious!</u> Neighbor came over demanding $300 to fix his car/truck in two days. A police officer sent him away, but he said he had proof John was trying to sell his stereo for $85 at Expo. John protests too much and I have no reason to believe him. Would that I could. He was cooking up brews (candles, black light bulbs, skull/reaper theme) all over his room with Anarchist's cookbook. Was copying car bomb sections. Why?? I don't' know if I can hold out til Upward Bound . . . at the edge. Lost it with grandpa yesterday. Rush was the last thing I needed. Just took Xanax again. I just got livid. Say hi to Senja. She doesn't write to me. Just to Yvette."

I was lucky I didn't have to deal with Mom being addicted to anti-anxiety meds. Despite Mom's letters and expressions of love to Senja, Senja was harboring feelings that Mom didn't love her.

As always, though, Mom had multiple concerns to juggle. About John and the First Offenders program, she told me,

"Get this, two days after I signed the 'case plan,' I learn John's off probation and starting a whole new round with new charges. Therefore, we no longer qualify for their help!! Is the system great or what? Just when we get to know them and they us.

"Deb, are you going to fix the system? An article about one of four women juvenile judges in Iowa says they're so far behind and have no place to put incorrigibles. We'll see if they pull him out of Upward Bound. Remember how long it took to get 'help' anyway? I had requested right after the East High incident, and actually way before that—I'd talk to Dennis at Stillpoint way last summer before school. How they had room, but his P.O. and his counselor, Larry, thought it was unnecessary? They actually scoffed at me, what did I know, anyway, I'm just the mother."

A few people in these kinds of roles were dismissive of Mom, probably based on her scattered demeanor, or her penchant for non-sequiturs, especially when rattled. Hell, *I* could be dismissive of Mom for much the same reason. This was unfair of us, of course, as Mom went right on trying to figure out the right meds to be on, the right way to think of herself and her troubles:

"In case you're still skeptical about my ADD, Dr. Fordham just shook his head and laughed, and said, 'You are so ADD!' It's spaciness—mental hyperactivity—not physical. With endogenous depression. I have an actual dual diagnosis. Now, tell me I'm not a space cadet! Dr. Raju put me on Effexor a new anti-depressant with a 3-day half-dosage build-up time. Do you remember when those little blue pills made me suicidal years ago and your dad flushed them? Another type actually made me worse as well as those original white-and-yellows I took in New Guinea against my better judgment. The R_x manual is not kidding when they list suicidal tendencies as a side effect for just about all of them. They do turn depression into suicidal ideation sometimes."

Mom was right. She had bipolar II, and research would eventually find that people with bipolar could have a poor reaction to some anti-depressants with side effects, including agitation and suicidal ideation.[201] No doubt it was beyond frustrating. As her daughter, it was hope-draining just to witness.

Mom continued:

"Well, I believe Dr. Raju was negligent in not hospitalizing me for the shape I was in. Steve wondered, too, why he'd try out a new Rx under circumstances like that. I [am] totally wiped out with barely enough strength to get up to go to the bathroom and return to the couch for those three days. Didn't even celebrate Isaiah's birthday. Missed one final. Was suicidal, but without energy to do anything about it."

Needless to say, it was extremely problematic if Mom's psychiatrist didn't hospitalize her when she needed it. With her history of suicidal thought and suicide attempts, it could be inexcusable. Mom had such a long history of getting inadequate mental health care that this kind of experience could be expected at this point.

And her family. They never stopped being judgmental and self-congratulatory, an added toxin to whatever difficulties Mom might be having. Mom wrote,

"Well, I believe the good Lord sent JaLee over Friday night. I told her to just fuss over Isaiah and basically leave me alone. I just wanted to sleep. She persisted, although I hadn't bathed in days. She took us to Lone Star and I perked up after a little food. She suggested I not take any more of those pills. I didn't. I did get a little energy on Sunday and

re-cleaned my office. Had motivation but really had to push myself physically.

"*Better today on no meds at all, but weak and tenuous. Now, no car, no ADC* [welfare check], *no food stamps, no Rx, no counseling or contact with them (unethical for a year) and I have to read Grandpa's Letter to the Editor, 'Don't Pick on Rush Limbaugh.' I won't send it to you, Deb. I really blew up at him. That's the last thing I needed just then—someone like him advocating a return to family values where families took care of their own. Spare me the hypocrisy! I just should renounce welfare and announce we're moving in with them June 1ˢᵗ. Grandpa totally devoid of original thought. He builds his day around Rush.*"

Thank goodness for our family friend, Ja-Lee, a Korean American woman who also struggled with poverty. Poor Mom: trying to get over the depression she'd lived with her entire life, a depression her family refused to understand, and having to deal with the hypocritical values they'd shine when the chance arose. They had never volunteered to help us with our problems, but they would be the first to endorse the policy that family should help family before welfare gets involved. *They were the worst.*

Mom's letter was long, and she finished with a nearly continuous concern for us. She said, "*Well, I'm getting a new 1978 Chrysler LeBaron, maroon, for $1600, nice.*"

Mom wrote again the next day,

"*Well, so much for that car—didn't quite make it 24 hours! Isaiah's 11 now. Proudly announced, 'I'm learning to sleep by myself' (two full nights, but not in a row). I'm now on Effexor, 75 mg, building up for three days halfway through. Now, I am waiting on AAA . . .*"

Another freaking lemon. Our whole lives, one piece of crap car after another. Isaiah took much too long to wean himself from sleeping by my mom, but it was another example of how all our mental health was affected.

When school got out in May, Senja went back to Iowa. From Iowa that month, Senja wrote, *"What's up? I'm getting fat, but don't worry, so are you, too."* She ended the letter by saying, *"P.S. I didn't mean the fat part,"* but since I was three hundred pounds at this point, it was not the right thing to say to me.

I ran into an eating disorder therapist and cried out about the bingeing symptoms that had been with me since I was eight years old. The man I was working with ruled out anorexia, but then he pondered bulimia. He said I may fit the diagnosis, but after he worked with me for a while, he decided I couldn't be called bulimic. It was true that I didn't purge by vomiting or overexercising, though I had done some of the latter for a while.

It was 1995, and my eating disorder didn't yet exist. I didn't know that he could diagnose me with an "eating disorder–not otherwise specified," and that's sort of what this man did. He did talk therapy with me for a couple of years, but without giving me a diagnosis. That would be impossible now. Binge Eating Disorder would come out in future versions of the *Diagnostic and Statistical Manual (DSM)*, a.k.a, "The Psychiatrist's Bible."

It was interesting how until I formally had a diagnosis according to the *DSM*, my eating habits weren't coming across as odd. Here I was shoveling all kinds of sweets and salty snacks along with soda pop into my mouth for a few days only to have a couple weeks of salads and exercise. Back and forth. Back and forth.

But the end result was still three hundred pounds. I looked like complete shit too. Some people look good heavier. My high school best friend was still attractive as she carried extra pounds. I was not. My face rounded out like a pie. My eyes seemed to disappear, so it was a good thing I had glasses to show people where to look. My whole shape was undesirable, and I felt the ugliest I ever had in my life.

Perhaps I was being fatphobic, and I did have body dysmorphia, but honestly, I look horrible overweight.[202] So, I was miserable and withdrawn from the opposite sex as well. No worries—they never paid me any of that kind of attention.

One of the things that made 1995 special was the wedding of Deborah MacGregor to a Hungarian man. She had invited me to be her maid of honor. I decided to make a trip out of it and travel back to Muenster, Germany, to see my host family, and then take the train to Hungary. I asked my brother Samuel if he wanted to go along with me. We would bring along Senja and Samuel's girlfriend, Yvette. I showed my brother and sister as much of Germany as I could, including a tour of Dachau. When we got to Budapest, a British taxicab driver took advantage of the fact we didn't know the currency well yet, and charged us over one hundred dollars for our ride.

I hated that I was so overweight for my friend's wedding. I was extremely self-conscious about how I looked compared to my slim, beautiful friend. I was jealous of her ability to find a husband while I still was not even dating. I shouldn't have been envious. The marriage didn't make her that happy or last very long. The Hungarians at the wedding would have said the marriage didn't last because we Americans didn't eat the sheep's brain that was being served for good luck during the reception, as was customary. I think it might have been more complicated than that. He was a heavy metal rock star and a journalist in Hungary, and he gave that up to be a waiter in the United States after they married, so he wasn't happy. He ended up returning to Hungary after they divorced.

A letter from Mom in July 1995 was representative of so many others:

"Isaiah went through that whole box of matches—I found the empty box out back with matches strewn all over. There were far more than can be accounted for with just sparklers. I told his P.O. And John. Humph! Last night he rigged up a phone, so he could hang out on the dike and still get his curfew calls. Yvette says he didn't come in until

about 3:00 after Samuel was home. Trouble is, he had lied about being down in the basement when I asked him where he was. . . . Turns out they were responding to John's request for some acid 'for David and him.' Dave says he got a note on his car seat asking him if he wanted any and he said he threw it away. He also refuses to give up smoking, so I told him if he was going to spend his resources on nicotine, I wasn't going to support his effort to get his GED. Incidentally, Isaiah has taken off and I haven't tracked him down yet."

I think it was decisions like taking away help for the GED as punishment that led me to suggest that Isaiah come and stay with me as well. Or just reading how things in general were going badly with the boys. I knew ToughLove was never going to cut it. I didn't want Isaiah graduating to arson.

Dad also wrote, piling on the difficulties:

"I'm writing this to tell you of our misfortunes lately: I lost a lot of work due to a bone spur on my right heel. It's very PAINFUL. I've got an arch support in place so I can resume work. And 800 mg 4x/day painkillers. Was using a cane and unable to move. Surgery is out, as is steroid injections. So . . . it looks like we won't make Aug. 6th ceremony, but hope prospects improve later this season. I'm sorry. It's a problem of $ (lack), pain (travel in a car for me is a torture over ten miles)."

"Also, I had my car broken into. It is figured somebody from a detective agency (of Ford & Chrysler hire) to figure out emissions secret. (It's no device by the way)! They found nothing. Also—a good reason for not being in Michigan. There's a price on my head—of sorts. What prompts this is the EPA's ethanol mandate for June 1, 1995."

I should have had lots of empathy for Dad's heel pain, since I would inherit it, but I was distracted by the other things he wrote, and how he was once again letting me down. He had missed my high school graduation ceremony, my college graduation ceremony, and now he was missing my master's degree graduation ceremony. It hurt my feelings. But he wasn't there for any of my siblings' ceremonies either, as far as that goes, and I knew rationally why he missed them.

I was also distracted by his claim that there was a price on his head. Obviously, there wasn't a price on his head. His paranoia never stopped though.

* * *

Updates from Mom continued to arrive describing, and usually lamenting, the yo-yo-like ups and downs Mom experienced with the boys.

"Isaiah's been so lovable lately. He rubbed my back yesterday in bed and made me a cup of coffee. He can sure be funny. I actually got John to laugh. His guard was down. Four Oaks sent home a book called, Before It's Too Late, *about antisocial traits*[203]. *It sure fits John. Unable to see other people's point of view."*

John was a teenager, and he was antisocial and rebellious, even relative to other teenagers, but he was not really a psychopath or a sociopath as Mom feared. I had conversations with John about the other boys in the Four Oaks program, and he teared up when he said they were the types to torture animals. I believed him.

* * *

Demonstrating her usual excellent judgment, Mom wrote:

"Deb, I know you must be a bit skeptical of my 'track record,' but I really want you to give Darrell a fair chance. Get to know him and you'll find an extremely sensitive, caring, loving man who loves all of us very much as his 'family.' I love the way he truly loves the Lord and just simply wants to help people—he's exactly my counterpart at being concerned with every kind of social problem there is—jails, mental hospitals, youth, substance abuse, elderly, sick, homeless, community, you name it, and he's interested. We are so compatible in every way. He even cut down his smoking to 2-3 cigs a day. Isaiah and John are responding absolutely unbelievably. I think the timing of John's Four Oaks & DJ is perfect. You wouldn't even know John."

Based on what John told *me*, he wanted to stop being involved with criminal justice because the other kids in the system scared him. It wasn't because of Mom's new boyfriend. But I knew she must be head over heels because she doesn't tolerate smoking, and this guy smoked. Oh well, I thought. Here we go again.

In a letter written the same day, Mom said,

"Is May 25th going to work for you to be at our wedding? Oh yes, I was telling you about Darrell (DJ). He has such a 'dry' sense of humor, sometimes he gets taken seriously and it results in a misunderstanding. But his humor is keen. You would be so proud of John the other night at the parents' meeting at Four Oaks. He suggested they cover the dysfunctional cycle and got himself chosen to 'volunteer' to do it. He presented it like an old pro, with professional style, humor, and he acted like he was enjoying it. Gave examples of how he used to be and I must say it was thrilling to listen to him. He is into a really positive cycle now and looks at other's needs. Darrell came along just at the right time, combined with what he is learning at Four Oaks."

Mom never married DJ, who turned out to be a dud.

Chapter Thirty-Three: Deb, Are You Going to Fix the System?

T HE SUMMER OF 1996 was exciting because I went back to Iowa to work for Upward Bound. Senja participated in Upward Bound that year, and so did John. I also spent the summer teaching my master's thesis in personality psychology to the Upward Bound students, focusing on the concept of "Possible Selves."[204]

Senja continued to live with me in Ann Arbor, but she spent August in Iowa with Mom. During that month, Samuel, his girlfriend, Yvette, and Senja got into a serious car accident. It wasn't fatal for anyone, but the consequences of the accident were a lot longer than anyone expected.

Senja wrote:

"Hey big sis, I could probably get money from this accident. I'm going to be wise about it. I'm pretty sure that I'll be okay . . . all that happened is just a really tensed up back . . . no broken parts anywhere. (I did bump my head and I couldn't talk right but that lasted for about an hour)."

Famous last words: *"I'm pretty sure I'll be okay and it's just a bump on the head."* Senja had a traumatic brain injury. It was not going to be okay. Combined with a couple TBIs to come, Senja was going to struggle mightily.[205] Head injuries are like an affliction for this family, a ever-growing part of our identity.

A very familiar, kind of letter came next: another description of an old used car Mom was buying. If only she could have afforded a decent car upfront, she wouldn't have had constant car expenses.

"Well, we have a new Oldsmobile. It was no doubt one classy buggy in its day (the operative word here is 'was'). It's gold and rust colored. It was originally gold and brown. Year? I don't know. Isaiah immediately proceeded to pull off the door closer thingy. Not a good sign . . . Sigh . . . It's a two-door with two heavy metal 'gates'—humongous things. It's a V-6."

Isaiah was going to spend August with me as well until school started, and Senja came back with me. The arrangement worked quite well, except Senja thought that Tappan Middle School was "snobby." The other kids there were upper middle class. I knew all about this culture clash, how hard it could be to adjust to class differences, and she indicated that it indeed was.

In August, Mom wrote:

"Isaiah, are you meeting new friends? People ask about you at church. Were you able to visit the church up there? That's where Pastor Walker and Ruth are from. Hey, maybe one of them is going up that way. We'll see. We sure had a wonderful lesson all week on Daniel. Full house every night. So perfect the Bible is. Remember how Jesus said to forgive 70 X 7? Well, that's 490 times and Jews had 490 years to accept the truth and they didn't (except those who converted, but as a whole, they didn't). There's so much precision, and the Old and New Testaments complement each other so for a total big picture."

The antisemitism in this letter wasn't subtle. I was reluctant to even show it to Isaiah. I knew she wasn't being intentionally antisemitic, and that the ideas were from her church. Mom and Dad had taken me to Rabbi Serber when I was a teenager for guidance, and his advice was so spot-on that it was a lifesaver for me at the time.

But at the end of August, things returned to normal. Isaiah went back to Iowa to live with Mom, and Senja came back to Ann Arbor to stay with me.

In September, Mom wrote Senja and me:

"John just got back from a week in Cedar Rapids for problems related to letting people know where he is. He's working at Industrial Fabrication now. I think that will be a good job for him. Richard [the neighbor kid] *has been staying here pretty much. He's turning into a really decent young man. He's offered to pay for laundry, and he said we've always been good to him ever since we moved in.*

Isaiah really changed his attitude. He was really grumpy about going to church (after all, I allowed him to go out for football). He's doing really well, and their team won their first game against West. He's an offensive guard. Looks so cute in his uniform . . . I'm pretty mad about whoever got into his Ritalin. It's absolutely gone. He's getting notes from school, although I'm really going to try to help him settle down now that we're organized. I can't believe what a roll I've been on. Samuel said John has said he was getting concerned about me."

It didn't sound like Mom had a solid handle on the boys despite how she may have briefly felt as she wrote the letter. She was probably trying to force Isaiah to go to church with her against his will, like she had with the rest of us. With the neighbor Richard, she was taking in outsiders again as a sort of a rescuer, and this always meant even less attention to her children. Still, I wasn't overly worried.

The call came at one o'clock in the morning on October 14, 1996. A nurse warned me that my brother David had attempted to kill himself, and it was very serious. She called back a half hour later and told me that he had died. Her first call had a tone that prepared me for the second call.

I didn't wake Senja up at first. Instead, I called Kyla and cried on her shoulder. She came over and helped me wake up my sister to tell her David had died. We immediately prepared to get home to Iowa.

I asked Senja to drive because I was shaking uncontrollably. It turns out she resented me for years for doing this.

When we got to Iowa, we learned the details of the story. David had taken a hose from a vacuum cleaner and connected it with duct tape to the back of his car muffler. He wound the other end of the vacuum cleaner hose into the car window.

Samuel tried to save him but opened the door too late. David fell to the ground, sustaining a perimortem injury to his forehead. He was already brain-dead when he arrived at the hospital, and they tried to revive him. They obviously couldn't.

The entire family was devastated by David's death. It didn't come out of nowhere, given his past suicide attempts, but I was defeated. I had hoped that all six of us would escape poverty.

David's funeral was well-attended, including by Dad. Many people in the community came to share their condolences with the family. Sweetie's son spoke. But Senja's reaction to David's death was odd. Two weeks later, back in Michigan, she wrote a note:

"Dear Deborah honey,

My day was fine. Was yours? Will you pick me up? Or are you going to sleep in lieu of last night's missing sleep? Either way, it's fine by me. Thanks for doing the dishes for me. That was muy thoughtful. Well, it's time to close this, my delicate rose. Love, Senja"

It was sweet and kind, and it makes sense that we would be treating each other tenderly right after losing our brother. But it was also strangely upbeat.

Dad wrote at the beginning of November to tell us he had put Senja on his health care plan through Walmart. In his letter he included,

"I'm not in the right frame of mind right now to discuss David—But feel free to talk or write to me about it. My conviction and faith is that he is in good hands and found the peace he truly wanted."

Mom wrote in early November, and she said,

"Oh, Sweetie's into crank. Just goes from bad to worse. Her sons both have cut her out of their lives. She's even alienated her adoptive brother. Sad. I haven't seen her since the day of the funeral when she said she'd come at 3:00 and no sign of her—no note, nothing. Her son says they were thinking of committing her."

Sweetie was using meth, the scourge of poor people. David may have had a meth problem before his suicide. He certainly had abused it. Now, I was worried about Senja and Isaiah.

Mom wrote in mid-November to say, *"Isaiah missed a lot of school last week. Back today (Monday). Cylert works. Isaiah does his homework."* This was a source of long-term disagreement between them. Although he seemed to perform better academically and behaviorally when taking his meds, Isaiah resented how he felt on Ritalin or Cylert very much. He was angry for having to take it.[206]

Mom continued:

"John & Dion [next-door neighbor] stayed up all night to clean the house, but Isaiah and Richard [the neighbor kid that mom was allowing to live with them] messed up right behind. Richard starts working Village Inn today so when he gets his first paycheck, it's going toward a sleeping room . . . Left a terrible mess all over the floors when his car started on fire—ashes and yuck all over and no effort to clean it up. Or do anything! Got violent videotapes to play all the time—really getting me depressed. Deb, I might need your help over Thanksgiving to ensure that he's making necessary arrangements, okay? My therapist says I need to do 3 things 1) Prozac daily, 2) journal daily, and 3) walk/exercise. Today, I took Prozac, but I think cleaning will count for exercise. Got the kitchen and bath floors scrubbed. What a mess!"

She complained a lot more about Richard and his ability to eat lots of food and leave a mess everywhere he went. Then she wrote,

"I can't afford him! He's worse than David! Attitude problem, too. And I'm missing my last $20 out of the bank envelope in my purse. Do I sound resentful? He doesn't cooperate . . . Don't be surprised if he's gone by the time you get here."

So, that was that. David was gone. The neighbor kid was an ass, but we always knew that. He was going to be a pain to evict. Sigh.

Mom sent a card to me and Senja before Christmas 1996: *"Hope you get this before you leave. You are, of course, feeling better, by now, but I'll fix some chicken soup for you, since you didn't get the chicken soup I poured into Yvette's email. Forecast is -10° so dress warm and take blankets along, just in case. Got a cell phone? See you soon."*

It was always good to get a note from Mom that sounded like a note from a mom. It was comforting and supportive.

At Christmas 1996, Dad sent a Christmas card with this update: *"Lost my one job, so kinda hurting right now for income."* Hmm. So, our family's deeper poverty can be linked to the fact that Dad only had one job, instead of two.

~

After I finished my master's degree in Social Work, my second two years of graduate school were heavily focused on finishing the requirements for my master's in Personality Psychology. Instead of being directed toward Social Work goals, I was taking lots of classes in the Psychology department and preparing to complete my master's thesis. To be clear, I was in a doctoral program in which I got my master's degrees along the way to completion of my doctorate.

I took Social Psychology with Professor Joe Veroff and Personality Psychology with Professor Abby Stewart. In both classes, guest lecturers spoke about their theories on all kinds of topics ranging from evolutionary psychology to racial socialization and gender roles.

In January 1997, Mom wrote, *"Working for Uncle Paul. Helps money-wise. Depression lifted. Somewhat just today."*

In February 1997, Mom added:

"I've been working for Uncle Paul, but I had quite a scare yesterday. I'd had a 'film' over my right eye for about a week, so I took a day off to see doc this morning . . . I think menopause is eroding what little is left of my brain cell function. It's all a neurological problem, I'm convinced, which just feeds the old depression which is inherent in my genes. Was really starting to get depressed but found pillbox with Prozac from my purse under the bed. Still can't find pharmacy bottle."

Then, at the beginning of March, Mom sent a postcard on which she said that her therapist got her on hormone replacement therapy, because *"I was going postal."* The importance of treating menopausal symptoms appropriately was not understood, apparently, by many of my mother's doctors, and I didn't realize it either. My mother probably had a condition called premenstrual dysphoric disorder,[207] a condition openly mocked by conservatives on Fox "News."

In March 1997, Mom wrote, "*Went to ACOA meeting Saturday. Very helpful. Fish are learning new tricks everyday (roll over, play dead, sing).*" Of course, I laughed at the notion of Mom's pet fish doing tricks, but I loved the way one of them came to the side of the tank and seemed to suck my finger when I put my finger to the glass. I liked her fish. She seemed to be in a better place. It was also very good that Mom was going to a group for people from dysfunctional families. She could get a lot of strong support from Adult Children of Alcoholics. I certainly had during college.

Mom wrote to us again in March:

"*Thank you for being my favorite daughters in the whole world. When I think of how little trouble you've been compared to your male counterparts, I'm just so proud of you both. Senja, your card will be late. I don't want to shock you by having it timely. I have a nasty headache—banged my head getting into Steve's car yesterday, but it's PMS time again. Doctor says no estrogen now—migraines have been 'estrogen headaches.' Should diminish in time. We'll see. Could be your problem, Deb? Too much estrogen? Got the Corsica fixed—just in time. Samuel's joint going out on his pickup truck over $400 worth (gulp).*"

Poor Mom and her migraine headaches. She's kept right on having them all her life.

Dad wrote again in April for my birthday. He announced:

"*I'm unemployed. And I need some information to present in court. I'm having the child support redone now that John and Samuel are above age 18. So your information is vital...*"

Then he took off asking all kinds of questions about how Senja was being financed. Suddenly, I had to round up paperwork for him. I was swamped at the end of the semester, so I felt guilty about how long it took me to get everything back to him that he needed. But it meant sharing all my student loan information with my dad, and I wasn't comfortable admitting how much my education was costing me. I eventually did though.

~

Based on my amazing experience in Germany, I encouraged Senja to apply for the Congress-Bundestag Youth Exchange, a scholarship program for a high school student to go to Germany for a year for free. It was highly competitive, but she applied and was accepted.

Mom was writing to someone named Mike in May 1997. Her letter was full of soaring language and fanciful talk. She sounded manic. She wrote:

"Lest your concern legitimately wander toward my mental state, I hasten to reassure you that manic depression is not my diagnosis, so this isn't a 'manic phase.' This is pure, raw, fresh JOY, emerging from the deep 'seeds of reality' planted in sorrow."

Right. I had been saying for years that Mom had bipolar II, and no one had been listening to me.[208] She apparently never told her mental health professionals what I suggested, or they had never listened to her.

She wrote Mike again later that month and sent a copy to me, boundaryless as usual:

"I really do believe there is no such thing as a lost cause! I kinda wish I'd written to John Wayne Gacy when he was alive. He was so hardened. Nothing like a granite test case to explore possibilities, huh? I did feel a spark of some kind of 'connection' with Jeffrey Dahmer—he seemed so repentant and eager to cooperate, stemming from a genuine empathy for the victims' families. Someone who worked with him was interviewed on TV, and commented on how helpful he was, motivated by his desire to help the families find resolution."

Lordy. Reading this made me upset with Mom. Maybe it was because I knew how evil serial killers were, but it was so irritating that my mother was naïve enough to believe she could write to them and make them anything but malicious. Something about her words really triggered me. I could tell it was a kind of mania that she was experiencing, a kind of expansive thinking one sees in mania and hypomania. She wasn't thinking clearly, but, again, her mental health providers hadn't identified her as having bipolar.[209]

In June 1997, Mom wrote a card in Germlish that said she had a migraine headache that had made her throw up twice, and it still hadn't gone away. She attributed the headache to it being her time of the month. By that time, I had inherited Mom's and Grandpa's migraine headaches, too, but they came all the time, not at only one time of the month. I was having as many as fifteen migraine headaches a month.[210] They were causing me to miss a lot of work. I'm not sure if I had more headaches than my mother and grandfather or not. I was taking all different kinds of preventative medications, but they still weren't putting Mom on one. I assume that was because she was on Medicaid.

~

In the fall, Isaiah arrived in Ann Arbor to start his eighth-grade year at Tappan Middle School with me as his guardian. Senja was in Germany for the Congress-Bundestag program, and she wrote home regularly. The first letter home, in August, sounded positively exuberant, except for scolding me for giving her a bad German accent. She was so proud of herself because she had climbed the Alps.

But there was an inkling that things would go badly when she said that on her way down the mountain she got *really* depressed and couldn't explain why. Her letter home on September 2 helped me understand what might be bothering her. She described her host brother:

"There's Hans. Let me describe him. He's 17. He only listens to techno music (the kind that gives most people headaches). His favorite color is orange. All of his girlfriends must be anorexically thin, and all other women are fat. He lies to and about me. Basically, he's a jerk."

She wasn't done though. She continued, *"Let me describe his grandpa. He's old, loves nobody (he even said that), hates Americans (therefore he hates me, hates women, loves to criticize.) He's an absolute asshole."*

She went on to explain that her host brother complained to his grandpa about having a foreign exchange student, so the grandpa tore into her host mother. No wonder she was miserable. She was in the middle of a dysfunctional family situation again.

~

In September, Mom wrote a letter to her father, Grandpa Meyer:
"This is in response to the letter you dropped off. First, it saddens me to see the cloud of anger and bitterness that surrounded you that day

especially when I think how the Bible says, 'Husbands, love your wives, and be not bitter against them.' Colossians 3:19.[211] You have allowed yourself to be bitter for all these years since I was 15 years old. I am 52 years old now. You figure out how much of your happiness (and your family's happiness) that has consumed. And for what? What's really sad to me is how you didn't even ask how your grandchildren are?... And how do you think Senja feels to be singled out and forced to listen to an embittered old man yammering about an irrelevant moment in history? Is that how you want to continue to defy the Bible two years later: 'Fathers, provoke not your children to anger, lest they be discouraged.' Colossians 3:21.[212] Enough already! If it helped anything, it might be tolerable, but it is intolerable. 40 years of the same ol' same ol' is all I can handle without vomiting it back up. I need a dad & the kids need a grandfather, not a bitter, hateful, whining, complaining, criticizing, negative, dark-brooding, seething, angry, wretch of a man who has replaced him. Give us back the old Grandpa."

Grandpa had written to all of us about his anger over being hospitalized for his mental health when Mom was fifteen years old. He resented that it had happened, although I'd heard the story, and he definitely needed inpatient treatment. He did need to let it go. He'd been hospitalized again when Mom was twenty-two, and he was probably angry about that too. Anyway, I was proud of Mom for standing up to her father. Usually, she just let him carry on.

~

Mom sent a postcard to Isaiah in September:

"Everyone is thrilled about your being in a school where you can be challenged to do your best, and to know that you can just start out with 3 As! Isaiah, have you ever had grades like that? You know you were capable of doing well, but now you are proving you can do it. Yes!! You know you have to work at it like anyone who wants that good feeling of satisfaction in doing well, but we know you have what it takes."

In September 1997, I was preparing for an exam in the middle of the night when something jolted my back. I was walking back to my chair to sit down and work, but I just crumbled. I couldn't even stand. It was too painful. The only thing I could do was lie there. I couldn't even crawl to get a blanket to cover myself. I laid there freezing overnight until the morning when Isaiah woke up. I asked him to bring my phone and a blanket.

I immediately called the doctor, and he said I had a few options but the best one was probably to call an ambulance to go to the emergency room. Next, I called my close friend, Sue, who also worked for the Center for Poverty, Risk, and Mental Health as a research assistant. We enjoyed regularly eating lunch together to talk about life in school and being single. I was grateful she answered the phone and helpfully agreed to come right over to meet me at the hospital.

In the emergency room, the doctor tried to make me stand up again. Sue says I literally turned green with the pain. I know I absolutely started screaming and shouting and begging to lie back down. The doctor got me back off my feet immediately and sent me home with a Fentanyl patch for pain.[213] I needed significant painkillers to be mobile. Fortunately for me, this was an era when painkillers were prescribed more easily.

A letter of Senja's from October helped further explain why she might be depressed. In school, she had to participate in a coordinated dance routine with eight other students, and the other students already knew the routine when she arrived. Senja felt clumsy and awkward. As an extremely clumsy and awkward person myself, I understood every bit how awful she felt.

She also explained that she was taking physics, chemistry, geometry, and religion in German. She estimated she understood 40 to 51 percent of what was being said. I thought that was remarkably good comprehension, but obviously not a good thing in an academic class setting.

Another October letter added:

"I want you to know that I quit Gymnasium, because they were such snobs. I can't survive in such an environment. Realschule is like the

difference between a university and a community college, but I don't care. I feel better here."

I understood how Germans did their schooling system. They used tracking. My sister was feeling the difference in social class between the schools.

But in November 1997, she sounded excited again, and eager to be there, describing the two big newspaper articles that were written about her with enthusiasm. She was right; they were major news articles.

~

That same month, my eating disorder therapist told me, "I don't think you have an eating disorder; I think you have something else." He was completely wrong. I did have an eating disorder called binge eating disorder, but the disorder hadn't been identified yet.[214] So, I went investigating medical causes for my eating issues. And there it was, right in my medical record: even though a doctor diagnosed me with polycystic ovarian syndrome (PCOS) in November 1994, I wasn't told until almost three years later that I had it.[215]

PCOS causes many symptoms, including hirsutism, infertility, weight gain, hair loss (from the top of your head), a distinctive apple body shape, cardiac problems and more. I was devastated to learn I had this disorder even as I was also relieved to finally have a name for a lot of what was wrong with me.

At first, the message boards I found for women with PCOS seemed like great places to go for information and mutual support. I was most concerned about the research showing we have a seven times greater likelihood of having a heart attack than typical women. But the message boards quickly became a dark and toxic place for me to be. Women with PCOS who could not have children would go on rants about women on welfare popping out baby after baby, while they couldn't have one. If your parents had been on welfare, it felt like an assault.

I compiled what I had learned from some of the wiser women with PCOS, and I started putting it to work. I created menus that were sensitive to insulin resistance. I got myself into a research study on metformin and PCOS, so I could get the drug prescribed to me.

I obtained laser hair removal, which is the only thing that ever works permanently on our faces.

I went on to have nearly a decade without a date. That's a slight exaggeration. I had one or two dates, but nothing where I felt like either of us was an attractive candidate. I developed an intense sense of hopelessness about anything ever getting better. I went into a deep funk about my impending life of loneliness without a mate.[216]

I used every weapon available to me to lose the weight I gained in graduate school. Otherwise, I would never get married. I hadn't missed any of the Disney princess movies. I fantasized about a Prince Charming.

~

In November 1997, I was contacted by the University of Michigan Pain Research Center to enroll in a study of painkillers. It took place from January to June 1998. They compared how Vicodin relieved my pain for three months versus how Fentanyl relieved my pain for three months.[217] Sweet Jesus, six months without pain!

I started an exercise routine in January 1998 that I faithfully continued each week through the rest of my time in Michigan until June 2000, eventually finding my way from three hundred pounds down to 150 pounds. I did weight training and aerobics twice a week and water aerobics once a week.

The dieting was extremely strict. I thought I couldn't eat any carbohydrates, so I followed an Atkins Diet. It was a lot of salads and hamburger patties. All the diet experimentation began while Senja was in Germany and continued for several years, but it was hard to stay rigorous in my self-care while also getting my doctorate.

I was teaching class, doing research, helping with admissions, writing my master's thesis, and going to parent-teacher conferences for Isaiah, who was getting in trouble in school. He struggled not to act out in class due to his ADHD. In particular, he poked his teacher in the stomach.[218] She didn't like it. She didn't realize he did this to everyone. And I mean everyone. But that didn't make it okay, obviously.

~

In January 1998, Senja wrote about a lot of the details of her life in Germany, and she seemed to be adjusting. She wrote about a teddy bear she received from an Iowa classroom. The teddy bear had a backpack, which she was asked to fill with souvenirs from the area and then return to the classroom. She seemed to like the task. Dad wrote that month as well, but throughout the letter he kept mentioning Vedic astrology as a treatment for PCOS. There was no way I was going to consult Indian astrology for help on PCOS, but thanks anyway, Dad.

In February, Senja wrote, "*I believe I've matured here. I'm practically a grownup. Do you wanna hear all my dreams and goals?*" She went on for several pages about her plans for college and travelling back to Europe. It still seemed like she was thriving there. I should have recognized that she was becoming manic. I should've had the training and experience to recognize what she was going through, but the sexual harassment I had experienced had interfered with that training. Senja was demonstrating tendencies that were concerning.

~

In February, Mom wrote to her dad, Grandpa Meyer. At the time, she was in Ann Arbor with Isaiah and me:

"*Keep your eye on the paper to see if you can see if John goes to court on that possession of marijuana charge and intent to deliver. He doesn't communicate with us. He'll be nineteen soon. Deborah and I were thinking of getting him a 'Get Out of Jail Free' card, like in the game Monopoly. There's a book called,* The Bible Code, *that you could check out from the library. If they don't have it, they could order it for you on interlibrary loan. It sure is fascinating. It's how everything is encoded in the Torah, the first five books of the Bible. It's been said that every hair is numbered, and the way those codes work out, it's amazing. They had the assassination of Rabin with the name of his assassin, and I believe even the date. I know you'd enjoy it.*"

Mom and Grandpa Meyer were able to connect when they talked about the Bible. Mom was still a biblical fundamentalist of one kind or another. It was sort of hard to pin down. But she also tolerated the fact that I didn't want to hear about the Bible anymore. Grandpa would have said college caused that. I went to a religious college. Of course, it didn't cause that. It was the lifetime of Mom and Dad's focus on the Bible that pushed me away. It was the fundamentalism itself.

~

In March, Senja wrote:

"I'm going crazy, Mama. . . .put me on an appointment list to see a shrink and get some Prozac. I'm getting MPD [multiple personality disorder][219] *. . . The devil child and the angelic woman in me are fighting with the loser (normal) personality of me about depression. My head is a battlefield and I'd like to die -now-. I want to shoot myself. . . Do you know that I value my life/health/happiness even less since I've been here? I think I'm cracking."*

I panicked upon reading this letter. Up until then, she had written extremely long letters that indicated she was homesick. At first, I wasn't too concerned, thinking she was getting closer and closer to the end of her stay. Now, she needed to come home, but I didn't know how to end the scholarship arrangement. She could terminate the program if she was in this much trouble, but it was over soon, so I thought maybe I should just arrange the mental health care from Michigan. But "soon" was July. Still four months away. It was devastating that something I thought was going to be edifying and helpful in her life was, in reality, harmful. This overseas experience was turning out a lot like Mom's had in New Guinea, but not entirely. Senja also told me that she started drinking and smoking while in Germany.

~

Mom wrote another letter to Grandpa Meyer, dated March 20:

"I guess John's doing okay. Watch the paper for any hearing. You'll know before I do. Isaiah's behavior is much better on 2 Cylert pills a day. I'm helping Deb hand out survey forms today. Deb's awaiting further tests, maybe Cushing's Syndrome, weight, facial hair? See you if and when I ever get back. Senja is really bored and lonely—it's like a tiny village there & she is not a happy camper. She'd love mail."

I appreciated her help on my research project as well as having her there to talk to Isaiah's teachers when they called about his behavior, which had indeed gotten better.

Senja's April letter sounded a bit better, but she said that she'd pierced her nose. Well, my best friend from college, Deborah Mac-Gregor, had had her nose pierced a couple of times, so this wasn't alarming in itself, given the fashion at the time.

Mom sent a postcard in April relaying that she was back in Iowa. Mom told me,

"I'm really excited about this new herbal stuff. I'm gonna get some to help with ADD, but I want to show you first how much it helps me."

I can't tell you how many often-expensive "remedies" Mom discovered outside the medical system that were "guaranteed" to treat whatever she had. The product might be guaranteed to treat a list of one hundred different ailments. Needless to say, Mom still had all the ailments she'd treated with these wonder cures. Now, she'd tell you that she couldn't afford to "maintain" the treatment, so that was why it failed. I am sparing you the letters where she complained the treatment tasted too bad. Yet she never thought the treatment hadn't been worth investing lots of money in in the first place. Every one of those treatments was somehow still worth what she paid for it, just to have it sit on her shelf apparently.

Mom wrote in May:

"Today, I got a violation from the Health Department! It was about that tan Aspen in the driveway, and how it's a health hazard. We were planning to junk it anyway, along with the other three junkers."

I pictured these ancient used cars broken down around the house. We didn't really have a yard, just a driveway, but it was home to two beaters. There was another parked across the street from the house. In fact, the city moved the parking from our side of the street to the other side of the street in about 1994, possibly in an effort to decrease the number of junked cars around our property.

Mom continued,

"Well, Senja can say she'll be home next month now. Will she remember how to speak English? What will be her summer plans? . . . I bet she could easily get something using her translating skills now. Also remind me to have you watch this video that I know will impress you about the language in the Bible. It is awesome. Everything is in types and antitypes, or like the mold and the Jello. I LOVE studying it."

Indeed, Mom and Dad had this in common. I heard from both of them, all the time, that studying the Scriptures was the key to life.

But she couldn't have been more wrong about whether I would love it.

Mom's letter continued:

"Well, I'm experimenting around a bit, and have been off the Prozac ever since I wound up in the emergency room that night with really pounding heart palpitations along with a migraine and severe nausea. I had taken it at the same time as the St. John's Wort (warns not to use them together, but Dr. Pangilinan had said it was okay) and I had tried it before with no effect)."

Mom's psychiatrist did her a huge disservice here by telling her she could take Prozac and the herbal treatment together, if that's what he did. He should have told her to take her medication and avoid the St. John's Wort altogether because mixing them is dangerous,[220] But naturally, what do you think Mom did when she decided which to take when she felt bad? That's right.

Mom wrote:

"Anyway, I decided to just go herbal instead. Well, predictably, I started to skirt around the edges of depression after a little over a week . . . However, in that week, I had practically rearranged the house singlehandedly, including bringing boxes up and down steps, hauling a dresser up the basement steps by myself, going for long walks, and in general, 'overgoing' a lot. Actually, I felt so good, I just got on a roll, but it says to get extra rest while your body is healing, and your body will win every time. So, I caught up on my sleep too."

Ah yes, of course, Mama. This was the all-too-familiar manic phase of her bipolarity. Why didn't her mental health professionals ever treat her manic phases?[221]

She added:

"I ended up short of sleep and depressed. My therapist discussed the pros and cons of going back on Prozac, but I wasn't ready to do that quite yet. Instead, I went to Dr. Short, the chiropractor, and he had just returned from a seminar, wherein he had gotten this new machine, he used on me. I have NEVER felt so good coming out of an adjustment before! My, that helped, although it hurt while he was doing it somewhat. In my neck, he told me this would jerk my hands, and sure enough, they were flipping all over the place (which was an indication that it was needed). We discussed how that could free up

the nerve supply in the 'depression' area and are both eagerly seeing what a full program of that would do."

That was total quackery.[222] No wonder it didn't have a long-term effect.

She continued:

"All of the above (herbs, chiropractic, exercise, counseling, etc.) should all work together to maximize health. I'm optimistic, anyway. However, this herbal barley stuff is supposed to clean you out while the barley that nourishes the cells tastes absolutely vile. Yuck. It's been so bad that I've psychologically just backed off of taking it. I just took some a while ago before I started this letter. It was wretched, but at least I'm back on it."

She raved about chiropractic appointments, but I have just not been impressed with my encounters with chiropractors. They haven't fixed my problems. She didn't discount the value of the herbal treatments because of their ineffectiveness. She just said she didn't take them properly. Maybe I should have asked the question, *Did you ever take the prescription medication properly?* But we didn't get that far. It was a moot point, anyway, because I think she was getting the wrong prescription meds too, so a comparison might not have been so informative.

~

Dad wrote to Isaiah for his birthday in May 1998. He apologized for being late due to his health:

"Today I had a seizure the doctor called a T.I.A.—transient is-chemic attack. There was no help or hope for the bio accident–caused depression. Years ago, your mother and I heard an expression, 'If you even saw the lowest glory of the three glories of celestial, terrestrial, and telestial, you'd commit suicide to get into the telestial.' Perhaps that's what David fulfilled in his own way. There was a special person unseen at his funeral. The same person that promised David that when your time comes, I'll come and get you. That promise was fulfilled. And that's my great hope and consolation, and it should be yours! That person was John the Revelator. The man who wrote the 4th gospel, 3 Epistles, and the mysterious Revelations. I've seen St. John in a transfiguration on July 20, 1972, and again I saw him as we started David's funeral . . . Brother David came to me in a dream and told

me 'You [Dad] have got to tell them [the family] what we know! You know. The truth. You've got to tell them . . .' Jeremiah 30:6 hints at our David."

It was hard to give Isaiah letters of Dad's in which he was delusional like this. Dad had never met St. John the Revelator. Not in 1972 and not at our brother's funeral. I *might* have just hidden this one from Isaiah. I was also beginning to feel like we needed to value our lives in the present, because there was no guarantee of an afterlife. I never sensed David after he died. He was gone. Dad is not the one he would have visited anyway.

Senja was back living with me, but she wrote me a note on July 18, 1998:

"Hey Sis, You're at work now and I'm here, really sick. After today, I realized 100% why you're so stressed out. Understandable, actually. I realize you worry about me, but you don't need to. I survived a year of hell, and deep inside I am truly happy to be back in the USA. You also managed quite a load with Isaiah, and I'll tell you, I couldn't do that. He's a load that busy people need tons of energy for. With proper care and time, he could amount to something more than a hyper thief."

I appreciated Senja's words of support, because it was true that parenting Isaiah was biting off more than I could chew. I didn't know how to deal with ADHD in the classroom much better than Mom, and it didn't seem like his teachers did either.

Senja gave me another beautiful card four days later. It was one of those cards intended for sisters and filled with eloquent and sappy words, but it was what she wrote inside that made me feel she loved me. She wrote:

"Thank you for letting me live with you. It's hard to say where I'd be today. You've encouraged me a lot (but don't go getting vain on us now). Not every older sister would let their bratty 14-year-old sister tag along through Europe. That's pretty cool of you. I've gotten to know you quite well, and you're very beautiful in every way . . . Keep in touch, or else I'll injure you (joking, Mr. Lawyer—I was NEVER abusive toward my older sister. She always snapped MY bra)!"

~

In October, Senja gave me a card with a letter that read, *"It was nice of you . . . to be so nice to me. Thanks."* She wrote that her medicine was "*helping a lot*" and that a "*couple of people have noticed.*" She also wrote, "*I have my concentration back as well. It all feels good.*"

But it didn't last. Literally that same month, that same medication started to make Senja feel suicidal, because she has bipolar disorder, not depression. By now, this is a recurring theme in our family. The paradoxical effect of antidepressants on persons with bipolar disorder was going to be discovered just a few years later, but it was still unknown at the time.[223] Her age may have been a factor as well.[224]

Senja was hospitalized following a suicide attempt later that month. Mom was staying with us to help take care of Senja and Isaiah at that point. Mom was also helping me with my dissertation, because it was a massive project, and I was overwhelmed. During this entire period, Mom's and my roles in our relationship flipped back and forth multiple times.

I had promised the National Institute of Mental Health that I would do a longitudinal, mixed-method, multi-site dissertation. It required complicated statistical analysis. It required transcribing more than one hundred interviews and analyzing them on software that I needed to learn. It required travel to other locations where I would need to spend time building a rapport. It was little wonder I got the grant. I promised something closer to what full professors propose for their research projects.

I hired some great research assistants, but I was still behind on the work. Senja's suicidal crisis occurred just as I was conducting my study, so I reacted to my sister's suicidality with anger, much as I had reacted to Mom's. I was personally hurt instead of reminding myself again that she had a mental health issue. I was somehow still not recognizing that this was just like a physical illness.

By January 1999, Senja wrote me a long letter apologizing for smoking in front of Isaiah. She had been trying to get him to quit, but was also smoking in front of him at other times. She realized that I wasn't making headway with him either. She also apologized for bringing her boyfriend into my bedroom while I was not home. She repeatedly said she was sorry for undermining me. She wanted me to know she was sorry because she wanted our relationship to improve again.

I deeply appreciated her letter, and I felt like our family was functioning as a team again. I didn't apologize to her for failing to act on her mental health crisis sooner. That's because I still didn't even recognize where I had dropped the ball. I was so busy I had failed to provide adequate mental health services in time, and it's hard to say what sort of long-term impact that had. I'm deeply sorry to Senja for not addressing her mental health crisis well. I was completely overwhelmed, so I stepped back to let Mom handle her crisis.

~

My stress level was through the roof. I can't recall the exact timeline of my dissertation. Since the study took more than a year to do, I already had the grant by this time, and all my time was spent managing my research project.

On October 4, 1999, Dad wrote me a letter:

"Lately, I had an offer to buy Relief Mining Co. stock at $5/share. ->Ultimate value $500,000/share. Very bad times. I am hoping I can buy some. If so, our family could be worth $40 million some day—I hope soon."

The Relief Mining Company was supposed to be related to the Dream Mine, a fantasy of many fundamentalist Mormons, including Bob Crossfield. It's basically a scam.[225] I knew it was a scam, so it was hard to read about Dad still believing it. Dad never had any money, so it would be horrible if he actually managed to waste anything on this.

In October, Dad wrote a letter to everyone, but he clearly wanted my attention drawn to some "official" paperwork.

"Enclosed is a Xerox of Iowa's persistent demands for $. If you guys are in Michigan—I'm in Wisconsin—why can't we get rid of them? Deb's already replied—I sent a package of Xeroxed documents showing Judge Langhoff's decree and signature, plus papers showing you guy's address. I'm whizzed over all this. My Chiquita canning job ended 2 AM October 5. I don't know when the bonus check arrives if it does. Did over 2 million cans of corn—a lot going to S. Korea. A bad year for ag: abundant and iffy quality corn . . . I was glad to hear that

your Mother and Paul went to Australia and New Guinea for old times' sake. Now, if we can just get your mom busy with Psalms 118:17 ['I shall not die, but live, and declare the works of the Lord']. "[226]

Dad was commenting on Mom's trip to the other side of the world with her brother, Uncle Paul. Paul wanted to see Australia, but his wife didn't care for traveling, so he asked Mom to go along, because she'd been in New Guinea in the 1960s as a missionary, and this would also give her the chance to revisit. The trip was healing for Mom, who was healthier on her return. My dad's appeal to Mom and Psalm 118:17 was one of his usual obsessions, present in so many letters.

"Working on Gospel of St. John, Romans, James, right now. Once you get the epistemology track laid, the theological train runs so much faster and smoother. And you can feel the spiritual power once you get 'epistemology literacy.' Wow! Some of the vexatious issues are un-kinked fast . . . Some of Laura's [Mom's] issues like the Sabbath observance, etc. can be better handled with my mapping system. Actually, the Bible of 774,000 English words can be condensed down to a manageable system rapidly. Scriptures are like raw material of oracles-mixed and mixed up. The system I have gets it all sorted and in order—easier to follow and to learn. See Hebrews 2:2-3.[227] *Think about my proposition of the epistemology system: There's plenty of room for personal growth here—a career, job, etc. Think of epistemology as the computer for the computer: an easy interchange between the sacred and the secular. I could use Deb's knowledge of grants and grant writing."*

My guess is that all of this follows to some extent from Dad's like-ly incomprehension when he read the Bible, which was often. This was a man, like countless others, who'd heard since early childhood that the Bible held all the important answers for mankind. The re-sult for Dad, whose schizoaffective disorder involved both paranoia and grandiosity, was his *"jêêl epistemology system."* Which, of course, explained *everything* with such precision that meaning and pur-pose were obvious. Delusions themselves aren't a "culture-bound" symptom, meaning that people everywhere appear to experience them, and at about the same prevalence. But the content of delu-sions most certainly *is* culture-bound,[228] and Dad's epistemological mapping is a good example of it. He was asking for help with grant writing, but there is no agency that sponsors delusions.

On October 11, 1999, Dad sent a very similar letter, in which he elaborated further on his system:

"Ask Mom when she's going to commit to Psalms 118:17? I just got done mapping more of the Bible—yes it's mappable once you get a format laid—like a railroad track for a train to run on. The tricky Christian argument of works versus grace versus faith, St. James versus St. Paul—things that divide people into warring sects of 'believers' . . . well I found the solution. And this unique map can absorb a huge amount of text. Think of a condenser or mop, into a consistent mapping system. The Scriptures state we adult parents have a moral obligation to teach the children 'light and truth.' Ok. But with the confusing and discordant state of affairs in the Bible, there's a hesitancy for me to teach—what? Error or worse?"

Does this sound like a man certain about what the Bible means? He continued:

"So over the years, I worked on this underground unsolved problem and found answers and solutions: the 'jêêl epistemology' system composed of 55 tables (see the Book of Habakkuk, Chap 2: 2-3 'vision on tables').[229] *In other words . . . all wisdom and knowledge can be formatted. I'm trying to make plain as possible what are parables, oracles, precepts, etc. that intimidate or baffle people. Also to anticipate further Scriptures like the Book of Truth. Think of $\Delta o55/\infty$ (Gµ= jêêl 55/tablet epistemology) as the central processing unit of a computer—a computer within a computer—a mind or soul of knowledge or truth. I hope Deb can slip me some tips on grants and grant writing."*

Again, there was no place to point him to.

Mom's letter from Australia came in mid-October. She announced, *"I hugged a dingo."*

My parents. I do love them.

Chapter Thirty-Four: PhD

I SUCCESSFULLY DEFENDED MY dissertation in June 2000. I listened to a lot of Eminem while writing it. He and I were the same age, and we were from the same social class and environment. I had earned my PhD, making me Dr. Deborah MacIntyre. Did that mean it was time for relaxation and fun? Of course not. I needed to pack for my move to St. Louis.

My new job started in July 2000. As a graduation present to myself, I bought LASIK surgery so I would not have to wear glasses anymore. At least not for a while. The tenure-track position I was hired for at Midwestern University came with a postdoctoral program. I was hired to focus on quality of care in mental health services. Perhaps that doesn't sound so exciting to others, but I was pumped. My task was to take the work that had been done in health care for physical health and create a model for mental health care and social services.

Meanwhile, my former roommate Kyla had been having problems with racial discrimination at University of Michigan, so she ended up transferring to University of Wisconsin–Madison for her doctoral studies. For example, one professor actually told her that she didn't "look like an engineer," and he was referring to her hair.

Dad sent a letter in July to Mom, Senja, and Isaiah. It wasn't appropriate content for Senja or Isaiah, in my opinion, so I confiscated the letter. Dad was proposing polygamy to Mom, with his wife and who knows what other women. He made the case:

"Plural marriage is an institution for women primarily. There are key principles: 1. Each wife must have religious liberty (Micah 4:5)."

I looked it up: "For all people will walk every one in the name of his god, and we will walk in the name of the LORD our God for ever and ever."[230] Hmm, that didn't exactly have the ring of religious liberty to it.

He continued:

"2) Each wife has proprietary rights over her marriage bed, 3) The wives decide among themselves who will sleep with the husband, 4) Each wife is encouraged to magnify her life as she is temperamentally suited, 5) She is primarily required to obey God in spirit and truth and be faithful in her covenant therein."

Then he told Mom (and intended to tell Senja and Isaiah) that his new wife, our stepmother, didn't know about the existence of the clitoris before he met her. I repeat, he intended to tell his son and his daughter that his new wife learned about her clitoris from him. When he sent an obvious disaster like this one, it was easier to forgive myself for keeping some of his letters from them.

There was more:

"In plural marriage, women can talk to each other comfortably about sensitive subjects without being threatened. This is the one key to plural marriage—it's a women's institution, and I'm not going to play fast and loose with it."

I was so disturbed by Dad's continued efforts to be in a polygamist marriage that I felt sick. It wasn't *my* business what Dad proposed to Mom. But how could he think it was appropriate to share that with Senja and Isaiah? I felt like I needed a shower.

He wasn't done:

"Also I suspect most women want to be loved—held, cuddled, 'a presence,' etc. So it isn't sex, sex, sex as most women accuse men. Diabetes trims the libido flame considerably, so I'm no threat in sexual advances. In the past you have questioned my commitment, so I will offer this. I have stayed the course—hard and painful on its way. In

the course, I have managed to open new vistas: 1. a system to organize truth, knowledge, and wisdom, 2. An open theatre to the 10 tribes of the North countries."

It bothered me even more that Mom found that invitation worthy of her attention. She had tolerated polygamy, embraced it for a time. She thought Dad's ideas sounded enticing, instead of delusional or just outright unappealing. I recall seeing a pegboard in Muenster, Germany, that Anabaptist polygamists used several centuries ago[231]. It was to show which wife the man picked that night. Just considering the misogyny of that arrangement made me sick.

Dad also wrote a letter specifically to me in July. He warned:

"Beware of the fact I may be laid off in the near future—affecting child support. 220 people to be laid off due to a business slump in the global machine tool industry. My company is part of Thiessen-Krupp Group in Germany. Trouble there and also in Brazil. I'm glad to get the low down on your plans but I am concerned. Permit me to be a dad and offer some advice. Education and accreditation are but one part of the mix. First, with Isaiah, get an astrological chart on him dealing with careers. He's experiencing a Saturn opposition, which is a fitful season of life. Second, your life. Yes, balance is in order, but balance carefully. This isn't a simple teeter-totter balance. Life is more complicated. You are experiencing a Saturn return—a 29-year cycle where the physical body will be premiere. Your body will be a ruthless dictator of your life and powers of decision."

This was ridiculous on the face of it, of course, but in retrospect it was spooky too, because it wasn't too much later that my body broke down and I was largely at its mercy. Nevertheless, Dad hadn't predicted this by looking at where Saturn was moving. I wasn't on a "29-year cycle." At all. Whatsoever. If my situation was predictable, it was by looking at my genetics and the effects of chronic stress.

More to the point, though, Dad would be laid off. Deeper poverty again. Dad's advice to get my brother's astrological chart done for his careers may have been the only parenting advice he ever gave me.

Samuel bought partial season tickets to the St. Louis Blues for me and his wife and himself, so I had a little bit of a ready-made social life: "Let's go Blues!" I didn't get the sense my fellow academics approved when I went to games with my brother.

Samuel was working in Cedar Rapids as an electrician for a major American food corporation. This was going to be his job for the next couple of decades. It was union, it was well-paid, and it was solid work. The downside was the hour commute each way. This was particularly a downside because Samuel was listening to Rush Limbaugh the whole time. At least he could fit in with his uncles and cousins who had money.

Otherwise, I was lonely in the evenings. I wanted a relationship badly. My heart ached from loneliness. I signed up for a dating service, but the only date I went on from the service was with a conservative football superfan. We didn't click. So, I tried to hint to coworkers that I was single, if they knew anybody. I was secretly paranoid that I would not be able to maintain my thinner body long term. I was right about that.[232]

I was assigned several different research studies to work on during my postdoc. Two colleagues, Dr. Donald Needham[233] and Dr. Lizzie Fell[234] worked together on poverty-related research, and I was their research assistant. This was partly because Dr. Needham knew me from my days at Michigan and had provided a recommendation for me at Midwestern. Still, I knew he picked me partly due to being attracted to me, which was awkward. I went to team meetings twice a week that were led by his research coordinator, Doug.

I focused on work to keep myself busy. There was always plenty to do. Hundreds of pages to read. Data to analyze. Plus, to bump up my salary, I had asked to teach one class each semester. Always an extra workload. I was going to be starting out with mental health policy. This was in my wheelhouse. I began teaching in fall 2000. It went so well that two of my students approached me about doing a research project together for their master's project. They wanted me to supervise, and I agreed. It was a busy first semester as a professional academic.

⁕

In August 2001, Mom sent me a postcard:

"Those Vocational Rehabilitation and Social Security Administration forms are killers but I'm working on them."

Mom had gone to a training to be a reflexologist, and now she needed help getting her business off the ground. In the 1990s, one idea frequently made by welfare reform advocates was that everyone could develop their own business. Mom would never make any money doing this, but she helped some people.[235]

⁕

Two Mormon missionaries started coming around, pestering me when I moved to St. Louis. I think it was because my cousin Simon lived in town, and he was a member. I felt like they were stalking me, so I started taking steps to officially leave the Mormon Church, a vexing process that I hadn't worried about until then.

I started attending Catholic conversion classes in the fall of 2001. I told myself it was for my grandma. But I think I was looking for a connection to a religion again after a long absence of a positive experience with one. I picked Catholicism because Grandma literally never cited the Bible to me. I didn't consider that Catholics could push their faith on other people in many other ways, such as limiting women's reproductive freedom[236] and limiting self-autonomy over the body in general—even taking away the right to die—because I hadn't been exposed to that side of it. Keep in mind, things like lack of television left me naive. I was trying to be sincere for Grandma, but this was complicated. Eventually, I couldn't accept those beliefs at all, so I later left that conversion behind.

September 11, 2001, was a clear, sunny day in St. Louis. I was watching the news while eating breakfast. I was running late for work that morning because I saw the report about the first tower just after it happened. The news was still on, so I then saw the second tower getting hit. I saw people jumping from the towers. I was traumatized by what I saw, and I didn't know what else to do but go into work. I wanted to talk to other people about what had happened.

It was disturbing to see my coworkers at the Mental Health Center react to the news of the terrorist attacks. Because they didn't react. They just nodded and turned back to their computers to work. Soulless. I had no one to talk to about what I'd just seen, what it meant. So I tried to do my work. Tried.

At Christmas, I went home to Iowa to visit family. I told Grandma MacIntyre all about the RCIA (Rite of Christian Initiation of Adults) classes I had been attending through the fall at the Catholic church in preparation for adult conversion. I wanted her to feel secure with my spiritual salvation before she passed away. Grandpa MacIntyre had been distressed about our family's salvation.

While I was in Iowa, Aunt Mary gave me a Reiki massage meant to open me up to relationships. Reiki is the Japanese massage in which the masseuse doesn't actually touch you.

I headed back down to St. Louis, and those of us on the homelessness research project held a holiday party at work. I had nowhere to be, so I volunteered to clean up, and so did the attractive coordinator, Doug. He invited me out for a drink afterward.

We went to McGurk's Irish Pub at around nine o'clock, but we closed the bar. We talked for hours. Doug was married, so I was not expecting anything to develop. But that evening really was completely different from anything I'd experienced before.

Doug moved in with me by the end of January 2002, and by April we were engaged. He'd never met anyone like me either, and he was actually thrilled with who he saw. He began mediation proceedings to end his marriage, and it seemed to me that the Reiki must have worked. We celebrated our twentieth anniversary in 2023.

Mom wrote to Cleo in January 2002, and she mentioned that she was still transcribing tapes from my dissertation project. There were apparently six left. I had turned in a dissertation, but the fact was that I was still doing a lot of analysis from it. I should have published many articles from this giant project, but I only published one or two because everything started to go wrong. Dr. Needham threatened that he would retaliate if I dated his research supervisor. He seemed jealous, but I wasn't going to let him control my life. I would soon see how he'd follow through on his threats.

Dad wrote in April:

"Mom says you're having back troubles. Better work on that; health is precious. She also said you're turning Catholic. All I'll say is go with your eyes open—No religion is perfect, so don't be disappointed if things fall short."

I hadn't considered how my conversion would impact my dad. I had begun to wonder if his strong hostility toward the Catholic Church had something to do with a childhood experience, like maybe with a pedophile priest? I was doing this mostly for my grandma. I'm not sure if I reassured Dad properly. He certainly didn't like Catholicism.

Doug was an atheist, so I was going to be marrying a man who didn't believe in God at all. This had come up as early as McGurk's, and I was so intrigued. My parents and grandparents would have thrown fits if they had known, but their input was no longer important given the precedent they'd set in the area of religious belief. I had flirted with the idea of being atheist too, and not just once. I mean, just look at my life experience with organized religion up to that point. I agreed with Doug that we would get married by the Ethical Society rather than by a church.

I was having serious back troubles. I ended up having a microdiscectomy[237] on my L4-L5 disc in May 2002, after which the surgeon said he'd rarely seen a disc quite so herniated. I was supposed to be getting a lot of work done, such as publishing from my dissertation, but I was mostly preoccupied with recuperating from the surgery. To appease my mother, I had been seeing a chiropractor prior to the surgery, and after I was healed, I started seeing her again. She was kind, and I liked the machines she used.

As a chiropractor's granddaughter, I may have broken a cardinal rule by getting back surgery, but I was still using a chiropractor's services. My mother couldn't complain. The surgery seemed to help my back too. For a while anyway. I thought about how I was allowing the feelings of my parents and grandparents to dictate my choices, like my conversion to Catholicism, like going to a chiropractor because it was easier than hearing about it from Mom all the time.

Just as we started planning our wedding, Doug's first wife left us a scary message in August 2002. Eric, his five-year-old son, couldn't seem to maintain his balance and kept falling down. Eric had been extremely premature, wanting little to do with almost all his third trimester and had remained in the NICU for ten weeks after birth. One of the consequences of this was some weakness on his left side, so some challenges to his balance had been recognized and were to be expected. But her next message was beyond anything we had anticipated. Eric had started to have much more frequent problems with stability, so his mom took him to the ER. Eric had a tumor on his brainstem, a *medulloblastoma*.[238]

Eric immediately had surgery, but his odds were not great because of the location of the tumor and the potential consequences of trying to remove it. They couldn't remove all of it safely.

The impact of surgery and chemotherapy was that Eric could no longer walk, talk, or eat without help. He was on a feeding tube but still had trouble keeping most of his food down. With extensive physical and occupational therapy, he relearned speech and large motor functioning, but he continued to require a wheelchair. He looked as if he were suffering a great deal much of the time.

We were all devastated. We were determined to ensure Eric received the best, most compassionate care. Many doctors and nurses and staff members fell in love with Eric as he started to slowly get better.

Chapter Thirty-Five: Getting Married

I N OCTOBER, DOUG AND I camped out in our car practically overnight in St. Louis's Forest Park. We wanted to reserve the Jewel Box for half price for our wedding. It's a magnificent glass greenhouse that was built nearly a hundred years ago and renovated two years before our wedding, which occurred in October 2003, a year after our campout.

In May 2003, Mom wrote a letter to her sister Cleo, Mom was visiting St. Louis to help us out during that busy year:

"I'm staying longer, coming home next Sunday. There is so much left to do. No wonder Deb was under such incredible stress. Doug and I are hoping to finish 'our' project while she's gone to Indiana University tomorrow. When I told her I'd cancelled my appointments and was going to stay, she just teared up and gave me such a hug of relief. There was no way she could have gotten this done. And the boys are so sweet. Eric is my honey."

I was getting further and further behind on the work I had to do for the university because of my back and my migraine headaches too. But I was tenure track at a major university, so I had a dozen balls in the air. Publish or perish. I didn't have time for my family.

※

The classes I taught were on social policy, mental health policy, and human diversity. They could be viewed as an extended refutation of the arguments made by Murray and his friends. The evidence is clear: Being poor *is* really bad.[239] From that starting point, I asked questions. Why is being poor relatively more expensive than not being poor? Shouldn't it be the other way around? You know, to help people or to match the circumstances with the means?

Well, why isn't it cheaper to be poor? Consider the "boots theory" of socioeconomic unfairness. Thomas Huffman[240] describes how when poor people can't afford the top of the line, they buy cheap stuff that ends up ultimately costing more in the long run:

A really good pair of leather boots cost $50. But an affordable pair of boots, which were sort of OK for a season or two and then leaked like hell when the cardboard gave out, cost about $10 . . . But . . . good boots lasted for years and years. A man who could afford $50 had a pair of boots that'd still be keeping his feet dry in 10 years' time, while the poor man who could only afford cheap boots would have spent a hundred dollars on boots over in the same time period and would still have wet feet.

My family had this problem exponentially. We bought many junk cars that cost more over time than a new one would have cost if we could have just afforded one outright. Mom's letters help to make that clear. This theory also applies to being able to buy in bulk and other cost-saving measures that require upfront cash.

For example, more careful analysis of expenses beyond food shows why low-income people are strained:

About two-thirds (63%) of families reported spending out-of-pocket for transportation. These families spent 14% of their total expenditures on transportation costs at nearly $333 on average each month. Even though transportation is a key expenditure for job retention and access to services, including healthcare, few family or individual level subsidies exist for families residing in poverty outside of broader government investments in transportation infrastructure such as bridges, roadways and public buses and train s.[241]

Transportation was estimated to take up 22 percent of a U.S household's budget of $30,000 in 2019, and that was mostly because people needed to keep putting money into older cars or rely on an unreliable public transit system.[242] The distance between where poor people live and where good jobs are located leads to high transportation costs as well.[243]

Senja wasn't writing as regularly because she was completing her bachelor's degree at a university in Michigan. Isaiah lived with his girlfriend's family in Iowa Falls, Iowa. John was living with his girlfriend in Waterloo. Mom was visiting me.

Naturally, I wanted Dad to walk me down the aisle, so I asked him to. He wrote me back three months before the wedding:

"We are bankrupt. I look like a freak with head bald and scarred and limping on a cane. Samuel might be a better bet to give you away, Deb. I'd throw somebody out like me if I were at my wedding. Also, I have a wound dressing and I look like hell. Yuk!!!"

In August, Dad wrote me a letter with mixed messages. On the one hand, he was saying, *"So, I'm good for nothing—not even to sleep under a bridge."* But on the other hand, he was grandiose:

"Even your dad is getting encouragement to build a website for epistematics—hopefully to conquer disease, solve true problems, and straighten out a problem people have overlooked: Rome partially fell due to its numeric system—The Arabics invented 1-9 integers but the key cog wheel invention was 0 (zero) and later the decimal point. Our civilization would collapse in minutes without 0 and the decimal point. My epistematics is like '0' and '.' for the oceans of information every day. I might get a free computer and watch out! . . . If I have my way. A computer to me is a tool and a weapon, not a plaything."

I felt bad for my dad. I knew he was a hardworking man. He was conscientious. I was proud of him when he was described as a man without guile. I didn't need him to be the inventor of a knowledge system. I knew he wasn't, and that was okay.

Our wedding was perfect, except for a few small hiccups. It was a sunny, crisp autumn day with big, fluffy clouds. I arrived thirty minutes late because I was waiting for Senja to get ready. She was being a diva and, if I may say so, a bit of a brat. She was supposed to be helping me to get ready, but it wasn't working out that way. Dad wasn't at the wedding. I was supposed to call him so he could be there by phone, but I forgot. Once I dried my tears over being late, the ceremony started. Our wedding took place at the Jewel Box and so, it was already decorated with a lot of plants. Our florist added lots of beautiful red, orange, and yellow lilies and perfectly selected complementary flowers.

I couldn't believe how nervous I was. Thankfully, our vows were simple. Deborah MacGregor did a reading we selected. The best part of the day was the reception, because it was an opportunity to see some friends I hadn't seen in quite a while. Phyllis Gray, Kyla, Denise, my aunt Nicky, Eri, Anita. I invited as many of my favorite people as I could.

Two weeks after our wedding, Deborah MacGregor's fiancée died of a heart attack at the age of thirty-two. He had been on the Atkins diet at the time, and some people were suspicious his diet contributed to his death. But either way, he was gone, so I dropped everything and went to Decorah to be with my best friend for a weekend. I didn't really have the time, but she mattered. It was heartbreaking, and feeling awful for my best friend, it really dampened the honeymoon phase after our wedding.

In summer 2004, I was now finished with my postdoc so I was a tenure-track assistant professor. Specifically, I was a research associate studying PTSD, quality of care, and lots of other things. But someone had attacked senators with anthrax in 2001, so my supervisor sent me to Washington, DC, to study the aftereffects of the bioterror attacks on the people who experienced them.

I threw up on the bushes of the Rayburn House building on my way to an interview. When I kept having to run to the bathroom, they sent me to the Capitol infirmary.

A nurse suggested, "Honey, could you be pregnant?"

I replied insistently, "Of course not."

I'd made a decision in my twenties not to have children. Since I had PCOS, I assumed that I was infertile. Moreover, I had already taken on many of the responsibilities of a parent. I had raised my younger brothers and sister. I had routinely changed diapers for five children starting when I was six. I had formal custody of Senja and Isaiah beginning when I was twenty-three. I felt like I never had a youth.

But I had a much more critical reason for not wanting to have children. My DNA is riddled with health and mental health problems. My father was diagnosed with schizoaffective disorder, although I think he may have had schizotypal personality disorder,[244] based on the fact that I am pretty sure that's my brother Samuel's diagnosis too.

Dad's physical health problems were extensive as well. His diabetes was wicked, with sugar levels in the 400s. I inherited the insulin-related endocrine disorder, PCOS, from him, no doubt.

Then, there's my mother's side. She's got bipolar disorder II. She has a serious case of ADHD, which may even have the most impact on her day-to-day functioning. She is plagued by chronic migraines. Her father had both these problems as well. Since Dad had a bad back, it's a tough call, but I think that bad backs are inherited from Grandpa too. I could also mention a litany of other miscellaneous health problems, like fibromyalgia (this one would kill me without expensive meds), arthritis, plantar fasciitis, and acid reflux, but I think you get the picture. Also, ask anyone with lower back pain what repeated puking does to that pain?

After collecting the rest of the research data in between rounds of heaving, I flew home from Washington, DC. The research was a success. You probably won't be surprised to learn people are more distressed by visible terrorism than bioterrorism—unless they have OCD.

Home was something of a nightmare. Eric had been fighting brain cancer for more than a year. He was in pain. He was throwing up on the hour. He had a feeding tube inserted, but he still lost weight to a frightening degree.

Since my constant vomiting and nausea were now disrupting my own ability to help, I saw the doctor again. This time, a pregnancy test was administered.

The doctor informed me I was pregnant.

I was floored. Not. Possible.

Describing my reaction to this news is difficult and complicated, so bear with me. Here's the reality:

Mom and Dad needed supportive living services for their mental health conditions, but they didn't get them. They needed income support from the government, because each of them needed to work only part-time to accommodate their mental illnesses. They needed physical and mental health care.

Society is not willing to meet any of these needs, not willing to pay for them. Society doesn't believe enough in people like my parents to consider them part of its "pro-life" policies.[245] Rather, society broke up my family. Police were involved. Child abuse investigators were called in. Mom and Dad lost custody of their children for long enough to traumatize already mentally ill people in unspeakable ways.

I knew all those things were true after my mom's childhood church turned Mom and Dad away following their request for charity. I knew so after everyone at my small-town school mocked me for using the free lunch card that was bright pink while theirs were green. I knew that after Ronald Reagan made up the myth of the Black welfare queen,[246] and then cut the Aid to Dependent Children of Unemployed Parents program we were on. We also lost food stamps and Medicaid. My brother died. My sister was given a permanent attachment disorder because of that separation.[247] No one is okay as a result of our upbringing. Almost all of us have complex post-traumatic stress disorder.[248]

I'm surprised Charles Murray didn't specifically say, "We wrote welfare rules that explicitly hurt two-parent families." Because they did. That's not why my parents split up, but I'm curious what would have happened if they had continued to receive welfare support as a two-parent family. Supposedly, this is what the Earned Income Tax Credit can do.[249] Provide income support to both parents while also rewarding work. Unfortunately, this wasn't around yet in the 1980s.

The State made clear that Americans were willing to pay more to split our family between two foster homes than they were willing to pay to keep us together as a family unit.

These were distant events, right? Too long to still be thinking about? The year 1981 was a lifetime ago, right? Not for me, and definitely not for Senja. She was an infant when this happened. She's over forty now, but she's riddled with complex PTSD, an attachment disorder, and more. She is seriously dependent on alcohol. She is chronically suicidal. That's not a real problem? What if she follows David's lead and also takes her life? She threatens to all the time. What about her kids?

If you are not willing to support people who are born into poor families, then I don't think you should rally the troops in defense of developing humans who are not yet born. I just don't. They have no feelings, no memory, and no thoughts. But the woman who is living is unwilling to make them into a human, for a variety of very good reasons, and, yes, occasionally a poor reason. That's the story. That's not the government's business, and it shouldn't be anyone else's.

Since I knew people who had grown up as unwanted children, like Sweetie, or unhappy, adopted children like my best friend, Deborah MacGregor, I knew how risky the adoption road was. I was secure knowing my child, should I have one, would never suffer this experience. On top of all of that, Doug needed me to be there for him, and for our sick son. Eric's younger brother, Elliot, needed attention too. Under the circumstances, he wasn't getting enough of it.

So, with all of that as backstory, I found myself in the shocking position at the turn of 2004 of being pregnant. I had taken birth control precautions. I was not supposed to be fertile. I was in a monogamous relationship with a husband who was busy enough with the two children he had.

There was no doubt in my mind. This embryo was *not* going to develop into a human being. There were a million things working against it, and no loving parent would do that to their offspring.

The pregnancy was making me extremely sick, as the bushes outside of the Rayburn House office building could testify to. Given how much pain the pregnancy was causing my back, I honestly don't know if I could have survived the pregnancy, because I would not have tolerated giving up the medications I needed, and I could never have tolerated the back pain. My back would not have toler-ated the weight gain. I know this because, when I gained weight, I experienced pain at levels that made me want to kill myself. That way neither myself nor a developing child would have lived.

Not that I must keep justifying my decision to abort an eight-week-old embryo.[250] It doesn't help to show me a picture, because I know I am rescuing my offspring and would not have been able to carry the pregnancy. But no one could take away my right to not be a parent if I didn't want to be.[251]I've never regretted my decision, although it still makes me sad to have had to make it. I mourn our loss as the loss that it is. It's not like it's ever an easy decision. It's not like I don't wish things could've been different. I would want the best for my offspring, like anyone else. That's why I'm comfortable with my decision.

In June 2004, close to the Fourth of July, Ronald Reagan died. Mom sent an email afterward.

"Anyone else rather sick of all of the hoopla surrounding the depar-ture of the man who caused so much of the trouble for the MacIntyre family? This pseudopatriotism is nauseating, and it does not want to go away. Even without a TV or paper, it has somehow permeated my world."

Mom had figured out after the foster care incident that Reagan spelled disaster for her family. He hated poor people of all colors, in case his black welfare queen stereotyping is ever seen as only racism.

Now, despite how contemptuous I was of him, I managed to miss all the hype about his death. I guess that was a benefit of being too busy to even sleep. Well, Mom, I'm told Nancy Reagan was really into astrology.[252]

In June, Mom was thinking about her reflexology business, which she had trained for through Vocational Rehabilitation. She made a pamphlet that described what her services provided:

"How does reflexology fit into all of this? These delicate connections necessary for survival still have certain 'trigger points' that send mes-

sages directly from the feet, hands and ears to corresponding organs or other parts of the body. Impulses travel along established channels or pathways in the body, sometimes called meridians. The reflexologist today combines the ancient art of massage with new techniques developed through years of research and observation. He or she may make use of an assortment of tools that will enhance his or her ability to speed up the whole process and make it more efficient. How much does it cost?"

Here was the point. Vocational Rehabilitation was being funded sufficiently to help my mom build her own business. She never made enough money to support herself with it, but she did provide a nice service to a lot of people.[253] In fact, a lot of people who typically couldn't afford a foot massage were able to get one at discounted prices or for free.

But she was trying to operate the reflexology business out of her house, the one I had lived in during high school. It still had steep steps that weren't customer friendly. Sure enough, Mom wrote:

"Also, Voc Rehab is finally coming through, and they are taking bids on finishing off the front porch, so people won't fall. Lowell fell and really hurt himself the other day. His leg got all infected where he gouged it, and with his diabetes it doesn't heal so well. It was the night of Isaiah's graduation. He hurt his arm, too . . . Obviously, I can't be having clients falling up the stairs!"

I didn't believe the theories behind reflexology—probably not even close—but I believed in the therapeutic benefits of a foot massage. I trust the endorphins and oxytocin that are released during the process are healing for people.

In a June email, Mom wrote:

"I went to volunteer at Allen [Hospital] tonight, and they just had brought in an ambulance. In fact, it came up behind me on the way . . . There was this Black family who were so upset that they had to have lost someone—in the same room where David died . . . It got a bit much for me, and we discussed it. Decided maybe it would be better for me in the gift shop . . . so I spent the afternoon in there. Tomorrow night I do the Aspire horse/disabled kids thing at Cattle Congress, and Saturday I have an all-day CPR/AED for the Professional Rescuer . . . then I can officially teach all the classes."

Mom was keeping busy with volunteer work. In fact, her volunteer work was keeping her busier than she had ever been before. Now that she didn't have any children to take care of, she was passionate about "giving back."

In early July, Eric developed complications and was hospitalized. Scans revealed what looked like regrowth at the site of the tumor, and the surgeons felt that the time to operate was right then in order not to give the tumor a chance to grow back any more than it had, since that would only make surgery more difficult. They operated. It wasn't regrowth. It was scar tissue from the first surgery, but Eric didn't tolerate the surgery well, following as closely as it did on the heels of the first. He developed a worrisome C *difficile* infection[254], and that only complicated matters. He didn't have an immune system available to fight it.[255]

Just a few days later, while Doug was there visiting him, Eric had a massive stroke and hemorrhaging in his brain. On July 23, 2005, Eric passed away.

I had a very hard time with Eric's death. Before the 2nd surgery, I had expected him to survive. He had been getting better. He died the same week I was supposed to be hosting a conference of the Working Class and Poverty Class Academics (WCPCA) at the university.[256] I didn't feel I could cancel the conference with attendees' plane tickets purchased. I wasn't there enough for my husband during this grieving period. I was numb and overwhelmed with my own issues. I threw myself into the conference to bury my feelings.

Meanwhile, I was supposed to be writing a grant called a K Award, a career award of the National Institute of Mental Health. I'd started writing it in 2002. It involved proposing three research studies that demonstrated new areas of learning for me and research priorities for them. One of the professors at Midwestern University, Ruiz Zamora[257], was listed as a mentor on this K Award He had knowledge of mental health research with minority populations. But he was a long way from being understanding about Eric's death. He expected me to have this grant written by the deadline. And he arbitrarily set the deadline. I felt he was urged by Dr. Needham.

⚜

Grandma MacIntyre passed away in September 2004. I had been closer to her than my other grandparents, so it was a tough loss. Her funeral was at St. Patrick Catholic Church, where we had gone to eat many meals when I was growing up. It felt awkward.

In October, Mom wrote that she had been in the hospital for cellulitis. She also said that her new psychiatrist told her that she wasn't even on a therapeutic dose of Lexapro, so he increased her dose. Then she sent an email in which she said,

"Just a quick note to let you know I wrote Aunt Nicky a letter and told her I was withdrawing from the family, at least for now, to regain my mental health from having been so put down as to have my little family called piglets at the government teat . . . I'm sure you are familiar with that one . . . I think this should help my mental health, too! I find that I wake up in the mornings with my jaw clenched thinking about it all."

Under the Banner of Heaven, by Jon Krakauer,[258] came out that fall, and Doug read it, like he had all of Jon Krakauer's books. One evening, he suddenly exclaimed, "Honey, these aren't just any crazy Mormons, these are *your* crazy Mormons!" Sure enough, the book included Robert Crossfield, or the prophet Onias, Mom's one-time polygamist husband.

The book was so intense for me that I couldn't read it carefully; I had to skim it. It was just too emotional and retraumatizing. We alerted Mom about the book, and it had a profound impact on her too.

Chapter Thirty-Six:
Losing My Career

FEBRUARY 2005 WAS ONE of the first deadlines set for submitting my K Award grant. I worked exceptionally hard to make that deadline. But Eric's death had taken a toll on our family. My post-doc had involved numerous publications that I was still working on. Teaching was time-consuming. I was flooded with some of the hallmark symptoms of PTSD after the Krakauer book.[259]

I was too preoccupied with work crises to notice right away. One of my coworkers, Dr. Nancy Sturmberg[260], was openly repeating what I had said just as I left the room, similar to how kids mocked each other in elementary school. Tim, my close friend from the University of Michigan, was also on faculty now; he was the one who told me about Dr. Sturmberg. I knew why she was doing it. Dr. Needham had egged her on as part of his guarantee to retaliate against me if I dated his research supervisor who was now my husband. Needham and Sturmberg were close that way.

Mom wrote in her email to her sister, Aunt Cleo:

"Sigh . . . When Dad [Grandpa Meyer] was lucid, he shocked me when he reflected that he thought we would have been better off under Hitler. I was shocked because I hadn't been indoctrinated by Rush. Dad never balanced his input with anything but fanatical right-wing radio, so it had to come from Rush. Did you ever imagine

*that one day you'd be parroting everything programmed into you,
and actually making excuses for horrible tortures [in Iraq], which
now I read included the death of a man hung by his wrists—with
them tied behind his back!! But people addicted to Rush say, 'Aw, give
'em a break—those troops are under a lot of stress!' Well, when their
'abuse'-a bit of light-hearted torture—puts such stress on a man in
that position that he dies—I have a problem with that!!"*

Since I had copies of the letters from my aunt, I had her notes on
the letters as well. My aunt wrote, "*Then why have the liberals failed
to get the poor out of their poverty?*" I suppose she was referring to us.

I wish I had seen her question at the time, so I could've responded
to it. The only people who had been trying to get us out of poverty
since we fell into it were liberals, and there were none of those in our
family. Aunt Cleo was a big part of my early childhood because she
read illustrated children's books to me that she wrote. We had other
nice connections, too, but they never carried over into adulthood.
It could be because her husband tried to molest me, and she'd spent
much of her life dealing with the shame of having a pedophile
husband, who also molested their children.

On the other hand, Mom's letter drifted into an earnest statement about how we're in the Age of Aquarius, a water sign, which
is feminine. And we're no longer under a fire sign like Mars, which is
masculine, like guns and bombs. She even associated former "***masculine ages***" [her emphasis] with fiery sacrifices on altars. It was astrological nonsense again, and that kind of stuff can be off-putting.

Other fundamentalists would insist that Mom's use of astrology
was the reason for her cursed life. They would claim she brought
evil spirits into her life or something bogus like that. There was no
way to win with this kind of belief system. What was the logic of it?
Seriously. The location of a planet in the sky controls your destiny?
Why? Explain how.[261]

In March 2005, my mentor and maternal figure for the past several
years, Carol Mowbray, called to tell me that she had terminal cancer,

and she didn't have much time left. It felt like the world was cracking up. I felt especially vulnerable losing Carol.[262] She was my rock.

I aimed to meet the June 2005 deadline for the K Award, but I still wasn't satisfied with my product. I had written an amazing grant for my dissertation, and I needed this grant to top that one. It just wasn't there yet. Now, I couldn't rely on Carol's help with the grant like I usually did. I turned to other major researchers in the mental health field to review my work, hoping for pointers.

In April, Ruiz Zamora came into my office at Midwestern University and crowded me at my desk. Since I was physically intimidated, I leaned backward in my chair as he towered over me. Zamora screamed at me that I didn't belong in academia, that I didn't have the talent to succeed as a professor, that I was useless and lazy because I wasn't meeting his arbitrary deadline. He was quitting as a primary mentor on my career award. Uncharacteristically, I burst into tears.[263]

When the tirade was over, I left my office, and the practicum supervisor, who was in the hallway, asked me what happened. Her office was next door to mine. She said the screaming was so loud it scared her. I told her that it scared me too. I went to the dean's office to tell him what happened, but he indicated there was nothing he could do. I believed Dr. Needham was behind each person's abusive behavior.

I continued to tweak the career award grant for what would now be the October deadline. Career awards could be submitted three times per year, so I was just moving back the deadline. It was hard to work on it without thinking about what Zamora had said, plus I had to replace him with another mentor, but I was determined to prove him wrong.

Carol Mowbray, the woman I credit with helping me finish my PhD, and a woman I felt was like another mother, died in August. I was asked to speak at a memorial event in her honor at the University of Michigan. It was the worst public speaking moment I have ever experienced. I completely crumbled in front of the crowd. I forgot what I planned to say. I had an anxiety attack.

I went back to St. Louis feeling extremely low about losing Carol and insecure about my academic future. I came to the conclusion that working for this dean of Social Work would be impossible. He was not supportive of me whatsoever as a faculty member. I couldn't believe it when the dean announced that Ruiz Zamora was being appointed the new dean of faculty. He had been verbally abusive to me just because I delayed submitting a grant following multiple significant losses in my life. The dean of faculty would have power over tenure decisions. There was no point in even staying at this school.

In November, Mom forwarded me an email from James Dobson and *Focus on the Family*. He was lying about why CBS was canceling the TV show, *Touched by an Angel*, claiming an atheist got the show canceled for using the word *God*.

Mom fell for his lies, and wrote:

"It's sad to have to align oneself with others one doesn't necessarily agree with, but you might want to take a look at this. Their premise is a bit faulty [I didn't realize the Constitution was based on the Ten Commandments. I had thought it was more framed with the five Indian nations alliance . . .]"

Mom had a good memory of the facts about this. The Constitution is not based on the Ten Commandments.[264] It was disturbing that she was tricked into initially thinking it was. But that's how indoctrination of the Limbaugh and Trump (and Dobson) variety works: say something completely false, and repeat it loudly and frequently, folks with similar, existing grievances find it convincing, and, if enough of those folks lack the education, native critical thinking, or sanity to know better, voila, you've got a rabid following.[265] Don't get me wrong. This dynamic can happen on the extreme Left too, but in the United States over the last forty-five years or so, it has been a decidedly, pungently, contemptuously right-wing phenomenon.

Mom continued:

"Without wanting to turn this into a 'Christian nation,' I do believe we should be able to use the word God if we so desire, and I

feel it was wrong to take that show off the air because of it. It was a popular show, and we did have freedom of religion written into our constitution, and this is not freedom."

I was finished for good with fundamentalist Christians running my life. I was done with their Scriptures constantly being recited to me. I didn't feel my relationship with God was particularly good at that moment anyway. He had taken Eric and Carol. I was about to lose my career, everything I had worked toward.

I wrote a fed-up email to my mother. It was very long. Even these excerpts are longer than many of the letters or emails I wrote to her.

*"I want you to think about what your Christianity has done to my life. I have had to endure sexual abuse at the hands of Crossfield's son [my first disclosure to her], I had to live in a freakazoid compound etc., etc., and in general, my mother had a religion addiction to try and treat her untreated mental illness, and it hurt me, and she sends me pro-Christian emails. And I still love her. As it happens, I am totally educated in my mother's beliefs, having been shoved into them all my youth. On the other hand, she hasn't a clue what I believe. I DONT try to change **her** religion, but she constantly bombards me with details about hers.*

"According to the National Science Foundation [in the year I sent the letter],[266] *70% of American adults do not understand the scientific method; the U.S. depends heavily on foreign born scientists at all degree levels, as high as 45% in engineering; Belief in pseudoscience is relatively widespread and growing; 46% did not know how long it takes the Earth to orbit the sun (1 year); 45% thought lasers work by focusing sound waves (they focus light); 49% believe antibiotics kill viruses (they kill bacteria); 66% don't believe the Big Bang theory is widely accepted by scientists; 48% believe humans lived at the same time as the dinosaurs;47% don't believe in evolution, which has been so widely accepted by scientists and much of the rest of the Western world for the last 150 years or so; 55% couldn't define DNA; 78% couldn't define a molecule."*

I was very upset, so I continued:

"Plenty of people could focus on the negatives of my family. According to many Christian groups, mental illnesses are excuses for laziness. And what about children being taken from parents? This is

a Christian attitude. No matter where I turn, including within social work, people who say they are Christian believe that children deserve 'the best homes.' They were a powerful lobby in the 1980s and 1990s, and they convinced the government to enact 'decency in parenting' rules.[267] *Needless to say, poor people weren't considered decent in any way, much less as parents. And since they are lazy, someone else should raise the children."*

Naturally, Mom didn't immediately write me back.

I was getting positively dizzy from the traumas and losses I'd experienced to that point, beginning in early childhood. Then Grandpa Meyer died in November 2005. He had been suffering from full-blown dementia for three years, but I believed it began many years earlier than this.

Dad wrote again, responding to a question of mine about his work history:

"My work history is a humdrum litany of cleanup, haul, paint on every job. Are you sure you want to know all that? The part of me that is still under development is more interesting and started when I was about 16. After 40 years plus, it's called epistematics (my word, the nearest word is epistemics, which I don't know the definition). Epistematics is one of my passions, and it has been a great help in understanding a number of complex topics . . . This is why I am trying to get your brothers interested in this as it is equivalent to Newton's development of calculus, which revolutionized science."

No, I didn't want to know about his fantasy, his fixed delusions. I have years of letters discussing that. I had wondered if he ever got a better paying job. The answer was clearly no.

Mom emailed her cousin and copied me:

"My daughter called tonight, drunk and stressed out, facing the uncertainties inherit in graduating college in a couple of months, while I was in the middle of this letter to Noam Chomsky when she called."

Mom was talking about Senja. The pattern in which Senja would drunkenly call Mom started early in college. We talked to her about her drinking, but she brushed everyone off, as problem drinkers tend to do.

Meanwhile, my situation at the university was deteriorating. I got an attorney, a very lousy attorney, and I sued Midwestern University for sexual harassment by Dr. Needham and hostile workplace by Dr. Fell. Curiously, some of my emails from Dr. Needham were suddenly not in my saved folder, something Dr. Needham could have arranged with the department IT guy.

Therefore, all the attorney got was a settlement of $75,000 with the promise of a nondisclosure agreement or NDA. The NDA was the rich man's way of buying my silence.[268] Therefore, they bought what they paid for: no mention of the name of the university, the parties involved, or much of what happened. But they cannot buy my silence about my life story. They didn't pay for that.

Mom wrote an email in December 2005:

"I went to a new woman doctor today—Dr. Garrelts—and I really like her! A great team approach—first time I've been asked, a couple of times, if I really wanted to try this new medicine . . . it's Lamictal, a mood stabilizer. Deb, you were right—she figured I was bipolar II, which also has a lot of ADHD symptoms . . . it was rather ironic that I forgot the medicine samples at the counter when I went to work . . . theoretically that won't happen after I take them! Well, I'm off to the Aspire therapeutic horse training program for disabled kids . . . I enjoy volunteering over there on Wednesday nights, and I got a new client from it . . . a woman with Bell's palsy. I just found some reflex points specifically for that, so I'm eager to try them out, too . . ."

Mom's bipolar II was finally being treated appropriately. Thirty-seven years after the onset of her symptoms, a doctor prescribed suitable medication.[269]

Chapter Thirty-Seven: You Can't Fight Personality Disorders

A FTER I LOST MY job, Doug wanted us to move near Minneapolis because his son's mother was moving there with Elliot, so she could be closer to family. I tried to get a different job as a professor of Social Work. In fact, I applied to none other than Luther College, my alma mater. But they asked questions about why I was leaving my previous position—questions that I could not answer because of the NDA. When I didn't get the job at Luther, my former advisor whispered to me that it was because of the red flags that came from my mysterious exit from Midwestern University. The NDA was ruining my life.[270]

There was no sense in applying to any other faculty positions, but I tried a couple of times. I didn't even get interviews. I was effectively blacklisted. I started applying to positions in social work. I found a job in St. Paul, doing social work/mental health. It would theoretically give me the opportunity to earn my professional license. Doug was also a social worker working with adults with serious mental illness and doing homeless outreach. In March 2006, I started my position as an adult rehabilitative mental health services (ARMHS) worker.[271] I had clients ranging from an eighteen-year-old boy with autism who loved to make monster masks to a middle-aged man with brittle diabetes and bipolar disorder who was struggling to manage both of his conditions. Another client had catatonic schizophrenia, so she froze up every few minutes, just like a statue. I remembered how Joel Slack said it felt to have catatonic schizophrenia when I worked with her.

Isaiah continued living with a girlfriend named Jacki,[272] who already had a toddler daughter. Senja was living in Ann Arbor and attending the University of Michigan School of Social Work for her master's degree. John was living with Sandy[273], the woman who would become his wife. Eventually, he would settle into a job at a lumber and packing company for many years.

Mom wrote in June. She said,

"Anyway, Isaiah and Jacki are still 'back when' and young and starry-eyed, and they are in the process of moving out of their house, and into the basement apartment there in Iowa Falls with her dad. Isaiah will still keep his apprenticeship, and will commute, although he can stay here every other night, which will give us a chance to practice with the band without the complications of personalities that don't blend, Her daughter getting into things, etc. . . . They seem happy with the idea. They had wanted to move in here, but absolutely not! I told him I'd be out at Independence [the state mental hospital] *in no time, and they'd just take over the house and I didn't want that. Period."*

I was proud of Mom. She was establishing boundaries, taking care of herself.

Dad wrote again, also in June:

"Anyhow, if you look at the Gospel of Matthew where the Devil tempted Christ with power over the kingdoms of the world, if only He would worship Satan. Well, Christ said a firm 'No,' and gave a 'why.' I was approached by the Devil, while in the service, and offered money, power, connections, fine housing, and the inside circle, if I would also follow him. And, I was within inches of that $1.5 million. Sure smells good to a poor man, but I said 'Hell No', and my life has been a battle of retribution ever since. There is a malignant hatred between us two, and if I had had my way, I would have demanded power from on high, and raised up an army, and cleaned house. But the powers on

High squelched that, and I was extremely angry for quite awhile. You might say God and me were on the outs with each other. But later I was told that Satan was going to use me (and my anger) to be the spark to set off the huge war he wants, and that it would involve secret combinations and alliances that reached into the far heavens, which if it went off, would have blown creation clean to hell."

Oh, Good Lord, Dad, I thought. *Enough*. Please, just stop. This grandiose fantasy just made me feel sorry for him. I wished he could hear himself. It was just the worst. Hearing him tell me he was a simple working man who studied the Bible a great deal would have been much less shameful. But what he said next really chilled my bones. Dad wrote,

"I am doing research on the internet right now, and if you saw the mapping connections on this huge issue, you wouldn't sleep at night ever again in comfort."

He was delving into the internet. This was frightening for some obvious reasons, but chiefly because of all the conspiracy theories, true crime, weird strangers, and cults for him to get involved with—not to mention just the sheer extremes of political discourse online.

In another email, the subject line was "Insights for your book." I had told him I was writing a memoir about mental illness in our family, that it was a long-term goal. This is what he wrote me:

"When I was an elementary school kid, I had a series of visions (see Isaiah 2:28-29)[274] depicting various prophetic subjects. These visions were so pronounced they left a searing impact on my psyche. They ran counter to many religious notions of my growing up years, and even to Mormonism. I can't relate to any Evangelical movement. You've asked me what brought me to Mormonism. Strangely, I had a vision of the Salt Lake Temple, but it had a dark cloud over it and looked gloomy and forbidden. Little did I know back then I would be associated with it by the proximity of the matter of yards of where I worked at the Visitor's Center. Strangely enough, just within the past few weeks, I finally learned more about the Temple's external stone symbols, which aren't necessarily what the critics claim they mean. From my epistematics training and insight, I understand the symbols at a greater depth than the critics."

Dad was describing a vision he had as a young child of the Mormon Temple in Salt Lake City, with a dark cloud over it. But he still went and joined the Mormon Church afterward? I doubted it, plus it didn't match his story from a previous letter. This was Dad giving me valuable information about his mental health without exactly intending to.

Dad wrote again with more insights for the book. This time, he said,

"I wouldn't have joined the military, and the excuse was the draft was coming so enlist and get it over with. Military hasn't changed my mind, and you kids were never pressured, were you?"

Isaiah was going to enlist in the Army in a few short years, not heeding his father's constant advice against it. He needed a way to support his family, so he enlisted in the U.S. Army even though we were in a war in Afghanistan.

Dad continued,

"There was a distance between me and the folks . . . On a test taken for self-esteem, going from 0-100, I scored a basement 4: rock bottom. Grandma tried to excuse that as a 'sickness' on my part. Strange her plans of living through her children (a terrible parental scheme) failed so miserably. I've heard others remark about it and if any of it got back to Grandma, she kept it to herself. That is probably why she buried herself in her university work, to assuage the pain and social standing. I had my own demon to fight, and got rid of it in 1969, just before the moon shot in July."

And Mom wrote in October:

"John got pulled over for going 106 somewhere . . . sigh. If he loses his license (distinct possibility . . .) it'll make it harder to find work when he finally terminates at APAC . . . they sure have kept him on a long time! I got someone to sign up for Senior Companions, so I get a free week's vacation coming up! YES!!"

Mom was thriving in her job as a senior companion. I had never seen her flourish like she was now. This job called on her to serve as a kind of case worker to senior citizens who needed extra care to stay in their homes.

Senja sent me a letter in November 2006 using the professional MSW letterhead that had been given to her by the University of

Michigan Alumni Office. I was so proud of her, and she seemed proud of herself. Her note was a Thanksgiving wish. Because she had to work over the holiday, she was going to be staying in Michigan. (She would repeat this for years. I won't be home for the holidays. Working).

I was honest with my clients and told them that I was one of them. I would try to explain what coping methods I used to help me succeed. Also, the agency I worked for believed in hiring people with mental illnesses as professional staff. My boss had borderline personality disorder.[275] It turned out that this was a problem though. She became suspicious of me. She began talking about me behind my back. I knew the workplace was going to get toxic if I tried to stay, so I looked around for another job. It was too bad because I enjoyed the work itself.

I hated letting down my clients by becoming one more professional who left them after working with them for only a short time, turnover being something that many of the ARMHS clients complained about. But I couldn't afford to be targeted at a job again. This woman was there first, and the new job would end up being better for me anyway.

I applied to Student Support Services[276] at Metropolitan State University in March 2007. SSS is a federally funded TRIO program that is intended to *"provide enhanced retention services to undergraduate students who are first-generation, coming from limited income backgrounds, and/or students with a disability."*[277]

Like many of the programs that came out of the War on Poverty, TRIO has always been subject to budget cuts. A lot of programs have been closed entirely while others have been cut back. Given what an enormous impact the program had on my life, it's always been hard to watch these programs be at the whim of political votes. **The Upward Bound program at Luther College was cut entirely.** Phyllis would have been crushed. She thought just her presence as a proud black educator in Northeast Iowa was changing society. She was right. I read Richard Wright's *Native Son* because of her.

Chapter Thirty-Eight: Another Generation

S USAN HAD THE PERFECT smile. Nice teeth, yes. But it was the way her cheeks drew up high and her eyes brightened. It made you happy too.

She came into my office in 2007 as a woman nearly fifty years old seeking to complete her college degree. She looked like she was in her late twenties, so I was initially caught off guard when she revealed the ages of her children, who ranged from five to eighteen. I was hired to be the Student Support Services counselor, but I had also been the SSS director for almost a year at this time. It meant working nearly around the clock to keep the program running. I believed in the cause, but I was tired and increasingly irritable.

I'd slog to work but then remember just what it meant to give back for what I had been given, and my whole attitude would improve. That's probably why the program likes to hire veterans of TRIO. Knowing we'd dedicate ourselves to TRIO and not worry so much about the pay. Students kept coming to my office with questions. Day after day. Hour after hour. Assignment after assignment. Class after class. So, I went from being a counselor to being a tutor. I could try and put that in professional speak. *"After conducting a needs assessment of the community, it became clear that what everyone needed most was tutoring."*

The university offered tutoring in writing and math. These students needed tutoring in Criminal Justice, Social Work, Research Methods, and Business. Not a lot of tutoring in most cases. Just enough to keep them on track. I did do a lot of counseling. But just as there were gaps in my own education due to poverty and trauma, the same was true for these women and men. From my office, I did my best to pass on what I knew to them.

Susan didn't need much tutoring at all. She had mostly earned As and Bs already. There was still plenty our program could offer to her, however. A national scholarship was available to worthy students to go to Europe for an educational trip. She wrote an outstanding essay. I wrote a letter of support. She was astounded when she was accepted. Again, her smile was contagious. It took some doing, but she managed to arrange childcare for her three children who still lived at home while she was gone over the summer. Once she returned, I knew she would never be the same. The leader inside of her was born. Susan was always meant to be an achiever, but life circumstances and poverty had held her back.

Susan became the secretary and then the president of the TRIO Student Union. She worked in concert with other TRIO students on campus. She joined other student organizations. She was always on campus for one event or another. Her daughters would often be with her. Her children were the sweetest girls, highly intelligent and polite. Susan went out of her way to enroll them in a Spanish immersion school. They were becoming fluent in Spanish from a young age in preparation for their futures. They were mature for their ages. Exposing them to this part of campus life certainly was not hurting them either.

I wrote to Dad to update him about my plans for the book, and he wrote an email in response:

"I have done some thinking about the poverty issue here in Iowa. A lot has to do with the culture. An agriculture economy that has outside investment to get it going, keep it going, and the products usually leaving the state. Iowa is an agricultural colony, much like our early colonies. . . It's a way of life."

I wanted to explain to Dad what I had learned about poverty. I wanted to talk to him about the theory of the culture of poverty and how he was talking about the structure of poverty. How in academia that is a specific theory of poverty. Let me paraphrase Philippe Bourgois, in the *International Encyclopedia of the Social & Behavioral Sciences* (2nd ed.).[278] The culture of poverty theory came about when anthropologist Oscar Lewis wrote about poor urban families in the 1960s.[279] He drew on popular Freudian beliefs and personality theory which dominated American anthropology after World War II. Lewis believed he had identified more than fifty traits that he claimed were shared by approximately 20 percent of the poor, including "orality," "strong present-time orientation," and a "high tolerance for psychological pathology." These traits were said to be transmitted from generation to generation within families. These traits were also said to prevent individuals from taking advantage of economic opportunity. In the end, Oscar Lewis sounded more like he was presenting, as Bourgois said, a "moralistic condemnation of the unworthy poor deeply ingrained in US popular ideology."[280]

Initially, I believed that Charles Murray was a culture of poverty theorist. His arguments about why poor people stayed poor seemed to target the behaviors of poor people in a similar way.

Then I read J.A. Banks, who wrote (also in the *International Encyclopedia of the Social & Behavioral Sciences*),

"Cultural deprivation and culture of poverty theorists believe that low-income students achieve poorly in school because the socialization in their families and communities does not equip them with the knowledge, skills, attitudes, and cultural capital essential for academic success in mainstream society."[281]

These theorists believe that low-income students can achieve if they are provided with early childhood experiences that will compensate for their family and community socialization.

In contrast, genetic theorists, such as Charles Murray and his *the Bell Curve* coauthor Richard Herrstein[282], believe that low-income students and ethnic-minority students do not achieve well in school because of their genes. Culture of poverty theorists would invest in Head Start and Upward Bound, while Murray would not.

Dad wrote more to me about the culture of poverty from his point of view:

"So no matter how intelligent a person is, there are heavy forces mitigating against the average person for economic security in Iowa. Education must be geared toward what is immediately vital to survive in this state. For example, education on business law, handling money, investments, debt, health issues, marriage issues, child raising, health care, elderly care, retirement issues, buying a car and a house. I never learned about any of the above. My parents were more interested in [me] playing a bass violin, religious devoutness, etc."

Dad suggested that there is a culture of poverty driven by a lack of education about practical life matters. Instead, he was raised with a focus on religious devoutness, something that didn't help him economically at all. It wasn't exactly what Oscar Lewis had identified, but it was helpful. The culture of poverty Dad identified came from religious fundamentalism.

Senja wrote about her memories of poverty as well. She focused on selling plasma:

"[Mom] has enormous, scarred pits in her arms from years of selling her plasma for a pittance to make much-needed money for the family. Eventually, the appearance of her arms gave her away, and she was promptly put on the 'do not let donate' list. But that didn't happen until the scars were too deep to ever heal. She would look forever like a heroin addict who preferred that one spot on the arm . . . at least in the eyes of people who might not know any better. When I turned 18, Mom took me to the plasma center and we sold our plasma together for $15 dollars a bag. The whole process took nearly two hours, and left me drained, tired, and hungry. But I returned, as she did so many times, because the second time I donated in the same week, I could make $25, which was just enough incentive for my poor soul to bring me back . . . week after week after week. I began to feel trapped; like it was a job I had to do, and not just some public service which benefited someone else's life. I needed the money. And I always resented how much the company turned around and sold the plasma for, when they had purchased it wholesale for so cheap. 'I've got five to stick' says one of the phlebotomists in my memory . . . [but] it was solely poor people who came to sell plasma. It was a sad, sad place to be . . . Nowadays, I donate (actually donate) my whole blood every eight weeks. I do it to

help out the community, but every time I get 'stuck,' I am inevitably reminded of the poverty which held a grip on us."

What are the health impacts of donating your plasma each week? I'm willing to bet there are mental health consequences for long-term depletion of plasma from the blood.[283] My poor mother wondered if she had chronic fatigue syndrome. Possibly, but another good culprit was poor nutrition and the chronic necessity to tap her life blood.

⧉

Mom wrote in July 2007:

"And Deb, I'm here to tell you that the best IS yet ahead! I'll be 62 soon, and I'm feeling better than I ever have in my life. I have more energy, 'stability' and some actual good habits, like washing my face with this apricot cleanse that Aunt Nicky left for me . . . then splashing on some toner that I got from Eri years ago . . . I'm finally getting 'round to using things up and taking care of myself."

I loved that her mental health was improving. She was envisioning more successes for herself and had already had some "wins," plus she had good social support in her life at the time.

In another letter, Mom wrote that she had officially quit the Mormon Church, difficult as that was bureaucratically.[284] The Mormon Church had dramatically affected her life and mine. Mom and I could add another experience to bond over.

⧉

Near her graduation in 2007, Susan came to me in a panic. She was going to lose everything. She was deeply ashamed when she whispered her problem to me. Her boyfriend—who was more of a common-law husband, and who was the father of three of her children—used marijuana for his back pain. He had been a hard laborer and construction worker throughout their time together. Now, he had been mistaken for a burglar in their neighborhood, and the police had followed him home and searched their place. They found the marijuana.[285] It wasn't a legal search, so her boyfriend wasn't going to be charged.

But she was losing custody of her children.[286] She expected me to have a judgmental reaction. There was no way that was going to happen. I'd smoked marijuana myself to treat multiple health problems. If we lived in another state, things might have been different. If she were a different race, things almost certainly would have been different.[287] The whole situation would probably have never happened if her boyfriend were white.

I was furious this was happening to her but helpless to do anything about it. I listened as Susan cried about losing her children. I listened as long as she needed me to. Thirty-some years ago my parents lost custody of their children—of me—for poverty-related reasons. They were even accused of using marijuana, falsely in their case. I had plenty of stories about my own use.

As white people, my parents were able to use their personal network and major media coverage to get an attorney who got back their children. They had the social capital and privilege to do that. Susan did not. As a Black woman without *any* privilege, she didn't have the means to get a good attorney and get her children back. She didn't know anyone who could help.

I wanted to hire an attorney, but I didn't really have the money at that stage of my life. If I had known of crowdfunding at that time, I would have known what to do. Susan was already my favorite student. It was easy for my own issues to influence my sympathies for her situation. Child welfare forced her boyfriend to move out before she could get her children back. All of this was going on as she tried to complete her undergraduate degree.

She continued to be superhuman. College classes. Extracurricular activities. Managing the child welfare system. Losing her partner of more than fifteen years in order to get her kids back. Outdated marijuana laws had a disproportionate impact on Black families and definitely weighed heavily on hers.[288] Susan persevered. She earned the coveted cap and gown. Her smile was beaming and so was mine. There were tears in our eyes.

My father died from a stroke at the age of sixty-one, in January 2008, mere months before his first grandchild was born. There was a small memorial service attended by his brother, his current wife, his first wife (Mom), and his kids. He had really looked forward to meeting his grandson. If it wasn't for that fact, I might have thought he had taken his own life. That's because he had sent me some gloomy messages on Facebook around Christmastime 2007. But he wanted to meet this baby.

Mom wrote me a letter in April enclosed with a copy of the book, *A New Earth: Awakening to Your Life's Purpose*.[289] Her note read,

"This book is powerful. It just brought the warmest hug I've had in a long time—from a total stranger named Rita. Tolle's other book, The Power of Now,[290] *is what helped me overcome so much depression (in part). No meds for about 4 years now."*

I am willing to mention the names of books that had given my mother purpose when she had struggled for years with depression. As Mom aged, she seemed to move into a more stable period psychiatrically in her life. I knew from the research of Courtney Harding that one third of people with serious mental illness have a tendency to sort of "age out" of the worst of their conditions.[291]

Tragically, Susan died of a heart attack in her early fifties, shortly after she graduated in 2008. Her little girls were going to have to grow up without a mother, after enduring foster care. Smart, traumatized little girls.

Susan was an example of the age tax of poverty and racism.[292] Another favorite student, who is also Black and in her mid-fifties, had such high blood pressure that her systolic numbers were in the 240s.[293] My own mentor, Phyllis Gray— another strong, Black woman—passed away in her early sixties from heart disease, years before she should have.[294]

These wonderful folks and my parents prove something critical in American society that I am endlessly trying to see identified. Racism is real and it takes a toll.[295] Classism is real and it is underappreciated.[296] Susan was gone before fifty-five; Dad was dead by age sixty-one. David was dead from suicide by age twenty-three.

Our culture is shortening some lives—whether it is by depriving Black women of their health by weighing them down with stress,[297] or by creating a toxic lack of empathy in white males that drives them to suicide and oppressive behaviors toward others,[298] including their own loved ones. No one had applied the rules of classism to my parents as coldly as their own family members. Common sense dictates that if you have to deal with an "ism," such as classism, as a whole host of our Black and Brown population does, then it is going to be at least twice as hard when you add in racism on top of that.[299] This seems to be a fact that huge swaths of the country cannot acknowledge.

Isaiah had his only son in May 2008. It wasn't much later that he decided to join the Army in order to support his family.

Mom wrote in May 2009:

"Jacki has to pack all by herself. Isaiah didn't get to come home as planned. Hasn't gotten paid yet either. Gotta love that behemoth called the Army, eh? He's in the Army now."

Isaiah was in the Army indeed. He was stationed in Afghanistan from January 2010 until January 2011. Then he returned for another year. Those years were hard on all of us because we worried all the time.

In January 2010, Mom wrote to her sister Cleo. My aunt added a note, right where Mom was saying liberals are not responsible for all social problems. The note read, *"Letting all the psych patients out without medication control."*

One of my aunt's heroes, Ronald Reagan, is the president most identified with letting institutionalized people out of hospitals without treatment or medication.[300] I would have loved to provide her with all the evidence that it was his administration that caused deinstitutionalization to grow into a huge problem.[301] Trust me when I say the people providing the underfunded community care to those seriously mentally ill people tended to be liberals, and they didn't appreciate losing the ability to hospitalize clients when it was needed.[302]

When these services become increasingly scarce, people in need commonly end up in one of three places: homeless shelters, jails, or emergency rooms. It costs an estimated $10,000 per year to offer community services to an individual, while paying to keep them in jail for a year, for instance, costs approximately $35,000 per person.[303] My numbers are no doubt old.

In March 2011, the National Alliance on Mental Illness released a report titled, "State Mental Health Cuts: A National Crisis."[304] The same year they released a second report, "State Mental Health Cuts: The Continuing Crisis," further detailing the trend toward defunding services. In each report, the organization pled with lawmakers to reconsider the decision to repeatedly slash funding for critical and necessary services, while documenting just how severe those cuts have been[305].

Between 2009 and 2011, states cut their mental health services by 9.5 percent (approximately $1.6 billion), and the cuts for 2012 were deep as well. There is variation across states, with some, like North Dakota, even increasing spending for the mentally ill. But the norm has been for states to try and balance their budgets by looking for savings in programs that serve this and other vulnerable groups.

In Michigan, the state government has dramatically cut mental health services, only to pay more to warehouse many of the same people in the criminal justice system. Detroit and its surrounding suburbs have lost 75 percent of their state psychiatric hospitals since

1987. The situation has become so drastic that the sheriff of the Wayne County (which includes Detroit), Benny Napoleon, called his jails the largest mental health institution in the county. Past research has shown that at least 30 percent of the population imprisoned in Wayne County has a serious mental illness. It's enough for the director of Michigan's Department of Corrections to state, "I've got institutions that are just packed with people who are very, very seriously mentally ill."

Since 2008, the state cut $50 million more from the mental health budget, and more than half of that money was cut from Detroit–Wayne County. In the meantime, Michigan's Republican governor at the time, Rick Snyder, cut taxes for corporations by 86 percent rather than address the crisis in mental health services that the criminal justice system is desperately trying to draw attention to. Of course, that's where Senja lives. That's where we can't get her any services.

Senja got married in 2007. She was pregnant with twins in 2010. They were born prematurely at twenty-four weeks, weighing approximately a pound each. Their survival was not assured at first, but Senja, her husband, and Mom took turns holding the babies skin-to-skin for better recovery. They ended up thriving.

Mom spent quite a bit of her time in Ann Arbor helping look after the babies. Doug and I drove to Michigan to meet my twin niece and nephew. To get there, I had to lie down flat in the back of our minivan, or else my back would hurt too much. It was truly scary traveling like that, but I was so excited and proud to meet my niece and nephew. Everything seemed positive, except Senja was spending nearly all her free time drinking beer in their garage. Mom and Senja's husband were doing a lot of the childcare. I was worried about her.

I guess I should have been worried about myself as well. My shattered family. Losing my career. My back continuing to give me grief since that first blowout at University of Michigan in 1997. It had been causing me significant and increasing pain since 2004. I had tried everything from chiropractic to surgery to steroid injections. I was also dealing with a new physical pain all over my body that was hard to describe. My doctor tested me for fibromyalgia, and said I fit the diagnosis, so she put me on Lyrica. This medication did help tremendously. Or, at least, missing a dose led me to feel such pain that I understood the value of the medication.[306]

All the various stresses led me to a suicidal depression in 2011. I was referred to PrairieCare, a large mental health agency in the area. I spent seven weeks doing intensive outpatient group therapy. The group therapists decided to refer me to an expert in trauma. Her name was Jane. She was a white-haired, grandma-like therapist who even ended her sessions with hugs. She practiced EMDR (eye movement desensitization and reprocessing[307]), and we talked about many of my traumatic memories. I think I got better.

Chapter Thirty-Nine: God Wants You to Write a Book

M OM TRIED TO WRITE her story about being drawn into the Mormon Church by her family and then sucked further into a polygamist cult by life circumstances. I wanted to help her get her story out. Mom really had gotten involved with a cult that was itself involved in crime, including murder some seven years later in Utah (see *Under the Banner of Heaven*).[308]

But Mom's story focused on religion. By the time I gathered journals and letters to write the book I'd thought about for years, I had a wider range of material to work with. In March 2014, I had to quit my job at TRIO to deal with my health. My weight had once again climbed back to 300 pounds because of my eating disorder. My heel hurt all the time from plantar fasciitis and a bone spur just like my dad's. My back and leg hurt constantly at balled-up-fist-level pain,[309] and I didn't know what to do about it, because a recommended second surgery on my back was risky. The surgeon was now proposing a fusion surgery,[310] which would lock together my bottom three spinal discs. It didn't sound like a good idea. My deceased chiropractor grandfather was whispering to me that I had made a mistake getting surgery the first time and that this surgery would be a definite mistake.

But I struggled to do my job in pain until I couldn't. I specifically could not handle sitting for any length of time. I had been allowed to take opiates to counteract that pain,[311] but I was struggling with tolerance to the pills and my pain was overcoming their helpfulness, making it feel like I needed more.[312] If I was building up a tolerance to painkillers, I was becoming addicted to them.[313] Since I still had problems sitting to do my job, I was missing a lot of work.[314] After two years of providing me the opiate prescription, my doctor decided to withdraw it.[315] I needed to deal with an opiate addiction, but I only half realized I had one.[316]

I started my road to recovery by exercising at Curves. I was prepared to lose weight the hard way yet again. But I quickly injured both of my shoulders by overdoing it on the arm exercises. This required surgery on each shoulder for torn rotator cuffs. The photos of the ripped-up shoulders were incredible to see.

My medical doctor proposed something to me called Physician's Neck and Back rehabilitation services. Someone had thought about strengthening backs and necks with specialized weight training e quipment.[317] I spent roughly seven weeks going from completely weak to the strength necessary to maintain my spine. It was the best intervention I'd ever had for my back. I wanted to shout about it with a bullhorn. This was my holy grail. I was exercising my way to health.

My family history was clearly controversial, and although my parents showed enthusiasm about telling our family's story, some of my siblings did not react as well. Samuel suggested he didn't understand why I was bothered by Charles Murray's mischaracterization of the poor and poverty. To me, this was like he was denying all the trauma we went through.

Our relationship started to decline. I learned that his life path of juvenile delinquency had apparently been easy to experience, even if it put others through a lot of misery. Since he had never left the working class, he had never experienced classism either.[318] I had actually mingled with people in the middle and upper classes enough to experience it.[319]

He never had people automatically assume that when you said you were on welfare that you had personally "made a bad choice to have a baby you couldn't afford." They wouldn't jump to that conclusion about him since he was a man. Of course, I doubt he spent much time talking about how his family depended on social programs his whole childhood. He was now a dyed-in-the-wool right-wing zealot, and a long history of welfare dependence just wouldn't do.

Mom was enjoying some of the benefits of old age. By her seventies, the bipolar had virtually disappeared. Her mood was much more stable. It's entirely possible that being in menopause helped her, since she always said that her menstrual cycle was heavily tied to her headaches and her moods. Perhaps her diagnoses included premenstrual dysmorphic disorder.[320] I wrote to a scientific journal on women's health about how this disorder may benefit from treatment by hormonal regulation, and they published it before I left academia. But I couldn't get my own family to listen to me about the diagnosis. Conservative media have mocked it as made up. I would ask Mom's conservative relatives who knew about her monthly weeklong migraine headaches if they also mock those.

Chapter Forty: Recovery

I N LATE 2015, MY trauma therapist, Jane, retired. I was nowhere near done processing my traumas yet, so I was devastated. Jane recommended that I address my eating disorder which she had diagnosed during our time working together. She referred me to the Emily Program for treatment.

I immediately went to the Emily Program for an evaluation, and by January 2016, I was enrolled in their intensive outpatient treatment program for people with binge-eating disorder or compulsive eating disorder (overeaters). I had to spend *six months* in intensive therapy before I finally had control of my symptoms.

For months, I couldn't stop bingeing at all, despite the intervention. This included eating together with the therapist for lunch every weekday for six months. That part of the intervention seemed especially useful and important. The therapist was actually with you while you ate. Our group processed a lot of emotions over lunch.

What also seemed to make a difference was learning about a concept called, "radical acceptance." It is a concept that comes out of dialectical behavioral therapy (DBT),[321] but fundamentally it derives from Buddhism. With radical acceptance, you accept the situations that are causing you pain but are outside your control, because refusing to accept the truth is more painful and has more negative consequences than accepting it. It prolongs your suffering to refuse to accept the reality of a bad situation.

I learned it wasn't the same as giving up. It was more like letting go. It was permission to stop struggling against impossible situations. There are all kinds of times you shouldn't use radical acceptance, such as when you are in an abusive relationship. You shouldn't use radical acceptance when you have some degree of control over a situation. But when you don't, it's invaluable.

Growing up with a mother who had her own eating disorder no doubt played a role in inheriting the issue. But running out of food about seventeen days into the month every month also led to chronic hunger. My body needed to understand that it wasn't living in a famine so I could stop bingeing as a response. I needed to accept my past and realize I currently had abundance.

In December 2016, I had surgery to have a spinal stimulator implanted in my back.[322] The surgeon put one electric lead on the left side of my thoracic spine and the other lead on the right side. Then, he put a battery pack in the area above my right buttock. I literally must recharge myself. I need to lie on a disc every few days for a few hours to keep the battery charged.

I was able to exercise more freely. I was able to travel moderate distances. I was able to sleep. I was able to stop complaining about how doctors would never give me pain medication. I managed to overcome the addiction to the pain medication. This all meant I entered 2017 without the physical agony that had haunted me for ten years. I was disappointed I was not pain-free, but the constant, small electrical shocks did a "good enough" job of changing my life. It can tickle or vibrate too powerfully, leading to itching, but life is full of trade-offs, right?

And until I relapsed in 2022, I stayed quite thin. The pandemic was so isolating that I fell back on old coping habits. I was starting to be overweight again, and my eating disorder was back. Worse than that, I didn't care. However, my therapist said it was a good sign that I wasn't skipping meals. So, hopefully, I will be back on track shortly.

I also participated for a year in DBT, the treatment created by Marsha Linehan. This therapy focuses on mindfulness, regulating emotions, and improving interpersonal relationships. It was especially helpful with my marriage. At DBT, I met my best friend, Anne, who is almost my mother's age.

I decided that I was going to get gastric bypass surgery for weight loss because I wasn't losing weight much at all, even with a personal trainer, and I wanted a more permanent solution to my problem. After my binge eating was in remission for a while, I joined a group at Emily Program for women who planned to get gastric bypass surgery.[323] I was influenced by Anne, who had gastric bypass many years earlier.

Many people get the surgery without going through the year of therapy first, and that's a mistake. You need to treat your eating disorder before doing this surgery.[324] If you don't, you'll gain the all the weight back and more not very long after the procedure. I was able to get a gastric bypass in April 2018. I lost 150 pounds—well, 175 pounds at one point, because I got down to 120 pounds. The weight loss helped with the back pain too.

But, as mentioned, my eating disorder was going to come roaring back during a harsh relapse in 2022, when I put half that weight back on. Worse than that, as I said, I didn't care. Maybe that was good, though. Could I learn to accept myself no matter what? My body dysmorphic disorder had finally been dogging me less since I was a chubby middle-aged woman.[325]

One internet positivity article I saw stated, "You had a hard life, you had some pain—okay cool, everyone does. Shake that shit off and get on with the fucking show."[326] That is a patently bogus statement. Not everyone has not had a hard life.

These are the eight commonly accepted categories of adverse childhood experiences or (ACEs): 1) child sexual abuse, 2) parental interpersonal violence, 3) parental child abuse or neglect, 4) community violence, 5) gun violence, 6) sexual violence, 7) bullying, and 8) teen dating violence.[327]

Complex PTSD or C-PTSD, is associated with experiencing long-term abuse, such as child neglect, child physical or sexual abuse, being held captive, or being a member of a cult. But recently, people have been connecting complex PTSD to children growing up in households with a high number of ACEs. Growing up with four or more is associated with a thirty-two times greater risk of having a behavioral disorder.[328] Specifically, four or more ACEs increased the risk of depression (4.5 times) and suicide attempts (12.2 to 15.3 times).[329]

Only a small portion of our population ever experiences four or more adverse childhood experiences as defined in the research. Specifically, that number is somewhere around 12 to 15 percent. Of course, not all ACEs are captured by the research. I would add genocide, for instance, based on my experiences working with refugees. But usually, when you add ACEs, it only adds to the total number of people who already have several.[330]

In fact, the calculations done by researchers show that while only 15 percent of Americans experience four or more of the adverse childhood experiences, a full 36 percent of Americans never experience any. That means one in three Americans are walking around having never gone through any of the major adverse childhood events. That's great for them but also increases the odds that they author an internet thought piece about shaking shit off and moving on. Another 25 percent have only had one adverse childhood experience.[331]

It is an accumulation of these experiences that leads to C-PTSD, which affects the portion of our population who have been subjected to repeated, long-term abuse or neglect. Foster children have twice the rate of PTSD as soldiers,[332] although they have changed the name of PTSD to PTS to reduce the stigma for soldiers to post-traumatic stress.

A few years ago, around 2018, my sister and I had a heart-to-heart conversation about the results of her recent neuropsychological examination. I was eager to hear them, because I'd been encouraging her for several years to see a mental health professional for chronic anxiety, impulsive behavior, and depression, to name a few issues.

I was especially worried about her because she lived far away from the rest of the family. Mom finally got mediocre but sufficient mental health care that helped her to recover after several serious suicide attempts. A concussion from a car accident ultimately convinced Senja to go for testing.

My sister said via text,

"I have developmental trauma disorder or complex PTSD,[333] and so do you. It isn't in the latest version of the DSM, but it should be at some point in the future. Well, it is sort of there, under other diagnoses, but there are additional symptoms, and the causes are not the same. I believe it is not in the DSM for political reasons."

We grew up in extreme poverty with a mother whose untreated mental illness equated to a childhood of chronic neglect, abuse, and family dysfunction.

I replied via text:

"No, you can't have developmental PTSD, if it isn't a diagnosis. If it is controversial whether to include it as a diagnosis, that's not what the neuropsychologist said, is it?"

She replied:

"Well, of course, it's a diagnosis. It's no different than any other disorder that took time to be identified and recognized. The reason they don't want to add it to the DSM is that it would then become a disability under the Americans with Disabilities Act, and then all of these children who have been subjected to long term neglect, abuse, and trauma will have rights in court to sue for programs and services. That basically means children in extreme poverty would have the right to sue to get out of poverty."

This is where she had me speechless. It was internally logical. The research has been done to show that extreme poverty affected the EEGs of children in a way similar to that of stroke victims.[334] Extreme poverty affects a greater portion of children in America than in several developing nations.[335] Still, I came back with another reason people don't want these kinds of diagnoses to be made.

I replied:

"There are disadvantages to having something become a diagnosis. Take Attention Deficit Disorder. It definitely identified a large number of children, and even adults, with a set of symptoms. Now, there are large numbers of people who believe the pharmaceutical industry has taken advantage of the diagnosis in such a way as to medicate generations of children rather than address social issues that might drive their symptoms.[336] Look what they do to African American children."

This time she was silent for a time until replying:

"I think the good outweighs the bad.[337] Recognizing that there are probably large numbers of people in this country experiencing this psychological condition gives them a chance to understand the true source of their symptoms of trauma."

The diagnosis is associated with a long list of symptoms,[338] some of which I have copied from the CPTSD.org[339] website that no longer exists: "emotional flashbacks; toxic shame; self-abandonment; inner critic; social anxiety; loss of meaning." (Similar information was later available from the CPTSD Foundation online: www.CPTSDfoundation.org).[340]

Now Senja had me thinking that maybe this diagnosis was a good thing. At the same time, however, it risked pathologizing people for their reactions to social abuse, like the failures of the child welfare system (social abuse term credit goes to sociologist Dr. Barbara Jean Peters, co-founder of the Working Class and Poverty Class Academics).[341] For example, ProPublica and NBC together recently did a special report on the fact that one in three Black families in the Phoenix area were getting visits from child welfare.[342]

Still, the trauma of childhood poverty was undeniable. People think extreme poverty is just having a little less cash than other people. They don't know. They just don't know. It is trauma to grow up this way, with all the adverse childhood events that can go along with it. As I calculated the eight ACEs Senja and I had, I understood why.

Then my sister said,

"You can be going along fine in adulthood, having survived what happened in childhood, when suddenly you hit a trauma, and everything rushes in. I know it's weird but I am actually joyful, even blissful, to have found this diagnosis. Because my symptoms finally make sense now."

In general, I'm inclined to think it's a good thing to diagnose people. People with the diagnosis can form support groups, online communities, and advocate for treatment. They can create public awareness campaigns to alert people that they might have the condition. Recognizing a diagnosis can be beneficial because it leads to specifically tailored therapies.[343] Still, the risks are there. A lurking pharmaceutical industry, for example. But, Mom's fears aside, even they can be helpful.

Now, therapeutically, what do we know about people with C-PTSD? They are walking wounds. Yes. Most importantly, they need to talk about what happened to them.[344] Doing so counteracts the years of shame, silence, and self-blame that surround those subjected to these experiences. *No,* they are not like everyone else. They haven't had "some" pain. They have pain so significant that researchers have found scores of neuro-endocrinological indicators in these people signaling their childhood and adult pain.[345] For example, inflammatory agents are increased in adults with these backgrounds.[346]

Everything I just said applies strongly to my brothers too. They also have complex PTSD, but I didn't realize that until close to 2020. And there's another variable that affects people in our family at a disturbing rate—traumatic brain injury. That could be a factor too.

Lots of people grow up in this kind of poverty or in struggling families without having any ill effects. This is because they have numerous protective factors in their lives: community members who reached out; better churches than we encountered; a teacher, or maybe even a few teachers; loving family members; school activities, etc. In my life, of course, this person who reached out was Phyllis Gray from Upward Bound. I deeply appreciated her investment in my well-being and outcome. Unfortunately, my family members proved that a couple of protective factors can be introduced and still not prevent the onset of C-PTSD in adulthood.

Damaged people have typically never been given space to emotionally react to what has happened to them or receive support from a community for it. In books like, *The Body Keeps the Score*,[347] we learn that bottling up these emotions leads to disease. People in pain have been hearing the same thing their whole lives. Don't talk about it because people don't tolerate listening to each other's pain very well.

Doug has been exceptionally supportive. However, we still suffered a period of separation in our marriage that can be directly linked to the effects of trauma and poverty from my childhood. It nearly resulted in our divorce.

We have faced many additional obstacles, including both the loss of Eric and a traumatic brain injury that Doug later suffered, and yet we celebrated twenty years together. We know we're stronger than ever because of what we've overcome together.

Epilogue

I HAD WAY TOO hard of a time writing this book. Doing so meant dwelling in the past for long periods of time, and I kept needing to address my trauma symptoms to travel there. But that process was obviously extremely good for me in the long run. My mental health is finally stabilizing for the first time ever. I'm heavily agnostic now, but I admit I asked God for help in finishing this book. It's complicated; one of the things C-PTSD is associated with is spiritual chaos.[348]

I am so proud of the person Mom has become. If she has taught me anything about how to cope with the world, it is to have gratitude. She surmounted all her family influences and church indoctrination to seek accurate and useful mental health treatment. She tries to provide social support to so many hurt people. She is spending her senior years as a content, productive free thinker. One of the public services she provides is to reassure her 80 year old best friend with schizophrenia that he is not going to hell, something he was taught as a child, and which still panics him daily.

I wish I had better news about her children. Starting with the youngest, Isaiah's time in the army resulted in a back injury during parachuting.[349] He developed an opiate addiction and overdosed a couple times.[350] But the rest of us only hear about him secondhand because he's not speaking to anyone. I just read that people with ADHD have been identified to have rejection sensitivity dysphoria, or an "unbearable" pain as a result of perceived or actual rejection, teasing, or criticism.[351] The good news about Isaiah is that perhaps as part of his recovery, he is running a veterans' wellness program that has the beautiful goal of saving lives.

Senja uses our traumatic background and her head injuries as an excuse to continue out-of-control drinking that pushes friends and family alike away.[352] Senja's drinking problem has led everyone to block her rather than endure another all-night barrage of more than 150 text messages alternating between being abusive and suicidal. Mom gets sad and anxious texts from Senja's innocent twins. No wonder Senja thinks Mom should have aborted all of us. We've tried numerous interventions. Please wish us luck.

John and his wife divorced, although their sweet little boy seemed to handle it well. John is caught up in the new Republican pastime of hating transgender people.[353] He was radicalized on the internet as so many have been. Having PCOS, which causes certain masculine traits, makes me feel a lot of empathy for transgendered people,.[354] I tried to explain the fluidity of gender in my own life, but he still displays hate.

Samuel, having been my closest brother, watched the harvest blood moon with Mom and me sometime around 2015, I think. The moon was so clear, so obviously three-dimensional. We all sat in awe. Then, I lost him completely, first to conspiracy theories from the internet, and next to Trumpism, which included neo-Nazism, QAnon, and white supremacy.[355] He believes what Charles Murray taught. He doesn't understand economic policy or lots of other things, like social media manipulation.

I had a stroke in 2022, which came with the depression that is common following strokes.[356] But there is no doubt that what was happening with Samuel contributed significantly to my mental state. I was treated with electroconvulsive therapy (ECT), and it mostly helped.[357] My memory is spottier now,[358] so it was good I was mostly done with the book.

Lies like, "The rich got their money by earning it, while the poor got what they deserved," or, "Work hard and you'll make billions," still drive fraudulent views of capitalism.[359] The greatest predictor of whether or not you will be rich as an adult is whether your parents were rich, not your ability at anything.[360]

People like Charles Murray didn't want any resources going to poor people, because those resources were starting to help people get out of poverty. Restorative justice worked with my brother.

Upward Bound worked with me, and it worked with Senja, Samuel, and Isaiah. However, most of the things designed to help us had been cut or were being cut, especially the poverty and mental health services. Neither my parents, nor Senja, nor David had or have really gotten necessary or sufficient treatment.

Gillian White wrote an article in the *Atlantic* about the poverty industry and its exploitation of the problem it's designed to fight. She cited poverty expert Matthew Desmond, who explains how the poor don't get the money that's supposed to be for them:

"What's kind of amazing to me is how much money is allocated to the poor on paper but doesn't reach them in practice . . . They use welfare funds to fund Christian summer camps, anti-abortion centers, marriage initiatives. Mississippi basically used it to . . . buy trucks . . . and build university sports stadiums."[361]

Many of us heard about how former Green Bay Packers' quarterback, Brett Favre, helped steer millions of Mississippi's welfare dollars for a sports center on his daughter's campus. That was my team. I was crushed. If I were to recommend one book on poverty, it would be Desmond's *Poverty, By America*.[362]

Repeatedly, Fox "News" implies that poor people have so many material goods that they must not really be poor.[363] You wouldn't know it from the biased coverage[364] that landlords are more than twice as likely to exploit their renters in high poverty areas.[365] My relatives who absorb that coverage should know better, considering their own family, but they are brainwashed too. It cannot be healthy for a democracy to have so many people who'll believe outright, flagrant, easily disprovable lies.[366]

I am a Midwesterner who doesn't drink coffee or alcohol, pretty much like my Mormon elders taught me. I drive a twelve-year-old gas-powered beater without a single bumper sticker (Doug has some great ones though). I want an electric car, but we can't afford one. I listen to the classic rock station preset on my factory-installed FM car radio. The Allman Brothers are still a huge favorite. It feels like I'm an average American.

My right-wing, Christian relatives are insisting that they don't have enough rights, yet they can control whether my employer covers the birth control pills[367] I still need for my PCOS and whether my preteen niece can control her reproductive future,[368] even if her life is threatened.[369] In too many states, my niece could still be forced to marry an adult man as a child bride.[370] A transgender woman Phyllis Gray and I love very much is facing a future of discrimination and potential violence.

I never dreamed that my education in Germany would be applicable to life in the United States, and yet later this year there is an election with a candidate who mimics Hitler in every way. He uses scapegoats.[371] He calls the free press enemies of the p eople.[372] He threatens his political opponents with jail and even the death penalty.[373] He even gives oxygen to neo-Nazis. and *they* think he supports them.[374] He directly quotes Hitler by talking about immigrants poisoning the blood of the nation. My book that was supposed to be about poverty ends noting our environment of authoritarianism.[375.] So, I am looking to young people to give me hope. They often observe their parents and see what needs to be done. Many of them are readers with teachers who are opening their eyes. This book is dedicated to them.

Additional Recommended Reading

Frank, T. (2004). *What's the Matter with Kansas? How Conservatives Won the Heart of America*. Macmillan.

Hartmann, T. (2020). *The Hidden History of Monopolies: How Big Business Destroyed the American Dream*. National Geographic Books.

Herman, E. S., & Chomsky, N. (1988). *Manufacturing Consent: The Political Economy of the Mass Media*. Pantheon.

McGirr, L. (2001). *Suburban Warriors: The Origins of the New American Right*. Princeton, New Jersey: Princeton University Press.

Pepper, D. (2021). *Laboratories of Autocracy: A Wake-Up Call from Behind the Lines*. St. Helena Press.

Quart, A. (2023). *Bootstrapped: Liberating Ourselves from the American Dream*. HarperCollins.

Stanley, J. (2018). *How Fascism Works: The Politics of Us and Them*. Random House.

Ward, J. (2023). *Testimony: Inside the Evangelical Movement That Failed a Generation*. Baker Books.

Yeung, B., & Grabell, M. (2021, February 3). How the history of Waterloo, Iowa, explains how meatpacking plants became hotbeds of COVID-19. *ProPublica*. https://www.propublica.org/article/how-the-history-of-waterloo-iowa-explains-how-meatpacking-plants-became-hotbeds-of-covid-19.

Endnotes

1. Risen, D. (2017, June 8). The war on the war on poverty. *Democracy Journal*. https://democracyjournal.org/magazine/6/the-war-on-the-war-on-poverty/

2. Murray, C. (1988). What's so bad about being poor? *National Review*, https://indexarticles.com/reference/national-review/whats-so-bad-about-being-poor-2/

3. Murray, C. & Herrnstein, R. (1994). *The Bell Curve: Intelligence and Class Structure in American Life*. The Free Press.

4. Murray, C. (1993). The coming white underclass. Originally from *U.S. News and World Report*. https://www.aei.org/articles/the-coming-white-underclass/

5. Murray, C. & Herrnstein, R. (1994). *The Bell Curve: Intelligence and Class Structure in American Life*. The Free Press.

6. Solomon, A. (2001). *The Noonday Demon: An Atlas of Depression*. Scribner Press.

7. Schizoaffective disorder: MedlinePlus Medical Encyclopedia. (n.d.). https://medlineplus.gov/ency/article/000930.htm.

8. Andersen, Kurt. (2017). *Fantasyland: How America Went Haywire: A 500-Year History*. Random House Books.

9. This is a pseudonym.

10. Mondimore, F. (2020, August 15). Can antidepressants cause problems for bipolar patients. *Psychology Today*. https://www.psychologytoday.com/intl/blog/bipolar-101/202008/can-antidepressants-cause-problems-bipolar-patients.

11. Gitlin, M. (2018). Antidepressants in bipolar depression: an enduring controversy. *International Journal of Bipolar Disorders, 6* (1). https://doi.org/10.1186/s40345-018-0133-9.

12. Villines, Z. (2013, March 8). Exorcisms and psychology: What's really going on? https://www.goodtherapy.org/blog/psychology-exorcism-demonic-possession-0308137.

13. This is a pseudonym.

14. Carroll, R. & Prickett, S. (2008). *The Bible: Authorized King James version*. Oxford Paperbacks.

15. Smith, J. (1823). *The Book of Mormon: Another Testament of Jesus Christ*.

16. Smith, J. (1879). *The doctrine and covenants, of the Church of Jesus Christ of Latter-Day Saints: containing the revelations given to Joseph Smith, the Prophet, for the building up of the Kingdom of God in the Last Days*. Greenwood Press.

17. Smith, J. (1878). *The Pearl of Great Price: Being a choice selection from the revelations, translations, and narrations of Joseph Smith, First Prophet, Seer, and Revelator to the Church of Jesus Christ of Latter-Day Saints*.

18. My mother's words from interviews with her about this time period.

19. [a]Ernst, E. (2000). Iridology: not useful and potentially harmful. *Archives of Ophthalmology, 118*(1), 120–121.[b]Münstedt, K., El-Safadi, S., Brück, F., Zygmunt, M., Hackethal, A., & Tinneberg, H. R. (2005). Can iridology detect susceptibility to cancer? A prospective case-controlled study. *Journal of Alternative & Complementary Medicine, 11*(3), 515–519.

20. Manoukian, M. (2023, October 13). The tragic story of the doctor who pioneered hand-washing. https://www.grunge.com/247211/the-tragic-story-of-the-doctor-who-pioneered-hand-washing/

21. Hawkins, E. (2020, June 1). Polygamist cult leader uses wives and followers to start bloody sectarian war. *Oxygen Official Site*. https://www.oxygen.com/deadly-cults/crime-news/ervil-lebaron-orders-rulon-allreds-murder-polygamist-cult.

22. Crossfield, R. C. (1969). *Book of Onias*.

23. This is a pseudonym.

24. This is a pseudonym.

25. This is a pseudonym.

26. Valley Fever awareness. (2023, July 12). *Centers for Disease Control and Prevention*. https://www.cdc.gov/fungal/features/valley-fever.html.

27. Herbert Woolston, C., & Frederick Root, G. (1913). Jesus loves the little children [Song]. Philadelphia, PA, United States of America.

28. Harvard Health. (2017, March 21). Depression and pain. https://www.health.harvard.edu/mind-and-mood/depression-and-pain.

29. Kapfhammer, H. P. (2022). Somatic symptoms in depression. *Dialogues in Clinical Neuroscience*, 8(2), 227-39

30. Ruth, J. (2018, June 16). It's time to stop normalizing evangelicals. *Medium*. https://medium.com/@julieruth/its-time-to-stop-normalizing-evangelicals-847ef451186c.

31. Dibdin, E. (2023, July 31). Understanding narcissistic abuse and breaking the cycle. *Psych Central*. https://psychcentral.com/disorders/the-narcissistic-cycle-of-abuse.

32. Wattenberg, B. J. (1987). *The birth dearth*. Pharos Books.

33. Martin, R. S., & Lakins, L. (2022). *White Fear: How the Browning of America Is Making White Folks Lose Their Minds*. BenBella Books.

34. Falk, D. (2020, April 29). The complicated legacy of Herbert Spencer, the man who coined 'Survival of the Fittest.' *Smithsonian Magazine*. https://www.smithsonianmag.com/science-nature/herbert-spencer-survival-of-the-fittest-180974756/.

35. Kazamias, A. (1966). Spencer and the welfare state. *History of Education Quarterly*, *6*(2), 73–95. https://www.jstor.org/stable/367420.

36. This is a pseudonym.

37. This is a pseudonym.

38. Gartner, J. F. (1969). *All about Pickup Campers, Van Conversions, and Motor Homes*.

39. Von Däniken, E., & Heron, M. (1968). *Chariots of the Gods? Unsolved Mysteries of the Past*. Berkley Books.

40. [a]Kristof, N. (1999, July 6). Alien abduction? Science calls it sleep paralysis. *The New York Times*. https://www.nytimes.com/1999/07/06/science/alien-abduction-science-calls-it-sleep-paralysis.html. [b]CSEWI. (2014, July 16). Link between sleep paralysis and alien abduction. *The Space and Astronomy Blog*. https://csewi.org/link-between-sleep-paralysis-and-alien-abduction/

41. Strong, J. (1890). *Strong's exhaustive concordance of the Bible*. Hendrickson Publishing.

42. This is a pseudonym.

43. Olfman, S. (2008). *The sexualization of childhood*. Bloomsbury Publishing USA.

44. This is a pseudonym.

45. Twitchell, James B. 1943–. Encyclopedia.com. (n.d.). https://www.encyclopedia.com/arts/educational-magazines/twitchell-james-b-1943

46. Warner, G. C. (1942). *The boxcar children*. Random House Books for Young Readers.

47. Fitzgerald, J. D. (2004). *The great brain*. Puffin Books.

48. Fletcher, J. (2020, October 15). *What to know about L-tryptophan supplements*. https://www.medicalnewstoday.com/articles/l-trytophan-supplements

49. Alexander, R. (2020). Contaminated L-Tryptophan and 5-Hydroxy-L-Tryptophan, eosinophilia myalgia syndrome [EMS], the 1989 epidemic and the 1998 warning. Alexander Law Group LLP. https://alexanderlaw.com/articles/2019/07/contaminated-l-tryptophan-and-5-hydroxy-l-tryptophan-eosinophilia-myalgia-syndrome-ems-the-1989-epidemic-and-the-1998-warning/

50. Brodie, F. M. (1971). *No man knows my history: The Life of Joseph Smith, the Mormon Prophet*. Alfred A. Knopf.

51. Baugh, A. (2017). The history and doctrine of the Adam-Ondi-Ahman revelation (D&C 116). In C. James Ostler, M. Hubbard MacKay, & B. Morgan Gardner (Eds.), *Foundations of the Restoration: The 45th Annual Brigham Young University Sidney B. Sperry Symposium* (pp. 157–188). Deseret Books. https://rsc.byu.edu/foundations-restoration/history-doctrine-adam-ondi-ahman-revelation-dc-116

52. Church of Latter-day Saints. (n.d.). What to expect when you visit the church's historic sites in Missouri. https://history.churchofjesuschrist.org/content/historic-sites/missouri/what-to-expect-from-your-visit-to-the-historic-sites-in-missouri?lang=eng

53. Lindsey, H., & Carlson, C. C. (1970). *The late great planet Earth*. Zondervan Publishing.

54. Stormer, J. A. (1964). *None dare call it treason*. Liberty Bell Press.

55. Barrett, S. (2014, August 23). Applied kinesiology: Phony muscle-testing for "allergies" and "nutrient deficiencies". *Quackwatch*. https://quackwatch.org/related/Tests/ak/

56. Andersen, Kurt. (2017). *Fantasyland: How America Went Haywire: A 500-Year History*. Random House Books. p.288

57. Berman, J. (2022). Conspiracy theory docuseries Shadowland might as well be the terrifying sequel to the U.S. and the Holocaust. *Time*. https://news.yahoo.com/conspiracy-theory-docuseries-shadowland-might-175101610.html

58. Cold Case Spotlight: Johnny Gosch. (2014, October 26). *NBC News*. https://www.nbcnews.com/feature/cold-case-spotlight/cold-case-spotlight-johnny-gosch-n234291

59. This is a pseudonym.

60. Lowery, G. (2010, November 15). Study: Low incomes make poor more conservative. *Cornell Chronicle*. https://news.cornell.edu/stories/2010/11/study-low-incomes-make-poor-more-conservative

61. Paterson, K. (2009). *Bridge to Terabithia*. Harper Collins.

62. Etebari, M. (2003, July 17). Trickle-down economics: Four reasons why It just doesn't work. United for a Fair Economy. https://www.faireconomy.org/trickle_down_economics_four_reasons

63. [a]Murray, I. (2019, December 5). One Iowa city where redlining's legacy still haunts. *Iowa Starting Line—Your Home for Iowa Politics*. https://iowastartingline.com/2019/12/05/one-iowa-city-where-redlinings-legacy-still-haunts2/[b]Segregation in Black Hawk County. Mapping Segregation in Iowa. (n.d.). https://dsps.lib.uiowa.edu/mappingsegregationia/segregation-in-black-hawk-county/

64. Seiple, E., Zitzner, A., Anthony, J., Dusil, R., Lehman, K., & P Martin, G. (2017, February). Racial segregation in Iowa's metro areas, 1990–2010. Public Policy Center, University of Iowa. https://ppc.uiowa.edu/publications/racial-segregation-iowas-metro-areas-1990-2010

65. Steadman, I. (2014, March 25). The dangerous new scientific racism. *The New Republic*. https://newrepublic.com/article/117884/nicholas-wades-troublesome-inheritance-new-scientific-racism

66. This is a pseudonym.

67. This is a pseudonym.

68. Anson, J. (1967). *The Amityville Horror*. Gallery Books.

69. Bult, L. (2020, October 23). Why American public transit is so bad. *Vox*. https://www.vox.com/videos/21529609/usa-public-transit-trains-buses-cars

70. He actually went by Uncle Dick, but I didn't know if people would believe my pedophile uncle actually went by this name

71. Twitchell, James B. 1943–. Encyclopedia.com. (n.d.). https://www.encyclopedia.com/arts/educational-magazines/twitchell-james-b-1943

72. Carroll, R., & Prickett, S. (2008). *The Bible: Authorized King James version*. Oxford Paperbacks.

73. [a]Billings, B. (2020). Megachurches can have mega problems: Insights from toxic leadership in modern megachurches" *Honors Scholars Collaborative Projects*. https://repository.belmont.edu/honors_theses/7[b]Wellman, J., E Corcoran, K., & J Stockly, K. (2019, September). Dissecting megachurch scandals. Oxford Academic. *High on God: How Megachurches Won the Heart of America*. https://academic.oup.com/book/36514/chapter-abstract/321252378?redirectedFrom=fulltext&login=false

74. This is a pseudonym.

75. Somers, J. (2022). The dark side of megachurches. *Grunge*. https://www.grunge.com/596092/the-dark-side-of-megachurches/

76. Gensler-Nic, K. (2020, May 14). "Church shopping" with chronic and mental illnesses. *The Mighty*. https://themighty.com/topic/chronic-illness/finding-church-mental-chronic-illness/

77. This is a pseudonym.

78. This was frequently stated by my mother growing up

79. This is a pseudonym.

80. This is a pseudonym.

81. This is a pseudonym.

82. Goldman, W. (1977). *The Princess Bride: S. Morgenstern's Classic Tale of True Love and High Adventure*. Ballantine Books.

83. Segregation in Black Hawk County. Mapping Segregation in Iowa. (n.d.). https://dsps.lib.uiowa.edu/mappingsegregationia/segregation-in-black-hawk-county/

388

84. Kinney, P. (2021, January 28). The history of Waterloo: A case study of race relations. Grout Museum District, Waterloo, Iowa. https://www.groutmuseumdistrict.org/about/news/the-history-of-waterloo-a-case-study-.aspx

85. Black Triangle in Waterloo, Iowa. African American Voices of the Cedar Valley. (n.d.). https://aa-voices-museum.uni.edu/black-triangle

86. [a]Stebbins, S., & Comen, E. (2018, November 9). The worst cities for Black Americans. *24/7* *Wall* *St.* https://247wallst.com/special-report/2018/11/09/the-worst-cities-for-black-americans-4/4/[b]Wind, A. (2022, April 10). Racial covenants still attached to Black Hawk County homeowners' properties. *Waterloo Courier.* https://wcfcourier.com/news/local/education/racial-covenants-still-attached-to-black-hawk-county-homeowners-properties/article_c44fb416-92d8-5e66-8228-20c8bd426a93.html

87. Library of Congress. (1968). Rath Packing Company, Sycamore Street between Elm & Eighteen Streets, Waterloo, Black Hawk County, Iowa. https://www.loc.gov/item/ia0405/

88. Kinney, P. (2021, January 28). The history of Waterloo: A case study of race relations. Grout Museum District, Waterloo, Iowa. https://www.groutmuseumdistrict.org/about/news/the-history-of-waterloo-a-case-study-.aspx

89. Frohlich, C. T. & Stebbins. S. (2015, October 6). The worst cities for Black Americans. *24/7 Wall St.* https://247wallst.com/special-report/2015/10/06/the-worst-cities-for-black-americans/

90. This is a pseudonym.

91. This is a pseudonym.

92. Cororve, M. B., & Gleaves, D. H. (2001). Body dysmorphic disorder: a review of conceptualizations, assessment, and treatment strategies. *Clinical Psychology Review, 21*(6), 949–970.

93. This is a pseudonym.

94. This is a pseudonym.

95. Brown, A. (2020, September 3). The changing categories the U.S. census has used to measure race. *Pew Research Center.* https://www.pewresearch.org/short-reads/2020/02/25/the-changing-categories-the-u-s-has-used-to-measure-race/

96. The Tragic Mulatto Myth. Jim Crow Museum. (n.d.). https://jimcrowmuseum.ferris.edu/mulatto/homepage.htm

97. This is a pseudonym.

98. This is a pseudonym.

99. Wy, T., & Saadabadi, A. (2023, March 27). Schizoaffective disorder. StatPearls, NCBI Bookshelf. https://www.ncbi.nlm.nih.gov/books/NBK541012/

100. This is a pseudonym.

101. [a]State v. Moses. (n.d.). Justia Law. https://law.justia.com/cases/iowa/supreme-cou rt/1982/65195-0.html[b]The Waverly Stranglings. (n.d.). *Unresolved*. https://unres olved.me/the-waverly-stranglings.

102. Lowrey, A. (2021, July 28). How government learned to waste your time. *The At-lantic*. https://www.theatlantic.com/politics/archive/2021/07/how-government-l earned-waste-your-time-tax/619568/

103. This is a pseudonym.

104. Russell. (2022). 4 reasons why do farmers detassel corn. *Farmer Grows*. https://fa rmergrows.com/why-do-farmers-detassel-corn/

105. Boustead, B. M. (2022, August 3). 'Corn sweat' is making the air in the Midwest oppressively muggy. *Washington Post*. https://www.washingtonpost.com/climate -environment/2022/08/02/corn-sweat-midwest-plains-heatwave/

106. Low, K. (2023). What are the effects of impaired executive functions? *Verywell Mind*. https://www.verywellmind.com/what-are-executive-functions-20463

107. Roggli, L. (2023, March 24). ADHD at the center: a whole-life, whole-person condition. ADDitude. https://www.additudemag.com/areas-of-life-health-relatio nships-career-adhd/

108. School desegregation in Waterloo, Iowa: a staff report of the U.S. Commission on Civil Rights. (n.d.). https://eric.ed.gov/?id=ED145058

109. This is a pseudonym.

110. Bagiella, E., Novack, T. A., Ansel, B., Diaz-Arrastia, R., Dikmen, S., Hart, T., & Temkin, N. (2010). Measuring outcome in traumatic brain injury treatment trials: recommendations from the traumatic brain injury clinical trials network. *The Jour-nal of Head Trauma Rehabilitation, 25*(5), 375.

111. Grabe, S., Ward, L. M., & Hyde, J. S. (2008). The role of the media in body image concerns among women: a meta-analysis of experimental and correlational studies. *Psychological Bulletin, 134*(3), 460.

112. Upward Bound program. US Department of Education (ED). (n.d.). https://ww w2.ed.gov/programs/trioupbound/index.html

113. Madowitz, J., Matheson, B. E., & Liang, J. (2015). The relationship between eating disorders and sexual trauma. *Eating and weight disorders: Studies on anorexia, bu-limia and obesity, 20*, 281–293.

114. Sefcek, J. A., Brumbach, B. H., Vasquez, G., & Miller, G. F. (2007). The evolutionary psychology of human mate choice: How ecology, genes, fertility, and fashion influ-ence mating strategies. *Journal of Psychology & Human Sexuality, 18(*2–3), 125–182.

115. Diamond, M. J. (1997). The unbearable agony of being: Interpreting tormented states of mind in the psychoanalysis of sexually traumatized patients. *Bulletin of the Menninger Clinic, 61*(4), 495–519.

390

116. This is a pseudonym.

117. Arabi, S. (2023, April 26). 6 things people don't realize you're doing because you're a complex trauma survivor. *Thought Catalog*. https://thoughtcatalog.com/shahida-arabi/2023/04/6-things-people-dont-realize-youre-doing-because-youre-a-complex-trauma-survivor/

118. This is a pseudonym.

119. This is a pseudonym.

120. This is a pseudonym.

121. This is a pseudonym.

122. [a]Haney-Lopez, I. (2014, January 11). The racism at the heart of the Reagan presidency. *Salon*. https://www.salon.com/2014/01/11/the_racism_at_the_heart_of_the_reagan_presidency/[b]Williamson, V. (2021, January 15). The austerity politics of white supremacy. *Dissent Magazine*. https://www.dissentmagazine.org/article/the-austerity-politics-of-white-supremacy[c]Phillips, K. (1991). *The politics of rich and poor: Wealth and the American electorate in the Reagan aftermath*. Harper Perennial.

123. This is a pseudonym.

124. [a]Eddy, C. (2015, December 16). A brief history of "Satanic Panic" in the 1980s. *Gizmodo*. https://gizmodo.com/a-brief-history-of-satanic-panic-in-the-1980s-1679476373[b]Yuhas, A. (2021, March 31). It's time to revisit the Satanic Panic. The *New York Times*. https://www.nytimes.com/2021/03/31/us/satanic-panic.html

125. Young women personal progress. (2009, January 1). https://www.churchofjesuschrist.org/study/manual/young-women-personal-progress?lang=eng

126. Schochet, P. Z., Burghardt, J., and McConnell, S. (2008). Does Job Corps work? Impact findings from the National Job Corps study. *American Economic Review*, *98*(5), 1864–1886.

127. O'Connor, C. (2014, April 15). Report: Walmart workers cost taxpayers $6.2 billion in public assistance. *Forbes*. https://www.forbes.com/sites/clareoconnor/2014/04/15/report-walmart-workers-cost-taxpayers-6-2-billion-in-public-assistance/?sh=82c4d9720b7e

128. Edwards, P. (2015, April 24). A brief history of the bizarre and sadistic Presidential Fitness Test. *Vox*. https://www.vox.com/2015/4/24/8489501/presidential-fitness-test

129. Davitadze, M., Malhotra, K., Khalil, H., Hebbar, M., Tay, C. T., Mousa, A., ... and Kempegowda, P. (2023). Body image concerns in women with polycystic ovary syndrome: a systematic review and meta-analysis. *European Journal of Endocrinology*, *189*(2), R1–R9.

130. Wright, R. (1940). *Native Son*. Turtleback Books.

131. This is a pseudonym.

132. Joyce, J. (1914). *Dubliners*. Wordsworth Editions.

133. Washington, B. T. (2001). Up from Slavery: An Autobiography. *The Outlook*. *66*(11), 649–654. http://ci.nii.ac.jp/ncid/BA90222863

134. [a]Wilson, William Julius. (1987). *The Truly Disadvantaged: The Inner City, The Underclass, and Public Policy*. The University of Chicago Press. [b] Kotlowitz, Alex. (1992). *There Are No Children Here: The Story of Two Boys Growing Up in the Other America*. New York: Anchor Books.

135. Cabrera, N. L. (2014). Exposing whiteness in higher education: White male college students minimizing racism, claiming victimization, and recreating white supremacy. *Race, Ethnicity and Education, 17*(1), 30–55.

136. Murray, C. (1988). What's so bad about being poor? *National Review*. https://indexarticles.com/reference/national-review/whats-so-bad-about-being-poor-2/

137. Fabian, R. (2023, August 9). The "Trauma Triangle" explains 3 classic roles trauma survivors fall into. *The Mighty*. https://themighty.com/topic/trauma/trauma-triangle-meaning/

138. Jelveh, Zubin, Kogut, Bruce & Naidu, Suresh. (2014). Economists aren't as non-partisan as we think. https://fivethirtyeight.com/features/economists-arent-as-nonpartisan-as-we-think/

139. Hartmann, Thom. (2022). *The Hidden History of Neoliberalism: How Reaganism Gutted America and How to Restore Its Greatness*. Oakland, CA: Berrett-Koehler Publishers, Inc.

140. Martin, P. Y., & Hummer, R. A. (1989). Fraternities and rape on campus. *Gender & Society, 3*(4), 457–473.

141. Swidey, N. (2016). The college debt crisis is even worse than you think. *The Boston Globe*.

142. Tait, V. (2020, July 5). Dismantling the myth of Tough Love. *Psychology Today*. https://www.psychologytoday.com/us/blog/pulling-through/202007/dismantling-the-myth-tough-love

143. Hoeve, M., Dubas, J. S., Eichelsheim, V. I., Van Der Laan, P., Smeenk, W., & Gerris, J. (2009). The relationship between parenting and delinquency: A meta-analysis. *Journal of Abnormal Child Psychology, 37*(6), 749–775. https://doi.org/10.1007/s10802-009-9310-8

144. Pointer, L. (2021, August 13). What is "Restorative Justice" and How Does it Impact Individuals. Bureau of Justice Assistance National Training and Technical Assistance Center. https://bjatta.bja.ojp.gov/media/blog/what-restorative-justice-and-how-does-it-impact-individuals-involved-crime

145. Gowen, A. (2023, March 20). Iowa's sharp right turn: From centrist state to 'Florida of the North.' *Washington Post*. https://www.washingtonpost.com/nation/2023/03/20/iowa-trump-gay-rights/

146. Earp, B. D., Wudarczyk, O. A., Foddy, B., & Savulescu, J. (2017). Addicted to love: What is love addiction and when should it be treated? *Philosophy, Psychiatry, & Psychology, 24*(1), 77–92. https://doi.org/10.1353/ppp.2017.0011

147. University of California–Berkeley. (2008, December 8). Poor children's brain activity resembles that of stroke victims, EEG shows. *ScienceDaily.* https://www.sciencedaily.com/releases/2008/12/081203092429.htm

148. Danziger, Sheldon, Sandefur, Gary, D., & Weinberg, Daniel. (1994). *Confronting poverty: Prescriptions for change.* Cambridge, Massachusetts: Harvard University Press.

149. Adult Children of Alcoholics/Dysfunctional Families. (2023, September 28). Welcome to Adult Children of Alcoholics & Dysfunctional Families. https://adultchildren.org/

150. We actually called them ACOA at the time

151. Whitfield, Charles. (1987). *Healing the Child Within: Discovery and Recovery for Adult Children of Dysfunctional Families.* Deerfield Beach, Florida: Health Communications, Inc.

152. Sher, L., & Kahn, R. S. (2019). Suicide in schizophrenia: an educational overview. *Medicina, 55*(7), 361.

153. Ciletti, N. (2023, October 2). What you need to know about Tough Love | *Better Help.* https://www.betterhelp.com/advice/love/what-you-need-to-know-about-tough-love/

154. Brock, D. (2005). *The Republican noise machine: Right-wing media and how it corrupts democracy.* Three Rivers Press (CA).

155. Licari, P. R. (2020). Sharp as a Fox: Are foxnews.com visitors less politically knowledgeable?. *American Politics Research, 48*(6), 792–806.

156. Her first name is real, but the last name is a pseudonym

157. Stroumsa, G. (1996). From anti-Judaism to antisemitism in Early Christianity. *Contra Iudaeos.* JCB Mohr.

158. Ferrell, D. R. (1995). The unmourned wound: Reflections on the psychology of Adolf Hitler. *Journal of Religion and Health, 34,* 175–198

159. [a]Gordon, P. E. (2017). The authoritarian personality revisited: Reading Adorno in the age of Trump. *boundary 2, 44*(2), 31–56.[b]Adorno, T. (2019). *The authoritarian personality.* Verso Books.

160. [a]Bendersky, J. W. (2020). *A concise history of Nazi Germany.* Rowman & Littlefield Publishers.[b]Longerich, P. (2012). *Holocaust: The Nazi persecution and murder of the Jews.* Oxford University Press

161. Richter, H. P. (2015). *Damals war es Friedrich.* Deutscher Taschenbuch Verlag.

162. Lemire, J. (2022). *The Big Lie: Election Chaos, Political Opportunism, and the State of American Politics After 2020*. Flatiron Books.

163. Murray, C. (1993). The coming white underclass. https://www.aei.org/articles/th e-coming-white-underclass/

164. Murray, C. & Herrnstein, R. (1994). *The Bell Curve: Intelligence and Class Structure in American Life*. The Free Press.

165. Surane, J., Abelson, M., Buhayar, N., Sam, C., Benhamou, M., and Keyes, G. (2022, July 26). Myth of 'free' checking costs consumers over $8 billion a year. *Bloomber g.com*. https://www.bloomberg.com/graphics/2022-bank-overdraft-fees-costing-c onsumers-billions/

166. U.S. Department of Education (ED). (n.d.). Student Support Services program. https://www2.ed.gov/programs/triostudsupp/index.html

167. Scull, A. (2021). "Community care": Historical perspective on deinstitutionaliza- tion. *Perspectives in Biology and Medicine, 64*(1), 70–81.

168. Sienaert, P., Dhossche, D. M., Vancampfort, D., De Hert, M., & Gazdag, G. (2014). A clinical review of the treatment of catatonia. *Frontiers in Psychiatry, 5*. https://d oi.org/10.3389/fpsyt.2014.00181

169. Newton, P. (2015, April 15). What Are learning styles? Should educators be using them? (J. Schrader, Rev.). *Psychology Today*. https://www.psychologytoday.com/u s/blog/mouse-man/201504/what-are-learning-styles

170. Haskins, R. (2016, July 29). Are conservatives serious about fighting poverty? *Brookings*. https://www.brookings.edu/opinions/are-conservatives-serious-about-f ighting-poverty/

171. Bagiella, E., Novack, T. A., Ansel, B., Diaz-Arrastia, R., Dikmen, S., Hart, T., & Temkin, N. (2010). Measuring outcome in traumatic brain injury treatment trials: recommendations from the traumatic brain injury clinical trials network. *The Jour- nal of Head Trauma Rehabilitation, 25*(5), 375.

172. Pointer, L. (2021, August 13). *What is "Restorative Justice" and How Does it Im- pact Individuals*. Bureau of Justice Assistance National Training and Technical As- sistance Center. https://bjatta.bja.ojp.gov/media/blog/what-restorative-justice-an d-how-does-it-impact-individuals-involved-crime

173. [a]Jones, D. K., & Dunn, M. I. (1995). 'Vampire syndrome': serum protein and lipid abnormalities related to frequent sale of plasma. *Journal of Family Practice, 40*, 288.[b]Starr, D. (2012). *Blood: an epic history of medicine and commerce*. Knopf.

174. Corrigan, J. D., Cuthbert, J. P., Harrison-Felix, C., Whiteneck, G. G., Bell, J. M., Miller, A. C., . . . & Pretz, C. R. (2014). US population estimates of health and social outcomes 5 years after rehabilitation for traumatic brain injury. *The Journal of Head Trauma rehabilitation, 29*(6), E1–E9.

175. Babiak, P. (2007). From darkness into the light: Psychopathy in industrial and organizational psychology. *The Psychopath: Theory, Research, and Practice*, 411–428.

176. Geismer, Lily. (2022, June 14). Bill Clinton did more to sell neoliberalism than Milton Friedman. *In These Times*. https://inthesetimes.com/article/bill-clinton-neoliberalism-milton-friedman-democrats-market-capitalism

177. Newkirk, V. R., II. (2018, February 5). The real lessons from Bill Clinton's welfare reform. *The Atlantic*. https://www.theatlantic.com/politics/archive/2018/02/welfare-reform-tanf-medicaid-food-stamps/552299/

178. Eisen, L.-B. (2019, September 9). The 1994 Crime Bill and beyond: How federal funding shapes the criminal justice system. Brennan Center for Justice. https://www.brennancenter.org/our-work/analysis-opinion/1994-crime-bill-and-beyond-how-federal-funding-shapes-criminal-justice

179. Faux, J. (2013, December 9). NAFTA's impact on U.S. workers. Economic Policy Institute. https://www.epi.org/blog/naftas-impact-workers/

180. Geismer, L. (2022, June 14). Bill Clinton did more to sell neoliberalism than Milton Friedman. *In These Times*. https://inthesetimes.com/article/bill-clinton-neoliberalism-milton-friedman-democrats-market-capitalism

181. Bailey, C. D. (2011). Does the Defining Issues Test measure ethical judgment ability or political position? *The Journal of Social Psychology*, 151(3), 314–330.

182. Hasson, Y., Tamir, M., Brahms, K. S., Cohrs, J. C., & Halperin, E. (2018). Are Liberals and Conservatives Equally Motivated to Feel Empathy Toward Others? *Personality and Social Psychology Bulletin*, 44(10), 1449-1459. https://doi.org/10.1177/0146167218769867

183. This is a pseudonym.

184. Fox Piven, F. & Cloward, R. A. (1971). *Regulating the Poor: The Functions of Public Welfare*. Vintage Books.

185. Bowser, B. (1985). Race relations in the 1980s: The case of the United States. *Journal of Black Studies, 15*(3), 307–324. https://www.jstor.org/stable/2784128

186. Collins, M. E., Bybee, D., & Mowbray, C. T. (1998). Effectiveness of supported education for individuals with psychiatric disabilities: Results from an experimental study. *Community Mental Health Journal, 34*, 595–613.

187. Kinoshita, Y., Furukawa, T. A., Kinoshita, K., Honyashiki, M., Omori, I. M., Marshall, M., . . . & Kingdon, D. (2013). Supported employment for adults with severe mental illness. *Cochrane Database of Systematic Reviews*, (9).

188. Mowbray, C. T., Bybee, D., Oyserman, D., & MacFarlane, P. (2005). Timing of mental illness onset and motherhood. *The Journal of Nervous and Mental Disease, 193*(6), 369–378.

189. Murray, C. (1993). The coming white underclass. Retrieved from https://www.aei.org/articles/the-coming-white-underclass/

190. Nelson, T. (2011, October 24). Why did the Des Moines Register censor Donald Kaul? *Blog for Iowa*. https://blogforiowa.com/2011/10/24/why-is-the-des-moines-register-afraid-of-donald-kaul/

191. This is a pseudonym.

192. Fitzgerald, L. F., Swan, S., & Fischer, K. (1995). Why didn't she just report him? The psychological and legal implications of women's responses to sexual harassment. *Journal of Social Issues, 51*(1), 117–138.

193. Thornton, R., & Timmons, E. (2015, May 18). The de-licensing of occupations in the United States. *Monthly Labor Review.* U.S. Bureau of Labor Statistics. https://www.bls.gov/opub/mlr/2015/article/the-de-licensing-of-occupations-in-the-united-states.htm

194. Jann, M. (2020, November 16). Adherence challenges with medications in patients with ADHD. *Psychiatric Times.*

195. Hallowell, E. M., & Ratey, J. J. (1994). *Driven To Distraction: Recognizing and Coping with Attention Deficit Disorder from Childhood Through Adulthood.* Simon and Schuster.

196. Antisemitic incidents on rise across the U.S., report finds. (2023, April 17). *PBS NewsHour.* https://www.pbs.org/newshour/politics/antisemitic-incidents-on-rise-across-the-u-s-report-finds

197. Specht, H., & Courtney, M. E. (1995). *Unfaithful Angels: How Social Work Has Abandoned its Mission.* Simon and Schuster.

198. This is a pseudonym.

199. This is a pseudonym.

200. This is a pseudonym.

201. [a]Mondimore, F. (2020, August 15). Can Antidepressants cause problems for bipolar patients. *Psychology Today.* https://www.psychologytoday.com/intl/blog/bipolar-101/202008/can-antidepressants-cause-problems-bipolar-patients[b]Gitlin, M. (2018). Antidepressants in bipolar depression: an enduring controversy. *International Journal of Bipolar Disorders, 6*(1). https://doi.org/10.1186/s40345-018-0133-9

202. Oliver-Pyatt, W. (2017). *Questions and answers about binge eating disorder: A guide for clinicians.* Jones & Bartlett Learning.

203. Samenow, S. E. (1998). *Before it's too late: Why Some Kids Get Into Trouble--and what Parents Can Do about it.* Crown.

204. Markus, H. R., & Nurius, P. S. (1986). Possible selves. *American Psychologist, 41*(9), 954–969. https://doi.org/10.1037/0003-066x.41.9.954

205. [a]Fleminger, S., & Ponsford, J. (2005). Long term outcome after traumatic brain injury. *BMJ, 331*(7530), 1419.[b]*What are the possible effects of traumatic brain injury (TBI)?* (2020, November 24). https://www.nichd.nih.gov/health/topics/tbi/conditioninfo/effects

206. Jann, M. (2020, November 16). Adherence challenges with medications in patients with ADHD. *Psychiatric Times*. https://www.psychiatrictimes.com/view/adherence-challenges-medications-patients-adhd

207. Premenstrual dysphoric disorder: Different from PMS? (2022, December 7). Mayo Clinic. https://www.mayoclinic.org/diseases-conditions/premenstrual-syndrome/expert-answers/pmdd/faq-20058315

208. Hall-Flavin, D. (2018, February 14). Bipolar treatment: Are bipolar I and bipolar II treated differently? *Mayo Clinic*. https://www.mayoclinic.org/diseases-conditions/bipolar-disorder/expert-answers/bipolar-treatment/faq-20058042

209. Dunner, D. L. (2003). Clinical consequences of under-recognized bipolar spectrum disorder. *Bipolar disorders, 5*(6), 456–463.

210. Tietjen, G. E., Khubchandani, J., Herial, N. A., & Shah, K. (2012). Adverse childhood experiences are associated with migraine and vascular biomarkers. *Headache: The Journal of Head and Face Pain, 52*(6), 920-929.

211. *Official King James Bible Online*. (n.d.). https://www.kingjamesbibleonline.org/

212. *Official King James Bible Online*. (n.d.). https://www.kingjamesbibleonline.org/

213. Schmidt, W. K. (2003). An overview of current and investigational drugs for the treatment of acute and chronic pain. *Pain*, 406–427.

214. Blum, D. (2023, May 31). What is binge eating disorder? What to know about causes and treatment. *The New York Times*. https://www.nytimes.com/2023/05/31/well/mind/binge-eating-disorder-symptoms-treatment.html

215. Cleveland Clinic Medical Professionals. (2023, February 15). *Polycystic ovary syndrome (PCOS)*. Cleveland Clinic. https://my.clevelandclinic.org/health/diseases/8316-polycystic-ovary-syndrome-pcos

216. Fabian, R. (2023, August 9). The "Trauma Triangle" explains 3 classic roles trauma survivors fall into. *The Mighty*. https://themighty.com/topic/trauma/trauma-triangle-meaning/

217. Hale, M., D'Andrea, D., Yang, R., & Niebler, G. (2012). Efficacy and tolerability of hydrocodone extended-release tablets for the treatment of moderate to severe pain in opioid-treated patients with osteoarthritis or low back pain. *The Journal of Pain, 13*(4), S84.

218. Jacobson, R., & Kahn, A. (2023, July 12). ADHD and personal boundaries in kids. *Understood*. https://www.understood.org/en/articles/adhd-personal-boundaries-in-kids

219. Pedersen, T. (2022, January 4). Dissociative Identity Disorder (DID): 5 myths busted. *Psych Central*. https://psychcentral.com/disorders/dispelling-myths-about-dissociative-identity-disorder

220. Lantz, M., Buchalter, E. N., & Giambanco, V. (1999). St. John's Wort and antidepressant drug interactions in the elderly. *Journal of Geriatric Psychiatry and Neurology, 12*(1), 7–10. https://doi.org/10.1177/089198879901200103

221. Guarnaccia, M. (2023). Bipolar II: What it is and what makes it different | Better-Help. https://www.betterhelp.com/advice/bipolar/bipolar-2-what-it-is-and-what-makes-it-different/

222. Hall, H. (2016). Adverse effects of chiropractic. *Science-Based Medicine.* https://sciencebasedmedicine.org/adverse-effects-of-chiropractic/

223. Gitlin, M. (2018). Antidepressants in bipolar depression: an enduring controversy. *International Journal of Bipolar Disorders, 6*(1). https://doi.org/10.1186/s40345-018-0133-9

224. Weintraub, K. (2023, July 25). Most antidepressants don't work on kids and teens, study finds. *STAT.* https://www.statnews.com/2016/06/08/antidepressants-teens-kids/

225. England, K. (2018, July 29). Utah's Dream Mine still has thousands of stockholders, supporters. *Daily Herald.* https://www.heraldextra.com/news/2018/jul/29/utahs-dream-mine-still-has-thousands-of-stockholders-supporters/

226. *Official King James Bible Online.* (n.d.). https://www.kingjamesbibleonline.org/

227. *Official King James Bible Online.* (n.d.). https://www.kingjamesbibleonline.org/

228. Suhail, K., & Cochrane, R. (2002). Effect of culture and environment on the phenomenology of delusions and hallucinations. *International Journal of Social Psychiatry, 48*(2), 126–138.

229. *Official King James Bible Online.* (n.d.). https://www.kingjamesbibleonline.org/

230. *Official King James Bible Online.* (n.d.). https://www.kingjamesbibleonline.org/

231. The Editors of Encyclopedia Britannica. (2023, September 14). Anabaptist | Definition, description, movement, beliefs, history, & facts. *Encyclopedia Britannica.* https://www.britannica.com/topic/Anabaptists

232. Davitadze, M., Malhotra, K., Khalil, H., Hebbar, M., Tay, C. T., Mousa, A., . . . & Kempegowda, P. (2023). Body image concerns in women with polycystic ovary syndrome: a systematic review and meta-analysis. *European Journal of Endocrinology, 189*(2), R1–R9.

233. This is a pseudonym.

234. This is a pseudonym.

235. Seelos, C., & Mair, J. (2005). Social entrepreneurship: Creating new business models to serve the poor. *Business horizons, 48*(3), 241–246.

236. Manson, J. (2021, May 27). The Catholic Church's abortion fight and what's behind it. *The New York Times.* https://www.nytimes.com/2021/05/27/opinion/catholic-church-abortion.html

237. Asch, H. L., Lewis, P. J., Moreland, D. B., Egnatchik, J. G., Young, J. Y., Clabeaux, D. E., & Hyland, A. H. (2002). Prospective multiple outcomes study of outpatient lumbar microdiscectomy: should 75 to 80% success rates be the norm? *Journal of Neurosurgery: Spine, 96*(1), 34–44.

238. [a]Medulloblastoma diagnosis and treatment. (2023, August 1). National Cancer Institute. https://www.cancer.gov/rare-brain-spine-tumor/tumors/medulloblasto ma[b]Johnston, D. L., Keene, D., Strother, D., Taneva, M., Lafay-Cousin, L., Fryer, C., ... Bouffet, E. (2018). Survival following tumor recurrence in children with medulloblastoma. *Journal of Pediatric Hematology/Oncology, 40*(3), e159–e163.

239. Schoenherr, N. (2020, November 14). Childhood poverty costs U.S. $1.03 trillion in a year, study finds. *The Source.* https://source.wustl.edu/2018/04/childhood-po verty-cost-u-s-1-03-trillion-in-a-year-study-finds/

240. Huffman, T. (2021, December 1). Understanding the 'Boots Theory' of socioeconomic unfairness. *MoneyWise.* https://moneywise.com/managing-money/budge ting/boots-theory-of-socioeconomic-unfairness

241. Haushofer, J., Conwell, J., Daniels, B., Lusk, J. L., Rothstein, J., Bitler, M., ... Fehr, E. (2014). On the psychology of poverty. *Science, 344*(6186), 862–867.

242. Power, M. (2019, September 4). The High Cost of Transportation in the United States. Institute for Transportation and Development Policy, Promoting Sustainable and Equitable Transportation Worldwide. https://www.itdp.org/2019/05/23/hig h-cost-transportation-united-states/

243. Neumark, D. (2019, January 22). Concentrated Poverty and the Disconnect Between Jobs and Workers. *Econofact.* https://econofact.org/concentrated-poverty-a nd-the-disconnect-between-jobs-and-workers

244. Rosell, D. R., Futterman, S. E., McMaster, A., & Siever, L. J. (2014). Schizotypal personality disorder: a current review. *Current Psychiatry Reports, 16*, 1–12.

245. [a]Godfrey, E. (2023, May 2). The new pro-life movement has a plan to end abortion. *The Atlantic.* https://www.theatlantic.com/politics/archive/2023/04/pro-life-ant i-abortion-roe-mifepristone-pill-ban/673763/[b]Moses, J. (2023, February 16). Author says 'pro-life' isn't quite accurate when it comes to forcing women to give birth. *NJ.* https://www.nj.com/opinion/2022/10/author-says-pro-life-isnt-quite-accura te-when-it-comes-to-forcing-women-to-give-birth-opinion.html

246. Sreenivasan, H., Weber, S., & Kargbo, C. (2019, June 1). The true story behind the 'welfare queen' stereotype. *PBS NewsHour.* https://www.pbs.org/newshour/show /the-true-story-behind-the-welfare-queen-stereotype

247. Zeanah, C. H. (1996). Beyond insecurity: a reconceptualization of attachment disorders of infancy. *Journal of Consulting and Clinical Psychology, 64*(1), 42.

248. Cloitre, M. (2020). ICD-11 complex post-traumatic stress disorder: Simplifying diagnosis in trauma populations. *The British Journal of Psychiatry, 216*(3), 129–131.

249. [a]Hamilton, L., Roll, S., Despard, M., Maag, E., Chun, Y., Brugger, L., & Grinstein-Weiss, M. (2022, April 13). The impacts of the 2021 expanded child tax credit on family employment, nutrition, and financial well-being. *Brookings*. https://www.brookings.edu/research/the-impacts-of-the-2021-expanded-child-tax -credit-on-family-employment-nutrition-and-financial-well-being/[b]Subramanian, C. (2023, January 16). You're not getting child tax credit checks anymore. Here's why. *Los Angeles Times*. https://www.latimes.com/politics/story/2023-01-03/child-tax-credit-expired-stimu lus

250. [a]Sharma, Y. (2023). Comparative embryology–principle, significance. *Microbe Notes*. https://microbenotes.com/comparative-embryology/[b]Gilbert, S. F. (2000). Comparative embryology. *Developmental Biology*. NCBI Bookshelf. https://www .ncbi.nlm.nih.gov/books/NBK9974/

251. [a]Rutherford, L. (2023, October 6). Opinion: The Constitution and women's rights. *St. George Spectrum & Daily News*. https://www.thespectrum.com/story/opinion/2023/10/06/your-turn-the -constitution-and-womens-rights/71083103007/#lneygdm6lijsnk67fp[b]Badger, E., Sanger-Katz, M., Miller, C. C., & Washington, E. (2022, July 28). States with abortion bans are among least supportive for mothers and children. *The New York Times*. https://www.nytimes.com/2022/07/28/upshot/abortion-bans-states -social-services.html[c]Ziegler, M. (2022, August 2). Why exceptions for the life of the mother have disappeared. *The Atlantic*. https://www.theatlantic.com/ideas/arch ive/2022/07/abortion-ban-life-of-the-mother-exception/670582/[d]McCammon, S. (2023, March 8). 5 Texas women denied abortions sue the state, saying the bans put them in danger. NPR. https://www.npr.org/2023/03/07/1161486096/abortion -texas-lawsuit-women-sue-dobbs

252. Grad, S., & Colker, D. (2016, March 7). Nancy Reagan turned to astrology in White House to protect her husband. *Los Angeles Times*. https://www.latimes.com/local /lanow/la-me-ln-nancy-reagan-astrology-20160306-story.html

253. Garrow, E. E., & Hasenfeld, Y. (2014). Social enterprises as an embodiment of a neoliberal welfare logic. *American Behavioral Scientist*, *58*(11), 1475–1493.

254. C. difficile infection - Symptoms and causes - Mayo Clinic. (n.d.). Mayo Clinic. https://www.mayoclinic.org/diseases-conditions/c-difficile/symptoms-causes/s yc-20351691

255. Michiels, E. M., Schouten-Van Meeteren, A. Y., Doz, F., Janssens, G. O., & van Dalen, E. C. (2015). Chemotherapy for children with medulloblastoma. *Cochrane Database of Systematic Reviews*, (1).

256. Hurst, A., Griffin, T., & Vitale, A. (2017). Organizing Working-Class Academics: A collective history. *Journal of Working-Class Studies*, *2*(2), 168–178.

257. This is a pseudonym.

258. Krakauer, J. (2003). *Under the Banner of Heaven: A Story of Violent Faith*. Anchor Books. http://ci.nii.ac.jp/ncid/BA68202805

400

259. Krakauer, J. (2003). *Under the Banner of Heaven: A Story of Violent Faith*. Anchor Books. http://ci.nii.ac.jp/ncid/BA68202805

260. This is a pseudonym.

261. McRobbie, L. R. (2016, January 5). How are horoscopes still a thing? *Smithsonian Magazine*. https://www.smithsonianmag.com/history/how-are-horoscopes-still-t hing-180957701/

262. Lebow, H. I. (2021, August 12). All about prolonged grief disorder. *Psych Central*. https://psychcentral.com/depression/all-about-complicated-grief#compl icated-vs-other-types-of-grief

263. [a]Hall, K.-M. (2021, September 27). A guide to PTSD triggers (and how to cope). *GoodRX Health*. https://www.goodrx.com/conditions/ptsd/common-triggers[b]Lo ckwood, A. (2023, October 7). 23 'Embarrassing' symptoms of PTSD we don't talk about. *The Mighty*. https://themighty.com/topic/post-traumatic-stress-disor der-ptsd/embarrassing-ptsd-symptoms/

264. [a]Ireland, C. (2016, December 13). The Constitution: An Origin Story. *Harvard Law Bulletin*. https://hls.harvard.edu/today/constitution-origin-story/[b]Klarman , M. J. (2016). *The framers' coup: The making of the United States Constitution*. Oxford University Press.

265. Lipka, M. (2020, August 18). Half of Americans say Bible should influence U.S. laws, including 28% who favor it over the will of the people. Pew Research Center. https://www.pewresearch.org/short-reads/2020/04/13/half-of-americans-say-bible -should-influence-u-s-laws-including-28-who-favor-it-over-the-will-of-the-people/

266. Besley, J., & Hill, D. (2020, May 20). Science and Technology: Public attitudes, knowledge, and interest. *National Science Foundation*. https://ncses.nsf.gov/pubs /nsb20207/public-familiarity-with-s-t-facts

267. [a]McGowan, B. G. (2014). Historical evolution of child welfare services. *Child welfare for the Twenty-First century: A Handbook of Practices, Policies, and Pro- grams* (pp. 11–44). Columbia University Press.[b]O'Neill Murray, K., & Gesiriech, S. (n.d.). A Brief Legislative History of the Child Welfare System. *The Pew Trusts*. https://www.pewtrusts.org/~/media/legacy/uploadedfiles/wwwpewtrusts org/reports/foster_care_reform/legislativehistory2004pdf.pdf

268. [a]Barmes, L. (2023). Silencing at work: Sexual harassment, workplace misconduct and NDAs. *Industrial Law Journal*, *52*(1), 68–106.[b]Altman, S. (2022). Selling Silence: The Morality of Sexual Harassment NDA s. *Journal of Applied Philosophy*, *39*(4), 698–720.[c]Lobel, O. (2018, January 30). NDAs are out of control. Here's what needs to change. *Harvard Business Review*. https://hbr.org/2018/01/ndas-are-ou t-of-control-heres-what-needs-to-change[d]Settlements, D. C. Rethinking the Silent Treatment: Discovering Confidential Settlements in a Post-# MeToo World.

269. Fritz, K., Russell, A., Allwang, C., Kuiper, S., Lampe, L., & Malhi, G. S. (2017). Is a delay in the diagnosis of bipolar disorder inevitable? *Bipolar Disorders*, *19*(5), 396–400. https://doi.org/10.1111/bdi.12499

270. Pagan, V. (2021). The murder of knowledge and the ghosts that remain: Non-disclosure agreements and their effects. *Culture and Organization, 27*(4), 302–317.

271. DeFelice, K. L. (2014). *Effectiveness of Adult Rehabilitative Mental Health Services in Mental Health Recovery.* St. Catherine University.

272. This is a pseudonym.

273. This is a pseudonym.

274. *Official King James Bible Online.* (n.d.). https://www.kingjamesbibleonline.org/ *Source says that the Bible verses my father referenced do not exist. I may have rewritten them incorrectly.

275. Lazarus, S. A., Cheavens, J. S., Festa, F., & Rosenthal, M. Z. (2014). Interpersonal functioning in borderline personality disorder: A systematic review of behavioral and laboratory-based assessments. *Clinical Psychology Review, 34*(3), 193–205.

276. U.S. Department of Education (ED). (n.d.). Student Support Services program. https://www2.ed.gov/programs/triostudsupp/index.html

277. US Department of Education (ED). (n.d.). History of the federal TRIO programs. https://www2.ed.gov/about/offices/list/ope/trio/triohistory.html

278. Bourgois, Philippe (2015). Culture of poverty. In *International Encyclopedia of the Social & Behavioral Sciences* (Second Edition). Retrieved from https://www.sciencedirect.com/topics/social-sciences/culture-of-poverty

279. Lewis, O. (1966). The culture of poverty. *Scientific American, 215*(4), 19-25.

280. Bourgois, Philippe (2015). Culture of poverty. *International Encyclopedia of the Social & Behavioral Sciences* (Second Edition). https://www.sciencedirect.com/topics/social-sciences/culture-of-poverty

281. Banks, J. A. (2001). The cultural deprivation or culture of poverty explanation. *International Encyclopedia of the Social & Behavioral Sciences.* https://www.sciencedirect.com/topics/social-sciences/culture-of-poverty

282. Murray, C. & Herrnstein, R. (1994). *The Bell Curve: Intelligence and Class Structure in American Life.* The Free Press.

283. Selvaraj, V., Gabel, T. L., & Ramaswamy, S. (2012). How plasma donation can affect your patient's pharmacotherapy. *Current Psychiatry, 11*(5), 59–60.

284. Larson, L. (2019, July 1). The Mormon Church vs. the internet. *The Verge.* https://www.theverge.com/2019/7/1/18759587/mormon-church-quitmormon-exmormon-jesus-christ-internet-seo-lds

285. Vitiello, M. (2019). Marijuana legalization, racial disparity, and the hope for reform. *Lewis & Clark L. Rev., 23,* 789.

286. Hill, R. B. (2004). Institutional racism in child welfare. *Race and Society, 7*(1), 17–33

287. Merritt, D. H. (2021). Lived experiences of racism among child welfare-involved parents. *Race and Social Problems, 13,* 63–72.

288. Turiano, E. (2015). War on Whom? Medical, Racial and Fiscal Critiques on the Criminality of Marijuana. https://digitalrepository.trincoll.edu/cgi/viewcontent.cgi?article=1038&context=trinitypapers

289. Tolle, Eckhart. (2008). *A New Earth: Awakening to Your Life's Purpose*. Penguin Books.

290. Tolle, Eckhart. (2004). *The Power of Now: A Guide to Spiritual Enlightenment*. New World Library.

291. [a]Harding, C. M. (2003). Changes in schizophrenia across time: Paradoxes, patterns, and predictors. American Psychiatric Publishing. https://psycnet.apa.org/record/2003-00335-002[b]Sit, D. (2004). Women and bipolar disorder across the life span. *Journal of the American Medical Women's Association (1972), 59*(2), 91.

292. Paradies, Y., Ben, J., Denson, N., Elias, A., Priest, N., Pieterse, A., . . . & Gee, G. (2015). Racism as a determinant of health: a systematic review and meta-analysis. *PloS One, 10*(9), e0138511.

293. Calvin, R., Winters, K., Wyatt, S. B., Williams, D. R., Henderson, F. C., & Walker, E. R. (2003). Racism and cardiovascular disease in African Americans. *The American Journal of the Medical Sciences, 325*(6), 315–331.

294. Anderson, N. B., Bulatao, R. A., Cohen, B., on Race, P., & National Research Council. (2004). Significance of perceived racism: toward understanding ethnic group disparities in health, the later years. *Critical Perspectives on Racial and Ethnic Differences in Health in Late Life*. National Academies Press (US).

295. Volpe, V. V., Dawson, D. N., Rahal, D., Wiley, K. C., & Vesslee, S. (2019). Bringing psychological science to bear on racial health disparities: The promise of centering Black health through a critical race framework. *Translational Issues in Psychological Science, 5*(4), 302.

296. Blacksher, E. (2018). Shrinking poor white life spans: Class, race, and health justice. *The American Journal of Bioethics, 18*(10), 3–14.

297. Boardman, J. D., & Alexander, K. B. (2011). Stress trajectories, health behaviors, and the mental health of Black and White young adults. *Social Science & Medicine, 72*(10), 1659–1666.

298. Racism, sexism, social class, and health—30 years ago and today. (2022, May 20). *Harvard School of Public Health News*. https://www.hsph.harvard.edu/news/features/racism-sexism-social-class-and-health-30-years-ago-and-today/

299. [a]Harrell, S. P. (2000). A multidimensional conceptualization of racism-related stress: Implications for the well-being of people of color. *American Journal of Orthopsychiatry, 70*(1), 42–57.[b]Zaidi, D., & Sederstrom, N. (2018). The racist underbelly of health disparities in America. *The American Journal of Bioethics: AJOB, 18*(10), 25–26

300. Thomas, A. R. (1998). Ronald Reagan and the commitment of the mentally ill: Capital, interest groups, and the eclipse of social policy. *Electronic Journal of Sociology, 3*(4), 1–13.

301. Grob, G. N. (1995). The paradox of deinstitutionalization. *Society, 32*(5), 51–59.

302. Kofman, O. L. (2012). Deinstitutionalization and its discontents: American mental health policy reform. *CMC Senior Theses*. Paper 342.https://scholarship.claremont.edu/cmc_theses/342

303. Carroll, H. (2016, September). Serious mental illness prevalence in jails and prisons. Treatment Advocacy Center. https://www.treatmentadvocacycenter.org/evidence-and-research/learn-more-about/3695

304. Honberg, R., Diehl, S., Kimball, A., Gruttadaro, D., & Fitzpatrick, M. (March 2012). State Mental Health Cuts: A National Crisis. *National Alliance on Mental Illness*. www.nami.org/budgetcuts,

305. Honberg, R., Kimball, A., Diehl, S., Usher, L. & Fitzpatrick, M. (2011). State mental health cuts: The continuing crisis. National Alliance on Mental Illness, https://www.nami.org/getattachment/About-NAMI/Publications/Reports/StateMentalHealthCuts2.pdf

306. Dellwo, A. (2022). How Lyrica works for fibromyalgia. *Verywell Health*. https://www.verywellhealth.com/lyrica-for-fibromyalgia-716073

307. Gillette, H. (2021, August 4). What is EMDR therapy? *Psych Central*. https://psychcentral.com/health/emdr-therapy#how-does-it-work

308. Krakauer, J. (2003). *Under the Banner of Heaven: A Story of Violent Faith*. Anchor Books. http://ci.nii.ac.jp/ncid/BA68202805

309. Balagué, F., Mannion, A. F., Pellisé, F., & Cedraschi, C. (2012). Non-specific low back pain. *The Lancet, 379*(9814), 482–491.

310. *L5 S1 Fusion Surgery: success rate & complications* (2023, September 13). Centeno-Schultz Clinic. https://centenoschultz.com/treatment/l5-s1-fusion-surgery/

311. [a]Franklin, G. M., Rahman, E. A., Turner, J. A., Daniell, W. E., & Fulton-Kehoe, D. (2009). Opioid use for chronic low back pain: A prospective, population-based study among injured workers in Washington state, 2002–2005. *The Clinical Journal of Pain, 25*(9), 743–751.[b]Gallagher, R. M., & Rosenthal, L. J. (2008). Chronic pain and opiates: balancing pain control and risks in long-term opioid treatment. *Archives of Physical Medicine and Rehabilitation, 89*(3), S77–S82.

312. Huxtable, C. A., Roberts, L. J., Somogyi, A. A., & MacIntyre, P. E. (2011). Acute pain management in opioid-tolerant patients: a growing challenge. *Anaesthesia and Intensive Care, 39*(5), 804–823.

313. Harned, M., & Sloan, P. (2016). Safety concerns with long-term opioid use. *Expert Opinion on Drug Safety, 15*(7), 955–962.

314. [a]Volinn, E., Fargo, J. D., & Fine, P. G. (2009). Opioid therapy for nonspecific low back pain and the outcome of chronic work loss. *PAIN, 142*(3), 194–201.[b]Pergolizzi, J. V., Varrassi, G., Paladini, A., & LeQuang, J. (2019). Stopping or decreasing opioid therapy in patients on chronic opioid therapy. *Pain and Therapy*, 8, 163–176.

315. Goesling, J., DeJonckheere, M., Pierce, J., Williams, D. A., Brummett, C. M., Hassett, A. L., & Clauw, D. J. (2019). Opioid cessation and chronic pain: perspectives of former opioid users. *Pain*, *160*(5), 1131.

316. Rose, M. E. (2018). Are prescription opioids driving the opioid crisis? Assumptions vs facts. *Pain Medicine*, *19*(4), 793–807.

317. Steele, J., Bruce-Low, S., & Smith, D. (2015). A review of the clinical value of isolated lumbar extension resistance training for chronic low back pain. *PM&R*, *7*(2), 169–187

318. Gamble, M. (2018, February 10). Classism: America's overlooked problem. *The Rutgers Review*. https://www.therutgersreview.com/2018/02/10/classism-americas-overlooked-problem/

319. Chang, A. (2018, September 12). The subtle ways colleges discriminate against poor students, explained with a cartoon. *Vox*. https://www.vox.com/2017/9/11/16270316/college-mobility-culture

320. Rapkin, A. J., & Lewis, E. I. (2013). Treatment of premenstrual dysphoric disorder. *Women's Health*, *9*(6), 537–556.

321. Linehan, M. M. (2015). DBT skills training manual (2nd ed.). Guilford Press.

322. Kumar, K., Taylor, R. S., Jacques, L., Eldabe, S., Meglio, M., Molet, J., . . . & North, R. B. (2008). The effects of spinal cord stimulation in neuropathic pain are sustained: a 24-month follow-up of the prospective randomized controlled multicenter trial of the effectiveness of spinal cord stimulation. *Neurosurgery*, *63*(4), 762–770.

323. *Gastric bypass (Roux-en-Y)*. Mayo Clinic. (2022, June 25). https://www.mayoclinic.org/tests-procedures/gastric-bypass-surgery/about/pac-20385189

324. Cheroutre, C., Guerrien, A., & Rousseau, A. (2020). Contributing of cognitive-behavioral therapy in the context of bariatric surgery: a review of the literature. *Obesity Surgery*, *30*, 3154–3166.

325. Ruffolo, J., Phillips, K. A., Menard, W., Fay, C., & Weisberg, R. B. (2006). Comorbidity of body dysmorphic disorder and eating disorders: severity of psychopathology and body image disturbance. *International Journal of Eating Disorders*, *39*(1), 11–19.

326. Cantor, P. (2016). Master your mind and your will master your life. *Medium*. https://medium.com/listen-to-my-story/master-your-mind-and-you-will-master-your-life-da356b1baac3

327. Oral, R., Ramirez, M., Coohey, C., Nakada, S., Walz, A., Kuntz, A., ... & Peek-Asa, C. (2016). Adverse childhood experiences and trauma informed care: the future of health care. *Pediatric Research*, *79*(1), 227–233.

328. Racine, N., Killam, T., & Madigan, S. (2020). Trauma-informed care as a universal precaution: beyond the adverse childhood experiences questionnaire. *JAMA pediatrics*, *174*(1), 5–6.

329. *What is Complex Post-Traumatic Stress Disorder, (CPTSD)?* | CPTSDfoundation. org. (n.d.). https://cptsdfoundation.org/what-is-complex-post-traumatic-stress-di sorder-cptsd/

330. Boullier, M., & Blair, M. (2018). Adverse childhood experiences. *Paediatrics and Child Health, 28*(3), 132–137.

331. Metzler, M., Merrick, M. T., Klevens, J., Ports, K. A., & Ford, D. C. (2017). Adverse childhood experiences and life opportunities: Shifting the narrative. *Children and Youth Services Review, 72*, 141–149.

332. Salazar, A. M., Keller, T. E., Gowen, L. K., & Courtney, M. E. (2012). Trauma exposure and PTSD among older adolescents in foster care. *Social Psychiatry and Psychiatric Epidemiology, 48*(4), 545–551. https://doi.org/10.1007/s00127-012-0 563-0

333. Maercker, A. (2021). Development of the new CPTSD diagnosis for ICD-11. *Borderline Personality Disorder and Emotion Dysregulation, 8*, 1-4.

334. University of California-Berkeley. (2008, December 6). Poor children's brain activity resembles that of stroke victims, EEG Shows. ScienceDaily. www.sciencedaily.com /releases/2008/12/081203092429.htm

335. Smith, C., & Chandy, L. (2014, August 26). How poor are America's poorest? U.S. $2 a day poverty in a global context. *Brookings.* https://www.brookings.edu/article s/how-poor-are-americas-poorest-u-s-2-a-day-poverty-in-a-global-context/

336. Massuti, R., Moreira-Maia, C. R., Campani, F., Sônego, M., Amaro, J., Aku-tagava-Martins, G. C., ... & Rohde, L. A. (2021). Assessing undertreatment and overtreatment/misuse of ADHD medications in children and adolescents across continents: A systematic review and meta-analysis. *Neuroscience & Biobehavioral Reviews, 128*, 64–73.

337. Rød, Å. N., & Schmidt, C. (2021). Complex PTSD: what is the clinical utility of the diagnosis? *European Journal of Psychotraumatology, 12*(1). https://doi.org/10.108 0/20008198.2021.2002028

338. U.S. Department of Veterans Affairs (n.d.). *Complex PTSD.* https://www.ptsd.va .gov/professional/treat/essentials/complex_ptsd.asp

339. www.cptsd.org Defunct link now goes to https://www.outofthestorm.website/

340. Complex Post Traumatic Stress Disorder Foundation Organization. www.cptsdfo undation.org

341. Social abuse was coined by Dr. Barbara Jean Peters, co-founder of the Working and Poverty Class Academics, which she spent a lot of her time organizing. She didn't always get to publish papers. She used this term regularly at our conferences.

342. Hager, E., Philip, A., Rappleye, H., & Mei-Ling, S. (2022). For Black Fami-lies in Phoenix, Child Welfare Investigations Are a Constant Threat. *ProPubli-ca.* https://www.propublica.org/article/for-black-families-in-phoenix-child-welfar e-investigations-are-constant-threat

343. Rød, Å. N., & Schmidt, C. (2021). Complex PTSD: what is the clinical utility of the diagnosis? *European Journal of Psychotraumatology*, *12*(1). https://doi.org/10.108 0/20008198.2021.2002028

344. Bacon, A. M., & White, L. (2023). The association between adverse childhood experiences, self-silencing behaviours and symptoms in women with fibromyalgia. *Psychology, Health & Medicine*, *28*(8), 2073–2083.

345. Kalmakis, K. A., Meyer, J. S., Chiodo, L., & Leung, K. (2015). Adverse childhood experiences and chronic hypothalamic–pituitary–adrenal activity. *Stress*, *18*(4), 446–450.

346. [a]Iob, E., Lacey, R., Giunchiglia, V., & Steptoe, A. (2022). Adverse childhood experiences and severity levels of inflammation and depression from childhood to young adulthood: a longitudinal cohort study. *Molecular Psychiatry*, *27*(4), 2255–2263. [b]Danese, A., Moffitt, T. E., Harrington, H., Milne, B. J., Polanczyk, G., 23Pariante, C. M., . . . & Caspi, A. (2009). Adverse childhood experiences and adult risk factors for age-related disease: depression, inflammation, and clustering of metabolic risk markers. *Archives of Pediatrics & Adolescent Medicine*, *163*(12), 1135–1143.

347. Kolk, B. V. der, MD. (2015). *The Body Keeps the Score: Brain, Mind, and Body in the Healing of Trauma* (Reprint). Penguin Publishing Group.

348. Wortmann, J. H., Park, C. L., & Edmondson, D. (2011). Trauma and PTSD symptoms: Does spiritual struggle mediate the link? *Psychological Trauma: Theory, Research, Practice, and Policy*, *3*(4), 442–452. https://doi.org/10.1037/a0021413

349. Edlund, M. J., Steffick, D., Hudson, T., Harris, K. M., & Sullivan, M. (2007). Risk factors for clinically recognized opioid abuse and dependence among veterans using opioids for chronic non-cancer pain. *Pain*, *129*(3), 355–362.

350. Bennett, A. S., Guarino, H., Britton, P. C., O'Brien-Mazza, D., Cook, S. H., Taveras, F., . . . Elliott, L. (2022). U.S. Military veterans and the opioid overdose crisis: a review of risk factors and prevention efforts. *Annals of Medicine*, *54*(1), 1826–1838.

351. Dodson, W. (2023, August 25). New insights into rejection sensitive dysphoria. *ADDitude*. https://www.additudemag.com/rejection-sensitive-dysphoria-adh d-emotional-dysregulation/

352. [a]Rogers, C. J., Pakdaman, S., Forster, M., Sussman, S., Grigsby, T. J., Victoria, J., & Unger, J. B. (2022). Effects of multiple adverse childhood experiences on substance use in young adults: A review of the literature. *Drug and Alcohol Dependence*, *234*, 109407.[b]Bjork, J. M., & Grant, S. J. (2009). Does traumatic brain injury increase risk for substance abuse? *Journal of Neurotrauma*, *26*(7), 1077–1082.

353. Natividad, I. (2021, June 25). Why is anti-trans violence on the rise in America? *Berkeley*. https://news.berkeley.edu/2021/06/25/why-is-anti-trans-violence-on-th e-rise-in-america/

354. Agana, M. G., Greydanus, D. E., Indyk, J. A., Calles Jr, J. L., Kushner, J., Leibowitz, S., . . . & Cabral, M. D. (2019). Caring for the transgender adolescent and young adult: Current concepts of an evolving process in the 21st century. *Disease-a-Month*, *65*(9), 303–356.

355. Oaklander, M. (2015, August 14). Here's why people believe in conspiracy theories. *Time*. https://time.com/3997033/conspiracy-theories/

356. Thomas, S. A., & Lincoln, N. B. (2008). Predictors of emotional distress after stroke. *Stroke, 39*(4), 1240–1245.

357. Kellner, C. H., Obbels, J., & Sienaert, P. (2020). When to consider electroconvulsive therapy (ECT). *Acta Psychiatrica Scandinavica, 141*(4).

358. Robertson, H., & Pryor, R. (2006). Memory and cognitive effects of ECT: informing and assessing patients. *Advances in Psychiatric Treatment, 12*(3), 228–237.

359. Watkins, S. (2021, November 12). Hard work keeps you at the top, says billionaire. *Investor's Business Daily*. https://www.investors.com/news/management/leaders-a nd-success/hard-work-keeps-you-at-the-top-says-billionaire/

360. DesRoches, D. (2019, May 15). Georgetown study: Wealth, not ability, the biggest predictor of future success. *Connecticut Public Radio*. https://www.ctpublic.org/education/2019-05-15/georgetown-study-wealth -not-ability-the-biggest-predictor-of-future-success

361. White, G. B. (2016, June 22). When Poverty Is Profitable. *The Atlantic*. https://w ww.theatlantic.com/business/archive/2016/06/poverty-industry/487958

362. Desmond, M. (2023). *Poverty, by America*. Random House.

363. Sheffield, R., & Rector, R. (2011). Air Conditioning, Cable TV, and an Xbox: What is Poverty in the United States Today? *The Heritage Foundation*. https://www.heritage.org/poverty-and-inequality/report/air-conditioning-ca ble-tv-and-xbox-what-poverty-the-united-states

364. Wildau, G. (2004, June 16). O'Reilly: "[I]rresponsible and lazy . . . that's what poverty is." *Media Matters for America*. https://www.mediamatters.org/bill-ore illy/oreilly-irresponsible-and-lazy-thats-what-poverty

365. Florida, R. (2019, March 21). How poor Americans get exploited by their landlords. *Bloomberg.com*. https://www.bloomberg.com/news/articles/2019-03-21/housing -exploitation-is-rife-in-poor-neighborhoods

366. Kelley, M. B. (2018, November 13). STUDY: Watching Only Fox News Makes You Less Informed Than Watching No News At All. Business Insider. https://www.businessinsider.com/study-watching-fox-news-makes-you-less-in formed-than-watching-no-news-at-all-2012-5?op=1

367. Marshall, K., & Leu, C. Employers to decide if OTC birth control will be covered at no cost. (n.d.). https://www.mercer.com/en-us/insights/us-health-news/employer s-to-decide-if-otc-birth-control-will-be-covered-at-no-cost/

368. Taylor, K.-Y. (2022, July 6). Abortion is about freedom, not just privacy. *The New Yorker*. https://www.newyorker.com/news/our-columnists/abortion-is-abou t-freedom-not-just-privacy

369. [a]Osmundson, S. (2023, March 17). Tennessee must change its abortion law. *The New York Times.* https://www.nytimes.com/2023/03/16/opinion/medical-exceptions-abortion-tennessee.html[b]McCammon, S. (2023, March 8). 5 Texas women denied abortions sue the state, saying the bans put them in danger. *NPR.* https://www.npr.org/2023/03/07/1161486096/abortion-texas-lawsuit-women-sue-dobbs

370. Padilla, M. (2023). The 19th Explains: Why child marriage is still legal in 80% of U.S. states. *CT Mirror.* https://ctmirror.org/2023/07/15/child-marriage-legal-18-states/

371. Ben-Ghiat, R. (2020). *Strongmen: How They Rise, Why They Succeed, How They Fall.* Profile Books.

372. Lee, B. X. (2019). *The dangerous case of Donald Trump: 37 Psychiatrists and Mental Health Experts Assess a President, Updated and Expanded with New Essays.* Thomas Dunne Books.

373. Price, M. L., & Riccardi, N. (2023, October 5). Trump's intensifying rhetoric offers insight into how he might govern again as president. *AP News.* https://apnews.com/article/trump-violent-rhetoric-retribution-authoritarians-2024-39e090680a33c0869312e79bcef106e8

374. Davis, C. R. (2022, January 14). Yale history professor Timothy Snyder told Insider he fears American democracy may not survive another Trump campaign. *Business Insider.* https://www.businessinsider.com/timothy-snyder-fears-democracy-may-not-survive-another-trump-campaign-2022-1?op=1

375. [a]Chrisinger, J. (2022, January 9). Opinion: What authoritarianism would look like in America. *Des Moines Register.* https://www.desmoinesregister.com/story/opinion/columnists/iowa-view/2022/01/09/what-authoritarianism-would-look-like-america/9088584002/[b]Reich, R. (2023, June 15). The five elements of fascism. *Robert Reich.* https://robertreich.substack.com/p/the-five-elements-of-fascism[c]Corn, D. (2023, September 14). How right-wing groups are plotting to implement Trump's authoritarianism. *Mother Jones.*

Acknowledgements

THERE ARE SO MANY people I want to thank and I lost my file stuffed full with names and gratitudes, so I sincerely hope I don't forget anyone I intended to thank. Let me begin with my parents who helped me gather materials, sat for interviews, wrote me their input, and generously offered support where maybe not all of my siblings did (except John). I still want to thank my siblings for their help and input to whatever extent they were able to provide it. My husband has been consistently behind me on this project from the start, through all of the ups and downs, including financially supporting me through writing. I am deeply appreciative to him for editing assistance and emotional support. I love you and we make a great team. I want to thank my stepson for being patient with me as I was an absent parent while writing.

Speaking of editing assistance, since this book was two books at one point, it has had a lot of editors. I would like to deeply thank Carol Reavy as the first editor of the *When We Were At Your Mercy* book. I am especially proud of her excellent work as she was a Luther College Upward Bound student with me. George White, a former Los Angeles Times reporter and editor, added helpful contributions to the book, *When We Were At Your Mercy,* that really strengthened the book. Steven P. Miller was given *The Poverty Experts* to edit along with a copy of *When We Were At Your Mercy* for reference. He really brought what was becoming chaos into focus by reminding me of my original purpose, to tell my family's story of poverty in response to Murray, so he helped me create, "*What's So Bad About Being Poor?*," including it's very title. Steven contributed so much that I am frustrated at my own limited writing ability to show effusively enough my praises for his skills and assistance. I have seen others give him his props for a job well done and trust me, I cannot match their eloquence. He's a master. Finally, I have Sara DeGonia who I deeply appreciated for knowing the rules. She could cite me exactly why she put that comma where she put it, and she did with a file that showed me each rule. I felt so secure knowing we made the right choices. So, Steven, if you're reading the book and see something that conflicts with your recommendation, it's because Dr. Rules could cite me the exact rule. Thank you so much to you both.

It is because of the editing that I want to both thank and apologize to my dearest friends from graduate school. Referred to as Kyla, Denise, Eri, and Tim, by her real name as Sue, or not referred to at all (Diane), and you know who you are, my relationships with you are my most important I will ever have in my life aside from my marriage. It seems nonsensical not to have a book expansively talking about our adventures at professional conferences, our time working for admissions, our times at brown bags, supporting each other, but it became clear it was my family's memoir, not solely mine. I love and appreciate all of you and your friendships to this day. I never would have made it without you.

I want to thank my teachers, who for the most part, were outstanding and helpful. I had hoped to thank Mrs. Eskridge personally but when I returned to her, I found she had passed away. Mr. Schilke, thank you for your endless patience with my lack of practicing my violin. Melanie Hoffner, you're a rock star of teachers. Of course, Phyllis Gray, I wish you were still with us because your insights were incredible about this topic. She knew all about poverty brain and how it affects your ability to think. Bless you for all you did for our family, Phyllis. I would also like to thank Dr. Carol Mowbray, Dr. Lorraine Guttierez, and the University of Michigan School of Social Work for all they did for our family as well.

I also want to thank a whole host of friends stretching back all the way to elementary school, Carmen, has been a forever friend. Then, although I didn't name them accurately, Annette and Erica, have remained my friends through social media to this day. I appreciate them for sticking with me. I want to give a hearty thanks to Patrice M. who happily told me to use her name when I asked (I admittedly didn't ask my other friends for their privacy). I want to throw a bear hug around everyone at our own reunion someday. That also goes for the many friends who were not mentioned in the book, like Jason Z or Rick B. I definitely want to extend my heartfelt thanks to Roxanne who I was grateful to have that reunion with in Charlotte, NC recently. I want to thank the many other Upward Bound or Student Support Services (TRIO) students and staff I didn't get to mention in the book. Much love to you.

www.ingramcontent.com/pod-product-compliance
Lightning Source LLC
Chambersburg PA
CBHW030817090426
42737CB00009B/762